Canadian Pacific

The Story of the Famous Shipping Line

Trade is the spirit of life

George Musk

Canadian Pacific

The Story of the Famous Shipping Line

David & Charles Newton Abbot London

British Library Cataloguing in Publication Data
Musk, George
   Canadian Pacific
   1. Canadian Pacific Company — History
   I. Title
   387.5′06′571   HE945.C3

ISBN 0–7153–7968–2

Printed in Great Britain
by Butler & Tanner Ltd, Frome and London
for David & Charles (Publishers) Limited
Brunel House Newton Abbot Devon

Contents

Preface

This study has been prepared as a part of Canadian Pacific's centenary observances to record ninety-eight years of shipping activity by the Company. It is by no means complete, nor is it sufficiently documented to rank as a definitive history, but it should help to fix names and dates for future research.

The influence exerted by the political and strategic aims of governments made the early development of the Company more than a commercial operation and may justify the bias towards the earlier years of this story.

The information has been collected with the co-operation of a great many authorities, including the World Ship Society, Canadian Pacific Archives (particularly David Jones), my colleagues both active and retired, Lloyds of London, newpaper offices and libraries in Canada and the United Kingdom. Space precludes the mention of all individually, but I am specially indebted to Earl Marsh, Jack Shave and Ed Vipond, without whose help over a number of years the chapters on the Coastal and Lake services in British Columbia could not have been written, also to Deborah, who transcribed my scribbles and typed the manuscript. My thanks to one and all, but any errors or omissions are mine alone; corrections or comments would be welcomed.

The book is divided into four parts: Part One—the development of the shipping services; Part Two—stories of some of the more important vessels; Part Three—appendices giving the background to services taken over, lists of voyages, cruises, wartime losses, etc; Part Four—fleet lists.

George Musk
January 1980

Introduction

More than 300 Canadian Pacific ships are described in the following pages, ships which have played an outstanding role in the development of both Canada and Canadian Pacific. Beginning with small wooden steamboats built in Canadian Pacific's own shipyards 1100ft above sea level in the Canadian Rockies, the record traces the expansion over some ninety-seven years to modern oil tankers of 250,000 tons; fleets which made the names Empress, Duchess, Princess and Beaver synonymous with the Canadian Pacific transportation system. Ships with names such as *Kyoquot, Illecillewaet, Valhalla, Fort Steele* and *Princess Norah* (later to become a Queen, a Prince and finally a Beachcomber) portray the romance of water transport.

The story also tells of the major contribution made by CP ships in two world wars, when some 300,000 tons of company ships were lost, including the 42,000 ton *Empress of Britain*, the largest merchant ship lost in World War II.

Never before has such a wide variety of shipping services reaching across the world, been developed and integrated with an airline, railway and trucking operation to compare with the Canadian Pacific multi-modal transportation system.

Part One  Company History

1  The North Pacific 1886-1915

So ran the advertising slogan so well known between the two world wars. W. C. Van Horne, who built the Canadian Pacific Railway (CPR), said: 'Canada is in a backwater, we must put her on a highway.' George Stephen, the first president of the CPR, who was mainly responsible for raising the cash, said in a letter to Sir John A. MacDonald that he saw the company as 'a service stretching from Liverpool to Hong Kong'. The CPR was incorporated on 16 February 1881, to build a railway across North America to link the then separate settlements and make the Confederation of 1867 a reality.

Several important names will recur throughout this narrative. W. C. Van Horne at thirty-eight was already general manager of the Chicago Milwaukee & St Paul Railroad; he joined the CPR as general manager on 1 January 1882, and followed George Stephen as president, 1888–99. In October 1882 he persuaded his purchasing agent from the American railway, T. G. Shaughnessy, to join him as general purchasing agent for the CPR. Shaughnessy became the company's third president, 1899–1918. Henry Beatty, a partner in the North West Transportation Company operating ships on the Great Lakes, joined the CPR as manager of Lake Transportation Services in 1882. His youngest son, Edward Wentworth Beatty, later became the first Canadian-born president, 1918–42. Sir John A. Macdonald negotiated the British North America Act of 1867 through Parliament, and was Canada's first prime minister as well as the political champion of the transcontinental railway.

The story of Canadian Pacific's involvement with water transport began in 1882–3 on the waters of the Great Lakes. During the building of the transcontinental line the company bought and hired a number of small steamboats and barges to ferry men and materials to help with the work of construction (see page 264).

The first order for ships to be built for the company was placed in 1883, with two Clyde yards, Aitken & Mansell of Kelvinhaugh and Connell & Co of Glasgow. Three passenger and freight ships were ordered for service on the Great Lakes. From May 1884 until the railway along the North Shore of Lake Superior was completed in May 1885, the *Alberta*, *Algoma* and *Athabasca* provided the only link between the rail head at Owen Sound and the western line out of Port Arthur. Henry Beatty went to England to supervise the building of these three vessels (see page 104).

George Stephen also visited England in 1884 and endeavoured to interest the Colonial Office, the Post Office and the London Chamber of Commerce in persuading the government that a mail contract for a steamship service across the Pacific in conjunction with the railway would offer advantages over the Suez route for mails, commerce and strategy. As well as faster times it could also provide an 'all red route' to Australasia and the Orient. This expression derived from the practice, at that time, of printing maps of the world with the areas of British influence coloured red.

A year or two later imperial thinking was expressed by Sir Andrew Clarke, British inspector-general of fortifications:

Once a regular steamship service with the East by way of Canada and the Pacific is established, the whole Empire will be firmly knit together and the chain of communications between British stations will literally girdle the world.

The 800 ton W. B. Flint, *first of the chartered sailing ships to bring cargo from Yokohama to the terminus of the transcontinental railway at Port Moody, BC, on 27 July 1886*

Sir Andrew's hopes were fulfilled with the subsequent growth of Canadian Pacific.

In October 1885 the British Post Office advertised for tenders for the carriage of mail via Vancouver to Hong Kong. Canadian Pacific Railway offered a fortnightly service for £100,000 per annum, but because of a change in government combined with the fact that a mail contract by way of Suez already existed, the offer was not accepted. Nevertheless, the directors were able to report at the 1885 annual general meeting:

The negotiations with the Imperial Government of which the shareholders are already aware, for the establishment of a first-class line of steamships between the Pacific terminus of the railway and Japan and China, are still pending. The many advantages to Imperial interests and the sense of

security that would be created by a thoroughly efficient and purely British alternative route to the East, inspire the Directors with the belief that their proposals must soon be accepted by Her Majesty's Government. The question of connections with the Australasian Colonies is also receiving the attention of the Directors.

Speaking in the House of Lords on 29 April 1887, the Earl of Harrowby said:

This great Canadian Pacific Railway was, perhaps, the greatest revolution in the condition of the British Empire that had occurred in our time.... It had brought the Pacific ocean within fourteen days of the English coast. Vancouver could only be reached before that in between two and three months. The Canadian Pacific Railway sent in a tender for a fortnightly service.... I cannot believe that the Government would really reject a proposal to take possession of the Pacific by means of a great line of mail steamers sailing under the auspices of our venturous Canadian brethren.

Sail

While the search was being made for suitable steamers for the Pacific service, immediate steps had to be taken to provide traffic for the railway, which was nearing completion.

Messrs Everett Frazar & Co were appointed to act as agents in Japan and China. Seven sailing ships were chartered and the first to arrive at Port Moody on 27 July 1886, only three weeks after the first train had crossed the continent, was the wooden barque *W. B. Flint*. Built in 1885 at Bath, Maine, she was 178ft in length with a beam of 35ft and a gross tonnage of 835. Fifty-two years later, in March 1937, she was set on fire at Seattle for the recovery of metal scrap.

According to the 'Vancouver News', her arrival caused 'much talk and interest'. Her main cargo consisted of more than a million pounds of tea, mostly consigned to Hamilton, Toronto and New York. A special effort was made to speed this traffic over the railway, and delivery was made in New York on 9 August, only forty-nine days after leaving Yokohama!

Bringing more than $1\frac{1}{2}$ million pounds of tea, the *Flora P. Stafford* arrived at Port Moody on 27 August, and reported that she had been chased by Chinese pirates at one stage of her journey. The third ship to arrive was the Australian barque *Zoroya*, reaching Port Moody on 17 September. The fastest crossing was achieved by the German barque *Bylgia*; she arrived on 13 October only $22\frac{1}{2}$ days after leaving Yokohama. The remaining three sailing vessels on this 'tea run' were larger, and the *Carrie Delap* arrived on 26 October with $1\frac{3}{4}$ million pounds. The *Eudora* arrived on 19 November and the *Frieda Gramph* in January 1887 with 1 million pounds each.

In that first and vital season the sailing ships brought more than 4000 tons of freight for the new railway. At the sixth annual meeting held in May 1887, the directors reported:

Although the railway was open for through-traffic for only the last five months of the past year, no less than seven cargoes of tea and other Chinese and Japanese commodities were brought to our line during that time by sailing ships consigned to the principal cities in Canada and to Chicago, New York and other cities in the United States, indicating that the expectations of the Directors as to a large and profitable trans-Pacific trade will be fully realised upon the establishment of a regular line of steamships and the fact that the tea already received has been transported across the Continent from Vancouver to Montreal and New York in from seven to eight days is evidence of the satisfactory character and condition of the railway.

Chartered Steam

At the time that the company was looking for steamships to replace the sailing ships, George B. Dodwell was the shipping manager of Adamson Bell & Co, a large merchant house with extensive connections in the Orient. Sir William Pearce, naval architect and controller of the John Elder yard (later to become Fairfields), was seeking employment for the *Abyssinia*, *Batavia* and *Parthia*, which he had accepted from the Cunard Company in part payment for two new ships. On 11 February 1887, an agreement was signed between Canadian Pacific and Mr Dodwell on behalf of Sir William Pearce for the three steamers to be placed on the Pacific under the management of Adamson Bell & Co for a trial period. Adamson Bell was also to represent the CPR in China, leaving Everett Frazar & Co to continue in Japan and New York.

The steamers were transferred to the Pacific and the service began in May 1887 and continued until the company's first Empresses appeared in 1891.

The 3600 ton *Abyssinia* sailed from Hong Kong on 17 May 1887, and from Yokohama on 31 May. Meantime, Vancouver had been established as the rail terminal in place of Port Moody, and the first transcontinental train arrived on 23 May 1887. The *Abyssinia* arrived in the Strait of Georgia on the afternoon of 13 June, whereupon, according to the 'Vancouver News':

The Mayor, the city band and hundreds of people gathered on the wharf to welcome the steamer. Unfortunately the vessel anchored in English Bay for the night and did not tie up at the new Canadian Pacific wharf until next morning.

On board were twenty-two first-class and eighty Chinese

The 3000 ton Abyssinia, *the first chartered steamship arriving from the Orient with passengers and cargo on 14 June 1887*

steerage passengers, three bags of letters, eleven packages of newspapers plus 2830 tons of cargo, mostly tea bound for Chicago and New York. A small trial shipment of tea reached New York on 21 June, when it was transferred to the *City of Rome* and arrived in London on 29 June, only twenty-nine days from Japan. Also on board the *Abyssinia* was a pioneer consignment of silk, sixty-three packages for New York and two for Montreal (see page 213). The *Parthia* arrived next, on 4 July, with a large consignment of tea, 5000 sacks of rice, and thirty-six bales of silk. The *Batavia* was not ready to make the third sailing as planned, and the *Port Augusta* was chartered for one round voyage. Westbound, these vessels carried chiefly cotton goods and flour.

When the *Parthia* made her second trip to Vancouver she carried Sir Francis and Lady Plunket, the first distinguished passengers to travel the new Canadian Pacific route; Sir Francis was the British Minister to Japan. On her return trip the *Parthia* carried the brother of the King of Siam who was returning home after visiting London for Queen Victoria's Jubilee celebrations.

Although the first season's operations ran at a loss, the directors were able to report: 'The service fully justified expectations as to the value and importance of the trade to be developed.' Another angle on the scale of this achievement is illustrated by a report in the 'Vancouver News': 'The *Parthia* brought ten sacks of mail and Postmaster Miller and his assistants were kept busy sorting all night.' In the following year the directors reported: 'Freight traffic to and from China and Japan continues to increase, but the present steamers have very limited passenger accommodation.'

14

By 1888 large numbers of Chinese passengers bound for the United States were being carried; to meet competition from the Pacific Mail Company and the Orient & Occidental Line running out of San Francisco, twelve voyages were continued southward from Vancouver to the American port. However, this business virtually ceased when the United States clamped down on Chinese immigration. In 1890, the *Danube* was chartered and placed on the Vancouver–San Francisco run, but in the following year the company withdrew from this coastal service, which was thereafter handled by the Union Steamship Company.

In 1888, the *Abyssinia*, *Batavia* and *Parthia* made thirteen sailings and these were supplemented by six sailings made by the chartered steamships *Zambesi*, *Port Adelaide*, *Albany* (two), *Duke of Westminster* and *Aberdeen*, the first large steamship fitted with triple expansion engines. Of even more importance was the fact that her cargo included 237 packages of silk. In all, more than 250 first-class passengers, 14 million pounds of tea as well as 560,000 pounds of raw silk were brought into Vancouver.

With the entry into service of the new Empresses, the chartered steamers were withdrawn during 1891. The *Abyssinia* sailed from Vancouver on her seventeenth and last Canadian Pacific voyage on 28 January. The *Batavia* completed her fifteenth round trip when she sailed from Vancouver in March. The *Parthia* remained in service until 20 August 1891, when she left Vancouver on her twentieth and last Canadian Pacific voyage.

First Mail Contract

Although it was announced in Vancouver in 1887 that an agreement had been reached with the British government and that three steamers were to be ordered from the Fairfield yard, it was not signed because the government considered that the existing service on the North Atlantic was too slow. However, two years later, it appeared that an improvement on the Atlantic was imminent and the directors were able to announce at the ninth annual meeting on 14 May 1890:

> A contract with the Imperial Government was concluded in July providing for a mail subsidy of £60,000 for the Company's proposed line of steamships between Vancouver and China and Japan.

The contract was for ten years with a four-weekly service across the Pacific, the British government paying £45,000 and Canada £15,000. A condition in the contract called for gun platforms to be built into each Empress, and 4.7in guns supplied by the Admiralty were to be stored at Hong Kong and Vancouver so that these ships could quickly be converted into armed merchant cruisers.

Transit time was not to exceed 684 hours from Hong Kong to Quebec between April and November, and 732 hours from Hong Kong to Halifax between December and March. There was a penalty of £500 if a ship or train failed to start on time, plus £100 for each additional twenty-four hours' delay. The penalty for late arrival was £100 for each twelve hours. In contrast, payment for today's airmail services is much simpler: Canadian Pacific Airlines share in carrying mails with other airline companies to and from Hong Kong and on other routes, receiving payment on a ton/kilometre basis.

In those early days of the railway, delays of up to forty-eight hours were not unknown, but because the Empresses were always able to make up time on their run across the Pacific, they established a remarkable record for fifteen years without penalty.

First Empresses

Meanwhile, on 12 October 1889, an order had been placed for three 6000 ton vessels. It may have been that Sir William Pearce had chartered the earlier ships in the hope of getting the order for the Empresses. Unfortunately Sir William had died, and his superintendent engineer, A. D. Bryce Douglas, had moved to become managing director of the Naval Construction Company by the time the order was placed; consequently, the *Empress of India*, *Empress of Japan* and *Empress of China* were built by the Naval Construction & Armaments Company of Barrow, which became part of Vickers-Armstrong (Shipbuilders) Ltd who launched the *Empress of England* in 1956 and the *Empress of Canada* in 1960.

During the building of the ships, Van Horne, who had by now become president, was represented at the shipyard by Henry Beatty, T. G. Shaughnessy and Maitland Kersey. R. B. Angus, a member of the original railway syndicate, suggested that the ships should be named after China, India and Japan. Van Horne, in agreeing with this suggestion, said the series could be continued with the names Russia, Germany and Austria for later ships.

The maiden voyages of these three famous ships were

The first ocean liners built for the CPR joined the trans-Pacific service in 1891. One of three sister ships, the 6000 ton Empress of Japan *(1891–1922)*

made in 1891 via the Suez Canal and the company advertised tours 'Around the World in 80 days—$600' (see page 127).

When the *Empress of India* ran her trials in January 1891, the company's red-and-white chequered house flag was unfurled for the first time. Van Horne, president of the company, said later that he designed the house flag partly to be different from any in use and partly that it might easily be recognised when hanging loose. It had no historical or heraldic significance. Someone suggested that it meant 'three of a kind', but Sir William said that would not be a big enough hand for the CPR for which only a 'straight flush' would be appropriate. The flag was added to the buff funnels of the ships in 1946.

16

Athenian (1897–1907)
Tartar (1897–1907)

In 1897 the *Athenian* and *Tartar* were bought from the Union Line to meet the demand for the movement of prospectors from Vancouver to Alaska on their way to the Yukon gold-fields. Both steamers had been built by Aitken & Mansell of Glasgow for the mail service of the Union Line between England and South Africa. They were iron single-screw steamers with compound engines. Both ships were re-engined in 1889 with triple expansion engines, which increased their speed and at the same time reduced their fuel consumption.

The *Tartar* was taken over on 28 December 1897 and

from an occasion when she had been used as a royal yacht by Queen Victoria. The first sailing up the coast to Alaska was made by the *Tartar* on 28 April 1898. Because the Gold Rush was falling off, the vessels were withdrawn after they had made only six voyages each.

After being laid up for several months at Vancouver, the *Athenian* and the *Tartar* made a few sailings to supplement the Pacific Empresses. The *Athenian* made a trip to Vladivostok and Hong Kong, where she was again laid up. The *Tartar* made her first trans-Pacific crossing in December 1898, and on her homeward run she carried 600 Japanese to Hawaii, the first Canadian Pacific call at Honolulu.

Around this time the Americans were having problems in the Philippines and the company was able to charter the two vessels to the United States government in July 1899 to carry troops and supplies. The *Athenian* was also used for the same purpose in the Boxer Rebellion. The *Tartar* returned to the Pacific route in May 1900 and the *Athenian* followed in 1901. A serious attempt was now made to integrate these two ships with the Empresses in order to handle the increasing amounts of cargo offering on the Pacific. An average of twenty-four sailings a year was achieved.

The *Athenian* left Vancouver on 22 August 1907, on her last Canadian Pacific voyage. On 17 October 1907, the *Tartar* was in collision with another Canadian Pacific ship, the *Charmer*, and had to be beached at English Bay, British Columbia.

The Pacific 1906–14

The Pacific fleet was strengthened in 1906 by transferring the *Monteagle*, one of the Beaver Line vessels bought in 1903. She was refitted at Liverpool to carry ninety-seven cabin class plus a large number of steerage passengers. She sailed via the Cape of Good Hope and left Hong Kong on her first trans-Pacific voyage on 2 May 1906.

When the first Empresses were placed on the Atlantic in 1906, the schedule of the Pacific Empresses was cut from twenty-one to nineteen days. With good connections this enabled mails to be carried from London to Hong Kong in twenty-nine days. However, the Pacific Empresses were already fifteen years old, and the new schedule left no margin for emergencies. Early in 1907 mail from the United Kingdom arrived at Vancouver four days late and the *Empress of Japan* was unable to reach Hong Kong on schedule, thereby incurring the first

the Canadian Pacific house flag was seen for the first time at Southampton when she arrived on 29 December.

At about this time Canadian Pacific Telegraphs had ordered forty-five miles of three-wire submarine cable from the Telegraph Construction & Maintenance Company. This was to establish a telegraph link between the mainland and Vancouver Island. The cable, weighing 230 tons, was loaded on the *Tartar*. They left Southampton on 5 and 12 February 1898 to sail round the Horn to Vancouver. The submarine cable was laid by the *Tartar* on 6 April between English Bay, Vancouver and Departure Bay, Nanaimo, on Vancouver Island.

When the *Tartar* arrived at Vancouver on 1 April she still had some furniture aboard bearing the royal arms penalty payment. Later in the year, Arthur Piers, manager steamship lines, announced plans for new ships for the Pacific, but as the next mail contract lowered the speed requirement the order for new ships was held over.

At this time the CPR was preoccupied with building its North Atlantic service and was no doubt thankful for the delay. However, severe competition out of San Fran-

cisco by new steamships of the Toyo Kisen Kaisha Line finally forced action and an order was placed with the Fairfield yard in 1911 for two 17,000 ton vessels. With a speed of twenty knots and luxurious passenger accommodation, the *Empress of Asia* and *Empress of Russia* soon restored the company's position on the Pacific, when they entered service in mid-1913 (see page 132).

First train arriving in Vancouver on 23 May 1887

2 The North Atlantic 1884-1915

Although the activities on the Pacific were more evident, the Atlantic connection was always in the minds of George Stephen and Van Horne. By 1884, well before the transcontinental line had been completed, arrangements had been made with the Beaver Line for the handling of traffic to and from Liverpool, and through the Robert Reford Company of Montreal with the lines they represented (the Donaldson Line to Glasgow, and the Great Western, Thompson and Ross lines), to other United Kingdom ports. The Allan and Dominion lines were, at this time, tied in with the Grand Trunk Railway.

The ever-exuberant Van Horne wrote on 8 September 1885 to Harry Moody, deputy secretary of the CPR in London:

I regard it as almost certain that before a great while we will have our own steamship connection across the Atlantic, and with the steamship service on both oceans and the trans-continental service as well, the line would be most effective.

George Stephen, beset with the problem of finding finance, and striving to ensure that the railway remained solvent, was a little more cautious. He wrote to Macdonald on 29 January 1886:

I had a visit from Andrew Allan this morning and gave him roughly my ideas as to what would be necessary to perfect the Liverpool end of the CPR. At first he was startled, but breathed easier before he left me and after he understood me better. He now knows that nothing but the very best and fastest ships will be of any use to us, and that whoever owns them the CPR must have a substantial control over them so as to ensure a unity of action....

The annual report for 1886 stated:

The establishment of a first-class line of mail and passenger steamships between Canada and the United Kingdom, fully equal in speed and character to any now crossing the Atlantic, is under the consideration of the Dominion Government, and it is confidently expected that the necessary steps to this end will be taken immediately. Such a line, while being of the greatest possible advantage to Canada, would also be a most important supplement to the Pacific service contemplated by the Company, and could not fail to contribute largely to the trans-continental business of your railway.

Whilst prepared to use any of the existing Atlantic lines, both Stephen and Van Horne were adamant that new and faster ships were needed. On 10 September 1886, Stephen wrote to Macdonald:

My dear Sir John:
I had a chat with Tupper [Minister for Railways] this afternoon on the subject of the Atlantic Mail Service, and repeated to him in substance what I had already said to you on the subject. I most thoroughly agree with the view you expressed in your note to me in June last, while I was at Causapsal 'that the subsidized vessels must equal the speed of the best New York steamers.' To subsidize inferior ships, cattle carriers, and expect them to carry the Canadian mails and passengers, would be great folly, and result in *forcing* the CPR to seek an alliance with the New York lines for its through business, and rendering the short line railway from Montreal to Halifax useless....
The CPR cannot take up the Atlantic Service of

itself—it would not be politic were it possible. The CPR must be free to use all the lines on the Atlantic, both slow and fast, but while this is a necessity, we have an enormous indirect interest in the Canadian Service on the Atlantic being as good as any, otherwise, it goes without saying, we shall have to look to New York or Boston. I mention this pointedly, as I do not wish you or your colleagues to think that I am trying to secure a big subsidy for the CPR. If you stipulate for the proper service, I do not care who gets the contract, certainly the CPR Company will not undertake the service.

Van Horne—President

Stephen retired from the presidency in August 1888, although remaining on the board. In 1891 he was created a peer, Lord Mount Stephen, the first time such an honour had been awarded to a Canadian. Van Horne became president and was elected chairman in 1899.

The 1890s were busy years for the CPR; on 15 June 1892 a branch line from Sicamous on the main line had reached Okanagan Lake. By May of the following year the company's first river steamer, the *Aberdeen*, had been launched from its own shipyard at Okanagan Landing. This was the start of Canadian Pacific's Lake and River services in British Columbia (see page 93). When the railway reached the Pacific in 1886, it had an immediate effect upon trade to Vancouver Island and along the British Columbia coast. Control of such trade could feed the railway with important earnings, and in 1901 the CPR bought the Canadian Pacific Navigation Company and ordered its first Princess steamer—the beginning of the company's British Columbia Coastal Steamship fleet (see page 75).

Fast Line to Canada

Until the middle of the nineteenth century sail held sway on the oceans of the world, but in an incredibly short time the iron hull and the screw driven by steam power took over. The enormous population and the consequent trading potential of the United States attracted the largest and fastest steamers to the New York run. Many Canadians saw that a similar service to Canada would provide prestige and encourage future growth.

Geographically Canada had a tremendous advantage from the shorter and more northerly route through the sheltered St Lawrence—saving about 400 miles, or a day's steaming, over the more southerly route from the United Kingdom to New York. In theory this meant that smaller and therefore less costly ships should be able to make the same times as the faster ships on the New York run. However, ice and fog in the Gulf and rapids in the upper St Lawrence made it a treacherous route, causing the loss of many ships. It had the further disadvantage of being closed completely during the winter. This meant that an alternative port had to be available. Many, including Sir Sandford Fleming, the government engineer, advocated Portland, Maine, the nearest ice-free port to Montreal. But for political reasons a Canadian port, Halifax, was chosen.

The Allan Line placed its first steamship, the *Canadian*, on the St Lawrence service in 1856. Eastbound voyages would take between twelve and thirteen days and westbound a little longer. By 1881 the Allan liner *Parisian* could average eight- or nine-day crossings, but still could not match the speed of ships on the New York run.

The completion of the transcontinental line in 1886 emphasised the need to encourage immigration and thereby trade. Pressure on the government to encourage increased speeds on the Atlantic came from merchants and the CPR. Politicians and the press were advocating the 'fast line'. 'Twenty knots to Canada' became a slogan, but did not become a reality for many years. Speed was a very costly business for the early coal burners, an increase from say fourteen to twenty knots could double coal consumption, thereby reducing cargo capacity. Understandably the shipowners, who knew the costs and the risks involved, were anxious to proceed cautiously and did not consider the mail contracts high enough to offset the risks.

The Canadian government's request in February 1892 for tenders for a twenty-knot Atlantic service, plus their derogatory remarks about the existing services, prompted J. & A. Allan of Glasgow to write a long letter to 'The Times', 11 August 1894:

... when they [the Allan Line] could not undertake the more ambitious schemes of the Government, believing it would fail financially and disappoint the expectations of the Government. Allans offered, at less cost to the Dominion, to provide the highest class of service which in their view is suited to the St

Lawrence.... In trying to fulfill previous contracts the Allan Line had lost six mail steamers between 1860 and 64, after which they had secured an additional clause in the contract enabling their Masters to reduce speed if weather conditions required....

There were two weak links in the dream of a service from Liverpool to Hong Kong. The first was the lack of fast liners on the Canadian run and the second the difficulty of getting a good rail connection from the CPR main line to Halifax, the winter port. Both Stephen and Van Horne realised that a satisfactory service could be achieved only if these two links were raised to the standard of the Vancouver–Hong Kong service.

The 'Short Line'

The rail problem was perhaps the more difficult because it was involved with politics. Portland, Maine, was by far the nearest ice-free port to Montreal, but obviously the government could not agree to using an American port. Halifax was already connected to Quebec by the government-owned Intercolonial Railway, but this followed a circuitous route in order to stay on Canadian soil. At the time of Confederation a 'short line' to run across the State of Maine to connect with the transcontinental line had been promised by the government. Stephen was against the building of another line, but the political representatives of the Maritimes were threatening to vote against Federal relief for the CPR unless a commitment was given to build the 'short line'. Stephen sought a compromise. In exchange for building the line to Saint John, he obtained promises from Macdonald for running rights over the Intercolonial from Saint John to Halifax; the through-traffic would then be routed over the 'short line', the Intercolonial becoming, in effect, a local line.

Unfortunately the management of the Intercolonial and the Maritime politicians did not see eye to eye with Macdonald over these problems. Although the CPR built a railroad across Maine and, by leasing a number of existing lines, secured access to Saint John in 1889, the running rights and the through-traffic did not materialise as hoped. Despite the disappointment of the CPR, the Saint John 'Times Star' of 3 June 1924, commenting on the thirty-fifth anniversary, said:

Not only was there great jubilation on the day when the first CPR train arrived from Montreal via the 'short line', but to make sure that the Company appreciated their enthusiasm the citizens held a summer carnival and electric exhibition on 22 July to celebrate the opening.

The coming of the CPR to the city has been one of the greatest factors in its upbuilding and development.

Among his many efforts to get an improved service on the Atlantic, Stephen approached the Anderson family of the Orient Line in 1886 and tried to interest them in placing fast steamers on the run between the United Kingdom and the St Lawrence. As an added inducement there was the possibility of the service from Vancouver to Australasia as well as the CPR contract to Hong Kong. To help raise the necessary finance he also offered, with his cousin Donald Smith (later Lord Strathcona) to contribute £50,000 each, on condition that he succeeded in obtaining the promised running rights over the Intercolonial Railway to secure the 'short line' access to Halifax for the winter traffic. Because of the many interdependent factors, the scheme never materialised. There were difficulties in raising the necessary capital. The British government renewed the mail contract out of San Francisco for a further year. The Halifax connection could not be finalised; therefore the CPR went ahead and ordered its Pacific Empresses and the Andersons finally withdrew.

Writing to Macdonald on 28 October 1890, Van Horne said:

> ... a first-class Canadian Atlantic freight line is of the greatest possible importance to the Dominion of Canada and to its railways.... We are enormously handicapped, our rates are regulated, not by New York, but by the amount of freight offering here.... Another disadvantage is the uncertainty as to cargo space at all times....

By 1902 Shaughnessy, who had been president since 1899, had become completely disenchanted with the lack of enterprise being shown by the Atlantic lines sailing into the St Lawrence and was convinced that he could expect little help from the British or Canadian governments. Help from the British government was virtually ruled out because of the high mail subsidy that had to be paid to the Cunard Line to meet the new American threat posed by the International Mercantile Marine, set up by J. Pierpont Morgan, which included the White Star, Leyland and Inman lines. This was seen as a threat to the British merchant navy and the government felt obliged to help the Cunard Line with a loan and an increased mail contract.

The 'Montreal Gazette' of 3 October 1902 reported:

Pact with Morgan

The Imperial Government's arrangements with the Cunard Line is a decisive blow to the Fast Atlantic Canadian Line receiving financial aid from that quarter.... The Fast Line idea must be abandoned for the less ambitious scheme of a combined passenger and freight service.

Fortunately by this time the CPR was in a strong financial position. On 24 July 1902, Shaughnessy made an offer which was reported at the annual general meeting of the company in October:

When the subject of an improved Atlantic service between Great Britain and Canada was receiving consideration in London, your Directors thought it wise to submit to the Canadian Government, on behalf of the Company, a proposition to provide what they believe to be the best and most practical service under existing conditions.

The Company offered, subject to certain traffic arrangements, to establish a weekly service of twenty knot steamships between Liverpool and a St Lawrence port during the summer months, Halifax to be the Canadian port during the winter months, for a subsidy of £265,000 sterling per annum during the first ten years, with a graduated reduction during each of the two following periods of five years, the ships to be most modern in every respect and to be built specially for the route. In addition to this, the Company signified its willingness to furnish a fleet of modern freight steamers of 10,000 tons capacity each, sailing at a speed of about twelve or thirteen knots, serving Canadian ports.

Up to the present time your Directors have no information as to the policy likely to be adopted by the Government. It is evident, however, that whatever may be the outcome of the negotiations for the fast mail service, the rapid growth of your export tonnage and the necessity of being in a position to meet the rates of any of your competitors, make it imperative that your Company be so situated on the Atlantic that it can quote

through rates of freight and give through bills of lading without being compelled to negotiate for space and rates with independent steamship lines.

This offer was probably kite-flying to find out what sort of response the government might make, if any, or to entice one of the existing lines into selling.

An editorial in the 'Montreal Gazette' for 13 September 1902 said:

The Government's courage is not equal to the task of establishing a fast Atlantic mail service. This would be no surprise if events justified reports that instead of a really fast line Parliament is asked to aid a middling fast service. It is to be trusted that public opinion will be strong enough to prevent a big subsidy being given for a little good. A middling fast line will neither catch the first-class mails nor the first-class passenger. The only justification for a subsidy is that without it the best class of service cannot be provided.

The Beaver Line

Sir Alfred Jones of the Elder Dempster [Beaver] Line wrote to Henry Allan, a partner in the Allan Line at Glasgow, on 24 November: 'I think we should tell the CPR that if they are determined to secure boats, we would sell ours. Why not do the same?' Henry Allan replied:

I do not believe that the CPR have any real intention of purchasing either your fleet or ours. The suggestion of a possible purchase, which they have made to each of us individually, is simply a move in the game, calculated to prevent us carrying out our proposed combination, and offering the Government the service which they desire. Shaughnessy has made similar overtures to us on several occasions, and it seems practically certain that he does not mean business.

However, I take it from your letter that you mean to allow him to humbug you, and to cause you to delay taking any action to secure the Mail Service. In these circumstances we shall, of course, proceed to negotiate henceforward for our own account.

Humbug or not, within six years Shaughnessy had bought both lines for the CPR. The 'Montreal Gazette' of 18 February 1903 reported a speech by Van Horne:

As I have said before, Canada·has for some years been raising the sides of her hopper without enlarging the spout. We are simply trying to do our share of enlarging this spout ... we are apt to get left in chartering vessels when we need them most, so we propose we have our own. This is in no way an effort to compete for traffic from New York. Canadian Pacific has plenty of business for a line of its own, our object is to have our own ships.

On 23 February 1903, Shaughnessy confirmed the purchase from the Elder Dempster Company of its Canadian fleet of eight passenger and seven cargo liners, saying, 'The present purchase is simply the nucleus of our fleet'. With a speed of between only twelve and thirteen knots none of these steamers approached the dream of 'twenty knots to Canada', but at a stroke one competitor had been eliminated and the railway now had an Atlantic service of its own. The 'Montreal Gazette' commented editorially on 24 February: 'This action of the CPR should have a good effect on the trade of the St Lawrence and of Montreal. The roads interest will be to bring by its trains all the business it can get for its steamers and vice versa.' Sir Alfred Jones of the Elder Dempster Company commented: 'The CPR has taken a tremendous step in the direction of Canadian trade development.' John Torrance of the Dominion Line said: 'This gives Canadian Pacific the inside track over all other steamship companies and railways.'

The *Lake Manitoba* made her last sailing for the Beaver Line on 31 March 1903; and on 6 April, on board the *Lake Champlain* at Liverpool the handing over of the line to Canadian Pacific was signalled by the hoisting of the famous red and white chequered house flag. The *Lake Champlain* made the first Canadian Pacific sailing, arriving at Montreal on 26 April, delayed by the weather. The 'Montreal Gazette' of 25 April 1903 reported:

> The steamer *Lake Champlain* with 1322 passengers, fifty-eight of whom were Saloon, arrived yesterday evening at Halifax. The Captain reported that he had made several attempts to force a passage through the Gulf, but was driven back by ice; after two days of vain efforts trying to get through he decided to make for Halifax.

Together with the *Lake Erie* and *Lake Manitoba*, thirty-three sailings were made from Liverpool in that year, carrying 860 first-, 1634 second-, and 23,400 third-class

The aim to build a highway from Liverpool to Hong Kong was achieved in 1903. The 7000 ton Mount Royal, *one of the fifteen Beaver Line ships* (National Maritime Museum)

passengers. Twenty sailings were also made from Bristol. Although primarily a freight service, some 325 second-class passengers were carried in the first season.

In the following year the service from Bristol was switched to London and Antwerp, with the *Lake Michigan, Monterey, Montfort, Montreal, Montrose, Mount Royal* and *Mount Temple* sailing regularly out of Antwerp from 1904 until 1913, carrying 188,000 emigrants in the third class. When the vessels arrived in Montreal the berths were often dismantled and replaced with portable stalls to carry upwards of 1200 head of cattle to London for the Deptford Cattle Market.

Emigration

With its own steamships on the Atlantic, Canadian Pacific was in the enviable position of being able to pick up its passengers at Antwerp or a UK port, carry them to their destination in Canada, and sell them land on the Prairies. No other company could provide such a service. It also helped Canadian Pacific to realise one of its earliest aims.

Europe, with a population of some 350 million and the beginnings of an industrial society, provided an existing market for the development of railways. By contrast, when the CPR was built in the early 1880s, Canada, larger than Europe, had a mere $4\frac{1}{4}$ million people. Because traffic was, therefore, almost non-existent, land and dollars were given to the company as an inducement to build. From the start the CPR had to encourage the build-up of Canada to ensure traffic for the railway.

Only a year after the company was formed, Alexander Begg was appointed general emigration agent for the CPR with an office in London. Hundreds of advertisements were placed in newspapers and periodicals in the United Kingdom and on the Continent, inviting the farming communities to get in touch with Canadian Pacific for information about the possibilities in Canada. The press in Great Britain was supplied regularly with the latest news items from Montreal. The company also helped with the distribution of the 'Canadian Gazette', a periodical published specifically to spread information about the Dominion. In the early 1890s a travelling exhibition-van was used by the company to help publicise Canada in the remote villages of the United Kingdom. For the long winter evenings, sets of lantern slides were available for use in church halls or by professional lecturers. Canadian Pacific maintained close relations with all the steamship lines operating services to Canada plus thousands of steamship agents, and kept them supplied with posters and maps of the new country.

By the close of the nineteenth century, Liverpool had established itself as the gateway to North America. In addition to the British and Irish emigrants, Scandinavians were attracted to Liverpool by the short North Sea crossing and the fast rail link from Hull. Lloyd's List reported on 7 April 1903:

> Evidence of the great 'treck' to Canada has been very patent in the streets of Liverpool during the last few weeks. Crowds of emigrants of all nationalities have been thronging the streets and outside offices of the several steamship companies engaged in the Atlantic trade there have been large numbers of people waiting whilst their tickets were procured.

The first CPR advertisement appeared in Lloyd's List on 16 April 1903

Canadian Pacific Railway
(Atlantic Ocean Services)

Liverpool to Quebec & Montreal
SS Montrose   April 21
SS Lake Erie   April 28
Saloon from £10 Second Cabin £7 & £8
         Steerage   £5.10
For passage or Freight apply CPR
67 King William St. EC or
30 Cockspur St. SW.

An advertising leaflet dated 1904 declared:

> Third-class accommodation by this Line is unsurpassed by any other, all the compartments being heated by steam pipes, and having the best ventilation.
>
> Voyage outfit—Third-Class passengers supplied with all necessaries for the voyage free of charge. The outfit consists of Bed, Pillow, Blanket, Plate, Drinking Cup, Knife, Fork and Spoon, which are the property of the Company, and must not be removed from the steamer. Passengers are required to take care of and keep in good order their eating and drinking utensils, and on arrival at the port of landing, the Outfit must be left in the hands of the Company's Stewards.
>
> Third-Class Bill of Fare—Breakfast 8 am, Dinner 12.30 pm, Tea 5.30 pm, Supper 8.30 pm.
> Breakfast: Oatmeal porridge and milk, salt herrings, corned beef, hash, bread & butter, preserves, coffee. Dinner: Green pea soup, boiled salt fish and egg sauce, roast beef, boiled potatoes, cabbage, tapioca pudding.
> Tea: Smoked herrings, corned beef, pickles, bread and butter, preserves, buns, tea.
> Supper: Gruel, biscuits and cheese.

To encourage the flow of emigrant traffic the CPR opened a boarding house in Liverpool in 1908, where passengers could await their sailings.

In the early 1920s an agreement was reached with the British and Dominion Governments to share in a reduction of ocean rates for British immigrants—families, teenage boys, trainees and domestic servants. To meet the need for extra farm labour in 1923, when a bumper harvest had been predicted, special cheap ocean and rail fares were provided by the CPR; more than 11,000 'Harvesters' sailed to Canada under this scheme and many remained to settle in Canada.

Mennonites

In the mid-1920s more than 100,000 Mennonites in Russia were reported to be desirous of emigrating to North America. When, in 1922, the Canadian government removed its restriction on emigration, the Mennonites already in Canada and the United States raised funds for the transportation and settlement of their nationals from Russia. Canadian Pacific made a special through rate of $140 from a Baltic port to Saskatoon. In 1923 the *Bruton* made three trips from Libau, Latvia, bringing several thousands of these people to Southampton. A special quarantine camp was organised at Atlantic Park, Eastleigh, now Southampton airport. In 1924 the *Marglen* made two trips from Libau to Antwerp, where there was a similar quarantine camp. After a period of quarantine the Mennonites sailed to Montreal and travelled to Saskatchewan by rail. The CPR provided credit of more than $1¾m for some 21,000 Mennonites, every cent being repaid.

In a statement to the standing committee on Railways & Harbours, on 17 November 1932, President Beatty was able to say:

Since its inception it has been the foremost agency in Canada in the work of Colonization, immigration and the development of natural resources, expending for that purpose more than $100 million, a sum greater than that expended by the Dominion Government on similar work over the same period.

It has settled more than 30 million acres of land in the Western Provinces. . . .

In the autumn of 1903, Canadian Pacific moved its London office from the City to a new European headquarters in Trafalgar Square, where Archer Baker was the European traffic manager. The headquarters moved to Finsbury Square on 13 March 1978; the Trafalgar Square office is now being rebuilt.

The Allan Line reacted quickly to the powerful threat created by the purchase of the Beaver Line and ordered two 10,000 ton steam turbine vessels, *Victorian* and *Virginian* (see page 163).

Atlantic Empresses

Shaughnessy was well aware that the buying of a ready-made fleet was only a start, and that fast, new passenger liners would be needed to take full advantage of the

Off to a new home in Canada

The first Atlantic liner built for the CPR, the 14,000 ton Empress of Britain *(1906–30)*

through-route from Liverpool to Hong Kong and also to meet competition from the Allan Line's turbine steamers. In November 1904 an order was placed with the Fairfield yard for two eighteen-knot liners, the *Empress of Britain* and *Empress of Ireland*. These were the first liners to be ordered for the company's Atlantic service and, unlike the Allan Line, Canadian Pacific decided to stay with well-tried quadruple expansion piston engines. The 'Montreal Gazette' of 7 August 1905 said:

According to Mr Piers, the CPR's Manager of Steamship Lines, who arrived home Saturday from a seven weeks' trip to the Old Country.... The new CPR steamers will be named *Empress of Austria* and *Empress of Germany* and will be by far the finest steamships in the St Lawrence trade.

Although the names were changed before the launching ceremonies, the two Empresses did prove to be slightly

Fourways Inn

Fine dining in Bermuda

...ning at Fourways Inn is a heady experience
...d certainly not one to be missed by the visitor
...Bermuda. Acknowledged to be the finest dining
...ablishment on the Island, it is "... a fantastic
...at". *VOGUE MAGAZINE*

...he verdict: splendid" *GOURMET MAGAZINE*

Fourways Inn

You can dine in the main dining room, with its
weathered coral stone walls, chandeliers and
comfortably spaced tables sparkling with pristine
napery, crystal and flowers. Or, when evening turns
on the Bermuda stars, you might prefer dining in
the romantic garden courtyard, where the air is
filled with the scent of flowers and the soft sounds
of the fountain.

Fourways Inn is open at 7.00 p.m. nightly and for
gourmet brunches on Sundays and (in the season) on
Thursdays. Reservations are advised, so please
telephone (809-29) 6-6517.

*"the premier eating place in Bermuda is the restaurant
called Fourways Inn. Not only is its food first-class,
with service to match, but it offers dinner music that
may be the best in this hemisphere"*
CBS RADIO, 1985

"the Island's premier eating place"
ABC's GOOD MORNING AMERICA, 1985

Situated at the junction of Middle Road and Cobbs
Hill in the central parish of Paget, the Fourways
Inn is ideally located less than ten minutes from
the City of Hamilton.

bp
Christopher N.B. Brown, General Manager
No. 1 Middle Road, Paget – P.O. Box PG 294, Bermuda

larger and faster than their rivals. 'Twenty knots to Canada', talked of for twenty years was still a dream, however.

The introduction of the new liners on the Atlantic run soon justified the contention that the 'fast line' would help to create traffic. Passenger carryings clearly indicated that emigrant traffic also showed a preference for the faster ships. Canadian Pacific third-class carryings westbound from Liverpool:

	1905	1906	1907
Number of ships	3	5	6
Number of trips	24	43	48
Number of passengers	13,871	23,815	34,036

Steerage had completely disappeared. Although third-class accommodation was still crowded and plain by comparison with the spaciousness of first-class, dormitory style had given way to cabins, and lounges and dining saloons were provided. Chinaware had replaced the metal 'eating irons'.

Commenting on the new third-class accommodation the 'Montreal Gazette' of 14 May 1906 said:

> The third-class accommodation of old has been revolutionised in the present vessel ... the old order of discomfort which formerly reigned in the steerage department has been swept away. There is even a roped off sand playground for the little children.

The increasing speed of vessels also encouraged the maritime authorities to improve navigational aids, thereby reducing hazards. Insurance rates fell, which helped to increase cargo carryings.

The Allan Take-over

In 1906 the Allan Line negotiated a new mail contract for a weekly seventeen- to eighteen-knot service. This called for two new liners to complement the *Victorian* and *Virginian*, and it was this particular clause that gave Canadian Pacific its chance. The Allan Line had a large fleet, but unfortunately many of its ships needed replacing; the line did not have the financial resources both to do this and spend a large additional sum on two eighteen-knot vessels for the mail service. Canadian Pacific had two Empresses available and was able to persuade Allans to sublet the mail contract. This foreshadowed the end of the Allan Line.

Contract of Employment, Mark. 1

Mr Auld eventually became the company's European Accountant

There were other factors, at this time, which Shaughnessy probably saw as possible threats to the CPR. There were rumours of a joint service to Canada by the White Star, Dominion and Allan lines. As at previous imperial conferences, delegates to the 1907 conference were full of optimism and fervour for faster 'all red routes' and were carried away by Lord Strathcona's offer to organise a twenty-four-knot service to Canada. At the conference Lloyd George stressed the need for more detailed figures before the British government could commit themselves to a new mail contract for the Canadian service. Delegates' enthusiasm also tended to fade when they had to justify the finance of such schemes on their return home. The 'Montreal Gazette' had reported on 30 April 1907:

> A 24-knot service across the Atlantic and a fast service on the Pacific, cutting down the time to such

an extent that the route will practically command business, would be announced from the Meeting in London, attended by Sir Wilfred Laurier [Prime Minister of Canada].

And on 28 June:

The building of the CPR gave us an undiscovered Empire. It opened up million upon million of waste acres—it preceded population and drew in its wake immigration with great industrial awakenings and it breathed life itself into the nostrils of Canada.

But by 17 July 1907, under the heading 'The All Red Fake' the 'Gazette' went on to quote the British Treasury: 'We have invested £5 million in Cunarders and we are now asked to compete with our own capital by starting a service to Canada. One subsidy thus leads to another.'

The Allan Line was still the largest carrier on the Canadian run. In 1908 with eighteen liners it carried 49,000 passengers westbound and 28,000 eastbound, whilst the CPR with eleven liners had carried 46,000 westbound and 30,000 eastbound. Although the threat of new services may have been vague, Shaughnessy was undoubtedly influenced to get in first; and because of its greater financial strength the CPR was able to exert pressure on the Allan family.

In 1897 the Allan partnership had formed the Allan Line Steamship Company Ltd of Montreal. Sir Hugh Montagu Allan, grandson of Alexander Allan, owner of the brig *Jean* was, with other members of the family, still in control; the firm of J. & A. Allan of Glasgow had been founded in 1846. In great secrecy a number of meetings took place in 1908. The CPR asked the Royal Trust Company to act for them and appointed F. E. Meredith, KC of Montreal, an independent lawyer and skilled negotiator, to carry through the transfer arrangements. After preliminary plans had been agreed, the first act was to transfer the Glasgow firm's shares, and therefore control, to Montreal. This was later 'explained' as merely an arrangement to facilitate easier co-operation with the CPR in Canada.

By 6 July 1909, Meredith wrote to Sir Montagu Allan:

My clients are now ready to carry out the transaction that you have had under discussion with them during the past two or three months, namely, to acquire all the Capital stock of the Allan Line Steamship Company Limited, and to take it over as

a going concern ... at the price of £1,609,000. ...

On 8 September 1909, a formal agreement was signed between Meredith and members of the Allan board. This left four members of the Allan family with 500 shares each, plus J. S. Park, another director. The CPR was represented on the board by H. Maitland Kersey, who also had 500 shares. The remaining 57,000 shares were transferred to the Montreal Trust Company on behalf of their clients whose names were not disclosed (ie the CPR).

Secrecy during the negotiations was natural and necessary, but no official announcement was made until 1915. The Allan ships continued to sail under their own colours. Advertising was continued under the Allan name. Both companies chartered each other's ships in order to maintain advertised schedules. Co-operation gradually replaced the intense rivalry that had existed; victualling departments were centralised; one marine superintendent acted for both companies. This encouraged rumours of amalgamation, always to be strenuously denied. It may be assumed that Shaughnessy, out of respect for the Allan family and the prestige attached to the Allan Line, had no desire to publicise the take-over; there was always plenty of anti CPR feeling about without encouraging it. It also allowed the CPR to control two votes at any meetings between the lines for some years. Good luck also helped the CPR. Apart from members of the Allan family, few people knew the facts. After July 1909, when journalists or others asked if any merger or change was contemplated, it could be truthfully denied, since it had already happened and no further change was contemplated or needed. The position was also helped by the linking of the Grand Trunk Railway in many of the rumours.

The 'Saint John Daily Telegraph' 8 October 1909, reported: 'The sale of the Allan Line has been completed, purchase price said to be in the neighbourhood of $12 million. It is thought that the fleet will go to the Grand Trunk although there is a possibility that the CPR may be the purchasers.' Lloyd's List reported on 18 October 1909:

Sir M. Allan landed at Liverpool on Saturday 16th from the *Empress of Britain*. In an interview he stated that it was the first time that he had crossed in a CPR liner and that as he left Sir Thos. Shaughnessy had remarked that, of course, a report would get about that there was to be an

The 18,000 ton Empress of France *ex* Alsatian, *the flagship of the Allan fleet, which was taken over in 1909 and renamed in 1919*

amalgamation. He need hardly say that such was not the case and that the Allan Line would, as a matter of fact, continue as heretofore. The only change would be with regard to the personnel of the principals.

In October 1913, a brief mention appeared in the annual report: 'Your Atlantic fleet has in recent years been supplemented by the acquisition of eighteen steamships . . .' but still no mention of the Allan Line by name. The start of hostilities in 1914 pushed the rumours into the background.

The take-over of the Allan Line was officially announced when the CPR applied early in 1915 to the Railway Commission of the House of Commons in Ottawa for permission to operate its steamship and railway services separately.

Canadian Pacific Ocean Services

The 'Toronto Globe' of 26 February 1915 quoted from a statement by Sir Thomas Shaughnessy:

The Company is operating fleets of steamships on the Atlantic and Pacific oceans as well as on the Pacific coast and other inland waterways of Canada. These latter are connecting links between different sections of the railway line and are, therefore, essentially a portion of the railway system, and it is not proposed to change their status. The ocean fleets are, however, in a different class, engaged in competition with outside fleets. . . . The ownership and control of the steamship company will remain with the Canadian Pacific Railway Company, but the management and operation of the steamship lines will be vested in the Board of Directors of the Canadian Pacific Ocean Services Ltd. It is only another step in the direction of eliminating from the direct operation of the railway company of items that do not relate to the railway property itself.

At a meeting held in Montreal, G. M. Bosworth, vice-president of the CPR, was elected chairman and Major H. Maitland Kersey, who had been the CPR representative on the board of the Allan Line since 1909, managing director. The new company opened its head office at Waterloo Place, London, in July 1917.

It was not until 28 January 1930 that the general manager Canadian Pacific Steamships wrote to the secretary of the Allan Line confirming that solicitors had been instructed to proceed with the necessary legal formalities for the voluntary winding-up of both companies—ie, the

Allan Line Steamship Company and Allan Brothers & Co UK Ltd. The necessary resolution was passed at an extraordinary general meeting of the Allan Line shareholders at the Trafalgar Square office on 28 February 1930, whereby the oldest steamship line in the St Lawrence trade passed into history.

Canadian Pacific had begun as a railway enterprise, but from the outset the directors had always fostered the broadest possible interpretation of transportation in order to encourage any activity likely to feed traffic and therefore revenue to the railway. Shipping, hotels and communications were natural starters. All began as departments of the railway administration. The establishment of Canadian Pacific Ocean Services as a separate company to manage the ocean fleets foreshadowed the eventual separation of all the company's non-rail interests into individual profit centres.

All the lines sailing from New York and Canadian ports to Europe agreed in 1908 to the reciprocal use of return tickets. Passengers sailing to Europe in the spring could buy a return ticket valid on any other line.

By 1909 the two Atlantic Empresses had been equipped with high-powered radio enabling them to keep in touch with Poldhu in Cornwall and Cape Cod in Massachusetts during the entire voyage. With the increasing number of ships being equipped with radio a much improved ice-reporting service was provided for all shipping. Radio received much publicity in the following year when it was used for the first time to effect the arrest of an escaping criminal on board the *Montrose* (see page 160).

On 12 October 1910, the 'Montreal Gazette' said:

> A noteworthy feature of the present season of St Lawrence navigation has been the clockwork regularity with which the Canadian Pacific Railway Empress steamers have been arriving and leaving from this side. Since the opening of navigation, via the Belle Isle route, their time of arrival at Quebec has been within forty minutes of 3·30 Thursday afternoons and their departure has not varied ten minutes from 3.30pm of the following Friday.

Cabin Class

Most early steamships were designed to carry first-, second-, third- and/or steerage-class passengers. By the early 1900s some lines found that the first-class accommodation on their ageing vessels had ceased to attract passengers, who naturally preferred to travel by newer

and more luxurious ships. To compensate, some lines downgraded first to a new designation 'cabin', charging accordingly.

In 1910 Canadian Pacific was advertising the *Lake Champlain* and *Lake Manitoba* as 'one-class cabin' steamers. A few years later it was one of the first companies to design and build cabin-class steamers. The *Missanabie* and *Metagama* were launched in 1914. Shaughnessy, writing on 18 December 1914 to the manager-in-chief, CP Ocean Services, said:

> Your correspondence would seem to indicate that you consider the *Missanabie* a second-class ship,

The first cabin-class liners were ordered in 1913; the 12,000 ton Metagama

and that she is being handled accordingly. This is a mistake. We do not wish the term 'second-class' used in connection with either this boat or the *Metagama*. They are one-class boats and there is not a second-class stateroom on either of them.

The immediate implications of this new trend were rather lost sight of in the more pressing problems of the war.

Two other cabin-class vessels, ordered from Harland & Wolff of Belfast by the Hamburg Amerika Line just prior to the war, were taken over by Canadian Pacific and named *Melita* and *Minnedosa*, when they entered service in 1918 and 1919.

The Austrian Adventure

Tourism and emigration were contributing factors which took Canadian Pacific Railway observation cars into the Austrian Tyrol and their steamships into the port of Trieste on the Adriatic. In the early 1900s the Austrian state railway was in a bad way and was envious of the tourist traffic enjoyed by the German and Italian railways. One of several delegations set up to study the problem visited Canada and was impressed by the observation cars operated by Canadian Pacific. An agreement was reached in 1911 whereby the CPR had eight such cars built in Austria, similar in design to its own. The first three of these cars went into service between Vienna and Innsbruck in August 1912. Five more cars followed and all saw service until the outbreak of the war, when they were seized for use as hospital cars.

The flow of emigrants from Europe to North America was very heavy at this time, causing fierce competition between the steamship lines. The traffic from Central and Southern Europe was virtually controlled by the North German Lloyd Line and the Hamburg Amerika Line out of the north German ports. In an effort to solve some of the problems, the North Atlantic lines convened the first Atlantic Conference in 1908, which established a 'pooling agreement' for third-class traffic (see page 48). The stakes were high and the rivalry continued. The Austrian government was becoming increasingly concerned at the number of male emigrants leaving their country through the many different frontier stations, over which it had little control. Doubtless through its contacts made during negotiations over the observation cars, Canadian Pacific was able to persuade the Austrian government that if it was allowed to operate a steamship service out of the newly opened port of Trieste, the Austrian authorities could channel emigrants through that port and keep a check on numbers leaving the country.

Such an agreement was reached, but naturally when it became known, the German lines protested vigorously, with the result that Canadian Pacific withdrew from the westbound pool on 31 December 1912. In 1913 the *Lake Champlain* and *Lake Erie* were renamed *Ruthenia* and *Tyrolia* and during that year operated ten trips out of Trieste with calls at Naples, carrying 6415 passengers. But only two trips could be made in 1914. This service by the CPR was looked upon with growing dismay by the German lines, who started a campaign in the Austrian newspapers against the CPR, even going to the extreme of starting new papers to carry the message that Canadian Pacific was trying to capture and enslave Austrian peasants. The 'Financial Times' of 23 April 1913 said:

The Canadian Pacific Company will not give way, but are ready to agree to any reasonable terms put forward by their competitors so long as they retain their foothold in Trieste. This Company occupies the advantageous position that it is able to recoup a portion of any loss incurred in connection with its ocean business through the additional traffic in which it is engaged in transporting on its own railway. The German companies are not similarly situated.

An action in the Austrian High Court alleged that the CPR had played a major part in the emigration of 600,000 Austrians. It transpired later that the list of names had been bought from a registration bureau. Nevertheless the CPR office in Vienna was closed and the staff taken into custody, but later released. The 'Financial News' of 12 August 1913 reported:

The German Lines demanded that the CPR should withdraw entirely from their Trieste service, but the latter—as was to be expected from such a powerful and progressive concern—entered a direct negative, contending that there was no just reason for withdrawing a service which had for its aim and object the establishment of closer and more extensive trade relations between Austria and Canada. The advantages to Austria in the new Trieste–Canada service were felt by Canadian Pacific to be incalculable, for she gained considerably by retaining for her own territory a good proportion of the transportation of passengers and freight which had been hitherto practically wholly lost to the Austrian Empire through the deviation of such traffic through German ports.

The 'Financial News' of 22 October 1913 quoted an official statement issued by the CPR:

The CPR obtained its concession for emigration business in Austria purely as a carrying company. The tickets issued being almost entirely prepaid by friends and relatives in Canada or the United States and the passengers, therefore, would have left their native country in any case. . . .

The outbreak of World War I put an end to the deliberations of the lawyers.

Shortly after the war an attempt was made to revive the Mediterranean service in conjunction with the Navigazone Generale Italiana. Canadian Pacific made two voyages from Trieste in 1921, and two from Naples in the spring of 1922, with the *Montreal*. In both years more passengers were carried eastbound than westbound and the service was withdrawn.

3 World War I and After

When Lord Salisbury's government had granted the Pacific mail contract in 1887, the military value of the CPR was a vital factor, with Russia as the threat. When war did come in 1914, Germany was the enemy and, as part of her war effort, the company carried 450,000 tons of war materials to Russia via the Pacific service. Fifty-two ships of the Canadian Pacific fleet, with a gross tonnage of over 426,000 were in the service of the British Admiralty during World War I, as armed merchant cruisers, transports or cargo carriers. They carried more than a million troops and passengers, plus approximately four million tons of cargo. During the war, twelve ships were lost by enemy action and two by marine accident (see page 235).

Because of the danger from U-boats and mines, the Grand Fleet left Scapa Flow in October 1914. Winston Churchill, First Lord of the Admiralty, suggested that ten merchant ships be converted to simulate battleships of the Grand Fleet. While it was realised that the Germans would soon get to know of their existence, it was hoped that they would create confusion as to which were the real and which the false. The liners had to be heavily ballasted to reduce their freeboard, and wood and canvas upperworks were built on the decks. This work was apt to cause some amusement when a couple of ratings might be seen carrying a 12in gun and another with a twelve-pounder under each arm. Five Canadian Pacific ships were so converted:

Lake Champlain	became	HMS	King George V
Lake Erie	became	HMS	Centurion
Montcalm	became	HMS	Audacious
Montezuma	became	HMS	Iron Duke
Mount Royal	became	HMS	Marlborough

From a distance they no doubt appeared very realistic.

The 'special squadron' arrived in Scapa Flow in May 1915, and occasionally steamed into the Atlantic, but this posed problems since the battleships could steam at over twenty knots whilst the dummies could only average about eight knots. The squadron was paid off in September 1915.

Ten Canadian Pacific and Allan Line ships formed part of the first convoy from Canada, which left Gaspe Bay on 3 October 1914 with the first Canadian contingent of more than 30,000 men and 7000 horses. Many thousands of Chinese, recruited for labour battalions to work in France, together with large quantities of rice, were carried by Canadian Pacific from China to Europe. Several thousand horses were carried from North America to France through the agency of Messrs Meyer & Carpenter of New York. In addition to company ships on war service, Canadian Pacific managed for varying periods a large number of ships on behalf of the Ministry of War Transport.

Between 1915 and 1918, regular passenger sailings across the North Atlantic were maintained with the *Metagama* and *Missanabie*, supplemented as required by other vessels from the fleet. Twenty-four round trips were made in 1915, twenty in 1916 and seventeen in 1917. The cargo ships also continued on the Canadian route. By 20 August 1917, the Ministry of Shipping was able to write to Sir Alfred Booth, chairman of the Atlantic Conference:

The Admiralty now inform me that a fast convoy will leave Halifax for the West coast of the United Kingdom on or about the 4th September, and subsequently every eight days.

I shall be much obliged if you will give this information to the members of your Conference and

The 7000 ton Montezuma, *a Beaver Line vessel taken over in 1903. Fitted out as the dummy battleship HMS* Iron Duke *in 1915 (Imperial War Museum)*

ask them, while making mental notes of the approximate dates for their own guidance, to keep the matter secret [Letter in Liverpool University Archives].

After 1915 a skeleton service was also operated across the Pacific by the *Empress of Japan* and the *Monteagle*.

T. G. Shaughnessy lent, to the British government, Arthur Harris (later knighted for his services) with a staff of thirty to take care of chartering and shipping the large supplies of foodstuffs and other war materials. To buy these supplies, another CP man, Edward Fitzgerald, and more staff were also loaned to the government, and handled approximately $50 million of purchases. In England, the European general manager, George McLaren Brown, was loaned to the British War Office as assistant director-general of movements and railways. He was later knighted for his services.

Beatty—President

In the last year of the war, Edward Beatty, youngest son of Henry Beatty, who in 1883 had been instrumental in organising the shipping enterprises of the CPR, was appointed president at the age of forty-two; Shaughnessy continued as chairman of the company. Edward Beatty had graduated in law and joined Canadian Pacific in 1901. He was the first Canadian-born president, becoming the dominant personality for the next twenty-five years, six as president, eighteen as chairman and president and one as chairman: years when no fewer than twenty-three ships were to be launched for the company, including his great pride, the second *Empress of Britain*.

Post-war

The return to more or less normal conditions for shipping in 1919 resulted in no fewer than sixty-eight sailings from Liverpool, with other services from Bristol, Glasgow, London (with calls at Le Havre), and from Antwerp (with calls at Southampton).

The *Empress of Asia* and the *Empress of Russia* returned to the Pacific to join the little *Empress of Japan*, now twenty-eight years old. It had been intended that two new liners should be built for the Pacific service, but because of post-war shortages, construction was slow and expensive. It was not until May 1922 that the new 21,000 ton *Empress of Canada* left for the Pacific. Because of the long delays in shipbuilding the company bought

four German liners, which had been seized as reparations. The *Tirpitz*, renamed *Empress of Australia*, was chosen to partner the *Empress of Canada*.

The three other German liners, *König Friedrich August*, renamed *Montreal* II, *Prinz Friedrich Wilhelm*, renamed *Montlaurier*, and *Kaiserin Auguste Victoria*, renamed *Empress of Scotland*, joined the North Atlantic service during 1921 and 1922.

The *Empress of France* and *Empress of Scotland* inaugurated a regular service from Hamburg with calls at Southampton and Cherbourg in 1922. In the following year Southampton became the home port of the Empresses with a limited number of sailings starting from Southampton and calling at Cherbourg. Some sailings from Glasgow were routed via Belfast, the *Tunisian* making the first call on 25 March 1922. The last direct sailing from Glasgow was made by the *Montclare* on 21 August 1931, after which these calls were maintained by Liverpool sailings being routed via the Clyde and Belfast until 1939.

Canadian Pacific Steamships

The name of the operating company was changed from Canadian Pacific Ocean Services to Canadian Pacific Steamships on 8 September 1921, heralding a period of intense activity. The passenger and freight traffic organisation of the CPR became traffic agents for CP Steamships. The change in style was also marked by the disappearance of the black tops, which had been a feature of the buff funnels since 1906.

In the autumn of 1922, a uniform classification of the company's passenger fleet was adopted whereby the Empress designation indicated the express service carrying first-, second- and third-class passengers. The cabin-class ships were given names beginning with *M*: *Marburn*, *Marglen*, *Marloch* and *Marvale*. By 1923 the fleet had been fitted with radio direction-finding apparatus. Its chief use was in saving time when ships ran into fog. On her first voyage after being so fitted, the *Metagama* ran into dense fog off Belle Isle and navigated by means of bearings provided by the apparatus.

The great earthquake at Yokohama marred the year 1923, when the *Empress of Australia* received worldwide publicity (see page 143).

Cruises

The company entered the cruise business in 1922, when the Frank C. Clark Travel Agency of New York chartered the *Empress of Scotland* for a seventy-four-day cruise to the Mediterranean. The accommodation sold so quickly that it chartered the *Empress of France* to leave a week later. In the same year Canadian Pacific operated two twenty-seven-day cruises to the West Indies.

In the following year Frank Clark chartered the *Empress of France* for the first round-the-world cruise and the *Scotland* for a Mediterranean cruise. The first Canadian Pacific cruise from the United Kingdom sailed in the same year, when the *Marloch* was chartered by the British delegation to the International Baptist Congress at Stockholm. From 1924 CP operated its own cruises except for the charters to Travel Savings Ltd in 1963 and 1964.

The Duchesses started eight-day 'miniature cruises' from Montreal and Quebec to New York in 1931. These allowed fourteen hours in New York, with a round trip fare from $50. The cruises were extended to nine days in 1935. Four cruises ran in July and August each year until the outbreak of World War II. From 1932, eight- to fourteen-day summer cruises, often advertised as '£1 a day' cruises, ran from UK ports to the North African coast, Spain and the Canary Islands. The 'Monts' and the *Melita* were used regularly until the fun and games stopped in 1939.

Because of political troubles in China and Japan, the 1939 world cruise was diverted and the *Empress of Britain* became the first CP ship to visit Australia and New Zealand. On her 1939 and last world cruise she called at St Helena, one time home of the exiled Napoleon, on her run from Cape Town to Rio de Janeiro. The first post-war cruise was made by the *Empress of Scotland* II in 1950, from New York to the West Indies. In the following year she made a cruise from Southampton, the first CP sailing from Southampton since 1939.

In 1963 Canadian Pacific and the Union Castle Company each acquired a one-third interest in Travel Savings Ltd, which was marketing low-cost cruises, to be purchased on an instalment basis, in the United Kingdom and South Africa. In October 1963, the *Empress of Britain* was chartered to the Travel Savings Association and made twelve cruises out of Liverpool and two from Cape Town. The *Empress of England* was also chartered to TSA in November 1963 and made six cruises from Cape Town. Canadian Pacific withdrew from Travel Savings Ltd in October 1964. (For details of the 557 cruises made from 1922 to 1971, see page 226.)

In the 1920s the company opened stores at Glasgow, Liverpool, London and Southampton to serve the deck, engine and catering departments. These were self-financing and enabled the purchasing department to buy in bulk and ensure that suitable stores were always available. The Liverpool store included a beer-bottling plant and a linen repair shop. On the closure of the Atlantic passenger service in 1971, the store and contents were sold. It had also been company policy to run its own shops on board the passenger liners, and from 1960 the hairdressing saloons were also operated by the company.

When the *Montrose* sailed from Liverpool on 27 July 1924, a call was made on the following day at Queenstown (later Cobh). Calls at this port continued until 1930, by ships either on the Liverpool or Antwerp service.

When the *Melita* arrived in Antwerp on 14 November 1926, she was the 10,000th ship to enter the port that year, beating all previous port records. Captain A. H. Notley and his staff were entertained at the Hôtel de Ville; in return the burgomaster and other prominent Antwerp citizens were entertained on board the *Melita*. W. D. Grosset, managing director for Canadian Pacific in Belgium, was made a Knight of the Order of King Leopold.

In the mid-twenties Canadian Pacific embarked on its biggest shipbuilding programme to that date. Five cargo liners, plus four Duchesses, the most up-to-date cabin ships of their period, were ordered. Between 27 September and 23 November 1927 seven vessels totalling more than 72,000 tons were launched. This is thought to have been a world record both for the number of ships and the tonnage launched by a private shipowning company in so short a time. Eleven ships totalling 134,898grt were launched in a year and two days. HRH the Duchess of York launched the *Duchess of York* on 28 September 1928, the first member of the Royal family to sponsor a merchant vessel.

Nineteen twenty-nine was a year of great activity for Canadian Pacific. The Atlantic fleet had been strengthened by the four new cabin-class Duchesses. These 20,000 ton liners were the largest vessels docking at Montreal. With a fleet of fourteen passenger liners, 127 Atlantic voyages were made, a company record.

In addition, the new 26,000 ton *Empress of Japan* had

been launched for the Pacific service.

The British Institute of Naval Architecture presented its gold medal for 1929 to John Johnson for his paper 'The propulsion of ships by modern steam machinery'. Mr Johnson was the chief superintendent engineer for Canadian Pacific Steamships and a distinguished exponent of high-temperature high-pressure steam practice. He was responsible for the machinery in many of the company ships.

Steam Propulsion

By the 1930s Canadian Pacific became recognised as one of the leaders in the use of steam propulsion for ocean liners, particularly with the advanced economy of Scotch boiler installations. The 'Marine Engineer and Motorship Builder' said in an editorial in March 1931:

Modernised in 1927, the *Empress of Australia* with the comparatively conservative steam conditions of 220lb pressure and 630°F, had her performance improved from $16\frac{1}{2}$ knots on 205 tons of oil per day to $19\frac{1}{2}$ knots on 150 tons per day ... The *Montrose*, built in 1922, with her two sisters *Montclare* and *Montcalm*, was originally fitted with 12,500 SHP double-reduction geared turbines taking steam from Scotch boilers at 215lb pressure and 550°F. These three ships have had their original propelling machinery replaced by modern single-reduction geared turbines of Parsons latest reaction type. Simultaneously, improved superheating plants have been installed ... Collectively these improvements have resulted in the guaranteed economy of 20% in specific fuel consumption, equivalent to a reduction of no less than 450 tons oil fuel for the round trip on the Liverpool Canadian service. By applying the same principles even more economies were achieved in the *Empress of Canada*, modernised in 1929. Diesel electric generators were installed and the existing Scotch boilers, formerly supplying saturated steam, were fitted with superheaters ... The additional steam thus released for propulsion resulted in a power increase from 20,000 to 26,000 SHP with a simultaneous reduction of the specific fuel consumption for all purposes from 1.13lb to 0.70lb of oil per SHP per hour—truly a remarkable achievement in a relatively new ship.

And in June 1931:

The best performance of marine steam machinery so far realised is that of the Canadian Pacific liner *Empress of Britain*, which returned a specific fuel consumption of 0.57lb oil per SHP per hour for all purposes on her recent trials, the working pressure of her steam at the turbine throttle being 375lb psi and the final temperature 700°F.

Tourist class

Restrictions introduced by the North American governments brought the post-war emigration boom to a halt during 1924 and 1925. To make use of the surplus accommodation it was agreed that part of the old third-class space could be improved and that $15 should be added to the round trip rate for a new 'tourist' class. By avoiding the connotation of third class it was hoped to attract relatives to visit North America and settlers to visit their homes in Europe, as well as holiday-makers. The cheap rates soon became popular, but the companies found difficulty in finding the necessary public room and deck space needed to create a new self-contained class. Some cabin space was also converted and this led to much argument between the lines regarding the classification of various ships. The problems were eventually sorted out and new ships were built with tourist-class accommodation as a standard feature.

Off-line Calls

To meet the special needs of parties, off-line calls could sometimes be arranged. After leaving the Clyde on 14 April 1923, the *Marloch* called at Lochboisdale, South Uist in the Outer Hebrides to embark 300 emigrants for Canada. After leaving Glasgow on 20 April 1923, the *Metagama* called at Stornoway on the Isle of Lewis when more than 300 settlers were embarked. When the *Minnedosa* left Montreal on 5 May 1925, she sailed for Pauillac on the Gironde River, where a party disembarked to make a pilgrimage to Lourdes and Rome, whilst the *Minnedosa* continued her voyage to Antwerp. On her way to Liverpool the *Montclare* called at Clew Bay, Westport, County Mayo, on 26 July 1928, to land more than 100 pilgrims to the shrine of St Patrick at Croagpatrick, which had been the scene of an annual pilgrimage since AD 441. This was the first time that passengers had been landed at Westport from a large Atlantic liner.

In 1929 a party of 'Lewismen' sailed from Montreal

in the *Minnedosa*, which made a special call at Stornoway on 15 June, for the opening of new municipal buildings, made possible by two 'Lewismen', T. B. Macauley of Montreal and J. Bain of Chicago, after a fire had destroyed the buildings in 1924. The millennial celebrations of the Icelandic parliament were made the occasion for a party of Icelanders from Canada. They travelled on the *Montcalm*, which made a special call at Reykjavik on 20 June 1930; the party returned home on 4 August in the *Minnedosa*.

Below Decks, 1930

The following extract is reprinted from the 'Hotel, Catering & Institutional Management Journal', by courtesy of the editor and the author, Mr John Crowley. The author worked on board the *Duchess of York*, one of four sister ships built in 1927. Having a natural tendency to roll, they were referred to affectionately as the 'Drunken Duchesses'.

These cabin ships with hot and cold running water in all cabins had accommodation for 580 cabin-, 480 tourist- and 510 third-class passengers. To look after the passengers there could be some seventy waiters, eighty stewards and stewardesses, plus half-a-dozen chefs and fifty kitchen staff. Actual numbers would vary according to the number of passengers being carried.

Pay and conditions

The crew would sign articles for the voyage and the contract terminated as soon as the vessel was tied-up in the home port. I don't suppose that anybody ever read or queried the terms of the contract, 'glory hole' lawyers were unheard of; we all had a sharp awareness that indiscipline at sea would not be tolerated. A record of employment was registered in your discharge book, right through from kitchen boy to chef. A prospective employer could scrutinise your personal record, and a bad discharge in your book could keep you unemployed for a very long time.

The pay for an assistant cook was £7.35p per month. A kitchen-boy working the same hours received £3.25p per month, later increased to £5.40p, usually after two years. Uniform was not provided; laundry was free only when the ship was in Canada.

The **Duchess of York**, *one of four 20,000 ton cabin liners built for the St Lawrence route in 1927*

Living quarters for assistant cooks, kitchen-boys, stewards and bell-boys were located in a honeycomb of 'glory holes' in the bow of the ship, most below the water line and sleeping up to twenty, in two-tier steel bunks. The furniture consisted of one wooden table and two wooden forms; metal lockers 18 × 18 × 18 inches were provided for personal possessions; your suit hung on the end of your

bunk. Senior staff lived above the water line on the working alleyway in an area known as 'Tin Town'. The chef had his own private room and the rest were in tiny cabins sleeping two or four.

There were no recreation rooms or dining rooms for the crew at sea. Kitchen staff ate on the work tops, using empty boxes for seats, the waiters mostly ate standing up in the kitchen. The chef ate in his office or his room, one of the kitchen-boys acted as his valet. The chief steward also enjoyed VIP treatment and had his own waiter. In spite of the pay and conditions there was a wonderful team spirit.

A Typical Day at Sea

The assistants and kitchen-boys were up at 05.30, and fifteen minutes later would be coming up the companionways like commuters from the underground. The first chore was to give the stewards their breakfast, egg and bacon Thursdays and Sundays. Then the mise en place for breakfast for a thousand people, lighting the charcoal grills, and the kitchen-boy on soups may be starting to cut ½cwt of paysanne garnish for minestrone. The two sittings for breakfast put the pressure on three sections, two in the still-room preparing thousands of rounds of toast, waffles, griddle cakes, eggs and gallons of coffee, hot milk and tea; the third section prepared the fried eggs and grilled bacon and omelettes, over two hundred. After breakfast the assistants formed into a cleaning squad to thoroughly clean the kitchen with boiling soapy water, scrubbed and refreshed with clean boiling water. If there was to be a captain's inspection (we had two a week) we were kept very busy until 10.30 hours.

We returned to the kitchen at 11.00 hours having washed and changed and were now ready for the next onslaught—lunch, the soup section having already sent the beef tea to the promenade deck.

A very extensive à la carte menu was offered to the Cabin passengers including a large cold buffet table. A reduced menu was offered to the Tourist class and table d'hôte to the Third class. There was a great respect for craft skills; the larder cooks and confectioners were superb craftsmen and sailing-day buffets were often a mini salon culinaire. The bedroom stewards did all the carving on the hot-plate and the cold buffet; the bell-boys acted as runners to replenish the buffet.

Lunch would be over by 14.00 hours and it was then customary for the chef to allocate any food that had been left over for the waiters, the kitchen staff having made their own arrangements. The chef then left the kitchen for his room, leaving the senior kitchen staff to act out a time-honoured perk. Many of the senior stewards, who made substantial tips, paid to be 'looked after'; these perks were referred to as 'bloods' or 'hoodles', a fee having been agreed between the parties concerned. The grill cook would barter steaks with the larder chef for seafood salads or with the entrée cook for special entrées, the vegetable cook provided vegetables for all three. Although this may appear to have been a sordid exercise, one must remember that there was no tronc, it was a way of supplementing poor pay and it maintained an entente cordiale between restaurant and kitchen that was not only psychologically important, but was a relationship not found in hotels.

After lunch the assistants and kitchen boys prepared allocated mise en place for dinner at 19.30 hours. In the larder they would prepare hundreds of cocktail canapés for early evening cocktail parties. The vegetable section might have hundreds of potatoes to turn, crates of beans to string, peas to shell, but there was always a fantastic spirit. The senior cooks were recalled at 16.00 hours, when there was a hectic run-up to dinner, which in the Cabin Restaurant was a formal affair with an orchestra playing in the gallery.

When we had finished our dinner at about 21.45 hours, the senior staff departed for 'Tin Town' and the assistants formed into three gangs, washing, scrubbing and squeegeeing the kitchen. We then reported to the vegetable preparing room to put three-quarters of a ton of potatoes through the machines. The chef usually looked in to be treated with the greatest respect, especially at 23.00 hours, when he would say, 'The rest of the day is your own—and don't forget there is an hour on the clock'. (This when we were sailing east.)

The night before the ship docked we would work through the night, following the tradition that you never took a dirty ship into port. We washed every square-inch of the paintwork, burnished the stove tops until they gleamed as new, pickled and polished every piece of copper equipment; next morning we collected our cards.

If the ship could be tied up at one minute to midnight then we lost the next day's pay; the shore gang beavered away on overtime not only to get the ship tied up before midnight, but also to establish the fact that union brotherhood is pure industrial mythology. 'I'm all right Jack' will forever be a human frailty.

Part of the magnificent cold buffet table offered to passengers at lunchtime

Into the 1930s

Before leaving for the Pacific, the new 26,000 ton *Empress of Japan* sailed on her maiden voyage to Quebec from Liverpool on 14 June 1930, returning to Southampton (see page 148). The highlight of that year was undoubtedly the launch of the 42,000 ton *Empress of Britain*, by HRH the Prince of Wales, on 11 June. She sailed on her maiden voyage from Southampton on 27 May 1931, the largest, fastest and most luxurious liner ever to ply the St Lawrence (see page 184).

Because of the depressed state of world trade an agreement was signed with the Canadian National Railways on 21 October 1931. This provided, among other things, that Canadian National would act as agents for Canadian Pacific Steamships for the sale of passenger tickets and the booking of passenger and freight traffic to and from Canadian Atlantic ports; and that CP passenger ships sailing to and from Saint John would call at Halifax, both westbound and eastbound. Cargo ships sailing from Saint John would also call at Halifax on eastbound voyages.

New York–Bermuda

An entirely new venture was introduced in 1931, when the *Duchess of York* made fifteen trips from New York to Bermuda between January and May, with a minimum fare of $70 for the round trip. In the following year the *Atholl*, *Bedford* and *York* made eighteen trips between them. The *Bedford* made four trips during February 1933, but these were on account of Furness Withy & Co, who chartered her to run alongside their ship *Monarch of Bermuda*, while they were awaiting delivery of the *Queen of Bermuda*.

In July 1931, the company announced the formation of the Canadian Australasian Line, jointly with the Union Steamship Company of New Zealand. Canadian Pacific had at last fulfilled the ambitious platitudes uttered by governments and imperial conferences for so many years about fast steamer services to link outlying parts of the empire—the 'all red route' (see page 209).

By 1933 the Atlantic fleet had been reduced to nine ships: *Empress of Britain*, *Empress of Australia*, four Duchesses and three Monts. This fleet averaged more than eighty sailings a year until 1939. In 1938, the last full year before the war, fifty-five sailings were made from Liverpool, with fifty-two and forty calls at Greenock and Belfast respectively. Thirty-two sailings left Southampton with twenty-five calls at Cherbourg.

Two Canadian Pacific liners were chartered for the Royal Tour of Canada, by Their Majesties King George VI and Queen Elizabeth in 1939: the *Empress of Australia* from Portsmouth and the *Empress of Britain* from St Johns NF (see pages 145 and 190).

Also in the early thirties, the CPR bought a site on Bruton Street, Berkeley Square, London, with the idea of building an hotel. The site included the Two Chairmen public house; in order to retain the licence, the pub was run by the sales department of steamships for several years. Unfortunately the plan to build the hotel did not materialise, the site and the pub being sold in 1936.

Princesses Elizabeth and Margaret on board the Empress of Britain *meeting their parents on their return from Canada in June 1939*

4 World War II and After

All British merchant ships were liable to requisition by the Ministry of Shipping, a department of the government concerned with the transport of vital supplies, munitions and troops. Canadian Pacific shipmasters had been supplied, in advance of the outbreak of the war, with sealed envelopes marked *A*, *B* and *C*, only to be opened on receipt of radio signals. They contained instructions for the conduct of the vessels concerned in the event of various stages of the war at sea. Control of shipping routes was vested in the Royal Navy and at all the Commonwealth ports a naval officer assumed control of the movements of all ships. The convoy system was not put into effect immediately because of the shortage of escorts.

Compensation was paid by the ministry at agreed sums per gross registered ton per month, owners being responsible for wages, provisions, normal insurance, deck and engine room stores and maintenance. Fuel, water, pilotage, port charges, stevedoring and the victualling of troops and passengers were the responsibility of the ministry.

Canadian Pacific had always co-operated with the Royal Navy and the Royal Canadian Navy in encouraging seagoing staff to undertake the special training required to qualify as officers in the Royal Naval Reserve. At the outbreak of World War II, some forty Canadian Pacific officers held commissions in the Royal Naval Reserve. Temporary commissions were granted to others and to a number of engineer officers. By the end of the war Canadian Pacific officers had achieved the following ranks: commodore—two; captain—six; commander—six; lieutenant-commander—seventeen; lieutenant—eight. Captain R. W. Jones RD, Commander H. F. C. Sanders DSO, DSC and Bar, Lieutenant-Commander A. F. Campbell, Lieutenant R. Antrobus, and Lieutenant

G. P. Thornton were killed in action. Commander G. P. Billot DSO was severely wounded.

Captain W. S. Main has recalled how he became Canadian Pacific's first naval prisoner of war when his submarine was attacked by depth charges. He was taken to a camp under German Army control at Wilhelmshaven, but was later transferred to a camp under the control of the German Navy. By one of the interesting coincidences of wartime he was surprised when a German officer, Lieutenant Hoppe-Garten, addressed him by name. When questioned the German said: 'The last time I saw you, you were the third officer on the *Empress of Britain* and you showed a party of Germans, who were travelling to Canada and the USA, around the bridge.'

A few weeks later Hoppe-Garten approached Captain Main during a roll-call and said: 'The white lady has gone—bombed and sunk.' He was, of course, referring to the *Empress of Britain*. Lt Hoppe-Garten later served in North Africa, where he in turn became a POW and was sent to America, where he acted as an interpreter.

Duties undertaken by Canadian Pacific RNR officers included the command of convoys, fighter direction ships, destroyers, frigates, corvettes, trawlers and minesweepers. They served in every war area and their experiences ranged from grave to gay, from infinite monotony and boredom to high adventure. One, eventually captain of a corvette, never saw a shot 'fired in anger' throughout four years of patrolling. Others fought off raiders in E-boat Alley, shelled beaches, or escorted convoys, as directed.

Eighteen Canadian Pacific ocean ships plus two Canadian Australasian Line ships and two vessels from the British Columbia coastal service, with a gross tonnage of 367,418, were in the service of the British Admiralty during World War II. Only five of these vessels, with a gross tonnage of 89,543, returned to the company's service after the conflict. The Beaver ships, invaluable as fast cargo carriers, spent most of their time shuttling across the Atlantic. The *Beaverburn* was an early victim by torpedo in February 1940. The *Beaverford* was lost in the *Jervis Bay* incident on 5 November 1940. In 1941 the remaining Beavers made only nine crossings; the *Beaverbrae* and *Beaverdale* were lost by enemy action in March and April. The *Beaverhill* carried on alone until she was lost by marine accident on Hillyards Reef in 1944.

The passenger liners, whether from Atlantic or Pacific services, moved about the face of the seas at the direction of the Admiralty and became equally at home in tropical as well as northern ports. They served as troopships, armed merchant cruisers, prisoner of war carriers and passenger liners; or on special missions such as the expedition to Spitzbergen with a demolition force to destroy the coal mines, the Madagascar landing, the removal of freed prisoners from Odessa and the evacuation of Narvik and Brest. They carried troops from Australia and New Zealand to Suez, from North American ports to North Africa; they saw the hell that was Salerno, were bombed at Oran, took reinforcements to Singapore, rescued Dutch from Batavia, ferried Canadian contingents from Canada to Britain, shipped landing craft in place of lifeboats for service in the Mediterranean and carried more than 6000 unescorted children from Britain to Canada.

In the fall of 1940, a British merchant shipbuilding mission visited North America and placed orders for standardised ships to be built in United States and Canadian yards to plans supplied by Britain. Most of these ships were to be 441ft × 57ft with a deadweight tonnage of 10,000 and a speed of eleven knots. During the war period Canadian yards built approximately four million tons of shipping for the Allied cause. In 1942 the Park Steamship Company was formed as a Crown corporation to expedite the movement of wartime supplies and to act on behalf of the Canadian government.

In all, 176 Park vessels—156 cargo ships and twenty tankers—were built and named after well-known Canadian parks. A number of these were handed over to Canadian Pacific Steamships for a single eastbound voyage for delivery to the United Kingdom. Others were managed and operated by the company as agents of the Ministry of War Transport for varying periods between 1942 and 1946, when they were returned to the War Assets Corporation and eventually sold (see page 237).

The prefix 'Empire' was adopted by the Ministry of Shipping for a large number of ships which came under its control during World War II. A number of these were managed by Canadian Pacific, mostly for single voyages but some for longer periods (see page 238).

Even before the Canadian Pacific Railway's Angus shops in Montreal had completed an order for 1400 Valentine tanks they received an urgent order for large marine engines and condensers. These were needed for the Royal Canadian Navy's escort ships, corvettes and frigates. Production drawings were completed in one month, and as floor area was released from the tank contract, sub-assemblies were begun and assembly lines developed. Seventy-five engines were built at a rate of six per month. This work had to be fitted in with the normal maintenance work on the company's locomotives and rolling stock.

On the outbreak of the war the chairman and president, Sir Edward Beatty, was appointed as the representative in Canada of the British Ministry of Shipping; to supervise in Canada all ships registered in the United Kingdom, neutral ships chartered by the ministry, and prizes of war engaged in its services. John C. Patteson, European general manager in London, was appointed director-general of supply services. Other members of the staff were loaned to various government departments for the duration of the war. Seventy-one steamship employees were decorated by the British or Canadian governments for conspicuous service, and 236 gave their lives.

Post-war Developments

Only five of the seventeen passenger liners which had been requisitioned returned to service. Eight had been lost by enemy action, one by fire, two had been sold to the Admiralty and the *Empress of Australia* I remained on trooping duties until scrapped in 1952. The *Aorangi* returned to the Canadian Australasian service, the *Princess Kathleen* to the BC coast, two Duchesses and the *Empress of Scotland* II to the North Atlantic. Liverpool was chosen as the home port, and the headquarters of the Steamship Co moved from London to the Royal Liver Building, Liverpool, in June 1948.

On their release from war service the two Duchesses returned to the Clyde to be upgraded to first-class status. Most of the state rooms were rebuilt and enlarged to carry two classes, 441 first- and 259 tourist-class—only 700 passengers instead of their original 1570. The hulls were painted white with a green riband, and the red-and-white chequered house flag appeared on the funnels for the first time. The *Duchess of Richmond*, renamed *Empress of Canada* II, made the first post-war sailing on 16 July 1947. The *Duchess of Bedford*, renamed *Empress of France* II, followed in September 1948. The *Empress of Scotland* II did not complete her last trooping voyage until 3 May 1948, when she too returned to the Clyde for a refit. She joined the two Empresses on 9 May 1950 and, because of her greater speed, was able to reopen the Clyde service with ten calls at Greenock. From eight round trips in 1947, Canadian Pacific were able to provide thirty-nine Empress voyages and carry 42,000 passengers in 1950. The return of the *Scotland* also enabled the company to offer its first post-war cruise, from New York to the West Indies in December 1950.

On Sunday 25 January 1953, the *Empress of Canada* II was gutted by fire whilst berthed at the Gladstone Dock, Liverpool. Fortunately the company found an immediate replacement, the liner *De Grasse* from the French Line, renamed *Empress of Australia* II. Her first sailing for Canadian Pacific was on 28 April 1953.

As early as 1944, in an air-raid shelter, under the head office in Waterloo Place, London, the company's technical staff, Messrs Johnson, Anderson and Evans, prepared the first of many draft specifications for new 20,000 ton Empresses. The placing of orders was delayed, partly on the assumption that prices would fall, as after World War I, and partly because of the threat of air transport, an unknown quantity. The arrival of a new liner from Home Lines in 1952 and orders by Cunard finally forced Canadian Pacific to place an order with the Fairfield yard for their first post-war passenger liner. At this time there was still a good demand for sea travel, but the *Empress of Britain* was not delivered until 1956, when air traffic across the Atlantic had almost caught up with sea travel.

The new ships, 640ft in length, with a beam of 85ft, were to be strikingly different from the pre-war Empresses. They had only one funnel and the emphasis was on tourist class with accommodation for 900, plus 150 first-class passengers. The *Empress of Britain* III joined the North Atlantic fleet in April 1956, to be followed by the *Empress of England* in 1957 (see page 194).

In order to reduce crossing times, the Clyde call was dropped for the 1956 season. This caused an outcry in Scotland and in Canada: the Scottish Tourist Board led a protest by many organisations including the Greenock Corporation; hundreds of letters and telegrams were dispatched; the Secretary for Scotland was called in to help. The Clyde call was reinstated in 1957.

The stop-gap *Empress of Australia* was sold in 1956, to become the *Venezuela*. For the 1957 season there were four Empresses on the St Lawrence route, the *Britain*, *England*, *France* and *Scotland*, and they made fifty-four trips out of Liverpool. The fleet was again down to three vessels in 1958, the *Empress of Scotland* being sold to the Hamburg-Atlantic Line to become the *Hanseatic*. The *Empress of France* was sold for scrap in December 1960, and the new 27,000 ton *Empress of Canada* III joined the fleet in May 1961—the third vessel to bear that name. Canadian Pacific now had, for the first time since 1939, three modern ships on the North Atlantic, providing a weekly service out of Liverpool with calls at Greenock during the St Lawrence season.

Until 1959 regular winter sailings had been made to St John NB, but between 1960 and 1963 these were much reduced and finally discontinued, except for one voyage each winter to New York via Saint John to position the *Empress of Canada* for her winter cruising season out of New York. In 1967 that voyage was made via Quebec instead of Saint John.

Corporate Symbol

The famous red-and-white chequered house flag, which had been in use since 1891, was replaced in 1968 by a new corporate symbol, a triangle to represent motion, blended with a circle for global operation and a square for stability, to publicise the company's multimodal transportation system. In the 1960s air traffic had begun to cut deeply into the North Atlantic passenger trade and to offset the falling demand an increasing number of cruises was operated (see page 226).

The *Empress of Britain* returned to Liverpool for the last time on 22 August 1964; in November she was sold to the Greek Line. The Liverpool–St Lawrence service was maintained with only two Empresses for the next six years, by which time air travel had made an even greater impact. The *Empress of England* was sold to Shaw Savill on 3 April 1970. The *Empress of Canada* continued for a further two seasons, making thirteen voyages each year.

After an investment of some $50 million rapidly rising costs of operating the new passenger liners, plus the ease with which the Atlantic could be covered in hours in-

The first post-war passenger liner, Empress of Britain III, 25,000

stead of days, brought Canadian Pacific ocean passenger services to a close when the *Empress of Canada* docked at Liverpool for the last time on 23 November 1971, ending eighty years of Empress tradition and sixty-eight years of passenger service on the North Atlantic.

Passengers arriving in Canada from Europe

	by sea	by air
1955	55,000	47,000
1960	56,000	149,000
1965	26,000	351,000

(Figures supplied by Statistics Canada, Ottawa)

This was the end of an era. For almost ninety years Canadian Pacific had achieved a very close relationship with Britain. As an international transportation company it had made a great contribution to trade and travel between the United Kingdom, North America, Australasia and the Orient. Liverpool had been a major port for CP ships for more than sixty years. The company had always bought extensively from the United Kingdom, and between 1883 and 1971 orders had been placed with British shipbuilding yards for

26 passenger liners	466,351
15 cargo liners	153,570
19 BC Coastal ships	80,518
5 Gt Lake ships	14,060
2 Bay of Fundy ships	5,663
6 tugs	1,403
	721,565grt

worth many millions of dollars to the British economy. Ships' stores and aircraft had also been bought in the United Kingdom. Much of the original capital to build the railway had been raised in the United Kingdom; by 1961 thirty-seven per cent of the voting stock was still held in Britain, attracting some fifteen million dollars each year in interest.

In August 1961, the Air Transport Board of Canada granted a licence to Canadian Pacific Airlines to fly to London, but because CPA was unable to obtain landing rights from the British government the licence was withdrawn in 1965. At that time the Canadian government reallocated the international routes giving Great Britain to Air Canada, the government airline, thus forcing CPA to fly its London-bound passengers to Amsterdam, where they had to change planes.

This refusal by the British government—in addition to the irritations of the seamen's strikes, when it became impossible to know when a ship could sail, tying up all three Empresses in Liverpool in August 1960—caused big losses to the company. As chairman and president, Norris R. Crump visited the United Kingdom for meetings with the British Council of Shipping, the National Union of Seamen and British government ministers, but was unable to secure the interest and co-operation needed to reach worthwhile agreements.

Mr Crump, who had joined the company in 1920 as an engineer and had successfully organised the changeover from steam to diesel-electric locomotive power in the 1950s, had been appointed president in 1955. Disillusioned with the lack of interest in the United Kingdom, he addressed the Canada Club of Lancashire on 2 April 1962:

Liverpool has been a major port for Canadian Pacific Steamships for the last half century and I hope that, in spite of labour difficulties, our association will continue to be close.

But we must be realistic, particularly with the intense competition faced by all shipping companies in the world today, and indeed by exporters of this country whose production is so essential to the economy. Therefore, my Lord Mayor, I think you will agree that my company, a privately owned organisation, must reserve the right to leave the port of Liverpool for some port elsewhere in this country or some other country where some continuity of operation can be obtained, notwithstanding my company's traditional inclination and close financial affiliations with Great Britain. . . .

It is because of this long and close association, the great respect we have always held for Britain, that I was deeply shocked by the attitude taken by the British Government in refusing Canadian Pacific Airlines the right to land in London after Canadian Pacific had been designated by the Government of Canada under terms of an international bilateral agreement. By this action, the British Government has denied Canadian Pacific the right to provide direct air services between Vancouver, Edmonton and Calgary in Western Canada and London, England. Since some seventy per cent of air travellers between Canada and the UK are Canadian, this action appears to me, as a businessman, to be inconsistent with the wish voiced in many quarters for strengthened ties between Canada and Great Britain....

Passenger Conferences

Fierce competition between the steamship lines operating between Europe and North America in the late nineteenth and early twentieth centuries had led to the building of ever larger, faster and grander ships to attract passengers. However, the high season across the Atlantic was relatively short. This was even more evident on the St Lawrence route than on the New York route, and consequently for many months in the year voyages ran at a loss. The emigrant steerage business had passed its peak before Canadian Pacific appeared, nevertheless rewards were still very high and of particular importance to the CPR which was also in the railway and land business; the company's future depended upon the growth of Canada.

In addition to the normal seasonal fluctuations the emigrant business was also afflicted by the unpredictable changes of economic and political climate in North America as well as in Europe. In times of economic depression, agreements to maintain rates became vital in order to avoid rate wars which threatened to cripple the industry. British lines also felt the need to protect themselves from the American and Continental lines. The first bilateral and multilateral agreements were reached through the Liverpool Steamship Owners Association. By 1885 a North Atlantic Passenger Conference and a separate North European Lines Conference had been established, but agreements were short-lived.

In 1902 J. Pierpont Morgan had established the International Mercantile Marine, a consortium of the Atlantic Transport, Dominion, Ismay, Leyland and White Star lines; later it reached agreement with Albert Ballin and the German lines. This appeared as a formidable threat to British interests, which caused the British government to increase its assistance to the Cunard company.

Albert Ballin of the Hamburg Amerika Line had long been advocating a 'pool' agreement for steerage traffic and in 1904 some of the British and German lines met in Frankfurt, but without reaching a significant agreement. At this juncture Ballin and Heinrich Peters of North German Lloyd campaigned for a conference of all the lines, to cover all aspects of steamship travel across the Atlantic. At a meeting held in London in January

1908, the Atlantic Conference was established with a secretariat under Heinrich Peters in Jena. The Canadian trade was represented by the Allan Line, Canadian Pacific and the Donaldson Line. It was hoped that by fixing minimum rates based on the age, speed and gross tonnage of the various vessels for first- and second-class traffic, plus a 'pool' agreement for emigrant traffic, the lines would be able to operate under reasonable conditions and eliminate rate cutting.

'The Times' reported on 27 March 1908: 'The large German shipping companies propose to endeavour to draw into the "pool" all the lines in the trans-Atlantic trade in order to establish uniform principles and tariffs for the Atlantic service.' From the outset it was the policy of CP to play a major role in the affairs of the conference so as to protect the company's interests in the Canadian route against the more powerful lines on the New York route. The 1908 conference was the most successful attempt to secure agreement between the many different interests and was made to work until 1914, when the two German lines fell out over the issue of Austrian emigration. Cunard bought the Thompson Line in 1911 and entered the St Lawrence route with the *Albania*, *Ascania* and *Ausonia*.

At this time an attempt was made by the CPR and the Cunard Line to form a joint company to operate their combined fleets on the Canadian run, in order to strengthen their financial and bargaining position with the other lines. The plan did not materialise, probably because Canadian Pacific feared that such a joint venture would prejudice other steamship lines against the company's railway interests in Canada. By such fragile threads is history woven.

The outbreak of World War I had ended the conference, although a group of Allied lines continued to work together in Paris. In 1916 the Anchor Line, already associated with Cunard, had formed a new company, Anchor-Donaldson, and took over the Donaldson service from the Clyde to Canada.

A new conference was started in 1921, with a secretariat in Brussels and an office in New York. This was the Transatlantic Passenger Conference, which would liaise with the US Maritime Commission and file with them copies of all agreements on rates and fares. The main aims of the 1921 conference were: to establish berth rights in the home port for each line, secure agreement on minimum rates, and maintain the overall membership of the conference. The German lines rejoined the conference in 1922.

Another problem had arisen in 1922, when the Canadian government placed severe restrictions on immigration other than for farmers, agricultural workers and domestic servants.

A trend by the lines to reduce first-class accommodation to cabin, and cabin to third, caused many headaches as it became difficult to reach satisfactory agreements. Although CP was the largest carrier on the Canadian run it had to emphasise that it was the only transatlantic line without a direct service to the United States, that this placed it in a special position, and that in particular such changes in classes would seriously affect revenue from its new cabin-class Duchess ships. On 12 December 1927, Sir George McLaren Brown, European general manager, wired the conference: 'In view of the invidious position in which we find ourselves as a result of recent action of certain lines in advising changes in classes on some of their ships ... we hereby give notice of our withdrawal from all Atlantic Conference agreements.' And on 29 December: 'Cannot discuss any subjects Paris meeting until Lines return status quo existing prior creation regular Atlantic services of modern Cabin ships for exclusive Tourist Third Cabin....' Agreement was reached in 1928.

Despite conference agreements, competition was severe between individual lines and between the groups operating on the New York run, with their large carryings and giant luxury liners, and those on the much smaller Canadian route.

On the St Lawrence route CP had maintained an advantage in the size and speed of its ships over those of Cunard, but there was always fierce competition in Canada, the United Kingdom and in Europe to secure the larger share of passengers. Had this competition extended to rate-cutting there is little doubt of the injury that would have been inflicted. By the maintenance of rate agreements, competition took the form of active networks of travel agents supplied with attractive literature and good advertising to capitalise on the high standards of ship accommodation, splendid service and gargantuan menus at all meals. With its emphasis on service Canadian Pacific carried more passengers to Canada than all its rivals put together. By exploiting the shorter and more sheltered St Lawrence route—'39 per cent less ocean'—CP was also able to secure some traffic to and from the American Midwest, particularly with the 42,000 ton *Empress of Britain*.

The depressed state of world trade following the disastrous slump of 1929 had caused a serious drop in steamship earnings, both passenger and freight. The company's annual report for 1933 had stated:

Our fleet which was designed in some measure to facilitate the transportation to Canada of settlers approved for emigration by the Dominion Government is particularly affected by the decrease in the number of immigrants to Canada which declined from 133,141 in 1929 to 6882 in 1932.... During a period of unexampled world economic conditions it is natural that a severe strain should be placed upon the long established Passenger Conference Agreements under which the Atlantic Lines operate. In the Spring of 1932 the agreements were temporarily abandoned as a result of differences of opinion as to the value of low rates in the creation of traffic from the US and Canada.

The alarming shrinkage in carryings continued for another three years, during which time efforts were made to reach agreement on a reduction of the number of sailings, but with little success. Nor was a satisfactory relationship between ships and rates determined. In October 1935, the Cunard Steamship Company announced that it would bring the new 81,000 ton *Queen Mary* into service in 1936, but with its top class designated cabin instead of first class. At that time the Canadian Pacific fleet, with the exception of its one luxury liner, the 42,000 ton *Empress of Britain*, and its twenty-two-year-old *Empress of Australia*, consisted of smaller cabin-class ships. As a result of the action by Cunard, all first-class ships then operating changed to cabin class and it was no longer possible for a rate reduction to be secured by changing designation, a bone of contention until then. The CPR report for 1936 had said:

It is satisfactory to record that as the outcome of meetings held recently in Europe the long standing differences of opinion among the Atlantic Steamship operators with respect to the appropriate passenger rate classification of ships have been composed. This adjustment has involved the abolition, for the present at least, of the long established First Class designation on the Atlantic.

After the war, conference agreements were revised and

the first-class designation was resumed.

Sir George McLaren Brown had been a commanding personality for the CPR at meetings between the wars. In October 1936, at a meeting in Berlin, the opportunity was taken to mark his retirement; Mr Lister of the Cunard Line, in presenting Sir George with a silver salver, affirmed the charm and good humour with which he had always supported the conference system.

In 1939 there had been more than 100 passenger liners on the North Atlantic run. After the war, although demand was very high, the North Atlantic passenger service was virtually non-existent for some years because of the loss of ships and the liner requisitioning schemes which delayed the return to normal. There was also the competition of commercial air services which had not existed before the war. The domination of the passenger liner was about to enter its last decades with a diminishing share of the market and rapidly rising costs. Nevertheless in the post-war period most of the North Atlantic passenger lines resumed services with reconstructed or new ships and all were members of the conference which was re-established in 1946 with the secretariat in Folkestone. The lines on the Canadian service were now Cunard White Star, Donaldson Atlantic, Furness Withy and Canadian Pacific, which was able to resume with one ship in July 1947 and had three ships in service by May 1950.

Many people were not yet in favour of air travel and still preferred the luxury and 'gracious living' offered by the ocean liner. A series of strikes in the 1960s caused the delay or cancellation of many sailings, and with no alternative but to return home by chartered air flights, many found that air travel was not to be feared and not nearly so bad as they had expected. This undoubtedly accelerated the drift from ships to aircraft. By 1959 the airlines were carrying more passengers across the Atlantic than the shipping lines. Cunard withdrew from the Canadian trade, making its last sailing from Liverpool on 13 October and from Southampton on 14 November 1967.

With the falling numbers of passengers on the scheduled routes too many liners were placed on the cruise market. Liners designed for the North Atlantic were not ideally suited to cruising in the warmer climates of the Mediterranean or West Indies. Also, many of the ships were becoming outdated both in deck space and interior design. The North Atlantic Passenger Conference was dissolved in March 1975 and renamed the International Passenger Ship Association, with an office in New York; it was now chiefly concerned with cruising activities.

Since the formation of the conference all decisions taken at meetings required a unanimous vote, which protected the interests of the smallest lines. Its success is borne out by the remarkable measure of stability achieved by the conference over six decades in a business continually affected by economic and political changes, both in North America and Europe.

5 Cargo Services 1903-80

Before Canadian Pacific bought the Beaver Line in 1903, the CPR had had to fight against keen competition for the rail haul of both import and export cargoes. As soon as the company had its own ships on the Atlantic, close co-operation between rail and steamship freight departments ensured rapid transfers at terminal ports, and it was able to concentrate its energies in developing the ports of Montreal, Quebec and Saint John, for the movement of Canadian traffic. The Grand Trunk Railway had always favoured Portland, Maine, for winter traffic and the Intercolonial Railway had never made any really serious attempt to develop Halifax NS.

Although the passenger liners carried some cargo, the main freight service was started with the *Milwaukee*, *Monmouth*, *Monterey*, *Montezuma* and *Montfort*, from Bristol and the Millwall Docks in London, where the Beaver Line had been established for a number of years. Calls at Antwerp were started on 13 December 1903.

The London operation was moved to the Surrey Commercial Docks in 1913, and remained there until the docks were destroyed by enemy bombing raids on 7 September 1940. For the remainder of the war CP vessels were diverted to the west coast ports, Avonmouth, Liverpool and the Clyde.

To replace losses suffered during World War I and to maintain its wartime cargo services, Canadian Pacific ordered the 6600 ton *Montcalm* II from the Northumberland Shipbuilding Co, but she did not come into service until September 1917. The company also bought eleven other cargo vessels of between 5000 and 6000 tons from various shipping companies: the *Mattawa* and *Medora* in 1915, the *Miniota* and *Methven* in 1916 and 1917. Five more were bought in 1918: the *Montezuma* II, *Holbrook*, *Dunbridge*, *Mottisfont* and *Batsford*; of these the *Medora* and *Miniota* were lost by enemy action. In the spring of

1919 two further cargo ships, the *Bosworth* and *Bothwell*, were bought from the Shipping Controller.

Immediately after the war the *Methven* transferred to the Pacific service between Vancouver and Hong Kong. In 1920, the *Mattawa* sailed for the Pacific via Suez to join the *Methven* and other vessels on a new service between Hong Kong, Saigon and Singapore, which lasted until 1922. By 1920 regular cargo services were being operated to Canada from London, Avonmouth and Antwerp, with occasional sailings from Liverpool, Glasgow, Southampton, Hamburg, Le Havre and Rotterdam. In all, fifty-one cargo sailings were made with ten ships.

In 1921 a new service was started from Canada to the West Indies. Between December 1921 and June 1922, the *Sicilian* made five trips to Havana and Kingston with passengers and cargo. Between December 1921 and December 1925, the *Holbrook*, *Mattawa*, *Methven* and *Montezuma* made sixty cargo voyages to the West Indies. Many of these trips went to British Guiana to load sugar. The *Montezuma* II arrived at Montreal on 20 May 1922, with 6000 tons, the largest consignment. Molasses was shipped in puncheons carried in the 'tween decks from Barbados. Cocoa, rum and fruit were also carried. Among the chief exports from Canada were flour, oats, hay, potatoes, fish, beer and cement.

In 1923 it was decided for the sake of uniformity that all the cargo liners should have names beginning with *B*: *Balfour*, *Batsford*, *Bawtry*, *Belton*, *Berwyn*, *Bolingbroke*, *Borden*, *Bosworth*, *Bothwell*, *Brandon*, *Brecon* and *Bruton*.

The Beavers—1928

While the company had always envisaged a fleet of specialised cargo liners of the same size and speed so that

51

One of several cargo liners bought to replace World War I losses, the 5000 ton Montezuma II *(Imperial War Museum)*

a regular service could be provided, the building up of the passenger fleets had always taken priority; it was not until the mid-twenties that money was allocated for the building of new vessels designed specifically for the company's North Atlantic trade. With the entry into service of the five Beaver cargo liners (see page 180) in 1928, the ideal of a regular service became practical. A Beaver could leave Montreal every Friday morning and be ready to discharge in London on the second following Monday, enabling the company to gain control of an increasing quantity of high-class freight for its rail haul.

By 1930 all the old *B* ships had been disposed of and the new Beavers carried the company's cargo operations on the North Atlantic until 1939. By concentrating on London, Antwerp, Hamburg and Le Havre, an average of fifty trips per year were made, thirty-odd in summer to Montreal and the remainder to West Saint John NB in winter.

Before 1930, motorcars for export were boxed, but in the early thirties they began to move unboxed with great savings to the car industry. Canadian Pacific carried large numbers of cars to and from Canada.

Beavers 1946

In anticipation of expected wartime losses, draft specifications for new cargo liners were roughed out, in an air-raid shelter behind the Francis Hotel in Bath, by John Johnson, Andrew Henderson and Fred Evans of Canadian Pacific Steamships. Preparatory work between the company and C. A. Parsons Ltd indicated that geared turbines would be the most suitable, but when the time came the country's gear-cutting capacity was so committed to the war effort that the idea had to be abandoned, turbo-electric propulsion being selected instead. Mr Johnson flew to Montreal in the belly of a bomber for further discussions on the draft specification.

In 1943, before the end of the war was in sight, special authorisation was obtained from the government to place an order for four sixteen-knot single-screw cargo liners

One of five sister ships, the 10,000 ton Beaverdale *with the 'Royal Scot' stowed on deck, May 1933 (ASN)*

with the Fairfield Shipbuilding & Engineering Company which, because of heavy Admiralty commitments, sub-contracted the first three vessels to Lithgows of Port Glasgow, to be named *Beaverdell*, *Beaverglen* and *Beaver-lake*. The fourth, the *Beavercove*, was built at Fair-fields. These four sister ships were designed specifically for the company's London and Continental cargo service to Montreal in summer and Saint John NB in winter.

With a length of 497ft and a 64ft beam, the cargo ships had a gross tonnage of 9900. The six twin Sampson posts, four forward of the bridge house and two aft, gave the vessels a distinctive silhouette. Thirty derricks based on the Sampson posts and operated by electric winches served six holds. There were eighteen separate insulated compartments totalling 160,000cft. To forecast future trends of traffic, bearing in mind that a ship may well have a life of twenty years, is always difficult; but the changes wrought by six years of war made it even more difficult. One of the major provisions in the new Beavers was the large amount of refrigerated space provided in the expectation that the pre-war meat trade between Canada and Europe would be resumed. Unfortunately this was not to be and the reefer space remained relatively unused. Four of the holds had special electric fan ventila-tion for the carriage of apples and other perishable cargoes.

The main propelling machinery consisted of a single water-tube boiler supplying steam at a temperature of 850°F at a pressure of 850lb psi to a turbo-alternator. A re-heat cycle was introduced between the high and low pressure turbines. These four ships were among the largest ever to operate on a single main boiler. Three 400kw diesel generators supplied electrical power at 225 volts. Accommodation for the crew of sixty-four was situated amidships with steam heating in all cabins. The life-saving equipment consisted of four large steel life-boats, one fitted with a motor, plus a number of rafts.

The *Beaverdell*, the *Glen* and the *Lake* sailed for their maiden voyage in 1946, the *Beavercove* following in 1947. All four vessels joined the London to Montreal service.

With the Surrey Commercial Docks being put out of action during the war, the London dock office was estab-lished in the Royal Albert Dock on 1 April 1946, the *Beaverdell* being the first ship to sail from the Royals on 11 April.

To supplement the new Beavers the company bought two 9000 ton standard design single-screw steam-turbine Empire ships, the *Empire Captain* and *Empire Kitchener*.

Four 10,000 ton cargo liners were ordered in 1944 to replace war losses; this is the Beavercove (Skyphotos)

They were renamed *Beaverburn* II and *Beaverford* II and joined the North Atlantic service in 1946. Unlike the other Beavers they had accommodation for thirty-five passengers, which helped to relieve the great demand for passages to Canada immediately after the war. This accommodation was reduced in March 1948 to twelve and withdrawn completely in 1960. A third Empire ship, the *Empire Regent*, was bought in October 1952 and renamed *Beaverlodge*.

Sojourn on the Pacific

In August 1952 the *Beavercove* and *Beaverdell* were transferred to the Pacific for a service from Vancouver to Asian ports, including Yokohama, Kobe, Manilla and Cebu. Because of the difficulty of translating *beaver* into Oriental languages they were renamed *Maplecove* and *Mapledell*. On her second trans-Pacific voyage in December 1952, the *Maplecove* lost part of her stern frame and rudder in a storm which lasted nine days. On Christmas Day she was taken in tow by the tug *Island Sovereign* and arrived in Vancouver on 27 December. This service did not develop as well as expected, and after they had completed sixteen voyages from Vancouver both ships returned to the North Atlantic in July 1954; but they did not revert to their original names until December 1956.

In 1948 Antwerp became a regular port of call and between 1953 and 1958 Le Havre, Rotterdam and Hamburg were also added to sailing schedules. Between 1947 and 1967 some 200 calls were made at Canadian Pacific berths by Head Line vessels (see below) to load westbound cargo, chiefly from Liverpool although there were occasional sailings from Antwerp and one or two from Dagenham with Ford cars. Some forty of these sailings entered the Lakes.

Head Line westbound sailings loaded on CP berths 1947–67

	voyages		*voyages*
Carrigan Head (1959–66)	24	Ranmore Head (1950–67)	44
Fair Head (1963–7)	15	Rathlin Head (1954–66)	37
Fanad Head (1947–60)	6	Roonagh Head (1953–67)	37
Inishowen Head (1948–67)	15	Torr Head (1947–66)	20

Note: 179 from Liverpool, 13 from London, 6 from Antwerp. In addition, Carrigan Head made 2 eastbound voyages from Saint John to Liverpool in 1967.

The St Lawrence Seaway

The five Great Lakes, with Lake Superior at 600ft above sea level, all flowing into the St Lawrence River and on to the Atlantic more than 2300 miles away, have long fascinated man—first as a means of exploration and later as a highway for commerce, despite the drawback of a four-month winter close-down.

A single lock overcomes the 21ft drop between Lake Superior and Lake Huron, and in 1932 a new Welland canal was completed with eight locks, 800ft × 80ft with a depth of 25ft, to bypass the 326ft Niagara Falls between Lake Erie and Lake Ontario. A 35ft deep water channel is maintained from the Atlantic to Montreal enabling 26,000 ton vessels to navigate as far as Montreal; but between Montreal and Lake Ontario a series of rapids prevents navigation. The Seaway proper is in this 150 mile stretch of the river.

The first attempts to bypass the Lachine rapids with a three-foot canal go back to the 1780s and the fur traders. By 1904 a 14ft minimum had been achieved on all the canals on the north bank of the river, and by the 1930s, with the help of twenty-two locks, oceangoing vessels of around 1500grt could navigate into the Lakes. Much argument flowed back and forth on the need to enlarge and deepen the locks primarily to enable the large 'Lakers' to sail down to the St Lawrence ports instead of having to tranship their cargoes at Georgian Bay ports or Prescott. Some eighty to ninety per cent of the traffic on these waters consisted of the bulk movement of ores from Seven Islands and grains from the head of the Lakes. A secondary reason was to allow large oceangoing vessels access to the Lakes. In the end it was the urgent need for more hydro-electric power which finally got the Seaway started.

Once the Ontario and the New York hydro authorities had agreed on a joint power project, the Canadian and United States governments got together to begin work on the Seaway in the autumn of 1954. The new Seaway, one of the largest engineering construction works ever undertaken, was built on the south side of the river with only seven locks (800 × 80 × 27), five in Canada and two in the States. It was opened in April 1959 and dedicated on 26 June by Queen Elizabeth II and President Dwight D. Eisenhower.

Manchester Liners, the Fjell-Oranje Line and others had operated services into the Lakes via the old 14ft canals for a number of years. When it became clear that

The 4000 ton Beaverpine *(1962–73)*

the new Seaway was going to be built, the CPR decided that it could no longer afford to remain out of this trade.

Chartered ships for the Seaway

To gain experience, the company chartered small motor ships. In 1957 a start was made with two 1500 ton ships to operate from London, the *Otto Nuebel* and *Auguste Schulte*. Both made five voyages in 1957. These vessels used the old 14ft canals on the north side of the river. Two further vessels were chartered in 1958–9, to offer a service from Liverpool and London (see page 228).

When the new Seaway was opened in 1959, two 3000 ton vessels were chartered, the *Elise Schulte* and *Hermann Schulte*. They were painted in Canadian Pacific colours with the house flag on the funnels. By 1962 the service had expanded and nine Schulte vessels were on charter for varying periods during that season, providing a fortnightly service from London and the Continent plus a three-weekly service out of Liverpool to Montreal, Toronto, Hamilton and Detroit.

Beavers for the Seaway

By 1960 it had been decided to develop a new and smaller type of Beaver for this trade and in March 1961 the company bought a 2900 ton diesel vessel which had been laid down at the Sarpsborg Mek Verksted yard in October 1960 and was still on the stocks. She was launched in March and named *Beaverfir* by Mrs Buik, wife of the deputy managing director of CPSS. She made her maiden voyage on 6 July 1961, from Antwerp to Le Havre, Quebec and Montreal.

The *Beaverfir* was 374ft in length and had a six-cylinder Burmeister & Wain two-stroke oil engine fitted aft. Instead of the usual black hull of the older Beavers she was painted white with Canadian Pacific in large letters along the hull. In September 1962 she became the first Canadian Pacific oceangoing ship to sail into the Lakes. In April 1963 a special call was made at Southampton, when a seventy-seater Westland SRN2 hovercraft was towed out to the *Beaverfir* and the 150 ton floating crane was used to load it on to the deck.

Between 1960 and 1963 the seven 10,000 ton Beavers were sold. To supplement the Continental service into the Lakes, the *Roga* was bought from Aktiesel-skapet Asplund of Moss, Norway, on 9 August 1962. The *Roga* had been built in Moss in 1960 by A/S Moss Vaerft & Dokk. She was 355ft in length with a gross tonnage of 3964 and had a seven-cylinder B & W engine amidships. During her refit at Hamburg she was renamed *Beaverelm*. Leaving Antwerp on 1 September 1962 she made her first voyage for Canadian Pacific via Bremen and Hamburg to Montreal and Toronto. On 30 April 1965 the *Beaverelm* called at Le Havre to load a French Railways locomotive 030-C-841 for Montreal, and on 23 March 1967 two London Transport Routemaster buses were loaded with the aid of the floating crane 'London Leviathan'. They were bound for Expo 67 and one was named 'the Red Rose Tea Bus'.

Continuing the build-up of the new type Beavers, the 4500 ton motor ship *Mimer* was bought in January 1963, from M. Thorviks Rederi A/S Oslo, and renamed *Beaverash*. She had been built in Stockholm in 1958 by A/B Ekensbergs Varv and launched on 19 May. She had a seven-cylinder supercharged Burmeister & Wain engine placed aft, and was 375ft in length. After an overhaul in Antwerp which included the fitting of 6000cft of refrigerated capacity, she sailed on her first Canadian Pacific voyage to Zeebrugge, Bremen, Hamburg and thence to Saint John NB on 17 February 1963. When she left London, two voyages later, on 16 May, she made her first sailing into the Lakes. Her North Atlantic service was broken in September 1968 when she was chartered to Harrisons for a trip to the West Indies. The *Beaverash* continued in the Continental service until November 1969.

To Quebec in Winter

The 1960s saw the development of an important new factor in the Canadian trade. The St Lawrence River had traditionally been closed to shipping each winter and traffic had been handled by the east coast ports during that season. Attempts were now to be made by specially built ships, strengthened for navigation in ice conditions, with help from government ice breakers, to keep first the Port of Quebec and later Montreal open all the year round. To meet this new requirement, an arrangement was made for the *Eskimo* to load on Canadian Pacific berth at Liverpool for one voyage to Quebec in December 1960. In the following year a similar arrangement was made for the *Fort Chambly* at London and Antwerp, and both ships made one voyage to Quebec in December. These two ships made five winter sailings into the St Lawrence in 1962.

Both ships were chartered from Canada Steamship Lines and provided invaluable experience in St Lawrence winter trading conditions. They were specially ice-strengthened vessels, virtually ice breakers, and the *Fort Chambly* had a totally automated engine room controlled from the bridge.

In June 1961 an order was placed with the Burntisland Shipbuilding Company for a 4500 ton motor ship to be 371ft in length and specially strengthened for navigation in ice. The propelling machinery consisted of a six-cylinder two-stroke turbo-charged Fairfield Sulzer diesel. Accommodation was provided for a crew of thirty-nine. The keel was laid on 18 June 1961, and exactly one year later she was launched by Miss Janice Crump, daughter of the chairman of Canadian Pacific Railway, and named *Beaverpine*. On her maiden voyage from London on 24 October 1962 she sailed for Montreal, Toronto, Kingston and Hamilton. In January 1963 she became the first Canadian Pacific vessel to enter Quebec in the winter season. On 8 January the following year her master, Captain A. N. Bezant, received the gold-topped cane awarded by the port authority to the first overseas vessel to arrive at Quebec. A similar award was received from the Port of Montreal on her arrival on 1 January 1969.

A joint service from Bremen and Hamburg to Canada was arranged with the Ellerman Wilson Line in 1962, the *Beaverelm* making the first CP sailing of the joint service on 17 October. Early in the following year the 7200 ton *Lord Viking* was chartered to provide a summer service to Saint John and Halifax NS. Calls were also made at Newcastle NB and Bathurst NB, but the vessel was switched to the Great Lakes service in 1964.

One of the problems arising from the service into the Lakes was the very small number of voyages that could be made by vessels making the long and slow voyage during the summer season; coupled with the very depressed rate situation, the service became uneconomic.

Container Ships

Meanwhile an even more important and far-reaching innovation in freight handling was beginning to appear—the container. In 1964, Canadian Pacific Railway added a rail flat-car to its overnight passenger train between Montreal and Toronto for the movement of Express traffic in two standard-sized aluminium containers. In the following year, further insulated containers were bought by the Express Company and six

Beaveroak *being cut in half to allow a 57ft mid-section to be welded into position. On completion she was renamed* CP Ambassador

specially designed flat-cars were placed in service. From time to time experimental movements of containers were made on the *Beaverpine*.

To gain experience in the new handling methods, a number of vessels were chartered (see page 228) for varying periods including, in 1963, the *Anders Rogenaes*, a ship of 5500 tons, which was renamed *Medicine Hat* in 1964. The *N.O. Rogenaes* was also chartered and renamed *Moose Jaw*, both vessels being painted in company colours. They could each carry approximately twelve containers, which were stowed on the hatch covers.

Beaveroak (1965–70)

In January 1964 an order was placed with Vickers Armstrong for a 6000 ton cargo liner, 408ft in length and with a Clark-Sulzer turbo-charged diesel engine. She was launched on 31 March 1965 as the *Beaveroak* by Mrs G. H. Baillie, wife of the managing director for Europe of the Canadian Pacific Railway. Her maiden voyage began on 7 September from Antwerp for London, Montreal, Toronto and Hamilton. She was a new Beaver in many ways, being the first Canadian Pacific vessel designed to carry containers. Two Thompson cranes were installed between numbers 2 and 3 hatches to ensure speedy handling, and space was available for the stowage of approximately 100 twenty-foot containers. She was also specially strengthened for navigation in ice conditions, and engine-room automation and remote control were introduced for the first time. An electronic 'watchkeeper' or data logger scanned more than 200 sensing points of the main engines and auxiliary equipment, which monitored temperatures, pressures, power, fuel consumption, shaft speed and many other vital performance details. The 'logger' raised both visual and audible alarm on detecting any irregularities.

On 10 April 1967 a British Rail class A4 Pacific steam loco, 'Dominion of Canada', was loaded at London for presentation to the museum of the Canadian Railroad Historical Association at Montreal to commemorate Canada's centenary. Number 60010 was presented by Mr John Ratter of British Rail to Mr Geoffrey Murray, Acting High Commissioner for Canada, on board the *Beaveroak* at the Royal Victoria Dock.

In April 1970 the *Beaveroak* started a new container service from Greenock and Liverpool to Quebec, a return to the Clyde of the Canadian Pacific flag after an absence

of about eighteen months. On the following day, 9 April, she was the first Canadian Pacific container ship to call at Liverpool, where she joined a Canadian Pacific–Head Donaldson service to Quebec.

The first container ship service across the Atlantic was started by the Sea Land Co in 1966, others soon followed, concentrating mainly on New York, to the disadvantage of Canada and the CPR.

In 1967 Canadian Pacific appointed a co-ordinator to reorganise the activities of the company's foreign freight department, the European freight traffic department, Canadian Pacific Steamships and the Canadian Pacific Express Co for the handling of containers between Europe and Canada. At that time a few containers were being carried in the break-bulk vessels, which made handling slow and costly. Also there were approximately three times as many stuffed containers moving westbound as eastbound, necessitating the costly movement of empty containers from Canada. These and other problems had to be solved before an efficient container service could be established. At a meeting of the board of directors on 9 September 1968, it was decided that the break-bulk service on the North Atlantic should be phased out and be replaced by a container operation. While the company's shipping services were originally planned to feed traffic to the railway, they were now to operate as an independent profit centre, with their own marketing and sales policies. This was a turning point in the history of Canadian Pacific's ocean shipping activities. To implement this change the steamship headquarters were moved from Liverpool to Trafalgar Square, London on 5 February 1969.

As a result of many studies, the company placed an order in 1968 with the Cammell Laird yard, Birkenhead, for three 14,000 ton cellular ships to carry 700 containers each, the *CP Discoverer*, *CP Trader* and *CP Voyageur*, which entered service in 1971.

These three ships were built with class 2 ice-stiffening for winter navigation of the St Lawrence. A Burmeister & Wain two-stroke turbo-charged diesel, plus a transom stern and a Cammell-Laird-designed 'geometric ram bow' gave them a speed of twenty knots. Four built-in stabiliser tanks helped to reduce roll in bad weather. A six-tier deck-house, which included the navigating bridge, was built aft above the engine room to provide fully air-conditioned accommodation in single rooms for the crew of thirty-seven officers and ratings. The four cargo holds carried 503 20ft containers in six tiers, with

The launch of the 16,000 ton cellular container ship CP Discoverer *on 26 March 1971 by Mrs F. S. Burbidge, wife of the president, Canadian Pacific*

204 in two additional tiers on the pontoon hatch covers. This was later increased to three tiers, enabling seventy additional boxes to be carried.

Meantime seven ships were time chartered in 1969, plus four further vessels in 1970–1 (see page 229). The London operation was moved from the Royal Docks to the new container terminal at Tilbury, the *Emstroom* making the first sailing on 10 April 1969. By January 1970, groupage depots had been opened in Birmingham,

Bristol, Exeter, Leeds, Leicester, London, Sheffield and Southampton.

Wolfe's Cove Terminal

Quebec was chosen as the Canadian terminal, chiefly because ice was less severe than at Montreal. A wholly owned subsidiary, Transport Terminals Ltd, was formed to operate the new terminal. The rail link from

The CP Voyageur, *one of three cellular container ships built for the London–St Lawrence route*

the main line to the terminal ran under the Plains of Abraham, through the tunnel built in 1930 to serve the Empress berth at Wolfe's Cove. A 35 ton British-built Paceco Vickers Portainer crane, operating on a 1200ft long 50ft gauge track, was installed for loading and off-loading the ships. A spur road provided vehicle access between the quay and the super-highways. Astride the four track railhead and the 16ft roadway, a Transtainer crane from the same British company was installed to handle transfers from truck and rail cars. With the *CP Ambassador* alongside, the terminal was opened on 5 December 1970 by Robert Bourassa, Premier of Quebec. CP Rail moved solid trainloads of containers to Montreal in three hours and to Toronto in ten hours. It was this fast movement to inland destinations that made the

time-consuming effort of sailing through the Seaway uneconomic for overseas break-bulk ships.

The *Beaveroak* entered the Boele yard, Rotterdam, on 10 July 1970, to have a 57ft midships section added and to be converted into a fully cellular container ship, increasing her capacity to 322 boxes. To identify with this new type of operation a new name series was started, and when the *Beaveroak* returned to service on 2 October 1970 she was renamed *CP Ambassador*.

On 2 January 1971 the *Ambassador* received the gold cane for the first oceangoing vessel to arrive at Quebec. The *Ambassador* was the first Canadian Pacific vessel to use the new Seaforth container dock at Liverpool on 18 May 1972, thereby ending a long company association with the Gladstone Dock. On 22 April 1973, when some

420 miles east of Newfoundland, the *Ambassador* was on her way to Quebec in a violent storm, took on water and had to make a distress call. Two German ships, the *Buchenstein* and the *Walter Herwig*, took off the crew except for the master and chief engineer. On the twenty-third, the Russian tug *Kapitan Nochrin* started a tow to St Johns NF where they arrived on 4 May. After repairs the *Ambassador* left for Quebec on 14 July.

A similar conversion was carried out on the *Beaverpine* at the Boele yard on 2 September 1971. Her four general-cargo holds were converted into five cellular container holds to accommodate 20ft containers, 40ft boxes being carried on the hatch covers. She joined the Liverpool Quebec service as *CP Explorer* on 13 December 1971.

CP Transport (London)

To facilitate the movement of company containers between inland points and Tilbury, a subsidiary, CP Transport (London), was formed in 1972.

In September 1973 the London–Rotterdam service was extended to include calls at Le Havre, and by December of that year an agreement had been reached with Manchester Liners to rationalise container services to Canada. Manchester Liners withdrew its service from Felixstowe and Rotterdam and concentrated on the northern ports of the United Kingdom; CP ships withdrew from Liverpool and Greenock to concentrate on its London and Continental service.

As a result of this agreement the *Ambassador* was withdrawn and placed on hire. As the *Beaveroak* she had completed forty-two round voyages, and as *CP Ambassador* a further forty-five, before being sold to the Arion Shipping Corporation and renamed *Atalanta* on 24 December 1973. The *Explorer* was also withdrawn, having completed twenty-eight round trips plus fifty-three as the *Beaverpine*. She was sold on 28 December 1973 to the Arion Shipping Corporation and renamed *Moira*.

By the time the company's cellular container ships entered service in 1971, there was a surplus of container tonnage on the North Atlantic, plus problems with strikes in Canada and the United Kingdom, and it was some years before the operation became profitable. The piggy-back and container services on the railway were unified under the title Intermodal Services in 1974.

Mr R. Y. Pritchard, managing director, was elected chairman and managing director, Canadian Pacific Steamships in November 1976.

Racine Terminal

As Montreal and its hinterland have always generated the largest part of Canada's import–export trade it is not surprising that, with the development of year-round facilities by the port, container activities increased. Together with the increasing costs of rail movement it became cheaper to carry containers all the way to Montreal by sea rather than by rail from the east. Canadian Pacific moved its container operation in 1978 to a new, common-user container terminal, at the east end of Montreal's harbour, operated by Racine Terminals (Montreal) Ltd, a subsidiary of Canadian Pacific Steamships.

The *CP Trader*, was the last Canadian Pacific vessel to leave the Quebec terminal, on 9 November 1978, while *CP Discoverer* was the first to arrive at the new terminal on 17 November.

When the *CP Voyageur* arrived on berth 39 at Tilbury on 28 December 1979, she had completed 138 round trips in nine years. The *Beaverglen*, 1946–63, had achieved only 149 round trips in her seventeen years of service! In December 1979, the 19,863dwt container ship *E.R. Brussel* was chartered from Ernst Russ of Hamburg and renamed *CP Hunter*. Adding Hamburg to the Rotterdam, London, Le Havre schedule improved the service from Germany, the Scandinavian and Comecon countries.

Freight Conferences

By 1904 Canadian Pacific had joined with the Allan Line, Dominion Line and Manchester Liners as members of the Canadian East and Westbound Freight Conferences. As with the Passenger Conference, the system worked more easily in times of prosperity, but came under strain when trade was bad. The preponderance of raw materials and foodstuffs moving eastbound compared with the higher rated manufactured goods moving westbound also caused problems.

CP (Bermuda) Ltd

In 1964 Canadian Pacific's ocean shipping activities were undergoing a period of contraction. Faced with diminishing prospects for the passenger operation on the North Atlantic, and with the replacement of the post-war Beaver fleet with smaller vessels, studies were made of the expanding markets for large-capacity tankers, general-purpose bulk carriers and special-purpose bulk

The launch of the Lord Strathcona *on 15 November 1966, by Mrs I. D. Sinclair, wife of the chairman and chief executive, Canadian Pacific*

carriers. These studies indicated potential in these areas, sufficient to provide attractive rewards and further diversification.

At the executive committee meeting of the board of directors of the CPR held on 5 June 1964, W. J. Stenason, assistant to the president, made a presentation recommending the company enter into negotiations with Shell and Texaco for time-charters on two 50–60,000dwt crude tankers; Stenason also recommended placing orders for the construction of these two vessels in Japan and at the same time advocated discussions with major US steel companies to assess opportunities for larger-capacity bulk carriers in an attempt to secure contracts for the movement of Canadian resource products.

In October 1964 a wholly owned subsidiary, Canadian Pacific (Bermuda) Ltd, was formed to own, operate and charter oceangoing bulk carriers. The 'Guardian' of 26 October 1964 quoted Norris Crump, chairman of the CPR:

The incorporation of the new Company reflects the growing importance of world trade in bulk commodities and in particular, the growing

importance of Canadian exports of bulk commodities by water to Europe, the USA and Japan.

To distinguish this new class of vessel a new series of names was started. Thirteen of the first nineteen vessels were named after senior company officers, others were named to commemorate trading partners, Canadian ports, historic forts of the Royal Canadian Mounted Police, and the Hudson's Bay Company.

As this was to be a worldwide operation, the choice of headquarters was important. Bermuda, the oldest British colony, had a long association with shipping, including a Royal Naval base and dockyard between 1797 and 1956. Today more than 120 ships belonging to over sixty companies are registered in Bermuda and fly the Red Ensign. In addition to government exemption from taxation for a number of years, Bermuda offered excellent back-up facilities with legal and accounting firms of international repute, good telephone and telex communications, together with the necessary air services for the rapid movement of personnel.

In December 1964, following the conclusion of charter

negotiations, the newly formed company CP (Bermuda) ordered two 65,000dwt tankers, the *Lord Mount Stephen* and *Lord Strathcona*, from Mitsubishi Industries in Japan, scheduled for delivery in late 1966 and early 1967. Because of changes in load line regulations the vessels were increased in size to 71,000dwt each before delivery.

In June 1965 a secondhand 15,000dwt bulk carrier, the *Modena*, built in 1959 in Yugoslavia, was purchased for $1,550,000. Renamed the *R. B. Angus*, she was chartered for the movement of lead, zinc and forest products from British Columbia to Japan. Pine Point Mines, a subsidiary of Cominco and the MacMillan Bloedel Company, were the charterers. While this vessel was owned by CP (Bermuda) it was decided to operate her from Liverpool, adding to the fleet of seven owned vessels and eleven chartered vessels already so operated by Canadian Pacific Steamships for itself and for the CPR. This continued Canadian Pacific's policy of using the expertise of British seamen and ship operators. The vessel was manned with British officers and a Chinese crew.

The *R. B. Angus* was lost in a storm on the Pacific on 17 December 1967, all of the thirty-nine-man crew being rescued by *No 18 Yasaka Maru*, a Japanese fishing vessel. Two American doctors were parachuted from a US military plane to attend the rescued crew. The *Adelfotis* was chartered in to complete the *Angus* charters.

In January 1966 the Canadian Pacific board approved the purchase of two 28,000dwt forest product vessels, the *H. R. MacMillan* and *J. V. Clyne*, to be built by Mitsubishi Heavy Industries of Japan at a total cost of $10,780,000. These vessels were chartered to MacMillan Bloedel for a period of eight years. They were specially equipped to handle forest products, having straight-sided holds and wide hatches. The installation of Munck gantry cranes provided for automated handling. They entered the West Coast–Europe lumber trades.

The *Lord Mount Stephen* was launched in Nagasaki, Japan, in August 1966 and upon delivery in November 1966 she was chartered to Shell. The *Lord Strathcona* was launched in October 1966 and upon delivery in February 1967 was chartered to BP. On 1 May 1967, while the *Lord Strathcona* was on her first visit to a British port, Lord Strathcona, a grandson of the man after whom the ship was named, presented a silver rum keg and goblets to the ship.

Following an earlier unsuccessful attempt to enter the coal trades in 1966, approval was given to an arrangement whereby Nippon Kokan Kaisha (NKK) would construct two 55,000dwt bulk carriers for CP (Bermuda). At the same time CP (Bermuda) entered into an agreement with the Marubeni Trading Corporation of Osaka and NKK whereby the first of these two vessels would, under a contract of affreightment, move four voyages of coal a year from Hampton Roads, Virginia, to Japan, returning with iron ore from Australia to the US east coast and Europe. The second vessel would move coal and iron ore under a ten-year contract of affreightment from the Vancouver area or Australia to Japan. In August 1967 the *T. Akasaka* and the *W. C. Van Horne* were ordered from NKK through Marubeni after completion of negotiations.

In June 1967 the board approved the construction of a 16,000dwt log and lumber carrier, the *Pacific Logger*, for operation under a ten-year contract of affreightment to C. Itoh & Co for employment in the movement of logs and lumber from the US Pacific northwest and British Columbia to Japan. The cost of the vessel was estimated to be $3 million. She was delivered on 5 September 1969.

The *Pacific Logger* damaged her tail shaft during a bad storm in the Pacific in December 1974 and had to be towed 2350 miles from the Aleutians to Mizushima, Japan, where a new shaft was fitted. She was first picked up by the US coastguard cutter *Balsam* on 20 December 1974, when an attempt was made to reach Adak Island. Meantime a 10,000 ton Japanese tug, *Amaryllis*, had been chartered and arrived on 28 December, reaching Adak with the *Pacific Logger* on the thirtieth. Permanent towing arrangements were then made for the long tow to Shiogama, Japan, reached on 13 January 1975, when the *Logger* was unloaded. The final tow to Mizushima was made by the tug *Hyogo Maru*, and the *Logger* returned to service in February 1975. Her name was changed in February 1977 to *Fort St John* to bring her into line with other units of the fleet.

In June 1967 approval was also obtained for the construction of one additional 28,000dwt forest-product carrier, the *N. R. Crump*, chartered to a subsidiary of MacMillan Bloedel, the Canadian Transport Company.

On 26 January 1968, the *H. R. MacMillan* was delivered. The *J. V. Clyne* followed on 26 April. Both vessels entered service carrying lumber and other forest products from British Columbia through the Panama Canal to British ports. The *N. R. Crump*, ordered later than her sister ships, did not enter this service until 31 May 1969.

Robert Lynch was appointed as the first president of CP (Bermuda) on 1 May 1969.

The 72,000 ton Lord Strathcona, *passing the Royal Liver Building, Liverpool*

N. R. Crump, chairman (left), and I. D. Sinclair, president (right), with Captain D. F. Tranter on board the W. C. Van Horne

(opposite) The W. C. Van Horne, a 57,000 ton bulk carrier named after the second president of the CPR (Skyphotos)

The 250,000 ton VLCC I. D. Sinclair, *1974*

Following this period of rapid expansion, in which eleven vessels were acquired in four years, there was a pause in undertaking new commitments until early 1970. In March 1970, it was decided that it would be desirable that the tonnage operated by the company be gradually increased from approximately 800,000 tons to between 1,400,000 and 1,500,000 tons. Since it was becoming impossible to secure a position in Japanese shipyards until late 1972 or 1973, it was felt that prompt construction commitments were required by CP (Bermuda) in order to avoid a significant interruption in its new tonnage programme.

In April 1970, orders were placed for two 120,000dwt bulk carriers from NKK in Japan for delivery in the fourth quarter of 1973 and the first quarter of 1974. An option, declarable before 31 December 1970, was secured

The Port Hawkesbury, *253,000 tons*

for one additional vessel of the same size and specifications, to be delivered in the second quarter of 1974. The price for the first two vessels, the *E.W. Beatty* and the *D.C. Coleman*, was fixed at $13,150,000 each.

On 21 November 1969 the *T. Akasaka* was delivered to be followed in June 1970 by the *W. C. Van Horne*.

The VLCC ordered in October 1968 was delivered some three months early on 15 July 1970. The *W. C. Van Horne* was delivered on 9 June 1970, registered in Hong Kong, and took up employment carrying coal from Vancouver and Australia to Japan for Marubeni.

By September 1970 it was felt that the escalation in tanker and bulk carrier charter and freight rates could not be maintained in the tanker sector beyond the mid-seventies, but that similar rates for bulk shipping would continue to escalate over the long term. It was also felt that building costs would increase as a result of world-wide shortages of bulk carriers. The option for the third 120,000dwt bulk carrier, *W.M. Neal*, for delivery in August 1974 was therefore exercised.

The orders for these 120,000dwt bulkers were the first

The lauch of the 253,000 ton T. G. Shaughnessy *on 26 October 1970, by Mrs W. J. Stenason, wife of the then chairman, Canadian Pacific Steamships*

69

orders placed by the company without back-to-back long-term charters. In view of the uncertainties of the market these vessels were placed on time-charter but with a considerably shorter term than had been the policy with previous new buildings. The policy now was to fix for not longer than three years in order to minimise exposure to cost increases and currency fluctuations. At that time escalation clauses, except for wages and insurance, were not common in charter parties.

The *E.W. Beatty*, delivered in September 1973, had been fixed in the previous April to Japan Lines. The *D.C. Coleman*, delivered in January 1974, had been fixed in the previous July to Kawasaki Lines, and remained under this charter until July 1975. In August 1974 the *W.M. Neal* was delivered, having been fixed to Showa Denko KK of Tokyo for three years. The *E.W. Beatty* and *W.M. Neal*, after their initial time-charters, were operated in the spot and short-term markets, primarily in the US Gulf grain trades. A three-year time-charter to Skjelbred was fixed for the *D.C. Coleman* in August 1976.

The *T.G. Shaughnessy* ordered in October 1968 was delivered three months early, on 28 January 1971. Because of extremely tight conditions in the tanker market, the *Shaughnessy* was fixed for three months and able to earn a substantial profit before taking up her ten-year charter to Gulf Oil.

In March 1971, anticipating the replacement of the ageing world product carrier fleet, CP (Bermuda) entered that market with the ordering of three 30,000dwt product carriers from Van der Giessen in Holland. These vessels were built with the intention of operating them in the short-term market. The first, the *G.A. Walker*, was delivered in March 1973, seven weeks late. She made two voyages and was then fixed to the Exxon Corporation of New York for three years. The *W.A. Mather* and the *R.A. Emerson* were chartered to Shell in May 1971 for five years while still under construction. They were delivered in July and November 1973 respectively. All three vessels were operated in the short-term market after their initial charters. Meantime Maple Shipping (London) had been reactivated and CP (Bermuda) used this company 'as a reference point for all brokerage needs' (see page 73).

In August 1972 a further two 30,000dwt product carrriers were ordered from the Van der Giessen yard at a cost of $11½ million each. After their delivery in March

The 31,000 ton product carrier Fort Coulonge

The launch of the Fort Nelson *on 28 May 1975 by Mrs Pritchard, wife of the chairman of CP Ships Ltd*

and November 1974, the *Fort Macleod* and *Fort Steele* traded in the spot market.

A further very large crude carrier (VLCC), similar in design to the *Port Hawkesbury*, was ordered on 1 September 1972, at a cost of $33,100,000. The *I.D. Sinclair* was delivered from NKK in July 1974, having been fixed on a three-year time-charter to Hilmar Reksten. However, in April 1975, Reksten defaulted on the charter party and the vessel lay in the Gulf from December 1974 until June 1975. After an out-of-court settlement had been reached the *Sinclair* was chartered to the Exxon Corporation of New York for one year, and afterwards traded on the spot market.

The ordering of the five product carriers and the VLCC marked a turning point in CP (Bermuda)'s assessment of the market. The company believed that the market for these vessels would continue to expand and present even more favourable opportunities in the future.

Hence its decision to order vessels without firm business, thereby indicating its willingness to accept the inherently riskier position of short-term operations, balanced against the premium rates expected in the 'spot' (short-term) market.

On 12 July 1973, CP (Bermuda) ordered three 35,000dwt geared bulk carriers designed for the forest products trade, from the west coast of Canada to Europe or the US east coast. They were ordered from the Sanoyasu Dockyard in Japan at a cost of $10,300,000. The *Fort Nelson* was delivered in August 1975, and after initially trading on the spot market was chartered to Aspen for one year. These vessels were equipped with Hagglund cranes as opposed to the Munck gantry cranes that had been fitted to the earlier forest product carriers. The second vessel, the *Fort Calgary*, was delivered in March 1976 and traded in the spot market. The third vessel in this series was sold, while under construction,

On 29 May 1980 the Fort Assiniboine *was sponsored by Mrs Margaret Vines (left), wife of Roger Vines of Alcoa, Australia. The company was represented at the ceremony by Mr and Mrs Joplin. Fred Joplin joined Canadian Pacific in 1947 and rose to become vice-president operations and maintenance for CP Rail. In July 1976 he was named president and chief executive CP (Bermuda)*

to the Leda Shipping Company of Liberia. Both the *Fort Nelson* and the *Fort Calgary* are currently on time-charter to Industrial Opportunities Inc carrying prefabricated homes.

Three more 30,000dwt product carriers were ordered from Van der Giessen on 7 July 1973, at a cost of $15,900,000 each. This order brought the fleet of product carriers to eight vessels. The *Fort Edmonton, Fort Kipp* and *Fort Coulonge* were delivered in February 1975, July 1975 and February 1976 respectively. After three spot

voyages the *Fort Kipp* was time-chartered to Kuwait National Petroleum Corporation for one year. The vessels have since been employed on the spot market.

While the operational fleet of CP (Bermuda) had not been expanded in 1972, during the year 1973 the fleet grew from ten to fourteen vessels and to nineteen by the end of 1974, when there were also eleven new buildings under supervision.

In late 1973, due to the Arab oil embargo, shortages of fuel were felt. Several vessels on time-charter were slow-steamed. By early 1974 negotiations with the charterers had succeeded in introducing bunker surcharges on the contracts of affreightment for the *Pacific Logger, W.C. Van Horne* and *T. Akasaka.* In early 1974 CP (Bermuda)'s expansion plans were reviewed in the light of oil prices and the reopening of the Suez Canal scheduled for later in the year. It was decided to drop further VLCC and product tanker projects.

In August 1974 CP (Bermuda) ordered two 60,000dwt gearless Panamax bulkers from Burmeister & Wain in Copenhagen, Denmark. These vessels were similar to the *T. Akasaka.* At this time world shipyards were full, consequently the price paid, approximately $26 million each, was high.

The *Port Vancouver* was delivered in January 1977, and since that time substituted for the *W.C. Van Horne* on the Marubeni Pacific Rim contract of affreightment, since the latter ship was a better slow-steamer and more marketable on the spot market. The *Port Quebec* was delivered in April 1977, and it alternated between spot employment and the Marubeni Hampton Roads contract. These changes to the Marubeni contracts enabled the *W.C. Van Horne* and *T. Akasaka* to be employed in the spot market.

In September 1974, the company ordered three 28,000dwt geared bulkers from the Sanoyasu yard. As with the *Port Vancouver* and *Port Quebec* they were ordered near the peak of the shipbuilding market. The *Fort Kamloops* was delivered in October 1976, the *Fort Victoria* in February 1977, and the *Fort Yale* in August 1977. All vessels took up spot employment upon delivery. The *Fort Kamloops* and the *Fort Yale* were later fixed on a time-charter to Sanko in June 1978.

Early in 1975, a wholly owned subsidiary, CP (Bermuda) Marketing Services, was established in London to provide marketing and chartering advice for the Bermuda fleet, reflecting the increasing importance of these activities.

The company sought to counter the effects of inflation on fixed-price charters entered into prior to 1973. In mid-1975 the *Lord Mount Stephen's* charter was terminated and the vessel laid-up in Scotland from September 1975 until March 1976. The *Lord Mount Stephen* and *Lord Strathcona* were later fixed on time-charter to Amoco for the carriage of crude oil from the Montrose field in the North Sea.

In late 1975, in order to improve the marketability of the *E.W. Beatty* and the *D.C. Coleman*, these vessels had eighteen feet cropped from their radar masts, which allowed them to pass under the Huey P. Long Bridge on the Mississippi River to load grain. The *E.W. Beatty's* ballast tanks were modified to give her access to the coal-loading chutes of Hampton Roads, Virginia. In 1975 slow-steaming was introduced to the fleet charterers' requirements for fuel conservation.

The *H.R. MacMillan* was detained in Basrah, Iraq, in a dispute over the quality of her rice cargo. From March 1976 until March 1978 the vessel awaited discharge. When released, she sailed to the Far East for dry-docking. The vessel was sold to Pender Shipping Corporation in June 1978.

In 1976 the company was successful in terminating the Canadian Transport Company charters for the *J.V. Clyne* and the *N.R. Crump*. The C. Itoh charter for the *Pacific Logger* was also terminated by mutual agreement.

On 1 July 1976, Mr A. F. Joplin was appointed president and chief executive officer of CP (Bermuda).

In October 1976 the company ordered three 22,000dwt geared bulkers from Sanoyasu. The *Fort Walsh* was delivered in January 1978, the *Fort Carleton* and the *Fort Hamilton* in March 1978. All were operated on the spot market after delivery.

In the third quarter of 1976, taking advantage of the temporary strengthening in the dry cargo markets, the company period-chartered five of the seven vessels available at that time at rates which proved to be in excess of continuing spot market levels. The *D.C. Coleman* was chartered to Skjelbred of Norway, the *Fort Nelson* and *Fort Calgary* to IOI and the *J.V. Clyne* and the *N.R. Crump* to Star Lines.

In 1976 and 1977, in a search for alternative markets, CP (Bermuda) successfully entered the company's product carriers in the vegetable parcel oil trades in both voyage and berth-term charters at rates which exceeded the average product tanker market. In October 1977 agreement was reached with Gulf Oil to allow the *T.G.*

Shaughnessy and the *Port Hawkesbury* to undertake slow-steaming on a trial basis.

In March 1978, the fleet was reorganised so that the container vessels no longer formed a separate unit but were coupled with the other vessels to give three divisions of ten to twelve ships each.

Captain P. A. Woods of the *Fort Calgary* suggested to the City of Calgary that his ship be linked with the Fort Calgary Park, which had been opened to mark the founding of the North West Mounted Police Fort in 1875. In May 1978, Norris Crump, a former chairman of Canadian Pacific, presented the city with a plaque from the officers and crew of the *Fort Calgary*.

Early in 1979 the *J.V. Clyne* and *N.R. Crump* were sold to the Korean Shipping Corporation and two 30,000dwt Imco class III product carriers were ordered from the Sanoyasu yard, for the carriage of caustic soda solution. An option for a further two sister ships was exercised in May 1979.

In 1980 five bulk carriers were bought and renamed *Fort Norman*, *Fort Fraser*, *Fort Douglas*, *Fort Erie* and *Fort Nanaimo*.

Following increasing international labour and organisational problems following the nomination of Bermuda as a 'flag of convenience' country, coupled with the uncertain future of the Bermuda Register, it was decided in mid-1980 that all vessels would gradually be transferred from the Bermuda Register to the UK and Hong Kong Registers.

Maple Shipping Company

Maple Shipping was originally formed in 1960, to arrange the charter of vessels to augment the Canadian Pacific Steamship transatlantic liner service and to provide ships for the movement of steel and motorcars to Canada, returning with grain from the Great Lakes. With containerisation overtaking conventional liner trades the need to charter extra 'tween-deck tonnage disappeared and with it the prime function of the old Maple Shipping Co. However, the name and company were preserved in case of need for the future.

By the early 1970s it was apparent, with the growth of the CP (Bermuda) tramp fleet, and also with the requirements of other subsidiary companies within the Canadian Pacific group for shipbroking services, that it made sense to restore an active shipbroking company.

In consequence, Maple Shipping was reactivated in October 1971. A branch office was opened in Vancouver in April 1972. Meanwhile Maple Shipping in London, with a seat on the Baltic Exchange, could offer full ship-broking services.

To assist the immediate development of Maple Shipping in Vancouver, CP (Bermuda) consigned its vessel agency activities in Western Canada in general, and Vancouver in particular, to Maple, as at that time it had various ships operating on the Pacific which were regular callers at Vancouver and environs. It was intended that Maple would initially be involved in marketing tonnage available from CP (Bermuda), developing new projects with in-house shippers and owners, developing projects with various other companies in connection with Canadian Pacific, and acting as a broker in the general marketplace.

After April 1973 the thrust of Maple in Canada changed radically, as the handling of CPB ships became a minor factor in the context of revenues earned. The company developed into a major force in the Vancouver shipping scene, attending some 250 vessels a year in an agency capacity, as well as handling between 5 and 6 million tonnes of export resources such as sulphur, potash, ore concentrates and coal in a forwarding capacity. It was also involved during 1979 in some one million tonnes of dry-bulk chartering.

Maple in Montreal, with a less spectacular development, nevertheless represents an active reefer consortium, acting as its exclusive chartering agent on the east coast of Canada and the Maritimes, as well as being an exclusive broker in Canada for a major heavy-lift owner, and acting as a competitive broker.

In 1977 considerable reorganisation of Canadian Pacific shipping activities saw the creation of a separate company, Maple Shipping (UK) Ltd. The original Maple Shipping became a division of Crossworld Freight (in turn a subsidiary of CanPac International Freight Services), while Maple Shipping (UK) Ltd became a subsidiary of CP Steamships. Both companies have separate directors and operate independently, but the total Maple approach has been maintained. During this reorganisation less emphasis was placed on the representation of house business and full emphasis given to developing outside and competitive contacts. All three offices—Vancouver, Montreal and London—have developed fast under this new strategy.

6 *British Columbia Coastal Services*

Canadian Pacific Navigation Company

The earliest steamship service on the British Columbian coast was provided by the Hudson's Bay Company with its steamer the *Beaver*, which arrived from England in 1836. In 1877 Captain J. Irving started a service from New Westminster to Yale BC, at the head of navigation of the Fraser River. In 1882 he obtained a contract to carry freight and passengers to help in the building of the Canadian Pacific Railway. Soon afterwards he was able to amalgamate his own Pioneer Line with the Hudson's Bay fleet to form in 1883 the Canadian Pacific Navigation Company (no connection with CPR).

Speaking at the annual general meeting in May 1887, Van Horne said:

I beg to call the attention of the Directors to the very unsatisfactory state of our steamship connections at the Pacific terminus. . . . It would be nearly as great folly, after building a railway across the continent, to stop short of providing the connections necessary to bring to it all the traffic within reasonable reach, as to fail to provide sufficient rolling stock.

The CPR realised from the start that a good steamship service was necessary to connect the end of rail on the

The last link with the Canadian Pacific Navigation Company ended in 1935, when the forty-eight-year-old Charmer *was dismantled* (World Ship Society)

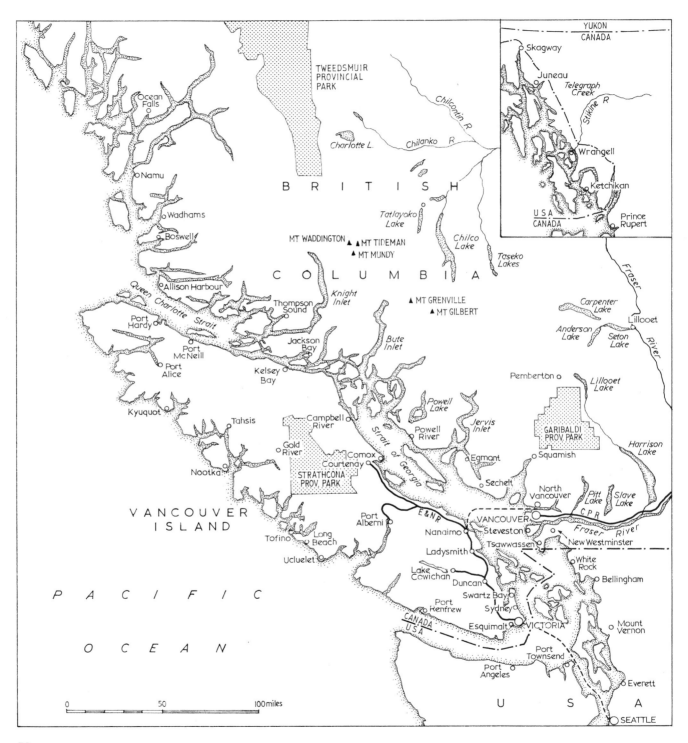

mainland to Vancouver Island. In 1893 an order was placed with William Denny Bros for the *Prince Rupert*. Before she could reach the Pacific coast, opposition from the CPN Company and other local interests forced the CPR to reconsider. When the *Prince Rupert* reached Tenerife she was recalled and laid-up at Plymouth before joining the Digby–Saint John service for the Dominion Atlantic Railway (see page 115).

By 1898 the Vancouver–Victoria service had further deteriorated and a change of feeling had occurred in business circles. Various bodies approached the CPR to improve the service. At about this time the Hudson's Bay Company, which had a large holding in the Canadian Pacific Navigation Company, was anxious to sell. On 10 January 1901 the CPR secured a controlling interest in the CPN Company. The formal transfer took place on 15 May 1903, when the red-and-white chequered house flag was hoisted on the vessels of the fleet, nine screw steamers and five paddle steamers.

Among the paddle steamers was the *Princess Louise*, the first of a line of thirty-two Princesses on the BC coast, plus two on the Bay of Fundy, *Princess Helene* and the *Princess of Acadia*. Captain J. W. Troup, then superintendent of the company's Lake and River Steamers, was appointed to reorganise the coastal fleet which grew, under his twenty-seven years as manager, into one of the finest coastal fleets in the world.

The first ship to be built for Canadian Pacific's new service was launched by Swan, Hunter & Wigham, Richardson's Wallsend yard, on 18 November 1902, and named *Princess Victoria*. She sailed round the Horn to Vancouver, where she arrived in March 1903, when she was promptly dubbed 'Troup's Folly'. This vessel proved an immediate success, with her speed of twenty knots plus, thanks to engines designed after those constructed for a unit of the Swedish Navy. She carried the broom at her masthead, being the fastest vessel in the coastwise service until the arrival of the *Princess Charlotte* in 1909. Although over the years there was a great deal of senti-

Captain J. W. Troup (left) born Portland, Oregon 1855, son and grandson of Columbia River steamboat captains. He joined the CPR in 1897 as superintendent of the BC Lake & River steamers. In 1901 he became manager of the coastal service and in the next twenty-seven years built the Princess fleet into one of the finest coastal fleets in the world. He retired in 1928 and died on 30 November 1931. Sir George McLaren Brown, born on 29 January 1865, in Hamilton, Ontario, joined the CPR in 1887, moving to London in 1910 as general manager for Europe. He was awarded the KBE in 1919, retired in 1936 and died on 25 June 1939 (BC Provincial Archives)

mental prejudice over the '*Old Vic*', undoubtedly, the *Charlotte* was the faster of the two.

CANADIAN PACIFIC RAILWAY COMPANY

STEAMSHIP LINES

OFFICE OF THE GENERAL SUPERINTENDENT
BRITISH COLUMBIA COAST SERVICE
VICTORIA, B.C. July 28/04.

Captain P. J. Hickey,
    Master, Str. *Princess Victoria.*

Dear Sir:

  In taking command of the *Princess Victoria* I wish to impress upon you the necessity for extreme care in the protection of life and property.

  Please attend carefully to boat and fire drill, see that your equipment is in good shape and that all officers and men are carefully instructed. Observe carefully the regulations for preventing collisions at sea (give all vessels a wide berth). Do not neglect Article 16 of these regulations which requires that 'every vessel shall in a fog, or in a heavy snow or wind storm go at a moderate speed, having careful regard to existing circumstances and conditions'. While we have a published schedule, bear in mind that the Company do not wish any risk whatever run in order to maintain this schedule, take no chances in foggy or stormy weather. Should you arrive late we will take care of the mails and traffic with other steamers. It is needless to say we shall expect you to be on the bridge yourself in passing through Vancouver Narrows, also to take charge whenever possible in passing through Active Pass, and invariably when the tide is running strong. You are expected also to take charge yourself in entering and leaving Seattle harbor, and in entering and leaving Victoria harbor. Please arrange your watches so that there shall be one of the Mates standing watch with the regular officer when under way between Point Wilson and Seattle in either direction.

  See personally that a good lookout is kept. Do not allow your lookout to converse with passengers when on duty. See that your night watchmen are attentive, particularly in the matter of precautions against fire. Let them report to the bridge at least once every hour. Do not fail to order your watertight doors closed when running in thick weather. Maintain thorough discipline throughout the ship, and report to me if you are having any difficulty or need any assistance.

               Yours truly,
               (sgd. J. W. Troup)
           General Superintendent

The Esquimalt & Nanaimo Railway

The Esquimalt & Nanaimo Railway had operated steamship services from the east coast of Vancouver Island to Vancouver from 1889, and when the CPR bought the company in 1905, two of its passenger steamers, the *City of Nanaimo* and the *Joan*, were added to the CP fleet.

The Triangle Service

The famous Triangle Service really developed from the speed of the '*Old Vic*' and the fertile imagination of Captain Troup. After a refit in Esquimalt she was placed on the Victoria–Vancouver run, making a round trip each day. This left her with time to spare, and in June a new schedule was devised—the 'crazy run', with the *Princess Victoria* leaving Victoria at 07.30 hours, returning from Vancouver at mid-day, and leaving Victoria again at 19.00 hours for a round trip to Seattle. This meant steaming for approximately sixteen hours, and sailing 280-odd miles in each twenty-four hours.

  Captain Troup soon saw the possibilities for further development and, in September 1908, the 'triangle' proper was established with the *Princess Victoria* and *Princess Royal* sailing in opposite directions around the 'triangle'. The Seattle leg was operated at night. This became one of the most important services of the coastal fleet for the next forty years. The *Princess Kathleen* and *Princess Marguerite* took over from the *Victoria* and *Charlotte* from 1925 until World War II, when the Seattle overnight run had to be withdrawn and was never resumed. A 'tri-city' service was substituted after the war.

Princess Mary (1901–19)

The *Princess Mary* was the first Princess to be converted to oil fuel, in March 1911; other conversions followed quickly. The main advantage was the saving of manpower in the boiler rooms, faster refuelling and almost continuous availability. Coal burners had to be taken out of service for half a day each week to draw the fire.

  On 19 May 1911 the *Princess Alice* was launched, the first Princess designed to burn oil fuel. However, for her voyage from the Clyde to the Pacific coast she burned coal, being converted back to oil fuel on arrival. She joined the *Princess Adelaide* on a night service between Victoria and Vancouver. Night services were particularly attractive to businessmen in those days, enabling them

The 2000 ton Princess Victoria, *the first ship to be built for the coastal service. During her forty-seven years she became known affectionately as the 'Old Vic' 1903–50*

to travel out of business hours and make an early start next morning. Another attraction in the case of the Victoria–Vancouver service was that the ships had all day to load and unload cargo. On some services there could be a bit of a scramble to keep to the tight schedules.

Princess Patricia (1912–37)

In 1902 Denny Brothers of Dumbarton had built the second passenger ship to be powered by steam turbines, the *Queen Alexandra*. She had three turbines driving three shafts. Originally the outside shafts were fitted with two screws, which were later replaced by a single screw. She ran on the Clyde until 10 September 1911, when she caught fire at Greenock. She was bought by Canadian Pacific and returned to Denny Brothers to be reconditioned; at the same time her superstructure was enlarged to provide enclosed lounges which increased

her tonnage to 1158g. She sailed from the Clyde on 12 January 1912, making the 16,000 mile journey to Victoria via Cape Horn in forty-three days and twenty-one hours, an average of 14.4 knots. She was then overhauled at Esquimalt and converted to oil fuel.

The *Princess Patricia* entered the Vancouver–Nanaimo run on 11 May 1912, and continued on that run until 5 May 1928, when she ran on summer cruises and acted as a relief boat until 1932, when she was laid-up at Esquimalt. The '*Pat*' had completed 7324 round trips between Vancouver and Nanaimo during her sixteen years on that run. She was replaced by the *Princess Elaine*, designed to carry sixty motorcars on her main deck.

Princess Maquinna (1913–53)

One of the best-loved ships on the coast was the *Princess*

In 1911 the CPR bought the 700 ton Princess Patricia, *which had been built in 1902 by Denny Bros of Dumbarton as* Queen Alexandra; *the second turbine ship to be built*

Maquinna, a steel vessel with fifty-four state rooms and good cargo space. She sailed on her maiden voyage on 20 July 1913, and served more than forty ports along the west coast of Vancouver Island for thirty-nine years. Before the days of cars and aeroplanes, all the scattered communities depended upon these small coastal ships for news, supplies and trade—their only link with the outside world. The tremendous reliance and importance placed on these steamers may be judged by the fact that with the coming of radio, newscasters would announce their position and next port of call each day.

On 10 August 1924, the *Princess Maquinna* left Victoria with a distinguished party including the Lieutenant-Governor of British Columbia, the Honourable W. C. Nichol, and Judge Howay of New Westminster, presi-

dent of the British Columbia Historical Association. The purpose of the trip was to unveil a monument in honour of the early explorers of Nootka Sound, a bronze tablet affixed to a cairn:

Nootka Sound, discovered by Captain Cook in March 1778. In June 1789 Spain took possession and established and maintained a settlement until 1795. The capture of British vessels in 1789 almost led to war, which was avoided by the Nootka Convention of 1790. Vancouver and Quadra met here in August 1792, to determine the land to be restored under the Convention.

After thirty-nine years' service along the west coast of Vancouver Island the *Princess Maquinna* was worn out and had to be laid-up at Vancouver, until she was sold to the Union Steamship Company who converted her hull to a barge. When she was finally broken up in 1962, her bell was presented to the Missions to Seamen Museum at Tofino on the west coast and her binnacle went to the Ucluelet Sea Cadets.

By 1913 there were twelve Princess steamers, ten of them having been built to the orders of Captain Troup. A magnificent coastal fleet had been achieved in twelve years. To meet increasing traffic it was decided to lengthen the *Princess Mary*. A new 40ft section was added to the hull in the Esquimalt yards, increasing her tonnage to 2155. At the same time twenty-four first-class cabins were added and she was converted to oil fuel. She returned to service in May 1914. In addition to the work on the *Princess Mary* a survey of the fleet had recommended that four new ships would be needed to meet expected traffic growth. Two turbine steamers were to be built for the 'triangle' service and two slightly smaller ships for the night run between Vancouver and Victoria.

Princess Irene and *Princess Margaret* (1914)

Captain Troup visited Scotland in May 1913 and placed an order with Denny Bros of Dumbarton for two Princess ships with geared turbine engines to give a speed of twenty-three knots. They were to be the largest and finest ships in the fleet.

The *Princess Margaret* ran her trials in October 1914, and in the same month the *Princess Irene* was launched. It was hoped that the *Princess Margaret* would leave for the Pacific after her trials, but it was now wartime and it was decided that the two vessels should sail together. In December both vessels were requisitioned by the Admiralty to become minelayers. Their elaborate furnishings were never to be used.

In April and May the *Princess Irene* made two minelaying forays and was at Sheerness, already loaded with mines for her third trip, when on 27 May she exploded and sank. Only one man survived, having been blown clear of the ship. A monument was later erected opposite the railway station in Sheerness. The *Princess Margaret* continued as flagship of the minelaying squadron and in 1921 was refitted as an Admiralty yacht. She was broken up in 1929.

The worst disaster on the coast happened on 23 October 1918 when the *Princess Sophia*, southbound from Skagway, ran into a snow storm and crashed on Vanderbilt reef. The gale-force winds increased and at high tide the stern of the vessel lifted; she turned over and sank on 25 October, with the loss of 343 lives.

Traffic boomed immediately after the war and replacements were urgently needed, but British shipyards had full order books and deliveries were slow because of shortages of materials. A local yard, the Wallace Shipbuilding & Dry Dock Company of Vancouver, thereby secured the order for a second *Princess Louise*. Her cabins were equipped with hot and cold water and her single funnel distinguished her from other Princess ships. She started service on the night run between Victoria and Vancouver, but during the summer transferred to the Alaska run.

Princess Kathleen (1925–52); *Princess Marguerite* (1925–42)

In 1923 the John Brown yard received the long-awaited order for replacements for the *Princess Irene* and *Princess Margaret*. The new Princesses both sailed from the Clyde to Victoria under the command of Captain R. W. McMurray and entered the 'triangle' run in 1925. They were equipped to carry thirty automobiles, which proved to be quite inadequate. The *Princess Patricia* had been on the Vancouver–Nanaimo run since 1912 and during that time traffic had continued to increase; there was also a growing need to be able to carry motorcars. A replacement was ordered from the John Brown yard in 1927, the *Princess Elaine*, designed to carry 1200 passengers and 60 cars. She entered service on 7 May 1928.

While in Scotland for the trials of the *Princess Elaine*, Captain Troup placed his last order for Canadian Pacific, for the *Princess Norah* designed for the service along the west coast of Vancouver Island and the Alaska run. Captain Troup had joined Canadian Pacific when they took over the lake and river boats of the Kootenay Steam Navigation Company in 1897, and had stamped his personality on the BC coastal fleet from 1901 until he retired in 1928. He became a legendary character. Captain C. D. Neroutsos followed Captain Troup as manager of the coastal fleet and in 1929 ordered two new ships, the *Princess Elizabeth* and *Princess Joan* to replace the *Adelaide* and the *Alice* on the Vancouver to Victoria night service. The new sisters had 207 cabins, a few of which had bathrooms, and there were twenty-eight single cabins with showers. There was also space for fifty motorcars. The following years were difficult ones. Traffic declined during the world depression and at the same time Canadian

Captain and Mrs R. W. McMurray with (on left) Captain J. P. Dobson. Captain McMurray joined the Atlantic fleet and in 1934 was appointed manager of the BC coastal fleet. In 1945 he moved to Montreal as managing director, Canadian Pacific Steamships

National tried to outdo the CPR with its new coastal service, but suffered heavy losses and withdrew the service in 1932.

Captain R. W. McMurray

Captain McMurray had joined the company's Atlantic fleet in 1910 and was later chosen to deliver two of the Princess steamers to the Pacific coast. Speaking of the coastal service in 1928, he said: 'The fleet was a happy combination of ocean going, coastal and river steamers,

with all cargo carried on the main deck, being loaded and discharged through freight doors in the ship's side.' In 1934 he succeeded Captain Neroutsos as manager of the coastal fleet and in 1945 was appointed managing director of Canadian Pacific Steamships in Montreal.

Records for the year 1938 show that the BCCSS fleet, consisting of fourteen passenger plus one cargo vessel with a gross tonnage of 56,642, steamed 676,984 miles carrying 878,290 passengers, 63,403 automobiles, 146,696 tons of cargo, and 256,696 tons by transfer barges. This was achieved with a staff of sixty-four deck officers with 265 ratings, and eighty-six engineer officers with 165 ratings. In the high season there were 580 on the catering staff.

The outbreak of World War II generated additional traffic for the fifteen ships of the coastal fleet, and in 1941 the *Princess Kathleen* and *Princess Marguerite* were requisitioned for service in the Mediterranean (see page 201). *Princess Louise, Princess Adelaide* and *Princess Norah* sailed for the US Army transport service to Alaska in 1942–3. Captain O. J. Williams became manager of the coastal fleet in July 1945 when Captain McMurray left for Montreal.

In 1946 two new turbo-electric ships were ordered from the Fairfield yard, *Princess Marguerite* and *Princess Patricia*, named after the two early ships of the fleet. The overnight run on the Vancouver–Victoria–Seattle service had been abandoned, so the new ships were designed as day steamers with only fifty-one cabins. A coffee shop proved more popular than the dining saloon. Provision was made for the carriage of sixty cars, but this again proved to be inadequate. The *Princess Patricia* made a fast run to Esquimalt via Panama, covering the 9626 miles in twenty-one days and thirteen hours, averaging more than eighteen knots and arriving on 3 June 1949. Also in 1949, the Typaldos Steamship Company of Piraeus bought the *Princess Charlotte, Princess Adelaide* and *Princess Alice* and renamed them *Mediterranean, Angelika* and *Aegaeon* for service in Greek waters.

By the 1950s the rapid growth of road and air services was responsible for a drastic change in the pattern of traffic on the coast. Demand for night travel had disappeared and with it the need for luxury accommodation. There was a growing demand for a fast means of moving an ever-increasing number of cars and trucks across intervening stretches of water. The West Coast Service was withdrawn in 1958. The Victoria–Vancouver night service, started in 1911, came to an end on 24 February 1959, when the *Princess Joan* made her last run. The 'tri-city' service was withdrawn in September 1960.

One gleam of hope remained: cruises to Alaska. In 1963 the *Princess Patricia* sailed into Esquimalt for a major overhaul. Designed as a day ship, additional accommodation was built on her car deck and upper deck, in all 152 cabins, 127 with private facilities, increasing her accommodation to 346 and her gross tonnage to 6062. She returned for her first summer cruise on 1 June 1963. She was chartered to Princess Cruises for winter cruising between Los Angeles and Acapulco in 1965–6

and 1966–7, and has since cruised each summer to Alaska for the CPR.

Black Ball Line

In 1953 the Black Ball Line (Canada) Ltd, of Puget Sound, began operating car ferries in Canadian waters between Departure Bay, Nanaimo, and Horseshoe Bay, Vancouver. By June 1960, the BC government had also entered the scene, building new terminals at Swartz Bay and Tsawwassen, south of Vancouver, and operating two new roll-on, roll-off ferries, with accommodation for 100 cars and 900 passengers each. Bow and stern doors allowed the ferries to turn round in less than half an hour so that a bus journey from city-centre Victoria to city-centre Vancouver could be made in $3\frac{1}{4}$ hours. Traffic increased rapidly! In 1958 the ferry services had been interrupted for a long spell by a strike of seamen, and in an endeavour to prevent future disruptions the BC government took over the ships and property of the Canadian Black Ball Line in November 1961.

After a retirement dinner on board the *Princess Patricia* on 6 September 1962 to honour Captain Williams, D. B. Prentice, superintendent engineer, and Harold Miller, catering superintendent, Harry Tyson took over as manager of the coastal service, the first time the post had been held by other than a master mariner.

In an effort to stem the tide, the *Princess Marguerite* went to Yarrow BC yard in 1972. Passenger accommodation on the upper deck was removed to make room for a further thirty-five cars, but this served only to aggravate still further the already crowded passenger space. After only two years on the Victoria–Port Angeles run it was announced in September 1974 that the ship would be sold, ending a seventy-year service between Victoria and Seattle by Canadian Pacific. The BC government stepped in and bought the *Princess Marguerite*, which it continued to operate, at a loss.

Over the years Canadian Pacific provided a number of distinct services on the Pacific coast. Many of the ships were built to serve a specific route, but all were at times switched to meet the demands of traffic and to cover vessels temporarily withdrawn for overhaul or repair (see page 229).

The Vancouver Pier B–C, originally built for the Pacific Empresses, is now being rebuilt as a convention centre and pier for ships in the Alaska cruise service.

The 1200 ton Motor Princess, *the company's first diesel powered vessel and also its first car ferry 1923–55*

Car Ferries

Canadian Pacific had pioneered the movement of motorcars as early as 1907 when there were two cars making occasional trips between Vancouver and Vancouver Island. The company required two days' notice of these movements, the cars being loaded on the foredeck of the *Joan*.

Motor Princess (1923–55)

In 1923 the *Motor Princess* was ordered from Yarrows. She was a wooden ship, 170ft long with two McIntosh & Seymour diesel engines driving twin screws. Fitted with side-loading doors in addition to fore and aft openings,

she could carry forty-five cars on two decks which were connected by a ramp. There was also accommodation for 370 day passengers. She was launched on 31 March 1923, amid much controversy. Even Sir Alfred Yarrow, head of the British Columbia yard, was annoyed that his son should have accepted the order and built such a monstrosity! The squat fat appearance of the car ferry compared badly with the sleek lines of the other Princesses. She was delivered only ninety-seven days after her keel was laid and started service on the Bellingham–Sydney route, but by 1925 had been transferred to the Vancouver–Nanaimo run. Later she ran between Sydney and Steveston.

When launched the *Motor Princess* was the first motor

Built for the Vancouver–Nanaimo service in 1950, the 7000 ton
Princess of Nanaimo *was transferred to the Digby–Saint John*
route in the Bay of Fundy in 1963 after being renamed Princess
of Acadia

ship built for the CPR as well as being their first motorcar
ferry. After thirty years' service she was withdrawn in
1953. On 16 September in the following year her bell was
presented to the Vancouver Sailors' Home, and on 17
January 1955 one of her lifeboats was presented to the
Indian Mission School at Tofino. After being re-engined
and rebuilt, so as to be almost unrecognisable, she
became *Pender Queen* for the BC Ferry Authority and
is now laid up.

Princess vessels built after 1924 usually provided
accommodation for a small number of cars, but in the
event there was never sufficient capacity to meet the
growing demand.

Princess of Nanaimo (1951–73)

The simple car ferry had come a long way by 1951 when
a modern 7000 ton car ferry appeared, the *Princess of
Nanaimo*. She was fitted with two sets of single-reduction
steam turbines generating 9000 horsepower and giving
a speed of eighteen knots, and was 358ft long. Much of
the boat deck superstructure had been prefabricated in
aluminium alloys and lifted bodily into position. Space
for 130 motorcars was provided on two decks, the cars
being still loaded through side ports. Three more decks
provided spacious accommodation for 1500 day passengers with a large observation lounge, a restaurant and
coffee bar.

Launched by Lady Anderson, wife of Sir John Anderson, a director of the Canadian Pacific Railway, on 14 September 1950 from the Fairfield yard, she left the Clyde on 2 May 1951 for her 9500 mile trip to Vancouver. Before entering regular service, courtesy calls were made at Vancouver and Nanaimo when more than 9000 visitors toured the vessel. Formal receptions were held in the evening when the mayor of Nanaimo presented an engraved plaque to the ship.

In 1962 rumours were rife that because of rising costs the coastal service would have to be cut back. At the same time the ageing *Princess Helene* on the Bay of Fundy was urgently in need of replacement. On 28 February 1963, the *Princess of Nanaimo* left the Pacific coast, after only twelve years' service, and sailed for Saint John, where, after being renamed *Princess of Acadia* to honour the people and history of the east coast, she entered the forty-three mile Digby–Saint John run on 29 April 1963 (see page 120).

Freight Services

Freight steamers served the ports along the coast to Skagway and the west coast of Vancouver Island, according to demand.

Princess Ena (1907–31)

Because of her broad beam the first cargo Princess was often referred to as the 'Blue Funnel Pup'. The marine superintendent at Liverpool, writing to the superintendent engineer at Vancouver, said:

> In my opinion she is the strongest little ship of her size that has ever been built. She made 10½ knots with 1160dwt on board on a 15ft draft during the trials. There was but one man in the stokehold, so you see she steams very easily. She has plenty of boiler power. Her engines are a simple compound job, good and solid for hard work. She has been inspected by a number of leading Coasting firms here, who were so pleased with her that they have laid down some vessels on the same lines.
>
> Lloyd's are greatly pleased with her, as when fully loaded she is a much better and more seaworthy vessel than the type of coaster generally built.

Only 195ft in length, she had a gross tonnage of 1368 and could carry 1300 tons of cargo with space for 800 head of cattle on her deck. She left the Mersey on 31 October 1907, and after a call at Montevideo for coal and water arrived at Victoria on 22 January 1908. At the beginning of World War I she acted as a supply ship for the Royal Canadian Navy. In March 1916 the little *Princess* carried urgently needed explosives to Vladivostok and returned to Seattle with a cargo of sugar-beet seed and sheep's intestines. On 28 June 1918 she made a second trans-Pacific voyage, this time to Kobe, returning to Victoria on 12 September 1918. In 1926 she was fitted with steel tanks to carry 75,000 gallons of fish oil, plus accommodation for five passengers. After twenty-five years on the coast she was retired and sold.

The *Nootka* bought in 1926 and the *Yukon Princess* bought in 1950, were also used for tramping along the coast until the mid fifties, by which time tugs towing barges had taken over. The *Nootka* would often carry coal to Skagway, Alaska, loading ore or asbestos concentrates for the return trip. Other cargoes on the southbound trip could be salmon from the Butedale or Namu canneries, newsprint from Ocean Falls, pilchard oil and fishmeal from the Queen Charlotte Islands. Voyages down the west coast of Vancouver Island might include calls at Nootka for cannery products and Port Alice for baled pulp and newsprint.

All the passenger vessels could also carry packaged freight and in the early days the night boats on the Vancouver–Victoria service would spend nearly all day loading Oriental cargo at the outer wharf for transhipment to Vancouver. After the arrival of the *Princess Elizabeth* and *Princess Joan* in 1930, less time was spent in port by the night boats. From Victoria they would often make day runs to Port Angeles or double back to Vancouver. From Vancouver they were often used for a day trip to Nanaimo.

Rail Box Cars

Another important part of the coastal service has been the ferrying of rail box cars between the transcontinental rail terminal at Vancouver and the Esquimalt & Nanaimo Railway on Vancouver Island. From 1889 the Dunsmuir Company, who owned the E&N Railway, had operated steamer services for passengers and freight from Victoria, Comox and other points on the east coast of Vancouver Island.

The E&N Railway built a transfer slip at Ladysmith,

The 2000 ton Nootka *was bought in 1926 for tramping along the BC coast to Alaska. She had been built in 1919 as the* Canadian Adventurer (World Ship Society)

some twenty miles south of Nanaimo, and reached an agreement with the CPR for the interchange of freight car traffic. The first car loads which were ferried between the then separately owned railways arrived in Victoria on 2 December 1900. The forty mile crossing was made by the tug *Czar* with *Transfer Barge Number 1*, which could carry twelve box cars. Both these vessels joined the CP fleet when the E&N Railway was bought in 1905. The slipway was bought in 1918 and continued in use until 1955.

Transfer barges were flat topped, fitted with rail track and could carry around fifteen rail box cars. A number of tugs were used over the years, *Czar, Dola, Nanoose, Nitinat* and *Qualicum*. The last Canadian Pacific tug on the coast was the *Kyuquot*, and after she was withdrawn in 1957, barges were moved, when necessary, under contract by the Island Tug & Barge Company.

The first carload of lumber was forwarded from the Coburn Sawmill, Shawnigan Lake, and was used in the construction of the Woodwards Store in Vancouver. This was the first of many thousands of carloads of lumber from various sawmills on the Island to be ferried across the Gulf to markets in Canada, the United States and overseas.

The E&N Railway acted as a feeder for services from the island, since almost four-fifths of the total carloads originating on the railway were transferred to the mainland, consisting mainly of lumber, forest products and coal. General merchandise, meat, fruit and butter made up the bulk of the return loads.

In the early days Victoria was the distribution centre for the whole Island and something like seventy-five per cent of freight cars ferried from the mainland were destined for Victoria; but over the years the proportion fell for various reasons. More traffic moved by all water routes via the Panama Canal. The Vancouver–Nanaimo

KYUQUOT

TRANSFER Nº4

VICTORIA BC

route was developed to serve the northern part of the Island. New highway services also appeared.

Early records are scarce, but the following figures indicate the growing importance of the E&N Railway service over Ladysmith.

| | Rail cars | |
	inward	outward
1907	2891	3471
1911	6745	6455

Because of the early importance of Victoria, a transfer slip was built at Thetis Cove, Esquimalt, about four miles from Victoria, the first rail-cars arriving on 12 April 1913. The slipway was abandoned in 1931 and used to rebuild the facilities at Ladysmith.

In 1920 a new slipway was built at Nanoose Bay, eighty-four miles from Victoria; this became known as the 'Jayem' after the initials of the manager of the E&N Railway, J. M. Cameron. The new port handled traffic to the north of the Island. After the abandonment of the facilities at Esquimalt, all barge traffic was handled over Ladysmith and Jayem until 1955. Growth in the lumber, pulp, plywood and paper industries on the Island are reflected in the following figures:

| | Rail cars | |
	inward	outward
1920	5215	10,474
1929	5624	15,208
1942	7459	17,282
1956	13,019	14,357
1961	7169	11,773
1971	10,687	11,504

The CPR acquired a wharf at Nanaimo in 1910 for its service to Vancouver. In 1947 this was rebuilt to include facilities for buses and trucks, but it had no rail connection. In 1955 a modern car ferry dock was built at Wellcox, within the city of Nanaimo, together with a railway marshalling yard.

A new type of ferry service was inaugurated. Instead of having to provide passenger ships with space for a small number of motorcars plus transfer barges and tugs for the movement of rail-cars, all were now combined in the new multi-purpose roll-on, roll-off vessel, designed

One of several barges to move rail box cars between the mainland and Vancouver Island

to handle passengers, buses, road-trailers, private cars, as well as rail-cars. In practice the rail-cars would mostly be handled on night runs, and road vehicles by day. After fifty-five years tugs and barges were no longer needed, except for relief work, when barges were moved under contract.

Princess of Vancouver (1955–   )

Mrs Arkle, wife of the managing director for Canadian Pacific in Europe, launched the *Princess of Vancouver* on 7 March 1954, from the Alexander Stephen yard at Linthouse.

The *Princess*, a 5500 ton twin-screw passenger vehicle and train ferry was powered by twin diesels on each shaft driving through hydraulic couplings, with oil-operated reverse reduction gearing. To facilitate manoeuvring, pneumatically operated remote controls were fitted in the wheelhouse, the wings of the bridge and the docking bridge aft. From these positions the electrically driven Voith-Schneider propeller, in a forward athwartship tunnel, could also be controlled. The surface of the main deck was flush with the tops of four rail tracks, enabling twenty-eight railway box-cars or 150 motorcars to be carried.

The ship was so designed that her scheduled service speed for her three round trips a day on the thirty-six-mile crossing between Vancouver and Nanaimo could be maintained with only three engines, enabling the vessel to remain in operation 362 days a year. Three days were allowed for hull cleaning. Two lounges on the boat deck and two on the upper deck provided seating accommodation for 770 passengers. There was also a coffee shop on the upper deck.

The *Princess of Vancouver* left the Clyde on 29 April 1955, with a cargo of 150 Ford cars for the trip to Vancouver, where she arrived on 5 June. To mark the occasion the mayor of Vancouver presented the ship with a plaque. In September 1972, the *Princess* entered the Burrard dry dock yard at North Vancouver for a refit. Four new General Motors diesels, totalling 8600hp, increased her speed to seventeen knots. The aft deck was modified to provide more room for oversized vehicles, and the rail tracks were renewed. On Sunday 20 June 1976 the 'Van' celebrated her twenty-first birthday with a party for a number of retired crew members and representatives from the World Ship Society.

The expanded vessel capacity and service provided by

the BC Ferry Corporation prompted Canadian Pacific to announce in November 1979 that the *Princess of Vancouver* would carry freight only between January and May 1980, with the passenger service to be resumed for the summer season.

Trailer Princess (1966–   )

In 1966 the CPR bought a tank landing craft which had been built for the US navy in 1944. She was refitted at Victoria to carry rail-cars and road-trailers. Renamed *Trailer Princess*, she was placed in service between Swartz Bay and Vancouver. To supplement this service the *Haida Transporter* was chartered from Kingcome Navigation Company in July 1969.

With the success of this type of operation an order was placed with the Burrard Dry Dock Company of Vancouver for a 3000 ton 380ft ferry based on the *Trailer Princess*. Built to carry 30 rail-cars, or 150 automobiles, or 50 trailers plus 260 passengers, she was powered by four General Motors diesels generating 11,500bhp driving twin screws to give a speed of eighteen knots and enabling her to make three round trips per day between Swartz Bay and Vancouver. The *Carrier Princess* was launched on 20 February 1973, and sponsored by Mrs R. Strachan, wife of the Minister of Highways BC. This was the first launch for Canadian Pacific from a BC yard since the *Motor Princess* left the Yarrow slipway in 1923.

Northland Navigation Ltd

By 1958 Northland Navigation Ltd of Vancouver was operating a tug and barge service along the west coast ports to the north and had qualified for a government subsidy. To augment its service the company bought the *Princess Alberni* and the *Queen of the North* from the CPR. In January 1959 it bought the remaining ships of the Union Steamship Company of British Columbia, which had been running into difficulties since the end of the war.

By 1977 Northland was handling package freight, pallets, containers and bulk commodities on a twice-weekly

(opposite above)
Canadian Pacific's first roll-on, roll-off ferry for rail-cars and road vehicles, built in 1955 for the Vancouver–Nanaimo run. The 6000 ton Princess of Vancouver *is still in service*

(below)
A war-time American tank landing ship bought in 1966 and renamed Trailer Princess *for the Vancouver–Swartz Bay run; she is still in service*

service with tugs and covered barges from Vancouver to Kitimat and other local ports. A subsidiary, Skeena Motor Carriers, ran road services out of Kitimat. In December 1977, Canadian Pacific announced that it had signed a lease agreement to take over three tugs, four barges and the trucking operations of the Northland Company from 1 January 1978 for a period of six years, with an option to buy outright.

Losses in 1978–9 caused the service to be withdrawn on 30 January 1980.

For fleet list see page 257.

The tug Ocean Prince *II with the barge* Northland Transporter, 1979

7 British Columbia Lake and River Services

BC Lake-River Steamers

For many years the lakes and rivers, flowing north–south, were the only highways in mountainous British Columbia, and later acted as important feeders to the transcontinental railway. The discovery of valuable deposits of gold, silver, lead, zinc, copper and coal attracted settlers to the area. Many from the United States travelled on the Columbia River boats. Experienced American river boatmen were among the first to build and operate boats on the Canadian rivers. Most of the boats plying these waterways were stern-wheelers together with a few small screw vessels. All had to be shallow draft and some, it has been said, needed as little as twenty-two

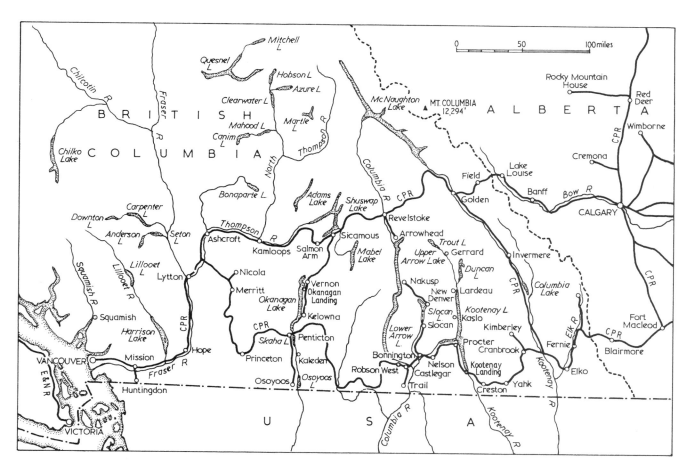

inches of water. Many landings were made by running the bow of the ship ashore and putting out a gangplank over which passengers and supplies, or the produce of mines and fruit farms, were loaded or unloaded.

Prospectors, loggers, farmers and hunters all knew that a flag or signal-fire would bring a steamer to the shore, between their regular stops on journeys up and down the lakes. Until the coming of the motorcar and aeroplane these river boats were the lifeline of the settlers. They were often comfortably equipped for passengers and were well known for the excellent dining-room service they provided. They could also act as travelling post office or bank. In the latter years of the service many communities were provided with wharves and docks built by the government. Ice and low water in the rivers could cause the suspension of steamboat services, thus isolating the settlements. The steamboats could push metal-sheathed barges into the ice, or reverse and allow the stern paddle to break up the ice, providing it was not too thick.

The completion of the transcontinental line in 1886, to the north of this area, placed Canadian Pacific in competition with J. J. Hill's Great Northern Railway, south of the border. To help develop the area and retain traffic in Canada, the CPR was eventually forced to build a second railway line from Medicine Hat through Nelson, Cranbrook and Penticton to the coast. The BC government was interested, and granted a charter, among others, for the Crow's Nest & Kootenay Lake Railway in 1888. Later renamed the BC Southern Railway, it had powers to build from Nelson to the Provincial boundary. In 1892 the CPR leased the Alberta Railway & Coal Company's line from Dunmore, near Medicine Hat, to Lethbridge, which could be extended westwards through Nelson to the coast when money became available.

The importance and size of the steamboat operations in this part of the country may be judged by the following report which appeared in the 'Kootenay Mail' on 7 October 1898: 'On Sunday there were six steamers, *Columbia*, *Lytton*, *Kootenay*, *Illecillewaet*, *Marion* and *Arrow*, waiting at the wharves at Revelstoke to load and unload the next day.' Recalling this era of steamboating on the treacherous Columbia River, and the beautiful Arrow and Kootenay lakes, the 'Vancouver Sun' of 11 May 1940 spoke of:

Paddle Wheelers that would float on heavy dew, ornate smoking rooms and dining rooms, that put

the luxurious Mississippi boats to shame, rapids that took six hours to negotiate against the current, one minute and six seconds or so with the current, and men who worked so hard that they never learned whether or not their ships had crew's sleeping quarters.

Canadian Pacific's development of steamboating centred on four main valleys, the Okanagan and Skaha lakes, the Columbia River and Arrow lakes, the Slocan Lake and the Kootenay and Trout lakes. Apart from commercial traffic, the tourist potential of the area began to be exploited in the early 1900s with round trips by rail and steamboat from Revelstoke. Visitors to Banff, for example, could sail south in the *Kootenay* or *Bonnington* from Arrowhead to Robson and then north on Kootenay Lake to Lardeau. The steamboats could also be hired for special outings.

Much highway building took place in the nineteen-twenties and thirties and by 1931 Nelson, Nakusp and Vernon had been linked by a bus service. To keep up with the growing number of road users, several of the steamboats on each of the lakes had by 1927 been modified to carry automobiles, from two on the *Slocan* to twenty-three on the *Nasookin*. For a few years this became an increasingly important feature of the services, but eventually road vehicles made the whole steamboat operation uneconomic, and a pleasant and romantic transport system died.

Okanagan Lake

The CPR opened a branch line from Sicamous, on the main line, to Okanagan Landing on 15 June 1892, and opened its own shipyard, 1100ft above sea level, in 1893. The company's first river steamer, the *Aberdeen*, was launched on 22 May 1893. This was the start of the company's BC Lake and River Services. The *Aberdeen*, a wooden sternwheeler 146ft in length, provided the CPR with a link to Penticton, sixty miles to the south end of the lake. By 1901 the *Aberdeen* was badly in need of repairs and in order to allow her to be withdrawn, the steel twin-screw vessel *York*, which was being built in sections in Toronto for service on Trout Lake, was diverted instead to Okanagan Landing, where she was launched on 18 January 1902.

The next to be placed in service was a much grander vessel, 193ft in length with accommodation for 400 passengers. The wooden sternwheeler *Okanagan* was

The 1000 ton sternwheeler Okanagan *launched in 1907 from the CPR yard at Okanagan Landing, BC*

launched from the CPR yard on 16 April 1907, and started a daily limited-stop service to Penticton. As soon as the *Aberdeen* had been given a new hull she returned to make three trips a week serving the local 'way' points.

The 'Vancouver Province' of 7 October 1928 reported:

An even greater feat than the building of a ship on an inland lake is the rebuilding of one. In April the *Okanagan* steamed into Okanagan Landing. Five capstans were placed on the shore near the railway tracks and to each capstan was attached a team of horses. Cables were placed around the ship and for a day and a half she was hauled inch by inch up the skidway until finally she was high and dry on the lake shore.

Workmen walked underneath her and removed her planking. This was to be an extensive overhaul, the largest job done on the Okanagan Lake for seven years.

The *Okanagan* continued in service until 1934, but from 1928 was mostly used for the freighting of goods traffic.

The Kettle Valley Railway was being built in 1911, and to help in the construction work a barge slip was built at Penticton. Two barges, fitted with rail track to take eight rail-cars, were built together with a new tug, the *Castlegar*, and placed in service in June 1911 to ferry materials from Okanagan Landing to Penticton. To cope with the growing traffic on the lake, the steel screw tug *Naramata* was launched from the CPR yard on 20 April 1914, to be followed by the 1700 ton *Sicamous*, which had been prefabricated at Port Arthur, Ontario. The *Sicamous* sailed daily, except Sundays, and with sometimes as many as fifteen intermediate calls, making a trip of ninety miles to Penticton. By leaving at 05.30 hours, she could make the round trip by 21.00 hours. Her crew might consist of a captain, mate, nine deckhands, two engineers, three firemen and two coal trimmers, a purser, freight clerk, chief steward plus ten stewards to look after a possible 500 passengers and the crew.

The last vessel to be built for the Okanagan service was the diesel tug *Okanagan* II. Prefabricated in Vancouver, she was launched on 18 February 1947, and handled the fruit crop to the railheads at Penticton and Kelowna. She made her last trip on 31 May 1972, which virtually signalled the end of Canadian Pacific's lake and river services.

	CPR service	Passenger licence	State rooms
Aberdeen	1893–1916	250	5
York[1]	1902–31	90	*nil*
Okanagan I	1907–34	350	33
Kaleden[2]	1910–17	40	*nil*
Castlegar	1911–25	20	*nil*
Naramata	1914–65	20	*nil*
Sicamous	1914–35	550	37
Kelowna	1920–56	?	*nil*
Okanagan II	1947–72	?	*nil*
Barge No 3	1914–26	8 car capacity	

Notes
[1] The *York* was transferred to Skaha Lake 1921–31.
[2] The *Kaleden* was first used on Skaha Lake, an outflow from the south of Okanagan Lake.

The Arrow Lakes

In 1893 the CPR began the construction of a spur from Revelstoke, on the main line, to Arrowhead at the head of the Upper Arrow Lake, in order to bypass a troublesome stretch of shallow water on the Columbia River.

Earlier the Columbia & Kootenay Navigation Company had brought Captain J. Troup from Portland, Oregon, to operate its steamboat service on the Arrow Lakes, from Revelstoke in the north to Northport, Washington, in the south.

On 1 February 1897, the CPR bought the entire fleet of seven steamers and ten barges of the Columbia & Kootenay Steam Navigation Company, including its shipyards at Nakusp, Nelson and Rosebery, plus its 'master builder' T. J. Bulger, who had also come in from Oregon, and Captain J. Troup. Canadian Pacific immediately launched a building programme which continued for the next thirty years. Shortly after the CPR took over, T. J. Bulger retired and his son J. M. Bulger succeeded him, while another son, D. T. Bulger, became shipyard foreman at Nakusp. In 1901, when Captain Troup was promoted to the management of the company's BC coastal fleet, Captain J. C. Gore became superintendent of the Lake and River Services.

The first sternwheeler launched by the CPR from the Nakusp yard was the wooden *Rossland* which sailed on her maiden voyage to Trail on 2 May 1898, and made a daily run between Robson and Arrowhead, 127 miles. One of the most famous Canadian Pacific sternwheelers, the *Minto*, was ordered for a proposed service on the Stikine River for the Gold Rush of 1897 (see page 102). She was built by the Bertram Iron Works of Toronto, and sent by rail in more than 1000 parts to Vancouver. Too late for the Gold Rush, she was diverted to Nakusp, where she was reassembled and launched on 19 November 1898, and in the following month took over from the *Rossland* for the winter service. After the severe winter of 1916–17, whenever conditions were bad, the *Minto* was operated only on the Upper Lake, leaving the Lower Lake to the small tugs *Whatshan* and *Columbia*.

By the 1940s passenger travel on the lakes had declined and the *Minto* and other vessels were mostly employed freighting farm produce, etc. She left Robson on her last round trip to Arrowhead on 23 April 1954. The Nakusp Chamber of Commerce hoped to preserve the vessel but cash was not forthcoming, and it was not until 1956 that a Mr Nelson had the hull towed to Galena Bay and began the work of restoration. The rise in the water level of the lake, after the building of a dam, condemned the *Minto*;

The 200 ton tug Okanagan II *was built in 1946 to handle the fruit crop between Kelowna and the railhead at Penticton, BC*

The last large vessel to be built by the Columbia & Kootenay Steam Navigation Co. Note sacks of ore on deck and fuel stack on shore

she was towed on to the lake and burned on 1 August 1968.

The *Bonnington*, one of the largest sternwheelers built in Canada, was launched by the CPR at Nakusp and entered service in July 1911. Two hundred and two feet in length, she had fifty-seven state rooms and could carry 400 passengers. Increasing road transport caused her withdrawal from service in 1931. The service on the Arrow Lakes continued with two tugs; *Columbia* II was launched from Nakusp in 1920 and sold in 1948, to become a houseboat at Robson West. A third *Columbia*, this time a diesel tug, was bought in 1948 and worked until 1954, when she was sold to Ivan Horie who had sailed her for the CPR.

	CPR service	Passenger licence	State rooms
Columbia I	1897–1920	nil	nil
Illecillewaet	1897–1902	?	nil
Lytton	1897–1903	?	?
Nakusp[1]	1897	?	?
Trail	1897–1900	?	nil
Kootenay	1897–1919	300	42
Rossland	1897–1916	300	45
Minto	1898–1954	225	34
Whatshan	1909–20	20	nil
Bonnington	1911–31	400	57
Columbia II	1920–48	?	nil
Columbia III	1948–54	nil	nil

Note
[1] The *Nakusp* was burned out on 23 December 1897, so was only in Canadian Pacific service for a few months.

The dining saloon on the 400 ton Kokanee, *which ran on Kootenay Lake 1897–1923 (Provincial Archives BC)*

Slocan Lake

The smallest Canadian Pacific operation on the lakes, Slocan was an important mining area, and the emphasis was on tug and barge operations. The CPR launched four steamboats and one diesel tug from their yard at Rosebery. The largest was the *Slocan* II, which plied the lake from 1905 until 1928, when she was sold to be used as a warehouse at a logging camp. She was replaced by the tug *Rosebery* I, which worked the lake traffic until 1943, when she was replaced by a diesel tug prefabricated in Montreal, the *Rosebery* II. After she was withdrawn in 1957, a service was provided, under contract by Ivan Horie, with the tug *Iris G*.

	CPR service	Passenger licence	State rooms
Denver	1897–1903	*nil*	*nil*
Slocan I	1897–1905	300	2
Sandon	1898–1927	50	*nil*
Wm Hunter	1899–1903	?	*nil*
Slocan II	1905–28	300	2
Rosebery I	1928–43	?	*nil*
Rosebery II	1943–57	?	*nil*
Barge No 18	1930–46		

Kootenay Lake

The CPR took over two sternwheelers on the Kootenay Lake when it bought the Columbia & Kootenay Navigation Company in 1897, the *Nelson* and *Kokanee*, as well

One of the best-remembered CPR sternwheelers, the 800 ton Moyie, which sailed the Kootenay Lake for fifty-eight years—1898–1956

as the shipyard at Nelson. Another famous sternwheeler, the 800 ton *Moyie*, a sister ship of the *Minto*, had been destined for the Stikine River, but was diverted and assembled at Nelson, where she was launched by Mrs Troup on 22 October 1898. She ran between Nelson and Lardeau until she was withdrawn in 1956.

In 1906 the 1000 ton *Kuskanook* was launched from Nelson, and started a limited stop express service, leaving the *Moyie* to make the 'flag' stops. Two more tugs followed and then, in 1913, the 200ft *Nasookin*, prefabricated at Port Arthur, was launched from the Nelson yard and made her maiden voyage on 1 June. Fitted with

112 berths and licensed to carry 550 passengers, she spent her later years ferrying motorcars across the lake. She made her last passenger voyage on 31 December 1931.

On 7 March 1928 the CPR launched its last Kootenay Lake steamboat, the powerful steel-hulled *Granthall*, shipped on ten flat-cars from Montreal. Her most important contribution was the barge traffic between Kootenay Landing and Proctor. With the withdrawal of the *Moyie* in 1956, the *Granthall* continued operations until 1957, when the service was contracted out to Ivan Horie, with the diesel tug *Melinda Jane*. Although the CPR continued to move rail-cars by contract with Ivan Horie for

100

some years, a steady decline in rail-car movements to and from Kaslo and Lardeau, coupled with rising operating costs, made the service uneconomic. From 1969 to 1974 southbound traffic declined from 1018 rail-cars to 121; and from 239 to six northbound. An application to discontinue the service in 1975 was unsuccessful, but after an appeal Canadian Pacific's steamboating service was ended on 16 December 1977.

	CPR service	Passenger licence	State rooms
Kokanee	1897–1923	200	9
Nelson I	1897–1913	?	?
Moyie	1898–1957	400	15
Ymir	1898–1928	20	nil
Proctor[1]	1900–1904	30	nil
Valhalla	1901–30	20	nil
Kuskanook	1906–31	450	37
Hosmer	1909–31	20	nil
Nasookin	1913–32	550	54
Nelson II	1913–19	40	nil
Granthall	1928–57	?	nil
Barge No 2	1914–39	15 car capacity	

Note
[1] Transferred to Trout Lake in 1904.

Trout Lake

Trout Lake, a small lake to the northwest of Kootenay Lake, was originally served by the CPR with the *Illecillewaet* on a daily run from Arrowhead to Beaton, on the northeast arm of the Upper Arrow Lake, thence by a ten-mile pack trail to Trout Lake City, at the head of Trout Lake. By June 1902 the CPR had built a rail link from Gerrard, at the southern end of Trout Lake, to Lardeau on Kootenay Lake. The steel-hulled *York* had been ordered in 1901 for a proposed service from Gerrard to Trout Lake City, but this tug had to be diverted to the Okanagan and a small sternwheeler, the *Victoria*, was bought for the Trout Lake service. In 1904 the *Proctor* was transferred to this run to replace the *Victoria*, which was beached and used as a wharf and freight shed for the *Proctor*. The *Proctor* was sold in 1917, but continued to operate on the lake.

The rail service to Gerrard ceased in May 1942. A large stationwaggon, fitted with steel wheels, maintained the service, in summer only, from the mid-1930s until abandonment. The rails were lifted and a public road built in their place in 1942.

	CPR service	Passenger licence	State rooms
Victoria	1900–1904	?	nil
Proctor	1904–17	30	nil

James Fitzsimmons of Nelson, for many years a captain with Canadian Pacific's lake steamers and later manager of the fleet, also a member for several years of the provincial legislature representing the Kootenay District, retired in 1935. On 22 April 1935 the 'Nelson News' devoted two pages to a valedictory address given by the captain to the Nelson Rotary Club, in which he said:

> The passing of Romance. With the extension of the Crow's Nest Line as the Kettle Valley Railway and its opening for through traffic in July 1916, the glory of the great river passed. Its work went from then to rails and locomotives. Below Revelstoke's bridges all the length of the Upper Columbia–Kootenay valley, from Boundary to Robson, railways parallel and cross it.
>
> Nothing is left between ungirdled, but the sublimely scenic and safely served waterways of the magnificent Arrow, Kootenay, Slocan and Trout Lakes. Gone are the days of six steamers tied all in a row at Revelstoke wharves, now only the ancient *Minto* plies a tri-weekly service between rail terminals. Gone are the days of white-water, runs of forced steam, of snags, sweepers, sand and gravelbars, rocks, ripples, low water, ice, bridges and all the romance and urge of the great river business in the days of Kootenay in the making.

For fleet list see page 257.

Houseboats

Another aspect of the CPR on the lakes was the three houseboats provided for holidaymakers or fishermen. In 1897 a wooden houseboat was built for the Okanagan Lake and sold in 1920. A second was built in 1901, for Shuswap Lake and sold in 1907. A third was placed on Kootenay Lake around 1910, and sold in 1919 to J. S. McGregor, who had it moored near Nelson.

The Kootenay boat was 50ft by 12ft and fitted with five state rooms, kitchen, pantry, dining-room and servants' state room. The upper deck was covered by an

Sternwheeler Sicamous *at Penticton, BC*

awning. For a small charge the boat could be towed to any point on the lake. Mail and supplies could also be delivered by the regular CPR lake steamers.

The Stikine River

At the time of the Klondyke Gold Rush in 1897, Canadian Pacific hoped to place a number of sternwheelers in service on the Stikine River between Wrangell, Alaska, and Glenora BC. Four steamers *Constantine*, *Dalton*, *Schwatka* and *Walsh* were built under the supervision of Captain Troup at Port Blakely near Seattle. Eight more steamers were ordered in Canada and six were assembled at the CPR freight yards at False Creek, Vancouver BC. They were the *Dawson*, *Duchesnay*, *Hamlin*, *McConnell*, *Ogilvie* and *Tyrell*. Most of these ships were completed too late to participate in the Gold Rush, and when the proposed narrow-gauge railway from Glenora on the Stikine to Teslin Lake BC failed to materialise, most of the ships became surplus and were sold. So far as can be ascertained, only the *Duchesnay*, *Hamlin*, *McConnell* and *Ogilvie* ever sailed on the Stikine River for Canadian Pacific. Two other sternwheelers built for this purpose, the *Minto* and *Moyie*, as already mentioned enjoyed more than half a century of service with Canadian Pacific.

8 Great Lakes Services

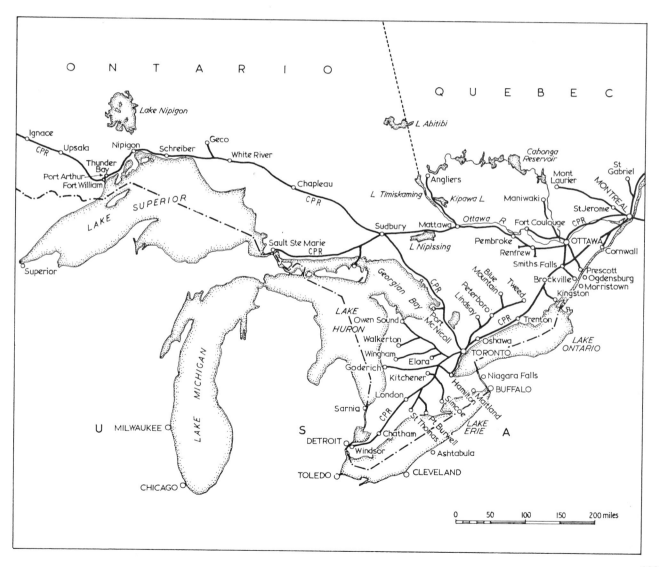

While the railway was still being built, Henry Beatty was persuaded to join the company. Beatty, a Scots-Canadian, had had long experience of shipping on the Canadian waters of the lakes and was a partner in the family business, the North West Transportation Company. In 1882 he became manager of Lake Transportation Services, the first of the company's many steamship activities. Over the years he was to exert his influence on a number of ocean as well as lake steamships.

Beatty's first job took him to Scotland to supervise the building of three ships ordered from two Clyde shipbuilding yards, Aitken & Mansell and C. Connell & Co. The vessels were constructed with special bulkheads amidships, so arranged as to allow the ships to be halved when they reached Montreal for transit through the small locks of the St Lawrence River canals. They were given distinctive Canadian names.

Alberta (1883–1946); Algoma (1883–5); Athabasca (1883–1946)

The *Alberta* and *Athabasca* were 260ft in length and had accommodation for 240 first-class passengers on the saloon deck, with space on the main deck for a large number of immigrants. They could also carry considerable quantities of cargo. The *Algoma* was slightly smaller. All three were launched in July 1883, and sailed across the Atlantic, arriving at Montreal during November. There they were halved and towed to Buffalo, where they were reassembled. Reporting on the *Algoma*, the 'Owen Sound Advertiser' of 24 April 1884 said:

> No such vessels have ever been seen on the Great
> Lakes but their excellence lies not in the
> gorgeousness of their furniture or the gingerbread
> work of decoration but in their superiority over all
> other lake craft in model construction and
> equipment and in their thorough adaptability for
> the business in which they will engage.

The first sailing was made by the *Algoma* from Owen Sound on 11 May 1884, with over 1000 passengers and freight. Sailings continued throughout the season, leaving Owen Sound every Tuesday, Thursday and Saturday, arriving at Port Arthur, Thursday, Saturday and Monday mornings. The lakes were closed to shipping during the winter. Some calls were made at Algoma Mills, at that time a railhead on Lake Huron, some 150 miles north of Owen Sound. As the railroad from Port Arthur

to Winnipeg had already been completed, the company was able to carry passengers and freight to the west, thereby earning valuable revenue whilst the railway line along the north shore of Lake Superior was still being built.

Lake Superior, the largest freshwater lake in the world, although mostly calm and beautiful, can be whipped into a sudden fury. One such storm occurred on the day that the 'last spike' was being driven at Craigellachie, although the actors in that drama were quite unaware of the other drama 1500 miles to the east. The *Algoma* had left Sault Ste Marie on Friday 6 November 1885, nearing Port Arthur early on the Saturday morning in a severe gale with violent snow squalls and visibility virtually nil. Suddenly the ship ran on to rocks smashing her rudder, which left her helpless, and she was forced further on to the rocks of Greenstone Island. The master, Captain Moore, was injured when the seas broke over the ship. While it was still dark the *Algoma* broke in two, leaving fourteen survivors on the afterdeck. Some of the crew, after an unsuccessful attempt to launch a lifeboat, reached the shore; the remainder stayed on board until the Sunday morning when the gale had passed and they were able to get ashore where they were looked after by local fishermen. The *Athabasca* had left Owen Sound on Saturday and on Monday fortunately noticed the distress signals on the island. Boats were lowered and the survivors taken off, and the news carried to Port Arthur.

The *Alberta* and *Athabasca* with the chartered *Campana* maintained the service and it was not until 1889 that a replacement was ordered from the Polson Iron Works at Owen Sound. Meantime the engine from the *Algoma* had been salvaged and was transferred to the new vessel, the *Manitoba*. The *Manitoba* was herself concerned in a rescue when, on 17 September 1928, she arrived at Owen Sound having rescued five survivors from the *Manasoo* which had foundered. The men had spent sixty hours on a life-raft before being sighted. After a number of years in freight service she was scrapped in 1951.

The *Alberta* and *Athabasca* were refitted at Collingwood, Ontario, in 1910 and 1911 and from then on were used chiefly for cargo. They were laid-up for various periods in the 1930s, but in 1937 a freight service from Milwaukee and Chicago to Port McNicoll provided work until the end of World War II. Long life was a feature of the lake steamers. The *Alberta* and *Athabasca* sailed for more than sixty years on the fresh waters of the lakes before being sold in 1946 to Florida interests.

The 2000 ton Alberta, *one of three vessels built for service on the Great Lakes in 1883*

They were then towed through the Chicago drainage canal and the Mississippi River for a further two years' work in the salt waters of the Gulf of Mexico before being broken up.

Owen Sound was and still is a thriving community, but in 1912 the eastern terminal for the lake service was transferred to a new railhead at Port McNicoll, about 55 miles to the northeast. The new terminal, being wholly controlled by the company and having better rail gradients, provided more expeditious handling for passengers and

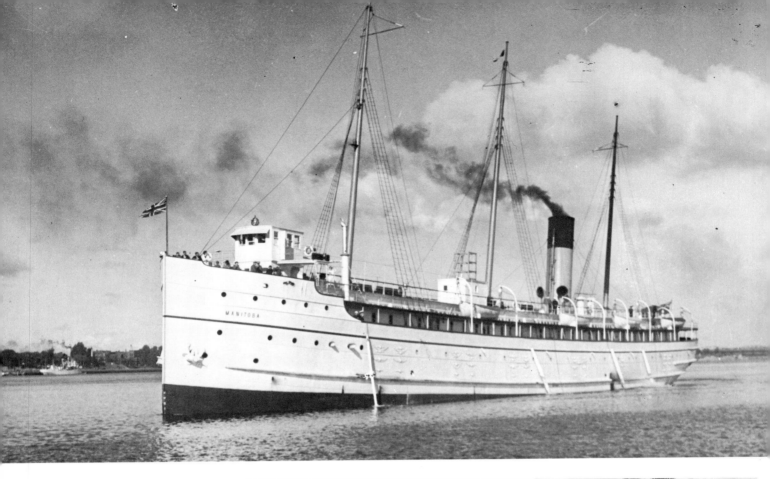

The Great Lakes steamer Assiniboia

freight. Access between train and steamer was across a well-kept formal garden.

Assiniboia (1907–68); Keewatin (1907–66)

In 1907 the two best-remembered lake steamers, the *Assiniboia* and the *Keewatin*, were built in the Fairfield yard. These too had to be built so that they could be halved for transit through the canals. They were 336ft in length, with berths for 279 passengers on two decks. The vessels boasted a flower lounge two decks high with a stained-glass skylight and many pot plants, a dining saloon seating 120, and a ballroom lounge with carved panels depicting various countries of the Commonwealth. Coal-fired quadruple expansion engines gave the vessels a cruising speed of fourteen knots. There was also

The 3000 ton Manitoba, *built at Owen Sound, Ontario, in 1888*

The dining saloon in the Manitoba

space for 147,000cft of cargo.

The *Keewatin* sailed from Greenock on 14 September 1907. She arrived at the Levis Docks on 5 October 1907, where she was cut in half. On 15 October she started her trip to Buffalo where she was rejoined before proceeding to Owen Sound.

Early in her career the *Assiniboia* had an exciting and dangerous escape from disaster. On 9 June 1909 she was in the Soo Lock waiting to be lowered twenty-two feet to Lake Huron. A second vessel, the *Crescent City*, was also entering to be locked down together with the *Assiniboia*. At the same time a freighter *Perry G. Walker* was slowly approaching the lock on the Lake Huron side. She would normally have tied up to allow the downbound ships to pass. For some unexplained reason the *Perry G. Walker* suddenly moved at full speed ahead, smashing into the lock gates. As the upper gates had not yet been closed, water, with the weight of Lake Superior behind it, crashed through the lock. The *Assiniboia* was shot out of the lock, completely out of control, hitting the *Perry G. Walker* as she passed. Fortunately, apart from damaged plates on her hull, she was little the worse for her experience. The *Perry G. Walker*, also out of control, spun round several times until she ran aground on a shoal. The *Crescent City*, loaded with ore, was swept past the damaged lower lock gate which tore a large hole in her side. She also hit the *Assiniboia* as she was swept along. American tug crews on the other side of the river saw the emergency and raced after the *Crescent City* and towed her into shallow water. Amazingly, all three ships were able to proceed under their own steam and no lives were lost, but the damaged Canadian lock was out of commission for a long time.

In 1946 the red-and-white house flag was painted on the funnels and in December 1950 the three wooden masts were replaced by two steel masts. Special fire bulkheads and a sprinkler system were also fitted. When overhauled during the 1953–4 winter, the *Assiniboia* was converted to oil fuel, had her stack shortened and boilers replaced. It was intended to convert the *Keewatin* in the following year, but the work was never started.

The two nights spent in a comfortable cabin, with a dining saloon famous for its fine food, made this leisurely and elegant mode of travel a delightful thirty-eight-hour break for passengers making the 3000 mile transcontinental rail trip. One night was spent crossing Lake Huron, then a fifty-five-mile sail up the St Mary's River to the Soo Locks, then the voyage across Lake Superior, out of sight of land for much of the time. In later years the round trip was often bought as a holiday cruise.

Rising costs of operation and ever more stringent safety regulations brought to an end more than eighty years of Canadian Pacific passenger service on the lakes in 1965. The *Keewatin* continued in freight service until November 1966, when she was sold for scrap. Fortunately she was saved from the torch and, in June 1967, she was towed from Port McNicoll by the tug *Amherstburg* to Tower Marina in Douglas, Michigan, to become a marine museum. The *Assiniboia* was not so lucky; she arrived at Port McNicoll after completing her last CPR voyage on 26 November 1967. In the following August she was towed to West Deptford NJ for conversion to a restaurant, but in November 1969 she was gutted by fire.

For fleet list see page 261.

The flower lounge on the Assiniboia*'s sister ship, the 4000 ton Keewatin*

Rail Ferries

Windsor–Detroit

By 1889 the CPR had extended its line from London, Ontario, to Windsor, Ontario, in order to provide a connection with the US railroads across the mile-wide Detroit River and so enable it to compete with the Grand Trunk service from Chicago to Portland, Maine.

The company ordered its first rail ferry steamers in 1889, two steel paddle-wheelers—the *Michigan* from F. W. Wheeler & Co of Bay City and the *Ontario* from the Polson Iron Works of Owen Sound. Both ships were launched in 1890, were 296ft in length, powered by compound two-cylinder horizontal engines developing about 170hp, and at that time were the largest car ferries operating on the Great Lakes. They had two sets of rail track enabling them to carry sixteen rail-cars each. It took about three-quarters of an hour to load, make the crossing and unload. In busy periods they could ferry 200 cars a day, but were rarely fully utilised and were sometimes hired to other railway companies.

At the start only freight cars were moved, but by June 1890 a passenger service was established from Montreal and Toronto via the Wabash Railway to Chicago.

The Detroit River tunnel was completed in 1910 and, by arrangement with the Michigan Central Railway in 1915, CPR freight trains were being hauled through the tunnel by electric locomotives. In the following year passenger trains were also using the tunnel. Both ships were laid-up in 1916, and by 1924 their machinery had been removed and they were sold to the Newaygo Timber Company of Port Arthur as wood pulp barges.

Pennsylvania–Ontario Transportation Company

Much of the coal used by CPR locomotives in Ontario was imported from the United States. On 16 February 1906 a company was formed as a joint operation with the Pennsylvania Railroad Company to own and operate ships to carry coal from Ashtabula, the Pennsylvania's coal port in Ohio, on the fifty-one-mile crossing of Lake Erie to the CPR at Port Burwell, Ontario.

The *Ashtabula* was ordered from the Great Lakes Engineering Works at St Clair, Michigan. She was 338ft in length, powered by two triple-expansion engines driving twin screws. Her main deck was fitted with four sets of rail track, taking six cars on each of the outer and seven on the inner tracks.

During the 1930s she suffered many periods of lay-up, but was saved by increasing traffic during World War II. Her southbound cargoes of grain, wood pulp and newsprint had always been much smaller than the northbound movement of coal. However, with the conversion of coal-fired locomotives to oil fuel and later the introduction of diesel-electric locomotives, the usefulness of this operation declined. Discussions regarding the dissolution of the company had already begun when the final decision was hastened by the loss of the ship when she collided with the *Ben Moreel* in Ashtabula harbour on 18 September 1958. The *Ashtabula* was later raised and dismantled at the yard where she had been built fifty-two years earlier. She was the last car ferry to operate on Lake Erie. The company was dissolved on 29 September 1961.

Toronto Hamilton & Buffalo Navigation Company

The CPR had a 27 per cent interest in the Toronto Hamilton & Buffalo Railway. In 1916 a branch of this line was extended to Port Maitland on Lake Erie in order to provide a ferry link with the New York Central Railroad, which owned the remaining 73 per cent of the TH&B Railway.

In 1915 the Navigation Company was formed, as a wholly owned subsidiary, to carry coal from Ashtabula, Ohio, to Port Maitland and thence by rail to the Hamilton steel plants. The *Maitland No 1* was built by the Great Lakes Engineering Works at Ecorse in 1916. She was similar in size to the *Ashtabula* and able to carry thirty rail-cars on four tracks. Unfortunately production in the Pennsylvanian coal-field declined and with the opening of the new Welland canal, allowing much larger vessels to pass between Lake Erie and Lake Ontario, the ferry service was suspended in June 1932, and the ferry laid-up. In 1942 her engines were removed and her hull converted to a wood pulp barge.

Canadian Pacific Car & Passenger Transfer Company

A ferry crossing between Prescott, Ontario, served by the Bytown & Prescott Railway Company, and Ogdensburg, New York, served by the Northern Railroad of New York, was started in 1854. The *St Lawrence* was placed in this service in 1863 and by 1874, was being operated by a coal merchant, I. D. Purkis. The Bytown

The 3000 ton Ashtabula *train ferry, which ran between Ashtabula, Ohio and Port Burwell, Ontario between 1906 and 1958*

& Prescott was reorganised as the St Lawrence & Ottawa in 1867 and in 1881 came under the control of the CPR. Its operations were integrated with the parent company in 1885. The CPR first served Brockville, Ontario, in 1881 when it took over the Canada Central Railway; by 1886, a Captain D. H. Lyon provided a ferry service between Brockville and Morristown, New York, with the *William Armstrong*. The ferry boats on these two services often switched routes to help out in times of peak traffics. On 17 March 1888, Captain Lyon amalgamated the two companies under the name Canadian Pacific Car & Passenger Transfer Company. By 1890 the traffic on both crossings was chiefly between the CPR and the New York Central, and by 1896 the CPR had concentrated its traffic on Prescott.

A new car ferry was ordered from the Polson Iron Works, Toronto, in 1916: a steel screw double-ended ferry, the *Charles Lyon*. Shortly afterwards all the passenger interests and the other ferry boats were sold. In 1929 the CPR bought the Prescott–Ogdensburg rail ferry *Charles Lyon* from the D. H. Lyon estate.

On 1 May 1930, the New York Central became joint owners with Canadian Pacific and a new diesel-electric tug, the *Prescotont*, was ordered together with a steel car-ferry float, the *Ogdensburg*. The tug was built by the Davie Shipbuilding Company at Lauzon, Quebec, and had a gross tonnage of 300 and a length of 117ft. She was also equipped as a fire-float. The *Ogdensburg* was built by the American Shipbuilding Company at Lorain, Ohio, and was 290ft long with a gross tonnage of 1405. She was fitted with three rail tracks and could carry seventeen rail-cars. The float had two rudders, which were synchronised with the rudder of the tug. When ferrying, the captain operated the tug from the pilot house on the bridge of the float which was equipped with controls identical with those on the tug. This was the only ferry in the world where the captain had direct control of the tug from the bridge of the float. This combination entered service on 2 November 1930.

This ferry crossing had always been an important link between US railroads and the CPR, particularly when the silk trains were rushed from Vancouver to New York (see page 213). In busy periods as many as 200 rail-cars were moved across the river in the course of a day. Newsprint, lumber, wood pulp and flour were the largest Canadian exports, while coal was the most important

The Incan Superior, *the 4000 ton rail-car transporter built in 1974 to move rail traffic from the Thunder Bay area to interconnecting rail lines serving the US mid-west*

northbound traffic. During the war the ferry was kept busy moving war equipment from Central Canadian plants to US ports, and US material through Canadian ports.

In addition to her duties pushing the float *Ogdensburg*, the tug maintained an open channel throughout the winter months between Prescott and Ogdensburg, by smashing the ice small enough to pass through the north channel, about three miles east of Prescott, where the Galops Rapids took care of the ice.

The transfer of rail passenger-cars was discontinued when a suspension bridge was opened between Prescott and Ogdensburg in 1958. Freight-cars continued to be ferried until 25 September 1970, when the Ogdensburg dock was destroyed by fire.

For fleet list see page 262.

The car float Ogdensburg *and diesel-electric tug* Prescotont, *which connected the New York Central with the CPR from 1930 to 1972*

Incan Marine

In May 1972 Canadian Pacific and the Inchcape Group of London formed a new company, Incan Marine, to design and develop marine-based intermodal systems in North America. In November of the following year Incan Ships was formed to be the operating company. An order was placed in 1973, with the Burrard Dry Dock Company of Vancouver, for a rail-car barge to operate between Thunder Bay, Ontario, and Superior, Wisconsin; the barge was named *Incan Superior*.

A sister ship was ordered in 1974 to be named *Incan St Laurent*, for service between Quebec City and Baie Comeau, but the proposed service ran into snags before the vessel left the Pacific coast. In June 1975 she was chartered to the Alaska Trainship Corporation to carry rail-cars between New Westminster and Whittier, Alaska. She was laid-up in Vancouver in 1976 and sold to Canadian National in January 1977 for service between Baie Comeau and Matane, on the south shore. She was renamed *Georges Alexandre Lebel*.

For fleet list see page 262.

113

The garden linking the CPR railhead at Port McNicoll and the Great Lakes steamer terminal

9 Bay of Fundy Services

The pioneer spirit has always been strong in Nova Scotia, and her people were well aware of the need to develop transportation services. The sailing packet *Sally* started one of the oldest regular services in Canada, on the forty-five-mile crossing between Saint John NB and Digby NS in 1784. Although only a short crossing, the bay, an arm of the Atlantic Ocean separating Nova Scotia from New Brunswick and the State of Maine USA, extends some 180 miles in length. It is difficult to navigate because of the tides, which at certain seasons have a rise and fall of over fifty feet, producing dangerous bores in the upper reaches and a heavy groundswell. The bay is also subject to severe gales.

The first steamship service started in 1827 with the eighty-seven ton *St John*. The Nova Scotia House of Assembly authorised a mail contract of £50 per year provided the operators maintained 'for not less than several months of the year steamboat services between St John and Annapolis'. In 1881 the Bay of Fundy Steamship Company began regular services and, by 1889, had the sternwheeler *Monticello* on this run. By 1889 Canadian Pacific rails had reached Saint John NB and the company was considering a steamer connection between Saint John and Digby, in order to move its passengers and freight to and from Halifax more quickly than was possible over the Intercolonial Railway. The company's failure to obtain running rights over the Intercolonial made the steamer service of even greater importance.

Dominion Atlantic Railway

The DAR had been incorporated on 22 July 1895 as a result of the take-over of the Yarmouth Annapolis Railway by the Windsor Annapolis Railway. The headquarters of the railway were in London and among the directors were John and Archibald Denny of the Dumbarton shipbuilding company, who had built the side-wheeler *Prince Rupert* for a proposed service between Vancouver and Vancouver Island for the CPR. The vessel had been ordered in 1893 in the name of Thomas Shaughnessy, because of expected opposition from the CPN Company and other interests on the BC coast. Before the ship had reached the Pacific, Shaughnessy decided that the time was not ripe and the vessel was diverted to the Digby–St John route for the DAR in 1895. Reporting on the *Rupert*, the 'Halifax Herald' of 5 August 1895 positively glowed:

> By this new enterprise the DAR can place its Halifax passengers in St John three hours ahead of the Intercolonial. On her first trip from Digby to St John she ran from wharf to wharf in 2 hours and 4 minutes, the fastest time ever made in Bay of Fundy waters.... On no vessel of her class are more majestic paddle wheels to be found.... She has two dining halls decorated and upholstered in the most sumptuous fashion.... The smoking room walls are panelled with leather studded with brass. The upholstery generally is green buffalo hide....
> Captain John Richards is one of the most genial, kind hearted, gentlemanly men that one could desire to meet.

A paddle-wheeler was not really suitable for the Digby–Saint John run. The Saint John River flowing into the harbour carried with it driftwood and other refuse from the many sawmills on the river. Floating logs and 'bobbers' (logs floating upright) caused much damage to the paddle floats. Every Sunday, and often nightly too, workmen had to renew the floats, a difficult and very cold job in winter.

The *Prince Rupert* would list badly when she met the

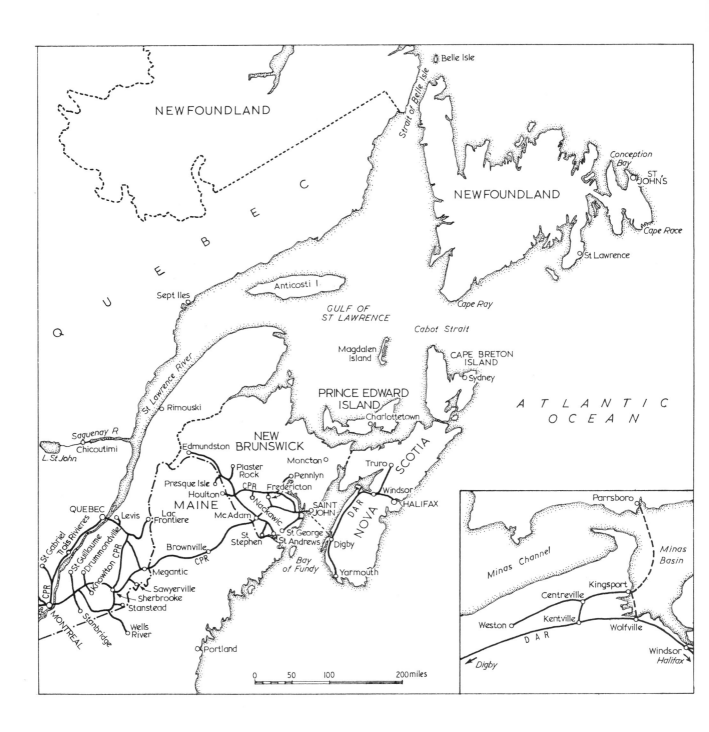

The 1000 ton *Prince Rupert, a side-wheeler built in 1894 for the B C coast, but transferred to the Dominion Atlantic Railway's Digby–Saint John run* (National Maritime Museum)

very strong tides in the bay broadside-on. Large casks of water were moved from side to side in an endeavour to counteract the list.

Digby–Saint John

On 13 November 1911 an agreement was signed leasing the Dominion Atlantic Railway to the CPR for 999 years from 1 January 1912. This included the steamship services operated by the railway. Canadian Pacific was primarily interested in the Digby–Saint John route and therefore disposed of the Yarmouth–Boston service by selling the *Boston, Prince Arthur* and *Prince George* to the Eastern Steamship Corporation on 20 August 1912.

The *Yarmouth* was retained on the Digby run, but the ageing *Prince Rupert* was soon replaced by the *St George*, a 2456 ton cross-channel steamer bought from the Great Western Railway in England in May 1913. She could carry 1100 passengers at over twenty knots. By 1916 the *Yarmouth* was replaced by the *Empress*, bought from the Charlottetown Steam Navigation Company of

Prince Edward Island. With a length of 235ft and a gross tonnage of 1158, she had been launched from the Swan Hunter yard at Newcastle in 1906. In May 1926 the *Empress* survived a very severe gale during which her superstructure, furniture and cargo were badly damaged.

Traffic grew steadily and in the late 1920s the need for a new purpose-built vessel for the forty-five-mile ferry service became urgent.

Princess Helene (1930–63)

In 1929 an order was placed with the William Denny shipyard at Dumbarton for a new steamer to be called the *Princess Helene*. She was 320ft long and 4035 gross registered tons. The *Princess Helene* was launched on 12 May 1930 by Miss Nesta Gillies, daughter of the general manager of Canadian Pacific Steamships in London. She ran her trials on 15 August and sailed on her maiden voyage from Greenock arriving at Saint John on 22 August. She began regular service between Saint John

Bought in 1916 from the Charlottetown Steam Navigation Co, the 1000 ton Empress *ran on the Digby–Saint John route until 1930*

and Digby on 27 August.

The *Princess* was propelled by two single-reduction turbine engines driving twin screws, which gave her a speed of nineteen knots. She was licensed to carry 1000 passengers and forty-five cars in the summer season, and thirty-five cars in the winter season, together with considerable quantities of packaged freight. Her passenger accommodation set a new standard for steamship services in the Maritime Provinces. The dining-room was fitted with tables for two, four and six people. There was a large smoking-room aft, and an observation room forward with large plate-glass windows and easy-chairs arranged in rows alongside the windows facing outwards.

Although the journey was short, many of the passengers liked to travel first class; forty-four state rooms, including two suites with sitting-room and bathroom, were included for travellers who wished to spend the night on board prior to an early morning departure from Saint John, when they might be tempted by the following:

118

| Breakfast Bill of Fare: |
| SS *Princess Helene* |

Baked Apple with cream

| Grape Fruit | Oranges |
| Corn Flakes | Shredded Wheat |

Rolled Oats

Fresh Fried Fish

Finnan Haddie

| Ham | Bacon |
| Sausage | Calf's liver |

Eggs, Boiled, Fried or Scrambled

French Fried Potatoes

| Jam | Corn Muffins |
| Toast | Marmalade |

Tea   Coffee   Cocoa

Known as the 'Digby Boat', the *Princess Helene* made the three-hour crossing of the bay with two return trips six days a week, with an extra trip on Sundays during the summer. During World War II, the *Princess Helene* remained on her peacetime route but carried many

The Princess Helene, *a 4000 ton ferry built in 1929 for the Digby—Saint John run*

civilians and troops in the war effort. She steamed 168,000 miles, and when the battle of the Atlantic was at its height she made the daily passage under escort of RCAF's coastal patrol bombers and anti-submarine ships.

In 1950, after twenty years of service, she was given a major overhaul. Some of her hull plating was renewed and she was fitted with an automatic fire sprinkler and fire alarm system. Her furnishings were also renewed at this time. A new dock, freight shed and car park were built on the Dominion Canal dock at Saint John in 1952, to enable the National Harbours Board to rebuild the Pugsley Wharf.

The *Princess Helene* was withdrawn in February 1963, after thirty-two years of service. In May she was sold, and left Saint John NB on 11 July under the name *Helene*, to become a car ferry in the Mediterranean after being renamed *Carina*.

119

Princess of Acadia (1963–73)

By this time motorcar traffic had grown considerably and the *Princess of Nanaimo* was transferred from the BC coast (see page 85). She was considerably larger than the *Helene*, being 358ft long with a gross tonnage of 6700, and she was able to carry 130 cars. She left Victoria on 28 February and arrived at Halifax on 20 March, starting her Digby run on 29 April 1963, after being renamed *Princess of Acadia*. During her first season, passenger carryings increased by more than 17,000 and the number of cars by more than 85 per cent. In November 1965 she was fitted with a bow-thruster whilst being overhauled at Lauzon, Quebec.

With the ordering of a new ship for the service, the *Princess of Acadia* reverted to her original name on 3 May 1971, although she continued in service until the day before the new *Princess of Acadia* II took over on 1 June.

It was intended that the *Princess of Nanaimo* would be sold, but at that time CP Rail was moving large numbers of cars and trucks from the big manufacturing companies to the Eastern Provinces including Newfoundland. As a part of the distribution system a twenty-three-acre compound was built adjacent to the CP Rail station at Saint John.

To handle this movement the CPR decided to convert the *Princess* into a vehicle transporter. The entire passenger accommodation on the saloon deck was removed to increase her carrying capacity from 130 to 225 full-sized cars. After her conversion she was renamed *Henry Osborne* and entered service between Saint John NB and St Johns NF on 14 November 1972. Unfortunately, after only six months on this route she ran aground in Saint John harbour on 16 May 1973. It was decided that she was not worth the cost of repair and she was sold for scrap. She left Saint John in January 1974 for Bilbao, Spain under tow by the *Hansa*.

Princess of Acadia II (1971–4)

Canadian Pacific ordered a 10,000 ton vessel from the Saint John Shipbuilding & Dry Dock Company in 1970. The *Princess of Acadia* was the largest ship of its kind built in Canada. Four hundred and eighty feet in length, with bow and stern doors for roll-on, roll-off operation, she had accommodation for 159 cars and 650 day passengers, with six day and two *deluxe* cabins, a self-service cafeteria, lounge bar, verandah and nursery for small children. She was powered by four diesel engines driving

Built in 1971, the 10,000 ton Princess of Acadia II *was taken over by the government in 1974*

twin controllable-pitch screws. The engines were similar to those used on CP locomotives. A bow propeller facilitated docking manoeuvres.

She sailed on her maiden voyage on 27 May 1971, when, at a special ceremony to mark the occasion, Richard Hatfield, Premier of New Brunswick, and Gerald Regan, Premier of Nova Scotia, unveiled a plaque bearing the provincial crests symbolising the service link between the two provinces.

The new *Princess of Acadia* was scheduled to make two round trips per day, the crossing taking only 2½ hours. When the order was given for this ship it was known that operating costs were rising rapidly and that it would be

difficult to make the service profitable; an understanding had been reached with the federal government that if this important link between the two provinces could not be made to pay then the company would be forced to ask for financial assistance and possibly have to sell the 10,000 ton, $8 million ship.

Unfortunately, losses continued to mount, and in 1973 the company announced that during the winter the service would be reduced to one trip a day. Because of the importance of the service, the government stepped in with a subsidy to cover the losses on the second trip. In December 1974 the federal government bought the ship and Canadian Pacific continued to operate her until 1

September 1976, when the service was turned over to CN Marine in accordance with a new policy established by the Federal Ministry of Transport, ending more than sixty years of operation across the bay by Canadian Pacific.

The Minas Basin

The Minas Basin is an area of great scenic beauty, on the northeastern arm of the Bay of Fundy. The Windsor & Annapolis Railway Company formed the Evangeline Navigation Company in 1893, to provide a daily steamship service between Kingsport and Parrsboro, across the

Between 1926 and 1941 the 200 ton motor vessel Kipawo *maintained a daily service across the Minas Basin, on the northeastern arm of the Bay of Fundy*

basin with the little twenty-five ton boat *Evangeline*.

When Canadian Pacific took over in 1912, the Dominion Atlantic Railway was operating this service with the *Prince Albert*, sailing between Wolfville, Kingsport and Parrsboro. She was retained until 1926, when a new 200 ton motor vessel, the *Kipawo* (*Ki*ngsport, *Pa*rrsboro, *Wo*lfville), was ordered from the Saint John Dry Dock Company. Replacing the *Prince Albert*, she

remained on this run until requisitioned in 1941 by the Canadian government to service military bases on the Newfoundland coast. The Minas Basin route was not reopened by Canadian Pacific after the war and the *Kipawo* was sold to Crosbie & Co of St Johns NF, who operated her between Conception Bay ports, where she is still in service.

For fleet list see page 260.

10 Tugs

Quebec Salvage & Wrecking Company

Canadian Pacific was a part-owner of this company, which was formed in 1914 for salvage work in the St Lawrence. The tugs *Gopher* and *Musquash* belonging to the Mersey Towing Company in Liverpool were requisitioned by the Admiralty in 1914, but were returned to Canadian Pacific shortly afterwards for transfer to Quebec. They left Liverpool on 3 June 1914, via Moville and St Johns NF, arriving at Quebec on 20 June. Both tugs remained with Quebec Salvage until they were sold; the *Musquash* in 1920 and the *Gopher* in 1923.

The company, including the tug *Lord Strathcona* and motor vessel *Traverse*, was sold on 30 September 1944 to the Foundation Company of Canada.

Mersey Towing Company

When Canadian Pacific bought the Beaver Line ships from Elder Dempster in 1903, it also took over the Mersey Towing Company plus the tugs *Beaver*, *Otter* and *Panther*. In 1906 the tender *Bison* with a passenger licence for 537 souls was added. In 1910 the *Gopher* and *Musquash* were built for the company and in June 1914 these two tugs were transferred to the Quebec Salvage and Wrecking Company. In 1915 two more tugs were built for the company, *Moose and Wapiti*. By 1947 all the tugs had been sold and the company was wound up on 26 May 1950.

For fleet list see page 262.

The tug Bison

The launch of the Empress of Britain *in 1930 and on tow northwest of Ireland after being bombed in 1940*

Part Two  Histories of Individual Ships

1 Pacific

The first Empresses

The three sister ships—*Empress of India, Empress of China* and *Empress of Japan*—were of almost 6000 tons and powered by two independent triple-expansion engines driving twin screws. They were the first and only twin-screw vessels on the Pacific until 1899. They were the largest and fastest passenger liners on the Pacific and their easily remembered names coupled with their graceful lines and reputation for good service soon established them as favourites with the travelling public.

Accommodation for 160 first-class passengers consisted mainly of three-berth outside rooms on the upper deck, plus four state rooms, with bedsteads instead of bunks, on the promenade deck. Forty second-class berths were provided aft, and 'tweendeck accommodation for steerage passengers, mostly Chinese, Japanese and Hindu immigrants, was arranged as required. As many as 700 steerage passengers were carried on occasions. There were no private toilet facilities and the three public rooms, a large dining saloon, a smoking saloon and a library/lounge, were exclusively first class. All furniture was either built in or secured to the decks.

The Figureheads

Each ship carried a figurehead: the *Empress of India* a likeness of Queen Victoria, the *Empress of China* a gilt dragon, and the *Empress of Japan* a green and gold dragon. It is thought that these figureheads were carved at Barrow-in-Furness, Kowloon and Yokohama respectively. Unfortunately only one remains, that from the *Empress of Japan*; this was bought by the 'Vancouver Daily Province' in 1925 and set up in Stanley Park, Vancouver. In the late 1950s, because it had begun to disintegrate, a fibreglass copy was made which still stands in the park. The original was rescued by the Maritime Museum which, in 1977, began a delicate job of restoration. The 700lb bell from the ship's foremast is also preserved in the museum. These three vessels cost $3\frac{1}{2}$ million. (The *Empress of Canada* III, the last passenger liner built by the company, cost about $22 million in 1960.)

The famous red-and-white chequered house flag flew for the first time when the *Empress of India* ran her trials in 1891. The company advertised tours 'around the world in 80 days for $600' for each vessel's maiden voyage, with calls at Gibraltar, Naples, Suez, Colombo, Singapore, Hong Kong and Vancouver, where passengers joined a Canadian Pacific Railway train for Montreal.

Over their long career, apart from meeting the normal quota of typhoons in the Pacific, the ships were lucky and did not suffer many serious accidents. However, because of the lack of experience at that time with electrical insulation in ships at sea, all suffered teething problems from faulty electric wiring. The most serious was a fire which broke out in the afterhold of the *Empress of Japan* in August 1892.

Many of the staff became closely associated over the years with a particular Empress: Captain E. Beetham was in command of the *India* for eight years, Captain H. Pybus the *Japan* for eleven years, and Captain R. Archibald the *China* for nineteen years. Writing in the 'Vancouver Province', Monty Roberts said:

To take command of one of the White Empresses of the Pacific, a man should have apprenticeship in sail, a kindly understanding of human nature, a sense of humour, a term on the Atlantic service, a long period at sea in a subordinate position, an affection for his ship and a patient philosophy.

Empress of Japan (1891–1922)

The *Empress of Japan* was launched on 13 December 1890, by Lady Alice Stanley, daughter-in-law of the Governor-General of Canada. She sailed from Liverpool on 11 April 1891, under the command of Captain G. A. Lee. After minor electrical troubles, which caused problems with her fans and refrigerating machinery, she arrived in Vancouver on 2 June with 145 first-class passengers and more than 2000 tons of cargo.

In August 1891 the *Empress of Japan* made the eastbound trip in ten days, thirteen hours, ten minutes, averaging 16.59 knots. Mails were then rushed by special train to Brockville, Ontario, thence to New York, where the steamer *City of New York* was held for half an hour before sailing to Liverpool. The mails reached London on 9 September, twenty-two days from Yokohama. Later she made the crossing in ten days, ten hours, a record which stood until beaten by the *Empress of Russia* in 1913.

The *Empress of Japan* sailed from Vancouver on 23 July 1914, and on reaching Hong Kong was fitted out as an auxiliary cruiser. She returned to company service in 1916, and made her three hundred and fifteenth and final crossing in 1922, arriving in Vancouver on 18 July. She was sold for scrap in 1926 after thirty-one years of continuous service during which time she had sailed more than two million miles.

A model of the figurehead from the Empress of Japan, *now standing in Stanley Park, Vancouver*

129

Empress of China (1891–1911)

The *Empress of China* was launched on 25 March 1891 by Lady Stafford Northcote, wife of the governor of the Hudson's Bay Company. She sailed on 15 July 1891 from Liverpool under the command of Captain A. Tillett, but with only a handful of passengers for the round-the-world trip. After a stormy passage across the Pacific she arrived in Vancouver on 23 September 1891.

In October 1907, while loading in Vancouver, water entered the engine room through an open valve. To prevent her from rolling over and sinking, the coal hulk

Robert Kerr was lashed alongside the *Empress* until she could be pumped dry.

The last to join the famous trio of the Pacific, she was unfortunately the first to leave. In 1911 it was announced that two new ships were to be built to join two of the old Empresses. Speculation as to which would be scrapped was ended when the *Empress of China* struck the Mera Reef, Tokyo Bay, on 27 July 1911. No one was injured but the ship had to be abandoned.

Crew of the Empress of China, *date unknown*

Empress of India (1891–1914)

The *Empress of India* was launched on 30 August 1890 by Lady Louise Egerton, sister of Lord Hartington who was chairman of the Naval Construction & Armament Company. She sailed from Liverpool on 8 February 1891, under the command of Captain O. P. Marshall, with more than 100 passengers. On her voyage from the Mersey to Hong Kong the *Empress* burnt 2436 tons of coal whilst steaming 10,096 miles in thirty-three days and seven hours, an average of seventy-three tons a day. On arrival at Hong Kong, while the vessel was painted and overhauled, many of her passengers travelled on to Japan to rejoin the ship at Yokohama for the final leg to Vancouver.

The sailing of the *Empress* from Hong Kong on 7 April 1891 for Shanghai, Nagasaki, Kobe, Yokohama, Victoria and Vancouver, marked the start of the ten-year mail contract and the regular trans-Pacific Empress service which lasted until the outbreak of World War II.

She left Yokohama on 17 April and arrived at Victoria on 28 April, a run of eleven days, seven hours, twenty-seven minutes, a record that was soon to be beaten by all the Empresses. Mayor Grant of Victoria presented Captain Marshall with a gold-inlaid punch set bearing the inscription: 'Presented by the City of Victoria to the Commander of the Canadian Pacific Railway's steamer *Empress of India* on her initial voyage to British Columbia, 18.4.1891.' After a three-hour stop at Victoria, the *Empress* sailed for Vancouver where 131 passengers disembarked together with 1800 tons of cargo, mostly tea and silk. Mail which left that evening for Montreal was distributed in London only twenty-six days after leaving Yokohama. The ship was officially welcomed by the mayor, who declared a civic holiday; a banquet was held that evening in the Hotel Vancouver.

In 1901 the Duke of York, later King George V, crossed to Vancouver Island, and it is said that he was so impressed by the high standard of efficiency and the personality of the *India*'s commander that he later supported the invitation which Captain Marshall received to become an elder brother of Trinity House in 1905.

In August 1903 the *Empress of India* became involved in a near-political incident, when among the passengers from Shanghai were some Chinese political refugees. During darkness the Chinese gunboat *Huang-Tai* appeared off the starboard bow and attempted to cross the bows of the liner. By quick action, the *Empress* re-ceived only a glancing blow from the gunboat while the starboard propeller of the *Empress* tore a hole in the side of the warship, causing her to sink. The crew were rescued by the *Empress*, apart from a group of officers who said that as they had failed to stop the *Empress* they preferred to go down with their ship, rather than be returned to Shanghai.

The *Empress of India* left Vancouver for the last time on 22 August 1914, her two hundred and thirty-eighth crossing. From Hong Kong she sailed under Admiralty orders for Bombay, where she was bought by the Maharajah of Gwalior who, at his own expense, had her converted to a hospital ship for Indian troops and renamed *Loyalty*. After her war service she was bought by the Scindia Steam Navigation Company of Bombay, but made only a few voyages to Marseilles before being laid-up and sold for scrap in February 1923.

Other Empresses

Empress of Asia (1913–41); Empress of Russia (1913–40)

The new Empresses had three masts and were coal-fired quadruple-screw vessels driven by direct coupled Parson's turbines, one high, one intermediate and two low pressure. Five hundred and ninety feet in length, they had accommodation for 284 first-class, 100 second-class, plus 800 Asiatic steerage passengers. The first-class rooms had brass bedsteads instead of the old-fashioned berths. Eight special suites had hot and cold running water. Five small holds were provided for valuable cargoes, particularly silk and tea. A mere $5 million paid for these two sisters, distinguished only by their wheelhouses—the *Asia* had portholes while the *Russia* had square windows.

The speed of the two new ships enabled the company to meet a request from the Philippine government for a call to be made at Manila. The *Empress of Russia* made the first call on 29 June 1914 and the *Empress of Asia* followed four weeks later. Unfortunately the outbreak of war interrupted the service, but it was reintroduced after the war and continued until May 1923. On returning to the Pacific service after World War I, both vessels appeared with grey and later black hulls and it was not until 1927 that the white hulls were reintroduced. The sisters ran on a regular schedule between Vancouver and Hong Kong, with the old *Empress of Japan* and the

The 17,000 ton Empress of Russia *joined the Pacific service in 1913*

Monteagle fitting in as best they could.

During 1919 and 1920 the accommodation on the Empresses was drastically altered to meet the rush of post-war traffic. The original second-class cabins were upgraded to make a total of 374 first-class berths. New second- and third-class accommodation was added, steerage numbers being greatly reduced. Total carryings in the 1920–21 season were more than double pre-war figures. Freight earnings also increased, tea and silk being the most important cargoes.

In the 1930s passenger carryings and cargoes declined rapidly. Artificial silks were coming on the market and the value of real silk had dropped from over $6 a pound in the 1920s to $1.30 by 1934. The big drop in value reduced insurance rates; consequently fast speeds were no longer important and the Japanese captured the trade by carrying direct to New York, via the Panama Canal.

The *Empress of Asia* was launched on 23 November 1912 by Mrs G. Bosworth, wife of the chairman of Canadian Pacific Ocean Services and vice-president of Canadian Pacific Railway. On 14 June 1913 she left Liverpool for her maiden voyage to Hong Kong via Madeira, Cape Town, Colombo and Singapore and arrived at Victoria on 31 August.

The *Asia* was requisitioned the day before World War I was declared, fortunately at Hong Kong, where she was quickly outfitted as an armed merchant cruiser in the Royal Navy Dockyard. As there were no Royal Marines available in Hong Kong her complement was made up with volunteers from a Pathan regiment who served for about six months. She then went on patrol in the Yellow Sea and the Indian Ocean, where she joined in the search for the German cruiser *Emden*, and later patrolled in the Red Sea. She was paid-off on 22 October 1915, and after an overhaul in Hong Kong she returned to the company's Pacific service in the spring of 1916. However, in May 1918 she was requisitioned for a second time for trooping on the North Atlantic, making five voyages from North America to Liverpool and one to Brest with US troops. She sailed on her final wartime voyage on 2 January 1919 when she left Liverpool with 1100 Canadian troops bound for British Columbia via the Panama Canal.

For the next twenty years the *Asia* remained on the trans-Pacific run and on one occasion made a round trip to Hong Kong in thirty-eight days, arriving at Vancouver on 12 November 1923. When eleven years old in July 1924, she made the fastest ever crossing by the two sisters, from Yokohama to Williams Head in eight days, fourteen hours, forty-eight minutes, an average of 20.2 knots.

On 21 February 1927, when the *Empress of Asia* was some 300 miles west of Victoria, a seaplane came alongside to collect from the purser a can containing newsreel pictures of the fighting between the Chinese and Japanese forces in the city of Shanghai. The seaplane took off for Seattle, where a land plane was waiting to carry the reels eastwards, thus saving twenty-four hours on their journey from the Orient.

Under the command of Captain G. Goold, she was in Shanghai when World War II broke out, and sailed two days later, arriving at her home port of Vancouver in October 1939. She continued making trips to Hong Kong on company service, meantime being fitted with a 6in anti-submarine gun and a 3in high-angle anti-aircraft gun. On 14 September 1940, while in the Gulf of Tokyo, more than a year before Japan entered the war, a Japanese bomber flew directly overhead and dropped a bomb that wounded several of the Chinese crew when it landed in the galley after penetrating two decks. The Japanese explanation that it was an accident had to be accepted. The cost of the damage was paid by the Japanese consul in Vancouver.

The *Asia* completed her three hundred and seventh crossing of the Pacific when she arrived at Vancouver on 11 January 1941 to learn that she was to become a troopship and would leave shortly to be converted for the job she had previously carried out twenty-two years earlier. This turned out to be the last scheduled crossing of the Pacific by an Empress, thus ending fifty years of Empress service between Canada and the Orient. (Today Canadian Pacific airliners fly from Vancouver to Hong Kong bearing names such as 'Empress of Hong Kong' and 'Empress of Tokyo'.) Travelling by way of Panama, Jamaica and Bermuda the *Asia* reached the river of her birth, the Clyde, in late March, and Liverpool on 24 March.

The *Empress of Asia* started trooping to the Near East in April 1941, leaving Liverpool and sailing via Freetown, Cape Town and Durban to reach Suez on the 24 June. On leaving Port Said on 29 June 1941, Donald Smith, the chief officer, invited two young naval officers

who were returning to England to sit at his table. One was Prince Philip of Greece, who travelled as far as Durban and there transferred to the *Empress of Russia* (see page 137).

In company with the *Empress of Japan* II and with 2235 troops in addition to her crew of 416, she left Liverpool on 12 November 1941, sailing via Cape Town and Bombay. She arrived off Singapore on 4 February 1942. The *Empress* had the stern position in the convoy through the Banka Strait on the east coast of Sumatra. Captain J. B. Smith, with reference to the *Asia*'s place at the end of the line, reported somewhat dryly: 'We had been allotted this position on account of our steaming difficulties, the ship almost invariably dropping astern of station when fires were being cleaned.' In a later interview Captain Smith explained:

> Well-trained Chinese firemen got the best out of the two coal burners from the Pacific Fleet, but by the time World War II broke out there was a real dearth of firemen accustomed to coal and after our Chinese firemen returned home we had to rely on what the Merchant Seamen's Pools could scrape up.

At 11am on 4 February the convoy was sighted by Japanese aircraft and a few near misses damaged two of her lifeboats. At the same time on the following morning the official report shows that:

> A large formation of Japanese aircraft passed overhead and disappeared in the clouds. Later they reappeared, seemingly coming from all directions and flying at both high and low altitudes. All ships in the convoy, including the escorting light cruiser and a sloop, opened fire. Bombs started falling all round the *Empress* and it was evident that the ship had been singled out to bear the brunt of the attack.

A stick of bombs scored the first hits, one going through the ornate dome over the lounge. A second bomb pierced the lounge and destroyed the radio equipment. Other bombs caused much damage to the engine room, including the auxiliary power plants, fractured pipes in the interior of the ship and started many fires. The chief officer reported that bombs had penetrated all decks, smoke and flames hindering attempts to control the fires which by 11.25am were out of control. The captain's report continues:

> At this time we were passing between minefields to the North and South of the swept channel. I

decided to swing the ship round and anchor close to the Sultan Shoal Lighthouse. At this time it was impossible to remain on the Bridge any longer on account of the smoke and heat.

One happy feature of the Japanese concentration on the *Empress of Asia* was that the other less badly damaged ships were able to get small boats away when the *Empress* was abandoned, thus keeping the loss of life to a minimum. The Australian sloop *Yarra* came alongside aft and took off well over a thousand troops and crew. By 1pm all personnel were off the ship. A later check showed fifteen military unaccounted for and one member of the crew dead as a result of injuries sustained in the bombing.

The deck and engine-room crew were later posted by the naval authorities to various small coastal ships to help in the evacuation of Singapore. Many of the catering staff volunteered for duty in Singapore hospitals and were later interned by the Japanese. Recognition of her service by HM the King was expressed in the award of the OBE to Captain J. B. Smith, the MBE to First Officer L. H. Johnston and a mention in dispatches for Chief Officer Donald Smith.

During World War II the *Asia* travelled 46,993 miles, carried 6839 troops, 1000 prisoners of war, eighty-four civilians and 3495 tons of cargo.

Empress of Russia (1913–45)

The *Empress of Russia* was launched on 28 August 1912 by Mrs W. Beauclerk, daughter of Sir Thomas Shaughnessy, president of Canadian Pacific Railway. With a party of round-the-world passengers on board, the *Empress* left Liverpool on 1 April 1913 for the Mediterranean, Colombo and Singapore and arrived at Hong Kong on 9 May.

She sailed on 21 May for her first Pacific crossing via Shanghai. At Nagasaki, between 8am and 2pm she took on 3200 tons of coal, an average of 533 tons per hour. All the coal had to be carried on board by human chains of Japanese coal-handlers. Then by way of Kobe and Yokohama (29 May) she arrived at Williams Head (Victoria BC) in nine days, five hours, twenty-nine minutes, beating the previous record, set by the *Empress of Japan* by more than twenty-eight hours.

After only a short spell in company service the *Russia* was requisitioned at Hong Kong on 22 August 1914, and with the *Empress of Asia* and *Empress of Japan* formed part of the squadron blockading German merchant ships in the Philippines. Later they transferred to the Indian Ocean. The *Empress of Russia* then met with the Australian cruiser *Sydney* on 13 November and took aboard 230 survivors from the German cruiser *Emden*. By December the *Russia* was on patrol duties in the Red Sea, but before long the naval authorities realised that these large liners were not being properly utilised. Accordingly she was paid-off at Bombay on 19 October 1915. She then proceeded to Hong Kong for refit before returning to the company's Pacific service on 12 February 1916.

The Empresses made an important contribution to the war effort at this time by carrying across the Pacific many thousands of Chinese who were being recruited for labour battalions in France. Early in 1918 a growing demand for more troop transports on the North Atlantic to carry American troops to Europe led to the *Russia* and *Asia* being requisitioned for a second time, when they made several voyages from North America to Liverpool with US troops.

The *Russia* left Liverpool on her last wartime voyage on 12 January 1919. Calling at Le Havre to pick up returning Chinese, she sailed by way of Suez to Hong Kong where she arrived on 22 February and then on to Vancouver arriving on the last day of March 1919. Her first peacetime voyage started on 10 April when, outward bound, she called at Manila and, homeward, at Vladivostok. Together with the *Empress of Asia*, the *Russia* quickly settled back into the routine schedule, averaging six trans-Pacific round trips a year with the old *Empress of Japan* and the *Monteagle* from the Atlantic fleet fitting in according to the demands of traffic. Both vessels appeared with grey and later black hulls and it was not until 1927 that the gleaming white hulls reappeared.

On 3 September 1939 the *Empress of Russia* sailed from Honolulu on the last leg of the eastward half of her voyage which proved uneventful, as were the six succeeding wartime round trips she made in passenger and cargo service across the Pacific for her owners. The only noticeable difference for the first fifteen months of the war was that she was 'defensively armed', sailed under naval instructions, had her crew augmented by DEMS ('defensively equipped merchant ship') gunners and, instead of her usual white hull and superstructure and the characteristic buff funnels, she was painted the dull grey that naval hands call 'crab fat'.

The delay in the call-up of the two sisters was probably due to the problems of securing suitable coal and the scarcity of firemen experienced with coal burners. When at Hong Kong on 28 November 1940, after her three hundred and tenth trans-Pacific crossing, she finally received her directive and, under the command of Captain M. J. D. Mayall RD, RNR, set out on a roundabout voyage to Vancouver by way of Wellington, New Zealand, Sydney, New South Wales, Auckland, New Zealand, Suva, Fiji and Honolulu. She had last carried troops twenty-two years before when she ferried 'doughboys' from the USA to the UK in 1918. The RAAF and RNZAF recruits she carried to Canada for their initial flying training enjoyed regular passenger amenities, as her conversion to trooping did not take place until she reached the Clyde where she returned via Panama, Jamaica and Bermuda, arriving on 18 March 1941. Within a week the 'Tail of the Bank' anchorage saw three Pacific Empresses, the *Asia*, *Russia* and *Canada*, within cables' lengths of each other. All three had been built in the same Clyde yard—Fairfields.

After being fitted out for trooping, the *Russia* left the Clyde in April 1941 on the Freetown–Cape Town–Suez route, necessitated by the closure of the Mediterranean route to Egypt. The return by way of Cape Town, Newport News and Halifax to the Clyde enabled transports to utilise the return trip bringing Canadian troops and cargo from the eastern seaboard of North America. By the time the *Empress* reached Puerto Rico, the Chinese crew had been confined to the ship (many countries would not allow Chinese crews ashore) for considerably longer than a normal voyage and their desire to stretch their legs was understandable. Not surprisingly some failed to report back on time and the *Empress* had to sail short of firemen. The officer commanding troops on board called for volunteers to act as trimmers from Puerto Rico to Newport News; among them was the young naval officer Prince Philip of Greece, who duly received a CPR trimmer's certificate.

Further trips to Cape Town and Durban followed, including one which extended to Bombay and Colombo. In July 1943 troops were carried to Philippeville, Algiers and Oran in support of the North African landing. By this time the *Empress of Russia* was thirty years old and the only large coal-burning transport left in service. Because of the great scarcity of good firemen and good steam coal she was transferred to special duties. On 14 October 1943 she made a special trip to Gothenburg to exchange prisoners of war. Union Jacks were painted on the side of the *Empress* and floodlights rigged to illuminate them at night. Sailing around the north of Scotland to the Skaggerrak she was met by a German minesweeper detailed to lead them through the minefields, and later by a Swedish naval officer to pilot the *Empress* into Gothenburg where they were officially welcomed by the Crown Prince of Sweden and the British minister. The exchange, supervised by the neutral Swedes, was made in two days, and the repatriates were returned to Leith and a tumultuous welcome on 26 October. Among the prisoners of war brought home was a Dieppe veteran, Captain R. R. Laird RCAMC, who before the war had been ship's doctor on the *Empress of Russia*. On this mercy trip the *Empress of Russia* was accompanied by the Swedish–American liner *Drottningholm*, originally the Allan liner *Virginian*, which Canadian Pacific had sold in 1920.

Then followed seven trips to Reykjavik, Iceland, for the RAF, including one trip to the Faeroe Islands. In April 1944 she was ordered to Rosyth naval base to provide accommodation for Russian naval crews who were to take over a number of British warships. After a short lay-up she sailed for Spithead where she arrived on Dominion Day 1944 to act as depot ship for the tugs busily crossing and recrossing the Channel in the great build-up that followed D-Day landings.

A precedent was created when the *Empress*, fitted with machine shops for repairs and baths for tugs' crews, etc, was selected as flag ship for the senior naval officer who, of course, brought his own staff aboard. He realised that the naval custom of piping the senior officer aboard, which he took for granted, seemed a little anomalous on another man's ship. So he ordered that a similar compliment be paid Captain Goold. Reminiscing some years later Captain Goold recalled that as far as he knew 'that was the first and only time a merchant shipmaster was piped over the side of a merchant ship by Naval Bosun's Mates and side-boys'.

By 31 October 1944 the *Russia* was back in the Gareloch, where she was laid-up until June 1945. At one time it was thought that she would be broken up but later it was decided to send her to Barrow-in-Furness to be refitted for the repatriation of Canadian troops and their families after the war. Before her overhaul was completed fire broke out on 8 September and swept through the centre of the ship. Declared a total loss she was broken up by T. W. Ward & Sons. During her second war she

had steamed 160,056 miles under five masters and carried 53,850 military personnel, 5486 prisoners of war, 904 civilians plus 6230 tons of cargo, half of which was carried in March 1944 from Reykjavik to Glasgow. Apart from her brightly lit passage between Scotland and Sweden, her service had been unostentatious.

Empress of Canada I (1922–43)

Fairfields received the order for the 21,500 ton *Empress of Canada* in 1919. More than 650ft long, she was much more lavishly furnished than the *Asia* and *Russia*. A feature of the new ship was the 110ft 'long gallery' stretching from the main staircase on 'A' deck to the first-class lounge. Panelled in Honduras mahogany, the gallery gave access to the principal first-class public rooms. At the after end the oak-panelled smoke room gave access to a verandah café. A 30ft swimming pool and gymnasium were situated on 'D' deck. The decoration of all the public rooms had been designed by George Crawley & Partners of London.

The first-class accommodation for 444 passengers had hot and cold running water and forty cabins had private baths and toilets. Two- and four-berth accommodation for second class was on 'C' deck, whilst third-class rooms were fitted with two, four and six berths. Kitchens, pantry and bakery were placed between the dining saloons. A separate kitchen was provided for the Asiatic steerage passengers. The vessel was also equipped with a laundry, hospital dispensary and barber's shop, and carried a manicurist and stenographer. Twin screws were driven by double reduction geared turbines and provision was made for conversion from oil to coal firing if necessary. J. H. Biles & Co, the consulting naval architects of London, supervised this, the largest ship built by Fairfields at that date.

Mrs G. M. Bosworth, wife of the chairman of CPOS Ltd, who had launched the *Empress of Asia* eight years earlier, sponsored the new *Empress* on 17 August 1920. It had been planned that she would leave for Vancouver by the following March, but strikes and shortages of materials and skilled labour in the post-war period delayed her departure. These problems plus the fact that costs had more than doubled because of the war made it uneconomic to build a sister ship. Eventually the *Empress of Canada* completed her sea trials at Falmouth and left on 5 May 1922 on her maiden voyage to Vancouver by the Suez Canal. Her troubles had not finished.

The Empress of Canada *i, a 21,000 ton liner from the Fairfield yard in 1922 for the trans-Pacific service*

Plans to welcome the largest liner to cross the Pacific had to be abandoned in both Victoria and Vancouver because a case of smallpox had been detected on board.

On her sixth round trip the *Empress of Canada* left Hong Kong on 3 May 1923 for Vancouver where she arrived on 17 June. On board were more than 1000 passengers, 3000 tons of cargo including twenty-five carloads of raw silk, and 500 tons of tea from Shimidzu. The 'Victoria Colonist' of 19 June said:

> There is the pride of knowing that this new trans-Pacific record will attract attention in every quarter where there is interest in shipping. It will add to the up-to-date reputation of the CPR and prove to the world that this Dominion continues to consolidate her place in commercial development.

On 27 June, prior to her sailing for Hong Kong, Captain A. J. Hailey and Chief Engineer J. Lamb were presented with a silver shield by Lieutenant-Colonel G. Kirk-patrick, chairman of the Vancouver Harbour Commission, inscribed:

TRANSPACIFIC RECORD, JUNE 1923

Presented to the Royal Mail Steamer *Empress of Canada* on the occasion of this vessel having broken all previous records between Yokohama and Vancouver.

Lieut-Commander A. J. Hailey RNR,
Master of the Ship.
James Lamb, Chief Engineer.
Time—8 days, 10 hours and 53 minutes.
Average speed, 20.6 knots.
Distance, 4179 knots.

In 1922 and 1923 Canadian Pacific had chartered liners to the Frank Clark Agency of New York for cruises, but in 1924 the company decided to operate its own seventeen-week world cruise with the *Empress of Canada*. She left Vancouver on 4 January 1924 for New York via Panama and Havana. This voyage was also sold as a cruise with the passengers returning to Vancouver by railway. The world cruise left New York on 30 January and sailed via Gibraltar and Suez, reaching Vancouver on 24 May, when she returned to her trans-Pacific run.

In 1928 the *Empress of France* was transferred from the Atlantic fleet whilst the *Canada* returned to the Fairfield yard for an overhaul. She was re-engined under the supervision of the company's chief superintendent engineer, John Johnson, with single-reduction geared turbines. Super-heaters were added to her boilers and diesel engines installed to run the ship's auxiliaries. As a sea-trial, a round trip to Quebec in August 1929 established a new transatlantic record of five days, fourteen hours, twenty-five minutes. The average daily consumption of oil fuel was 175 tons for 20.53 knots compared with a previous figure of 284 tons for 20.6 knots, a remarkable achievement.

On 18 September she sailed from Southampton for New York, Panama, San Francisco and Vancouver. Once again she was dogged by bad luck. When approaching Victoria in dense fog she ran on to the rock in Homer's Bay in the Juan de Fuca Straits. All the passengers were taken off by the *Salvage King* and *Salvage Queen*. With the help of tugs she was eventually refloated and taken to Esquimalt for repairs, which delayed her Pacific crossing until 2 November. On her next voyage she started calling at Honolulu westbound and in 1932 began regular calls both outward and homeward. One unfortunate result of this change in schedule was that the ship was used by smugglers of opium.

The *Empress* left on her one hundred and ninety-ninth and last company crossing of the Pacific on 2 September 1939. Like all other merchant ships at the time she carried two envelopes marked *A* and *B*, 'Not to be opened until officially instructed'. On the following day Captain G. Goold received radio instructions to open envelope *A*. The main instruction was to 'darken ship' which meant that portholes had to be blacked out and the ship painted grey as soon as possible. The voyage was uneventful and on her return to Vancouver she was fitted with a 6in gun aft, a twelve-pounder forward and four Bofors.

Sailing from Vancouver on 4 November 1939 she called at Manila and Hong Kong, where she was requisitioned on 29 November 1939 and cleared as HMT X5 on 8 December, for Wellington, New Zealand, to pick up New Zealand troops for Suez. Returning to Sydney,

Australia, she joined the 'multimillion-dollar' convoy of seven luxury liners, with the *Empress of Britain*, *Empress of Japan*, *Queen Mary*, *Aquitania*, *Mauritania* and *Andes*, totalling 276,918 tons. They left on 2 May 1940 and arrived in the Clyde in June. The *Empress of Canada* then made four trips to the Middle East including one transit of the Suez Canal to land troops at Alexandria on New Year's Eve 1940.

When she left the Clyde for Suez on 24 March 1941 as commodore ship in company with the *Duchess of Atholl*, *Duchess of York* and several other well-known liners, they were escorted by the battleships HMS *Nelson* and *Rodney*, two cruisers and eight destroyers—an indication of the importance of this particular convoy.

Next came a very different assignment, 'Operation Gauntlet', the Allied raid on Spitzbergen some 700 miles from the North Pole by Canadian and British forces in August and September 1941. The aim was first to capture two known German agents to prevent their reporting the raid by radio to the Nazis in occupied Norway, then to evacuate two thousand Russians to Archangel and Norwegians to the United Kingdom, and to put the coal mine and other facilities out of action. The main port of Barentsberg had to be left intact until the last possible moment.

Under the command of Brigadier A. E. Potts of the Canadian army, the raiding force consisted of some 650 Canadian troops from the Saskatoon Light Infantry, the Royal Edmonton Regiment, Royal Canadian Engineers, plus Norwegian and British specialists. As a precaution, before sailing, British troops with tropical kit were embarked in daylight only to be exchanged for the 'raiders' under the cover of darkness. Once under way, Captain Goold gave permission for the canteen to be opened but discovered a few minutes later that the ship was bound for Inveraray where the troops were to practise landings. A return to the Clyde a few days later involved the company in lengthy correspondence with Customs regarding the sale of bonded liquors, etc, aboard a ship not cleared for a foreign port.

The real action began on 19 August with an escort of HMS *Nigeria*, *Aurora* and three destroyers under the command of Rear-Admiral Vian. A call was made at Hvalfjordur, Iceland, to refuel the destroyers. Before reaching Spitzbergen, raiding parties were transferred to a destroyer and landed at selected points on the island where they were met by local Norwegians and led over the mountains to Barentsberg. Fortunately the German agents were quickly captured and the radio station taken over. The regular weather reports to the Germans were maintained plus a bit of extra information about low cloud and poor visibility to dissuade enemy aircraft. Among the Russians embarked for Archangel was one mother in labour; with sedation she was able to have her baby on Russian soil. Had the baby Russian been born on board the *Canada* the birth might well have been registered in the parish church of Stepney! A British mission and some French prisoners of war, who had been conscripted by the Germans for forced labour and later captured by the Russians, joined the ship for the return journey. Returning via Spitzbergen, where the mines and other important installations had been destroyed, 767 Norwegians plus the troops were then embarked for the Clyde, where they arrived on 7 September.

South again, the next voyage took the *Empress* to Singapore just before the Japanese raid on Pearl Harbor, and then on to New Zealand and home via the Panama Canal and Newport News where she had an extensive refit. Embarking Canadian troops at Halifax, she reached the Clyde on 22 March 1942. In the previous eight months she had been as far north as Spitzbergen and as far south as New Zealand in circumnavigating the world. Her next and last long voyage was to Bombay. Two trips to Oran with troops for the North African landings followed.

Luck was running out. Leaving the Clyde for the last time on 16 January 1943, the *Empress of Canada* reached Durban on 25 February where she embarked a very mixed group including representatives from the navy, army and air force, the Norwegian, Greek and French navies, the Polish army including seventy women, 500 Italian prisoners of war, plus her crew of 362 for return to the United Kingdom. The master's report of the loss reads in part as follows:

The voyage was without incident until 11th March, when I received wireless orders to proceed to Takoradi and giving me a new route. On the 12th I received another message changing this route, and on the afternoon of the 13th another instructing me to proceed direct to Takoradi.

At about 11.54pm on the night of the 13th March there was a heavy explosion and the ship immediately took a list to starboard of 15 to 20 degrees. The ship had been hit by a torpedo on the starboard side, abreast the after stokehold. This had

the immediate effect of putting main engines, steering gear and all electric light and power out of action. At about 12.10am I gave orders to lower away and abandon ship.

A second torpedo struck the ship on the starboard side below the bridge at about 12.50am and the ship started to sink rapidly. This torpedo capsized number 3 boat which had just been lowered and probably all the people in her lost their lives.

I had at no time seen the submarine that had sunk us but learned later that she had surfaced after the ship sank and gone alongside number 6 boat and taken aboard the Italian doctor.

Just before sunset on the 14th a Catalina came over us and signalled that help was on the way. In the evening of the 15th the destroyer *Boreas* and corvettes *Crocus* and *Petunia* picked up survivors and took them to Freetown. HMS *Corinthian* arrived the following morning and made a further search for survivors.

The total loss of life was 392 of which 44 were members of the crew.

In her seventeen years of company service the *Empress of Canada* had made two cruises, one North Atlantic trip, and 199 Pacific crossings. On war service she steamed 202,249 miles, carried 35,364 military personnel, 13,671 civilians, 500 prisoners of war plus 13,584 tons of cargo. It was later established that the fateful torpedo had been fired by the Italian submarine *Leonardo da Vinci* and that whilst she was attacking another Allied ship on 23 May 1943 she was sunk by HMS *Active* and HMS *Ness*.

The loss of the *Canada*, one of the worst sea disasters of the war, gave rise to much speculation. Some survivors had their suspicions about an Italian army doctor and claimed that his porthole had been seen open. Could it have been a coincidence that the submarine surfaced near the number six lifeboat and took the doctor aboard— the only survivor they picked up? Captain Bill Williams, who was a cadet on the *Canada* at the time of the incident, was told by a German radio officer after the war that the messages to change course, mentioned in the master's report, had been sent by German radio.

Empress of Australia I (1922–52)

The *Tirpitz* had been launched by the Vulcan-Werke AG

The Empress of Australia *i, the 22,000 ton German-built* Tirpitz,
which sailed on the Pacific and the Atlantic for Canadian Pacific

of Stettin, for the Hamburg Amerika Line on 20 December 1913; but for the war, she would have made her maiden voyage on the South America service on 29 October 1914. With a length of 615ft and a gross tonnage of 21,860 she was an unusual ship in many ways. The uptakes for her two forward funnels were on either side of a broad hallway linking the public rooms along the centre of the ship, and came together on the boat deck. Hydraulic transmission, designed by Dr Fottinger, had been fitted instead of the more usual mechanical gearing. Her turbines drove water pumps, the water then driving water wheels attached to the shafts. Her upper works were high and bulky; this made her top-heavy and had to be compensated with 1500 tons of permanent ballast. Rumour had it that she had been selected to carry the Kaiser on a triumphal cruise after the war. Although an unlikely story, work on her had been resumed at one period of the war.

The *Tirpitz* arrived in Hull in 1919, and was used by the Ministry of Shipping for trooping. In 1920 she made several voyages under Cunard management, eventually being laid-up at Immingham in February 1921. She was bought by Canadian Pacific on 29 July and renamed *Empress of China* III. On 20 August she was sent to Ham-

burg for refit and conversion to oil fuel; this work was completed at the John Brown yard on the Clyde.

When she joined the Pacific service her accommodation provided for 400 first-class, 165 second-class, 350 third-class and 650 steerage passengers plus a crew of 520. All the first-class rooms were fitted with bedsteads, and eight suites had bath and toilet facilities plus a box room. People travelled with seemingly vast amounts of luggage in those days. Two suites on 'B' deck comprised a dining-room, *salon*, bedroom, bathroom, maid's room and box room. The first-class dining saloon had a large central dome and was decorated in Louis XVI style with mahogany furniture; it had a musicians' gallery at the after end. The saloon could seat 330 and there were two small private saloons seating twenty each. A feature of the first-class lounge on 'A' deck was the absence of pillars, the roof and dome being built on the cantilever principle. The walls and ceiling were finished in green and gilt. Other furniture was in satinwood and a magnificent concert-grand sat in one corner. Two wide staircases and two lifts connected. the main entrance with all the first-class accommodation.

Renamed *Empress of Australia* I on 2 June 1922, she left the Clyde on the sixteenth, her first sailing under the chequered house flag, and arrived at Vancouver on 19 July to start her first Pacific crossing on 28 July. The company now had four large Empresses on the Pacific run, the *Asia*, *Russia*, *Canada* and *Australia*. Unfortunately the *Australia* proved disappointing as she was unable to develop her designed power and speed despite adjustments and new oil burners; her fuel consumption was very high and her performance never really satisfactory.

However, she achieved lasting fame on Saturday 1 September 1923. As she was about to cast-off from wharf at Yokohama, with coloured paper streamers thrown from ship to shore where several hundred people were waving goodbye to their friends, the first shocks were felt of the great earthquake that would devastate most of Yokohama. During the first five days more than 700 shocks were recorded, causing severe damage over an area roughly eighty by sixty miles. On the Saturday and Sunday, fires continued to rage over the entire city. It was estimated that a quarter of a million people died and two and a quarter million were made destitute.

A cable fouled the port screw and held the liner captive for some hours near the wharf, which had partly collapsed. Ropes and ladders were lowered to enable refugees to climb aboard. Patches of burning oil drifted about the harbour and after much manoeuvring on one screw the *Empress* was eased away from her berth and out to sea to a safer anchorage. On the day after the earthquake a count revealed that in addition to her passengers, the *Empress* had on board 592 Europeans, 705 Chinese and 604 Japanese. Captain Robinson's report reads:

> A violent earthquake took place, first a number of severe shocks, then the land rolling in waves apparently 6–8 feet high, like a succession of fast moving ocean swells, were plainly visible from the bridge. The vessel shook all over in a most terrifying fashion and also rocked very quickly and violently until it seemed as though the masts and funnels must carry away.

On the Monday morning the *Empress of Canada* arrived on her normal schedule and was able to provide the *Australia* with additional stores and take some of the refugees on to Kobe. On Tuesday a Japanese battleship, the *Yamashiro Kan*, arrived on the scene and Captain Robinson was able to persuade the admiral to send one of his divers to work on the port propeller of the *Australia*, which had been fouled by a $2\frac{1}{4}$in chain cable. This was

successfully cleared and Captain Robinson immediately steamed back into the harbour to continue relief work. Each morning, parties consisting of residents, passengers and ship's crew left the ship to search for and bring back women and children and injured from the outlying parts of Yokohama. Meantime other ships were taking refugees from the *Australia* to Kobe, where the Japanese had established reception centres. Captain Robinson's report continues:

> I should like to express my admiration of the conduct and calmness of the passengers, many of whom worked untiringly day and night among the sick and injured refugees of all nationalities. The lower decks and alleyways all over the ship presenting a most gruesome and heart-rending sight, crowded with hundreds of badly wounded among the rescued, half or partially naked and covered with dirt and blood, groaning and crying bitterly. . . .
>
> Up to the morning of Monday the 3rd we were entirely without news of the outside world, all telegraphic communication, either by wireless or land, being cut off.

Late on Saturday 8 September the *Australia* left with many refugees for Kobe, as by that time several Japanese and American naval vessels had arrived. The *Empress of Russia* was the first merchant ship, from the outside world, to reach Yokohama. The company had given $25,000 and offered to carry free supplies of food and clothing. The *Russia* carried supplies of food and medicines from the Canadian government, Canadian Red Cross and the Vancouver Japanese Association. Two Red Cross nurses from Vancouver also sailed in the ship.

Later, Captain Robinson was invested with the CBE and awarded the silver medal of the Order of St John of Jerusalem. British refugees and passengers on board at the time presented the *Empress* with a bronze tablet. When the *Australia* was scrapped in 1952 the tablet was rescued and presented to Captain Robinson, who was then eighty-two, at a special lunch in Vancouver (see photograph on page 144).

Although accommodation on the *Australia* found great favour with her passengers, the ship's engineers had a hard struggle to keep her on schedule, and her fuel consumption was far too high. She made her twenty-first and last voyage from Vancouver in May 1926, and leaving Hong Kong in August she sailed via Suez for the Clyde and the Fairfield yard for new engines and boilers.

PRESENTED TO THE
R.M.S. "EMPRESS OF AUSTRALIA"
BY THE PASSENGERS
TO COMMEMORATE THE HEROIC WORK PERFORMED BY
COMMANDER S. ROBINSON R.N.R.
AND
ALL THE OFFICERS AND CREW,
IN SAVING THE LIVES OF ALL ON BOARD, AND
RESCUING SURVIVORS OF THE EARTHQUAKE AND
FIRE WHICH DEVASTATED THE DISTRICT OF
YOKOHAMA, SEPTEMBER 1ST 1923.
THIS SHIP, FOR NINE DAYS, A VERITABLE
"HAVEN OF REFUGE" SHELTERED AND SUCCOURED
THOUSANDS OF HOMELESS AND WOUNDED.

Canadian Pacific was fortunate at this time to have as its superintendent engineer John Johnson, a distinguished exponent of high-pressure, high-temperature steam practice. He was awarded the 1929 gold medal of the British Institute of Naval Architecture for his paper 'Propulsion of ships by modern steam machinery'. The *Empress of Australia* was the first of many company ships where his ideas were to prove valuable; others included the *Empress of Canada*, the Beavers, the Duchesses and the *Empress of Britain* II. Single-reduction Parsons turbines and new boilers were installed in the *Empress of Australia*, together with diesel engines to drive the ship's generators.

It had been decided that the *Australia* would not return to the Pacific and she joined the North Atlantic service from Southampton on 25 June 1927. The Prince of Wales' standard was hoisted when she left Southampton on 23 July 1927, with the Prince of Wales, Prince George and the prime minister, Stanley Baldwin, who were visiting Canada to take part in celebrations commemorating the sixtieth year of Confederation.

The *Empress* was also used for cruising during the winter seasons, and on 2 December 1927 she left New York on the first of her four round-the-world cruises. From 1931 until 1939 she cruised from the United Kingdom to the Mediterranean and Scandinavia and from New York to the West Indies. In 1935, whilst on

---

Presented to the
RMS *EMPRESS OF AUSTRALIA*
by the Passengers
To Commemorate the Heroic Work Performed by
COMMANDER S. ROBINSON, RNR
and
ALL THE OFFICERS AND CREW
In Saving the Lives of all on Board, and
Rescuing Survivors of the Earthquake and
Fire which Devastated the District of
YOKOHAMA, SEPTEMBER 1st, 1923
This Ship, for Nine Days, a Veritable
'Haven of Refuge', Sheltered and Succoured
Thousands of Homeless and Wounded

Captain S. Robinson with the plaque that was presented to the Empress of Australia *to commemorate the rescue work during the earthquake at Yokohama, on 1 September 1923*

a cruise to South Africa and South America, she called at the 'lonely isle', Tristan da Cunha, and landed supplies for the islanders.

Her crowning glory came when she was chartered to take Their Majesties the King and Queen and their party of sixty-nine from Portsmouth, on Saturday 6 May 1939, to Quebec. For this special occasion the smoking room was converted into a private dining-room with a table and chairs borrowed from the Royal Yacht. The Royal Standard was flown from the foremast, the Admiralty flag on the main and the white ensign on the stern. A Royal salute was fired by the Home Fleet as the *Australia* and her escort squadron steamed between the lines. Planes from the Fleet Air Arm flew over, dipping in salute. The liner was escorted by the cruisers HMS *Southampton*, *Glasgow* and *Repulse*, and on entering Canadian waters they were met by the Canadian destroyers *Skeena* and *Saguenay*. For the entertainment of the Royal party a number of film shows had been arranged, and when His Majesty heard of this he insisted that everyone off-watch be invited. Severe ice conditions were met during the voyage; consequently the arrival at Quebec was delayed by two days.

The master of the *Empress of Australia*, Captain A. R. Meikle RN, RNR, realised the problems that would arise from the late arrival of the Royal party. After studying weather reports and local conditions he believed that a path could be found through the ice flows, but the captain of the Royal Navy escorting ships did not think that they would be able to manoeuvre through the winding channel in the ice. Captain Meikle radioed Sir Edward Beatty, president CPR, for permission to go ahead without the escort. In turn Beatty asked the British Admiralty, but they refused permission for the *Empress* to leave the escort and so the Royal party arrived late— one of the president's more difficult decisions. Captain Meikle was awarded the CVO, an order in the personal gift of the sovereign for services to the Royal Family.

The day before war was declared the *Empress* sailed from Quebec and was making for the Strait of Belle Isle when the expected news was received. She reached Southampton without incident and was immediately painted grey, armed with a 3in high-angle gun plus a few machine guns, and was fitted-out for trooping. Her first wartime voyage was to Colombo and then to Halifax to join a big convoy which included the *Empress of Britain* and the *Duchess of Bedford*, bringing the First Canadian Division to the United Kingdom. The Canadian com-

The dining table from the Royal Yacht Victoria & Albert *used on
the* Empress of Australia *for the Royal visit to Canada in 1939*
(The Times), *with a seating plan and menu for dinner on 13 May*

MENU

Consommé à l'Essence de Celeris

Sole Frite Colbert

Mignon de Bœuf Sauté Princesse
Haricots verts au Beurre   Salsifis au Gratin
Pommes Anna

Poularde du Mans Rôtie au Cresson
Salade de Legumes Variés

Pêches Melba
Petits fours

Savoury—Beignets Neufchâtel

Corbeille de Fruits

Demi-Tasse

Empress of Australia   *Saturday, May 13, 1939*

PROGRAMME

PLAN OF ROYAL TABLE AT DINNER
Saturday, 13th May, 1939.

Seat No. 1. G. F. Steward, Esq., C.B.E., Press Liaison Officer.

,,   2. Lieutenant-Commander Peter Dawnay, R.N.,
          Flag Lieutenant.

,,   3. Surgeon Captain Joseph A. Maxwell, R.N.,
          Medical Officer.

,,   4. Dr. C. P. Miller, Surgeon, Empress of Australia.

,,   5. Her Majesty The Queen.

,,   6. Mr. J. P. Dobson, 1st Officer.

,,   7. The Earl of Airlie, G.C.V.O., M.C.,
          Lord Chamberlain to The Queen.

,,   8. Commander Conolly Abel-Smith, R.N.,
          Equerry-in-Waiting.

,,   9. Lieut.-Colonel The Hon. P. W. Legh, C.M.G., C.I.E.,
          C.V.O., O.B.E., Equerry-in-Waiting.

,,   10. Surgeon-Captain H. White, C.V.O., O.B.E., R.N.,
          Medical Officer.

,,   11. Vice-Admiral Sir Dudley North, K.C.V.O., C.B., C.S.I.,
          C.M.G., R.N., Commanding the Royal Squadron.

,,   12. Lady Katherine Seymour, C.V.O.,
          Lady-in-Waiting to The Queen.

,,   13. His Majesty The King.

,,   14. The Lady Nunburnholme,
          Lady-in-Waiting to the Queen.

,,   15. Captain Michael Adeane,
          Assistant Private Secretary to The King.

,,   16. A. F. Lascelles, Esq., C.B., C.M.G., M.V.O., M.C.,
          Acting Private Secretary to The King.

,,   17. The Earl of Eldon,
          Lord-in-Waiting to The King.

mander-in-chief, General A. G. L. MacNaughton, travelled in the *Australia*. The convoy was escorted by the battleship *Resolution*, flagship of the senior naval officer and commodore of the convoy, HMS *Repulse* and *Revenge*; in mid-Atlantic they were met by the aircraft carrier HMS *Furious*. In thick fog the *Australia* lost the convoy and when she was eventually sighted by the destroyers the flotilla leader signalled 'Luke 15:6: Rejoice with me for I have found my sheep which was lost'.

More trooping voyages followed, and in April 1940 the *Australia* helped carry the first Allied troops for the Norwegian campaign. On 3 February 1942, the *Empress* arrived at Batavia to disembark 2431 army and air force personnel, and to embark many refugees from Singapore. Several voyages to Iceland and Durban followed. Towards the end of 1942 and in 1943 trips were made to North African ports, where she had been a welcome visitor on peacetime cruises. Although she had suffered many air attacks it was a friendly ship that caused her first accident. Leaving a convoy to enter Oran, she was badly holed by the SS *Ormonde*, but managed to stay afloat, and after being patched up returned to the United Kingdom for repairs. In October 1944 she sailed from Liverpool with 4944 Russian repatriates for Murmansk.

On 7 July 1945, the *Empress of Australia* sailed on her last voyage on active war service. Steaming via the Panama Canal, she called at Pearl Harbor and Eniwetok on the way to her former home port—Hong Kong— arriving on 4 September, six years and one day after the declaration of war. During her period of active service she had steamed more than 250,000 miles, carried 140,000 military personnel and 20,000 tons of cargo.

The *Empress of Australia* was now over thirty years old and no longer suitable for company service; she was therefore allowed to continue as a 'hired transport', making many trooping voyages to India, Korea and Hong Kong, adding another 400,000 miles to her total. On 30 April 1952 she arrived at Liverpool after completing her last voyage from Hong Kong. In May she was sold to the British Iron & Steel Corporation for scrap, arriving at Inverkeithing on 10 May 1952. Some of the magnificent panelling from her public rooms was used in the extension to the ex-servicemen's club at Rosyth.

During her seventeen years of company service she made twenty-one Pacific voyages, eighty-three Atlantic voyages, thirty cruises from New York and twenty-nine from the United Kingdom. All this was followed by another thirteen years on government service.

The largest Pacific Empress, the 26,000 ton Empress of Japan *II. As the* Empress of Scotland *II she sailed on the Atlantic after World War II*

Empress of Japan II (1930–42)
Empress of Scotland II (1942–57)

The announcement that a new Empress was to be ordered appeared in February 1928, and in June the contract was awarded to the Fairfield yard. With a gross tonnage of

26,032 and a length of 666ft she dwarfed the first *Japan* (5900grt, 456ft in length). Full advantage was taken of the new vessel's great beam of $83\frac{1}{2}$ft to create the impression of spaciousness, both in her public rooms and state rooms. At the forward end of the promenade deck a palm court and ballroom extended right across the ship. Red and black lacquered furniture made a striking contrast with the light-coloured natural-oak panelling. A large oval dome dominated the ceiling of the lounge, which was finished in pale mountain-ash and walnut. At the after end of this room was a large stage and a screen for film shows. The long gallery on the port side of the promenade deck was panelled in ash and walnut. The landing on the main staircase, between the promenade and 'A' deck, was decorated with a mural by P. A. Staynes, depicting the legend of the willow pattern.

Accommodation was provided for 399 first-class, 164 second-class, 100 third-class and 510 Asiatic steerage passengers. All the first-class rooms were fitted with bedsteads, and two deluxe suites had a veranda sitting room. A modern gymnasium on the boat deck was connected by lift to the large marble swimming pool on the main deck (29ft long and 20ft wide).

The whole of the propelling machinery was designed by John Johnson, the company's superintendent engineer. The new *Empress* was fitted with twin sets of Parsons' turbines driving twin screws. The 20ft solid-form bladed propellers, with a casting weight of thirty-five tons and finished weight of twenty-one tons, were the largest ever made at that time. Electricity for the auxiliary machinery and lighting was provided by four diesel generators. Ample provision was made for cargo, including 33,000 cubic feet of insulated space and 59,000 cubic feet of special stowage for silk cargoes. Part of the steerage accommodation could also be quickly converted to cargo space if and when needed.

Mrs Peacock, wife of E. R. Peacock (later Sir Edward), a director of the CPR, performed the launching ceremony on 17 December 1929, unfortunately in a thick fog. For her maiden voyage she made a trip across the North Atlantic to Quebec, under the command of Captain R. G. Latta, leaving Liverpool on 14 June 1930 and returning to Southampton. Her average speed for the Atlantic trip was 21.09 knots with a daily fuel consumption, for propulsion, of 154 tons, or 0.552lb per shp, which was considered very good. On 12 July she sailed from Southampton for Hong Kong via the Suez Canal.

The first commander of the new Pacific *Empress* was Captain S. Robinson, who thirty-five years before had been fifth officer on the first *Empress of Japan*, and who became famous in 1923 when, as master of the *Empress of Australia*, he rendered outstanding service in the rescue work during the Yokohama earthquake disaster.

The *Empress of Japan* II made her first crossing of the Pacific, from Yokohama to Vancouver, in eight days, six hours, twenty-seven minutes, establishing a new record. During a special reception for the new liner at Victoria, Captain Robinson was presented with a silver cigarette-case by the mayor. A banquet was held on board the liner to celebrate her arrival at Vancouver. The bell from the old liner was borrowed from the Merchants' Exchange for use by the toastmaster. The ship was later opened for public inspection, and seamen's charities benefited from the many thousands of admission fees.

The Pacific fleet now consisted of the *Empress of Asia*, *Empress of Russia*, *Empress of Canada*, which had just been re-engined, and the new *Empress of Japan* II. The speed of the latter two ships enabled a regular call to be made at Honolulu, although this added some 1500 miles to each trip, and brought the line into direct competition with the American and Japanese lines operating out of San Francisco. A seven-day schedule was maintained from Yokohama to Honolulu, a day faster than their rivals. From Honolulu passengers could still arrive in Vancouver before their competitors reached San Francisco, a much shorter journey.

Under the command of Captain L. D. Douglas the *Empress of Japan* was at Shanghai on the day that war was declared. Suspicions about the Japanese had made the Admiralty issue instructions when she left Vancouver that Kobe and Yokohama were to be bypassed. Passengers were put ashore at Shanghai and arrangements made for their passage to Japan. Word was put about that she was to sail for Hong Kong, but as soon as she was hull down, course was set for Honolulu. Arriving on 14 September, all hands were mustered to paint her funnels, masts and ventilators grey. She then sailed for Victoria, where her hull was painted grey and two rather old-fashioned guns were mounted. After making a round trip to Hong Kong by way of Honolulu and Shanghai, she was requisitioned on 26 November, and on 2 December sailed for Sydney, Australia. With a complement of 773 troops, travelling in great comfort in her peacetime accommodation, she sailed for Port Said via Colombo and Aden.

At the beginning of the war there was considerable trouble with the Chinese crew. They raised objections to sailing to a war zone and demanded double pay. They also held the conviction that soldiering was the lowest type of employment and they would 'lose face' serving the troops. More important perhaps was the loss of 'cumshaw', as the officers had batmen who would serve their morning tea! This led to an amusing situation. Morning tea was usually served at seven o'clock. The first day out the Chinese bedroom boys anticipated the batmen by five minutes. Next day the batmen started earlier, so the stewards stepped up by another five minutes. Eventually, some people found themselves being wakened at 5.30

with a most unwelcome cup of tea.

From Port Said the *Empress of Japan* returned to Australia and on 16 April, together with the *Empress of Britain* and *Empress of Canada*, joined convoy US3; this convoy consisted of seven luxury liners—the 'million dollar convoy'. The troops were disembarked at Cape Town on 26 May 1940, where the *Empress of Japan* took aboard the Chinese crew from the *Empress of Canada* for the return voyage to Hong Kong via Durban, Mombasa and Singapore. From Hong Kong two trips were made to Manila with evacuees. On 3 August she left Hong Kong for one of her longer voyages, 29,915 miles by way of Sydney, Wellington, Fremantle, Bombay, Suez, Durban and thence to the Clyde.

On 9 November 1940, when she was about 400 miles west of Ireland just two weeks after the *Empress of Britain* had been fatally hit in about the same position, she was attacked by enemy aircraft. Captain Thomas outmanoeuvred the enemy with the help of his Chinese quartermaster who, with machine-gun bullets raking the bridge, held the wheel and responded to every command of the captain without turning a hair. Only two bombs touched the ship, one hitting the railing aft and falling into the sea, the other striking the edge of one of the lifeboats forward and also falling into the sea. The explosion of the first bomb lifted the stern of the ship out of the water, damaging the rudder and the shaft bearings in the engine room. Captain Thomas brought the *Empress* into port under her own steam despite Lord Haw Haw's announcement over the German radio that she had been bombed, set on fire and left in a sinking condition. She was out of commission for the month of December whilst being repaired at Belfast.

Captain J. W. Thomas was made a Commander of the British Empire and Ho Kan, the Chinese quartermaster, was awarded the British Empire Medal for meritorious service. Later Captain Thomas recalled the imperturbability of Ho Kan:

> The veteran Quartermaster lost his calm when the announcement came that he had been awarded the BEM. He came to me in great excitement.
> 'Bottomside they say Ho Kan must go see King George for medal. No can do. What can say to King?' I told him that the King would do the talking and he could listen. That seemed to satisfy him.

In January 1941 the *Empress of Japan* sailed from the Clyde to Singapore via Cape Town and Bombay, returning to Glasgow on 15 May, after having made a call en route on 27 April at St Helena, a crown colony made famous by Napoleon's stay, 1815–21. In June she again sailed for Singapore after embarking 2993 troops but this time continued eastward and reached Vancouver on 29 August. During her overhaul the crew enjoyed some much-needed leave. The *Empress* returned to the Clyde via Panama. Her destination was once again Singapore, which was reached on 29 January 1942, after the fall of Hong Kong. More than 1200 women and children were evacuated and taken to Batavia.

Japan had attacked Pearl Harbor on 7 December 1941, and Captain Thomas was now in the anomalous position of commanding a ship bearing the name of the Allies' latest enemy; for reasons unknown the position continued until 16 October 1942 when her name was changed to *Empress of Scotland* II.

Practically the whole of 1943–4 was spent on a shuttle service across the Atlantic between Halifax, Newport News and New York on one side of the Atlantic and Liverpool or Casablanca on the other. It has been estimated that at this time the Germans had between sixty and one hundred U-boats in the North Atlantic; so successfully to transport nearly 72,000 troops on twelve round-trips was no mean achievement. On 18 November 1944 she sailed for Tasmania via the Panama, Sydney NSW and Wellington NZ, reaching Hobart on 9 January 1945.

The first voyage of 1945 was notable in that, from 'down under', the *Empress* made her way to the United Kingdom by way of the Suez Canal and the Mediterranean. The tenth of March saw the start of another 30,000 mile trip through the Panama Canal to Australasia and back through Suez for the second time in four months. One more short trip to Colombo and Bombay followed before the end of hostilities. However, before she was de-requisitioned on 8 May 1948 she steamed another 233,928 miles on the important duty of repatriating troops and civilians. During her eight and a half years of war service the *Japan* had sailed three times round the world and steamed more than 720,000 miles, probably more than any other merchant ship, carrying 258,000 passengers and 30,000 tons of cargo. During all this time, working under the most strenuous conditions, she spent only 125 days in repair yards. Her normal drill was to stock enough food to last seventeen weeks and replenish this whenever possible on the North American continent in order to conserve food stocks in the United Kingdom. More than twenty million hot meals were served from her kitchens.

The real record for the *Empress of Japan*, regardless of her astronomical mileage, lies in the smallest statistic in her record: 'Captains—two'. Not only was Captain Thomas in command from July 1940 until the *Empress* reached Liverpool on completion of her wartime duties in May 1948, but he had also been aboard ship from the outbreak as staff commander. Tom Patten, chief confectioner on the *Empress of Japan* II, recalls:

> On the morning after VJ-Day 1945, Captain Thomas called me to his cabin and after shaking hands said, 'Well it's all over and I think you should know, according to crew lists you and I are the only men to serve in this ship for the entire period of the war.'

A proud moment.

During a war personal acts of kindness stand out and are remembered with affection. Captain Thomas recalled a visit to Newport News:

> We had been on the run so much that practically all of us literally had holes in the soles of our shoes—and not much chance to replace them. With so little time in port and so much to do there was little or no time for shopping. What made it worse was that we were paid in sterling, and that didn't go very far in the United States. I happened to mention this problem to General Kilpatrick, US Commander-in-Chief of the area, and he very promptly called a local wholesaler, requested a 25 per cent discount, and next day shoes, graded to fit all who required them, arrived at the ship.

On another occasion, this time at Casablanca, the *Empress* being berthed alongside the pier, there was no anchorage.

> The wind was so strong the ship's lines could not hold her. Her manilla lines were old and even doubled would not hold. Remembering an old trick I asked for grass ropes. The shore staff had never heard of them but a bright young Army Officer turned up in the nick of time in a jeep with a US Navy trailer filled with grass rope he had 'won' from somewhere.

The *Empress of Scotland* spent the next two years under-going an extensive refit in preparation for her return to company service. This work was started in Liverpool but on 14 November she returned to the Fairfield yard on the Clyde where most of the work was carried out.

The promenade deck was enclosed for its entire length with deep windows to meet the more rigorous North Atlantic climate. The palm court was renamed Empress Room and it was intended that this should be used alternately by first and tourist passengers as a ballroom and cinema. The red and white chequered house flag was painted on the three buff funnels and the ribbon round the upper part of the white hull changed from blue to green. Her accommodation was reduced from 1115 to 663—458 first class and 205 tourist class. The overhaul completed, she was returned to the company in April 1950 and after running trials was finally accepted on 1 May.

The *Empress of Canada* and *Empress of France* had already returned to the Liverpool–Montreal service. The extra speed of the *Scotland* plus the fact that she would make Quebec her Canadian terminal, enabled her to re-establish the Clyde call, the first of two traditions which had been interrupted by the war. The second tradition, a weekly service out of Liverpool was also re-established. When the *Scotland* left Liverpool on 9 May 1950 for her first post-war voyage, she was the largest and fastest vessel on the St Lawrence service. In July she made a record crossing westbound in four days, fourteen hours, forty-two minutes and eastbound in four days, twenty-three hours and thirty minutes. She thus held the Pacific and the Clyde–Canada records. She made ten round trips on the North Atlantic between May and November. While the *Empress of Canada* and *Empress of France* maintained the winter service from Liverpool to Saint John NB, the *Empress of Scotland* sailed to New York to make her first ever cruise and the company's first post-war cruise. On arrival at New York on 19 December, her first peacetime visit, she was greeted by fire boats with their jets of water shooting 200 feet into the air, plus a noisy tooting welcome from the coastguard cutters, ferry boats and tugs. She was accompanied to her berth at pier 95 by the US destroyer USS *Ludlow*, the first time the US navy had taken part in a welcome to a merchant vessel. The mayor of New York sent a scroll of welcome and later Captain Shergold and other company officials lunched with the mayor in the New York City Hall.

Between December and March she made seven cruises from New York to the West Indies. This pattern was to continue for the next seven years. She made twenty-eight cruises to the West Indies including two from Southampton in 1951 and 1952. These two cruises from Southampton were also the company's first sailings from that port since 1939. In 1953 she made another cruise from Southampton, this time to South Africa and South America.

In the fall of 1951 their Royal Highnesses the Princess Elizabeth and the Duke of Edinburgh had been on a visit to Canada and were due to join the *Empress of Scotland* on 12 November for their return to the United Kingdom. The *Empress* was manoeuvring in Conception Bay where a northeasterly gale was blowing. In order to join the *Empress*, their Royal Highnesses left Portugal Cove in the 140 ton ferry *Naneco*. This mile-and-a-half trip took forty-five minutes owing to the strong swell. The heavy weather continued all the way to Liverpool where they arrived on 17 November.

In 1952 it was decided to make Montreal her terminal point in Canada. Accordingly, whilst undergoing overhaul at Liverpool in April, her masts were shortened by almost forty-five feet, to allow passage under the Quebec bridge on the 150 mile trip from Quebec to Montreal. She was the largest ship ever to enter the Port of Montreal when she arrived for the first time in May 1952.

The *Empress of Scotland* was now twenty-seven years old. During the nine years of service on the Pacific, she had made fifty-eight round trips from Vancouver to Hong Kong. Then had come $8\frac{1}{2}$ years' war service. From May 1950 to November 1957 she had made ninety round trips from Liverpool across the North Atlantic plus twenty-nine cruises. The *Empress* went into dry dock at Belfast on 1 January 1958, and on the thirteenth she was sold to the Hamburg Atlantic Line. She left Belfast under the name *Scotland*, and arrived at Hamburg on 22 January, to enter the Howaldtswerke shipyard for an extensive refit.

The *Empress of Scotland* had shared with the *Queen Mary* the distinction of being the last of the three-funnellers. Now she was to lose this distinction as the new company fitted her with two modern funnels. Her bow was replaced by a straight stem; a new bridge and superstructure were fitted, also a new main mast. In addition two decks made of aluminium alloy were added. This considerably altered her outward appearance. Internally her accommodation was now equipped for eighty-five first-class, and 1150 tourist-class passengers. On 21 July 1958, under her new name *Hanseatic*, she sailed from Cuxhaven for New York via Le Havre, Southampton

and Cobh. This was to be her route for the next few years with some cruising during the winter periods.

On 7 September 1966, whilst at pier 84 North River, New York, preparing to sail to Europe, a fire broke out causing extensive damage, but without loss of life. She was towed across the Atlantic by the tugs *Pacific* and *Atlantic* and arrived in Hamburg on 10 October 1966. Unfortunately she was found to be too badly damaged to be repaired and in November 1966 she was sold to Eckhardt & Co of Hamburg for break-up.

Canadian Australasian Line

Niagara (1931–40)

A triple-screw liner built at the John Brown yard in 1912 for the Union Steamship Company, she was 543ft in length with a gross tonnage of 13,000. Her propelling machinery consisted of two sets of triple-expansion engines driving the wing shafts, plus a low-pressure turbine taking the exhaust steam and driving the centre shaft. This was a popular combination at that time. The *Niagara* was the first passenger ship to be granted a Board of Trade certificate to burn oil fuel instead of coal, and is also believed to have been the first ship fitted with a passenger lift, which operated between the main and promenade decks. Accommodation was provided for 281 first-, 210 second- and 176 third-class passengers. A large amount of insulated space was also provided for the carriage of frozen meat, butter and chilled fruit.

Mrs Borden, wife of the Prime Minister of Canada, performed the launching ceremony on 17 August 1912. The *Niagara* left the Clyde in April 1913 for Auckland and Sydney and never returned to British waters. Because of the importance of the route between the Canadian west coast and Australasia she continued to run on her normal service throughout World War I and it was intended that she should be employed in the same way during World War II. When the *Niagara* left Auckland on 19 June 1940 she was carrying a large proportion of New Zealand's stock of small-arms ammunition destined for Britain, to help replace the losses suffered during the evacuation from Dunkirk. Also on board, but known to only a few, were 295 wooden boxes, each containing two ingots of gold valued at £$2\frac{1}{2}$ million in all consigned to the USA by the Bank of England to help pay for war supplies.

At 03.30 hours the *Niagara* struck a mine. Fortunately the weather was calm and the vessel remained upright, allowing all the passengers and crew to take to the boats

The 13,000 ton Niagara, *which ran on the Canadian Australasian Line, a joint service with the Union Steamship Co of New Zealand*

without loss of life. By 04.30 hours her screws were clear of the water, but it was not until 05.30 hours that she slid bow-first into the depths. By 11.00 hours next morning a coastal steamer from Whangarei arrived in answer to the SOS call.

The sinking took New Zealand completely by surprise; until then the war had always seemed a long way away, and it was some time before it was realised that the German raider *Orion* had sown a large minefield in the main shipping lane. Because of the value of the consignment and Britain's desperate needs at the time, an attempt at salvage was a matter of both secrecy and urgency. A small syndicate was formed in Australia to be led by Captain J. P. Williams (now Sir John) and Captain J. W. Herd. The *Niagara* was some 430ft below the surface, in an area famed for its bad weather, a prospect to daunt any but the most determined. The greatest depth that had been worked up to that date was 396ft by the Italians.

Captain Williams went to New Zealand in October 1940 to try to locate a suitable salvage vessel for the operation. As by this time shipping had already become 'scarce' the problem was not easy. Eventually a condemned thirty-eight-year-old coastal vessel, the *Claymore*, was found; the work of fitting her out was begun, but again because of wartime shortages this was very much a 'make do and mend' job. Meantime a new diving-bell was being built in Australia.

Work began in mid-December and although the *Niagara* had sunk only thirty miles from the shore, the wreck still had to be found by laboriously sweeping with a trawl. Sweeping could only take place on fine days and was further dangerously complicated by several mines being caught in the lines. Fortunately they were exploded before causing any damage, despite several hair-raising incidents. The wreck was finally located on 2 February 1941, lying on her side in 438ft of water. Next, moorings had to be arranged so that the *Claymore* could be held steady immediately over the wreck to allow the diver in his bell to descend and control operations. For this vital job two brothers had been recruited. Having fixed the position of the strong room, a hole had to be blasted through the hull and the structure of the ship. This work started in April and continued, whenever the weather was favourable, into September. At the same time debris caused by the blasting had to be removed by a giant mechanical grab worked by wires from the *Claymore* 400ft overhead from directions telephoned by the diver in his bell.

The first box was brought up by the grab on 13 October—a remarkable feat when it is remembered that the bell was still some considerable distance from the strong room because of the need to ensure that the cables from the bell were not fouled by the dangerous mass of twisted metal resulting from the blasting. The record for a day's catch was forty-six boxes, but this was a very exceptional haul. By December, 277½ boxes had been 'grabbed' out of the total of 295. One of the boxes had been smashed and a single bar was retrieved on one occasion. As it was becoming increasingly difficult to find any boxes among the debris, it was decided to call it a day and so end a most remarkable salvage job. Only just in time, as when the team returned to Whangarei they were greeted with the news of the Japanese attack on Pearl Harbor. Had the job not been completed there might have been more than the weather to contend with.

The *Claymore* too must have realised that her life's work had been completed; she sank in harbour a week or two after she had returned to Auckland. Of the thirty-five remaining bars, thirty were recovered between April and August 1953, when the Risdon Beazley Company with the *Foremost* 17 again dived on the wreck. During this period Captain J. P. Williams and Mr J. Johnston from the 1940 expedition were able to visit the scene.

Aorangi (1931–53)

With the success of the *Niagara* the service had prospered and a second liner was ordered; but World War I started whilst she was building and she was completed as an armed merchant cruiser and did not return to the company. The *Aorangi* was ordered from Fairfield's yard in September 1922. With a gross tonnage of 17,491 and a length of 580ft she was equipped with four Fairfield-Sulzer single-acting two-stroke engines, giving a total of

The 17,000 ton Aorangi *which also ran on the Canadian Australasian Line*

13,000bhp. This sounds very small when we think of the large amount of power developed on a single screw today. When tenders were called for a number of shipyards did not quote, claiming that the specification was unrealistic. However, in a very short time many large liners equipped with diesel engines were being built all over the world. The Fairfield Engineering Company, with no precedents to follow and no previous experience with diesel engines, was praised for its enterprise in undertaking the task. The *Aorangi* started a new era for large passenger motor ships. She was the first large motor ship on the Pacific and the first quadruple-screw passenger ship.

Accommodation was provided for 440 first-, 300 second- and 230 third-class passengers. A feature of the

after-staircase was an oil painting of Mount Cook by Julius Olsson RA. 'Aorangi' was the Maori name for Mount Cook. The main decorative feature of the dining saloon was a gross point tapestry panel of Calliope, the mythical mother of Orpheus and goddess of epic poetry. The *Aorangi* was launched by Mrs Houldsworth, wife of the chairman of the Union Steamship Company, on 17 June 1924. She sailed on her maiden voyage on 3 January 1925 from Southampton to Vancouver via Panama.

On the outbreak of World War II she continued to operate on her normal run and during the first eighteen months carried many Australian and New Zealand air trainees to Canada. She also carried New Zealand troops to Fiji in October 1940. She left Sydney in September 1941 for the United Kingdom, having been taken over for trooping by the Ministry of War Transport. As well as helping with the evacuation of women and children from Singapore, she also made a number of trooping voyages to India, the Middle East and the Mediterranean.

In 1944 she was refitted on the Solent as a mother ship to 150 tugs for the Normandy invasion. In this capacity she provided a floating engine repair shop, a hospital and accommodation for a reserve pool of personnel. Supplies of fuel, ammunition, water and victuals were also carried. From D-Day until the end of July 1944 she serviced more than 1200 vessels and many of the first casualties from the beach head were treated on board. In 1945 she returned to the Clyde to be refitted as commodore's ship for the Royal Auxiliary Fleet in the Pacific. For a time she was chart depot ship at Manus, in the Admiralty Islands, and was stationed at Hong Kong until April 1946.

On release from war service the *Aorangi* returned to Sydney for an extensive overhaul, which was prolonged by many strikes. To modernise the liner and to provide better facilities for the crew, the passenger accommodation was reduced from 900 to 486 (212 first, 170 second and 104 third class). She left Sydney on 19 August 1948 for her first post-war voyage, calling at Auckland, Fiji, Honolulu, Victoria and Vancouver. It soon became apparent that her earnings were inadequate and in December 1950 it was announced that the service would be withdrawn. After much negotiation the Australian, Canadian and New Zealand governments came to an agreement to subsidise the service on an annual basis.

By 1953 the *Aorangi* was twenty-eight years old, and when she arrived at Sydney on 8 June the service was finally withdrawn and the vessel sold to the British Iron & Steel Corporation for scrap. She left Sydney for the last time on 19 June 1953, and sailed to the Clyde to be broken up at the Dalmuir yard of Arnott Young & Co. Most of the crew were returned to Australia by air. An important sea link between Canada and Australia had ended, but Canadian Pacific continued the link with its airline service which began in 1955.

2 North Atlantic

Lake Champlain (1903–13)
Ruthenia (1913–14)

The *Lake Champlain* was perhaps the best-known of the Beaver Line ships taken over in 1903, and was built at the Barclay Curle yard in 1900. With a gross tonnage of 7392 and 446ft in length, she had accommodation for 100 first- and eighty second-class passengers. In May 1901 she became the first large merchant ship to be fitted with radio. A small cupboard $4\frac{1}{2}$ ft × $3\frac{1}{2}$ ft was built on deck behind the officer's cabin just aft of the mizzen mast, one side being formed by an iron bulkhead. It was made of matchboarding without windows and if natural light was required the door had to be left open. The apparatus, which sat on a green baize-covered table, consisted of a 10in induction coil working off current supplied from two six-volt accumulators. There were no tuning circuits, the aerial being connected to one side of the spark gap and earth to the other. Two balls, $1\frac{1}{2}$ cm diameter, were used to produce a 3cm spark. The aerial was slung from the mast head to the cabin, giving 110ft from the mast head to the spark gap.

There were no radio stations in North America at this time but contact was made with Marconi stations at Rosslare and Holyhead. Leaving Liverpool on 21 May 1901, two messages were passed to the Elder Dempster Company the next day when the ship was over eight miles from the receiving station near Holyhead. On the return voyage forty-seven messages were passed from the ship to Rosslare station. On her arrival at both Halifax and Montreal, she was invaded by reporters and members of scientific societies. After a visit by the Canadian government inspector of telegraphs, an order was cabled to England for two sets of apparatus for communicating across the Straits of Belle Isle.

In 1913 the *Lake Champlain* and *Lake Erie* were renamed *Ruthenia* and *Tyrolia* before being transferred to a new service from Trieste to Montreal. Unfortunately political problems and war put an end to the service (see page 31). On the outbreak of World War I, the *Lake Champlain* was first used as a troop transport and later taken over by the Royal Navy and fitted out as a 'dummy battleship' (see page 33). In 1915 she became a store ship at Scalpa Flow, being purchased outright by the Admiralty on 29 January 1916. Later she served as a naval oiler in far eastern waters until 1929, when she became a fuel jetty and pumping station at Singapore.

In 1942 she was captured by the Japanese and put back into service under the name *Choran Maru*. After being recaptured by Allied forces in 1945, when the oil tanks were replaced by primitive accommodation, she was employed transporting prisoners of war. On 30 October 1946 she ran aground in the Moesi River, being refloated in November. She was bought in 1949 by the British Iron & Steel Corporation (Salvage) and left Singapore on 3 April 1949, under tow by the tug *Englishman*. Arriving at Dalmuir on 18 June, she was broken up by W. H. Arnott Young & Co, forty-nine years after her launch.

Montrose I (1903–14)

The *Montrose* was another of the Beaver Line vessels that Canadian Pacific took over in 1903. Launched from the Middlesbrough yard of Sir R. Dixon & Co, she was 444ft long and 5431 gross tonnage. Originally designed as a cargo vessel with large refrigerated chambers, she was fitted with berths and made several trooping voyages to South Africa before taking up her North Atlantic duties. In 1900 she was chartered to carry the Dublin & Denbigh Imperial Yeomanry with their horses for the Boer War.

The 7000 ton Lake Champlain, which made the first Canadian Pacific sailing on the Atlantic in 1903

(opposite) Cutting from 'The Daily Telegraph' of 1 August 1910

Like the *Lake Champlain* she also received much publicity in connection with the early use of radio. The notorious Dr Crippen with his secretary Ethel Le Neve had fled the country, first to Holland and later Belgium, in an attempt to evade arrest for the murder of his wife. The *Montrose* left Antwerp on 20 July 1910 with Captain H. G. Kendall in command. He had been second officer on the *Lake Champlain* in 1901, when that vessel had been the first British merchant ship to be equipped with wireless. Captain Kendall's suspicions were aroused when two people in men's clothes were seen holding hands on deck. After further observation of the couple he radioed Canadian Pacific's Liverpool office on 22 July:

Have strong suspicions that Crippen London cellar murderer and accomplice are amongst saloon passengers. Moustache taken off growing beard. Accomplice dressed as boy. Voice manner and build undoubtedly a girl. Both travelling as Mr and Master Robinson.

Captain Kendall realised that action had been taken when a radio message to the *Laurentic* was picked up by the *Montrose*. In fact Inspector Dew of the CID had boarded the *Laurentic* at Liverpool and reached Quebec ahead of the *Montrose*. Disguised as pilots, Inspector Dew and two other police officers boarded the *Montrose* at Father Point and made the arrest. This was the first time wireless was used to arrest a fugitive criminal. As a reward Captain Kendall received a cheque, which he had framed and hung in his cabin. In August 1974 the original messages were auctioned at Bonham's in London for £1600. For the superstitious a story has it that when Crippen was arrested he cursed Captain Kendall, the ship and the spot the ship was on. Four years later the *Empress of Ireland*, with Captain Kendall in command, sank in approximately the same position.

At the time of the German invasion of Belgium in 1914 the *Montrose* and the *Montreal*, another ex-Beaver Line vessel, were in Antwerp. The *Montrose* was waiting to bunker and the *Montreal* was undergoing engine repairs, but had a supply of coal aboard. Captain Kendall, by

ARREST
OF
RIPPEN
AND
MISS LE NEVE.

APTURE · ON · THE
MONTROSE.

STANT RECOGNITION.

R. DEW DISGUISED
IN
PILOT'S UNIFORM.

FULL DETAILS
FROM OUR
PECIAL CORRESPONDENTS
BY
CABLE AND WIRELESS.

"Dr." Crippen and Miss Le Neve were arrested on board the Canadian Pacific Company's liner Montrose at nine o'clock (Canadian time) yesterday morning.

Our Special Correspondents supply the following details of one of most dramatic arrests that have ever been effected.

Wearing the uniform of a pilot, Inspector Dew, accompanied by four officers of the Canadian police, boarded the liner about two miles from Father Point.

Crippen was walking on deck. The inspector approached him from behind, and touched him on the shoulder.

Crippen turned round sharply, and there was a mutual recognition between him and the inspector.

"There's your man!" said Inspector Dew to one of the Canadian officers, and Crippen accompanied his captors to a cabin, where he was formally arrested.

"I am rather glad the anxiety is over" appears to have been the only remark he made. The inspector then went to Miss Le Neve's cabin. She was reading a book, and on looking up at her visitors immediately guessed what their purpose was.

She is said to have uttered a piercing scream, then grew suddenly calm, and submitted to arrest. Subsequently she collapsed completely. It is stated that the prisoners will return to England by the Royal George on Aug. 4.

N BOARD THE MONTROSE.

From Our Special Correspondent.

---

mixing medicine. He always appears anxious to be friendly with me. Le Neve never speaks to the passengers, and the man keeps a strict eye on her.

Both were anxiously gazing this morning towards Anticosti Island, and the man asked the distance to Quebec.

I have seen the man standing sometimes listening to the conversation of the French passengers, perhaps to try and catch any information.

Yesterday me and I came up the staircase together, just after lunch. We stood for a moment. Here I saw a French woman sitting on the cushions reading a French newspaper. I noticed that she was busy with an account of "Le Crime de Londres, curieuses suppositions de la police anglaise."

I noticed my companion's face began to twitch. Later I secured the paper, and hid it.

Yesterday morning when we were alone on deck, Le Neve fainted. We were 270 miles off Father Point at eight a.m. to-day (Saturday), and should arrive at Father Point about six or seven a.m. Sunday.

This is the only message I have sent to-day to the Press, and I send it in answer to your request. (Signed) KENDALL, Commander.

"MR. ROBINSON."

To the above information I am able to add from a reliable source that with the exception of captain and officers, the purser and the Marconi operator, nobody on board apparently suspected that Mr. Robinson was other than Mr. Robinson. He never apparently had an idea he was being watched from the moment of sailing. Neither the man nor his companion ever played at any of the usual deck games, and Le Neve usually seemed far from well. The papers containing accounts of the crime were removed from the reading-room. It was known that the suspect had a razor in his cabin, also small bottles of carbolic acid and peroxide of hydrogen, as well as a revolver and cartridges. Nothing was removed from the cabin, but a watch was kept practically day and night. The strictest censorship was also exercised on all Marconigrams coming to and from the vessel.

REPORTERS AT WORK.

Pending the arrival of the Montrose at Father Point the international delegation of journalists were puzzling their brains, exhausting their physical energy, spending their money, and risking nervous prostration in devising all sorts of schemes to reach the Montrose before the vessel touched land. Fast motor-boats and French-Canadian pilots were first engaged to put to sea at all hazards and meet the Montrose well in advance. I consented, on behalf of The Daily Telegraph, to take part in this enterprise, but withdrew later, on the ground that the Montrose would probably not allow us to come alongside. There was also a prospect that such a flotilla would alarm Mr. "Robinson," who might defeat the ends of justice by committing suicide.

The alternative plan to be the first with the news was to secure admission to the Montrose as shipwrecked sailors. A raft was constructed and arrangements made to tow the same across the liner's track fifty miles from Father Point. The pilots here declared that the plan was perfectly feasible, also that the captain dared not ignore the signal of distress. At the last moment, however, the deputation of three to whom the majority of the correspondents delegated the honour, responsibility, and risk of playing the rôle of shipwrecked sailors got cold feet, and refused point blank to embark. They were probably wise, because the dangers incident to fog and storm in July are seldom long absent from the St. Lawrence.

"It is understood," therefore, at the time of cabling, that a posse of Canadian police officials from Quebec, with Inspector Dew, who landed here from the Laurentic yesterday, the river pilot, and newspaper correspondents shall go aboard the Government tug Eureka, and board the Montrose immediately she arrives. Here, again, there was a prospect of alarming the mysterious Robinsons. Inspector Dew made it perfectly clear to us when he first landed from the Laurentic that he wanted to

---

this time marine superintendent for the company at Antwerp, had the coal and stores transferred from the *Montreal* to the *Montrose*, and with many refugees aboard she succeeded in towing the *Montreal* to the Nore, where the *Montreal* was anchored whilst the *Montrose* sailed on to Gravesend to disembark her passengers.

On 20 October 1914 the *Montrose* was sold to the Admiralty, who built a tangle of gantries on her deck and filled her holds with cement preparatory to sinking her as a block ship off Dover harbour, as part of the anti-submarine defences. Unfortunately, before the work was completed, a gale sprang up on 28 December and she broke loose from her moorings. During the night and after drifting through minefields, she drove ashore on the Goodwin Sands. Two tugs went out from Folkestone, and although it was impossible to save the ship, the watchmen on board were taken to safety. Her mast remained visible until 22 June 1963, having been used as a marker for Trinity House surveys.

The Empresses

An order was placed with the Fairfield yard in November 1904 for two 14,000 ton Empresses. They were the first ships to be built specifically for the company's Atlantic service. With accommodation for 310 first-, 470 second- and 500 third-class passengers, the *Empresses* were 548ft long. Six holds provided space for 5000 tons of cargo, including some insulated space for frozen meat. Coal-fired boilers supplied steam for their quadruple-expansion reciprocating engines driving twin screws.

A library, smoking room and a café were situated on the lower promenade deck. Two dining rooms occupied most of the saloon deck. The first-class saloon, panelled with mahogany, had a number of horseshoe-shaped tables arranged in alcoves along the sides of the saloon for small parties. In the ceiling a large oval opening gave a view into the café on the deck above. The music room, amidships on the upper promenade deck, featured a central ventilating column from which sprang a fine dome.

Empress of Britain (1906–24)
Montroyal (1924–30)

Launched by Mrs Arthur Piers, wife of the manager, CP Steamships Lines, on 11 November 1905, the *Empress of*

Britain sailed on her maiden voyage from Liverpool to Quebec on 5 May 1906. On her second voyage the *Britain* made the westbound trip from Moville to Rimouski in five days, twenty-one hours, seventeen minutes, a record. In the following years the two sisters clipped minutes off each other's records, with the *Empress of Britain* finally established as the faster of the two. Reporting the maiden voyage of the *Empress of Britain*, the 'Montreal Gazette' of 14 May 1906 said:

> The new mammoth liner of the CPR swung into her dock at ten o'clock on Saturday night, completing her maiden voyage from Liverpool in the fast time of six days seventeen hours, and considering the fact that one of the fiercest gales of the season was encountered on Wednesday, the quick voyage is regarded as highly satisfactory.

On her maiden trip the *Empress* carried 175 first-class, 473 second- and 809 third-class passengers.

Probably the first ever showing of a 35mm movie film at sea took place on the deck of the *Empress of Britain* in 1910, with a hand-cranked carbon-arc projector.

The first serious mishap occurred on 27 July 1912, when the SS *Helvetia* was rammed and sunk by the *Empress of Britain* in dense fog off Cape Magdelen in the Lower St Lawrence.

Shortly after the outbreak of World War I, the *Empress of Britain* was commissioned as an armed merchant cruiser. Her master, Captain J. Turnbull, continued as navigating officer with the rank of commander RNR. The liner joined Admiral Stoddart's squadron in the South Atlantic and later patrolled between Cape Finisterre and the Cape Verde Islands. It was realised that her passenger accommodation was wasted as an armed merchant cruiser, so in May 1915 she was paid-off and recommissioned as troop transport No 628. She carried more than 110,000 troops on war service to the Dardenelles, Egypt and India as well as many members of the Canadian and US expeditionary forces across the North Atlantic. Ending her war service in March 1919 she arrived at the Fairfield yard for a refit in July. Conversion to oil fuel increased her boiler efficiency and reduced her stokehold crew from 120 to twenty-seven.

During the overhaul her passenger accommodation was modernised, all the first-class rooms being fitted with running water and some having bedsteads instead of berths. The first-class lounge was enlarged and provided with facilities for concerts and film shows. A gymnasium was also included among the new features. The furnishings and decorations were specially designed by George Crawley & Partners of London.

A new Canadian Pacific venture started in 1922 when the *Empress of Britain* made two cruises from New York to the West Indies. The cruises were so successful that they were repeated in succeeding years. In April 1922, instead of returning to the Liverpool service, she switched to the new continental service from Hamburg to Quebec, via Southampton and Cherbourg.

By the 1920s cabin-class travel had become established, and in the autumn of 1923 yet another visit was paid to the Fairfield yard. The *Empress of Britain* was converted to cabin class and in April 1924 was renamed *Montroyal* to comply with company policy of giving cabin-class ships names beginning with *M*. Returning to the Liverpool service, she made eight trips a year through 1926. In the following year she transferred to the Antwerp–Southampton–Cherbourg–Quebec route.

The introduction of the luxurious new Duchess-class cabin steamers in 1928 and 1929 caused the twenty-three-year-old *Montroyal* to be withdrawn. A few days after the second *Empress of Britain* had been launched she was sold to the Stavanger Shipbreaking Company on 17 June 1930. Fortunately a part of the old *Empress* was rescued from the scrapyard when Mr Axel Lund, owner of the Sola Strand Hotel at Stavanger, bought the lounge from the shipbreakers and incorporated it into his hotel as the Montroyal ballroom. The beautiful woodwork built into the *Empress* in 1905 is still a feature of the building now housing the Norwegian School for Hotel Management.

Empress of Ireland (1906–14)

The *Empress of Ireland* was launched by Mrs Gracie, wife of the managing director of Fairfields, on 27 January 1906, and left Liverpool on 29 June on her maiden voyage to Quebec. The two Empresses established a great reputation for Canadian Pacific with their fast runs across the Atlantic. On 11 July 1913, Their Majesties the King and Queen left the landing stage at Liverpool on the Dock Board's *Galatea*, to review Merchant vessels, including the *Empress of Ireland*, anchored in the Mersey.

Tragedy struck the *Empress of Ireland* at approximately 2.30am on 29 May 1914, when most of the 1054 passengers and 413 crew on board were asleep. A few hours out of Quebec she was rammed by the 6000 ton

Norwegian collier SS *Storstad*. In less than fifteen minutes the liner sank and more than 1000 people lost their lives within four miles of the riverbank! Over 400 were saved by the *Eureka* and *Lady Evelyn*. Much conflicting evidence was heard at the subsequent inquiry, but it was established that the two vessels had sighted each other when more than three miles apart before thick fog had descended rapidly. When next seen, the collier, having altered course, was only a few feet away and collision was unavoidable. In 1964 the wreckage was located by skin-divers. Many items from the wreck, including the ship's bell, the helmsman's quadrant and the seven-ton main anchor, are now preserved in the Musée Maritime Bernier at L'Islet, Quebec.

Victorian (1909–22)
Marloch·(1922–9)

Construction of the *Victorian* had actually begun when it was decided to change the propulsion system to the then little-known turbine system designed by Sir Charles Parsons. Built in the Workman–Clark yard at Belfast, she was 538ft long with a gross tonnage of 10,629. Accommodation was provided for 470 first-, 240 second- and 940 third-class passengers, plus stowage for 8000 tons of cargo including some refrigerated space. The propulsion unit consisted of a high-pressure turbine and two low-pressure turbines driving three screws. Another innovation was the fitting of triple-bladed screws instead of the more usual four-bladed. The *Victorian* made her maiden voyage on 23 March 1905, and the *Virginian* followed a few weeks later. In September of that year smoke from forest fires drifting across the St Lawrence created a serious hazard to navigation and both ships became stranded for a few hours.

Keen rivalry existed between the two sister ships and the *Victorian* proved the faster, making a record crossing from Rimouski to Moville in five days and five hours in June 1906. By 1909, Canadian Pacific had secured financial control of the Allan Line; but this arrangement was kept secret and the ships continued to sail under the Allan Line colours until 1915. In fact the *Victorian* was not officially transferred to Canadian Pacific until 15 September 1928, when she was about to be scrapped. At the beginning of World War I both ships were requisitioned as armed merchant cruisers, serving first with the Ninth and later with the Tenth Cruiser Squadron.

Although the *Virginian* had also been taken over by Canadian Pacific she never sailed for the company. After her war service she was sold to the Swedish American Line to become the *Drottningholm*. Later sold to Home Lines as *Brasil* she became the *Homeland* in 1951, and was scrapped at Trieste in March 1955. After the war the *Victorian* was refitted by Cammell Laird and returned to the North Atlantic on 23 April 1920.

In a letter to the three St Johns newspapers dated 21 June 1920, Arthur Burrows of the Marconi Company wrote:

> In connection with the forthcoming Imperial Press Conference in Canada and the voyage of Canadian Pacific Ocean Services' SS *Victorian* commencing 20th July (when the ship will be carrying the delegation to the Conference from the United Kingdom), we are erecting, as you are probably aware, a wireless telephone station at Signal Hill, St Johns N.F, which will communicate with the *Victorian* which in turn is being fitted with the most powerful wireless telephone ever placed on board ship.
>
> It has struck me that it would greatly please the journalists travelling by this vessel if you would agree to give to our station at Signal Hill daily, a brief digest of not more than fifty words of any leading article appearing in the morning issue of your paper. I would quote you in the paper which we are producing on board ship.

The purpose of the conference was to discuss the empire's press services including the better use of wireless, telegraphy and telephony. It was an auspicious occasion for these experiments. Arthur Burrows, later to become well known as 'Uncle Arthur' of the BBC children's programmes, carried out many experiments on board. To demonstrate the possibilities to the delegates, the *Victorian* not only entertained her passengers throughout the voyage with concerts from the shore, but also permitted them to speak with friends they had left behind and those they were soon to see. For the first time at sea a morning and evening edition of the 'North Atlantic Times' was printed on board.

Amongst the outstanding performances were: the reception on the ship off Newfoundland of the national anthem, sung at Chelmsford in Essex, 2100 miles distant; the reception by Sir Bertram Hayes, commander of the *Olympic*, of an address of greeting delivered telephonically to him from the *Victorian* by Lord Burnham when the two ships were 510 miles apart; and the transmission of a gramophone concert from the *Victorian* to Newfoundland over a distance of 1200 miles. This was truly an epoch-making voyage.

On 8 October 1921, she set sail for warmer waters, when she was chartered for a trooping voyage from Southampton to Bombay. On her return from India she entered the Fairfield yard for conversion to cabin class and to have her engines replaced by lighter and more economical single reduction geared turbines. Provision was made for 400 cabin- and 560 third-class passengers. She was renamed *Marloch* on 23 December 1922, and Glasgow was to become her home port for an increasing number of voyages each year. She was transferred to the Antwerp–Southampton service in 1926, and when leaving Antwerp in a dense fog on 2 February she collided with and sank the *Whimbrel* off Flushing.

Laid-up at Southend in September 1928, she was sold to T. W. Ward & Co in 1929 and arrived at Milford Haven on 17 April; being subsequently broken up at Pembroke Dock. Panelling, inlaid with mother-of-pearl, was transferred from the ship to the board room of Ward's Sheffield office, where visitors still admire its beauty and craftsmanship.

As early as 1905 the Allan Line was thinking of building two liners to run alongside the *Victorian* and *Virginian*, but it was not until after Canadian Pacific had taken over that an order was placed with the Beardmore yard for the *Alsatian* and with the Fairfield yard for the *Calgarian*, in 1911. Because of the secrecy surrounding the deal, the Allan Line names, house-colourings and advertising were continued. Whilst the hulls and engine rooms were similar, the furnishings differed and an identifiable feature of the *Calgarian* was the placing of her promenade-deck windows in distinctive pairs.

With a gross tonnage of 18,400, the sister ships had accommodation for 263 first-, 496 second- and 976 third-class passengers. Both vessels had cruiser sterns, the first on the Atlantic, and large oval-shaped funnels, and both were driven by quadruple-screw turbines. They were also the first Atlantic liners to carry a motor lifeboat fitted with radio. Their furnishings were said to equal the best on the New York run. The first-class dining saloon extended the full width of the ship with a balcony at one end for a small orchestra. The designs for the lounge were based on the royal apartments at Hampton Court; three large bow-windows on each side and a full length skylight made this the most impressive room on the ship.

Calgarian (1914–18)

Launched on 19 April 1913, she had made only five Atlantic voyages before being requisitioned in August 1914, as an armed merchant cruiser (AMC) with the Tenth Cruiser Squadron. In 1917 she carried the retiring Governor-General of Canada, the Duke of Connaught, home to Devonport and on the return voyage the new Governor-General, the Duke of Devonshire. Captain H. Macmillan (later prime minister) was ADC to the Duke, and Lady Dorothy Cavendish (later Lady Macmillan) was also in the party.

On 1 March 1918, the *Calgarian* was torpedoed by *U19* off Rathlin Island.

Alsatian (1914–19)
Empress of France (1919–31)

The *Alsatian* was launched on 22 March 1913 and sailed on her maiden voyage from Liverpool to Halifax on 17 January 1914. After only seven Atlantic voyages she was requisitioned on 7 August as an armed merchant cruiser and joined the Tenth Cruiser Squadron patrolling off the Shetlands. She became flag ship for Admiral De Chair and later for Vice-Admiral Tupper. In 1915 the *Alsatian* was one of the first ships to be fitted with the new wireless direction-finding apparatus. After the squadron was retired in 1917, she spent the remainder of the war on convoy work across the Atlantic. To commemorate her wartime services a plaque was presented to the ship:

SS *Alsatian*

This vessel during the 'Great War' was flagship of the patrol between the Shetlands and Iceland and intercepted 15,000 ships. Escorted convoys numbering from 14 to 22 ships to and from America on many occasions. Was armed with eight 6in guns and two 12 pounder anti-aircraft guns.

Steamed while in War commission 266,740 knots and consumed 170,570 tons of coal. The vessel was reconditioned by the builders Wm Beardmore & Co Ltd and is now known as the *Empress of France*.

Meantime in 1915, Canadian Pacific Ocean Services Ltd

had been formed to manage the combined Allan and Canadian Pacific fleets. After her refit the *Empress of France* became the premier ship of the fleet and made her first voyage under her new name from Liverpool on 26 September 1919. In August 1920 she made a record run from Liverpool to Quebec in five days, twenty hours, six minutes.

From 1924 the company decided to sell and operate its own cruises and the *Empress of France* left for her second world cruise in January 1925. At Southampton on 30 October 1925 a silver cup weighing 157oz was presented to the *Empress of France* by passengers on the 1925 cruise in appreciation of a remarkably successful voyage of 34,000 miles. A smaller replica was presented to Commander E. Griffiths RNR. In the following years she made four cruises to the Mediterranean and in 1928 a cruise to South America and South Africa lasting ninety-two days. Midway between South America and South Africa on Sunday 25 February, the *Empress* called at Tristan da Cunha, and landed twenty tons of supplies for the islanders. The 'lonely isle' was also visited in 1929 and 1935 by the *Duchess of Atholl* and *Empress of Australia*. Captain E. Griffiths was in command of each of the three Canadian Pacific vessels visiting the island.

On returning from her first cruise in April 1922 the *Empress* was transferred to a new service from Hamburg to handle the growing emigrant traffic to Canada. On this service a call was made at Southampton where a Canadian Pacific office had been opened. The Hamburg call was dropped in 1928 and her home port became Southampton.

In 1923 HRH the Prince of Wales, travelling as Lord Renfrew, sailed in the *Empress of France*. During the voyage he played the drums in the ship's orchestra and autographed them.

The Beardmore yard was again visited in 1924, when the *Empress of France* was converted to oil fuel and fitted with bunker space for 3600 tons of oil. This enabled her to make the round voyage without refuelling and, more important, to reduce the number of firemen from 117 to thirty-four. At this time she was also fitted with the largest laundry to be installed in a ship. To meet changing conditions of travel her accommodation was reduced to 331 first, 384 second and 352 third class. In June she rejoined the Hamburg–Southampton–Cherbourg service. On her second trip press pictures of the opening of the 1924 Olympic Games at the Colombes Stadium, Paris, on 5 July were flown from Paris to Cherbourg to connect with the *Empress of France* leaving at 8pm. She arrived at Quebec at 10am on 11 July and the pictures were then rushed to New York.

With her hull painted white, she left Southampton on 31 October 1928 for a one-year stint on the Pacific to enable the *Empress of Canada* to be re-engined at Fairfields. Unfortunately the effects of the 1929 slump and the consequent falling-off of emigration resulted in the *Empress of France* being laid-up on the Clyde from 28 September 1931 until 20 October 1934, when she was sold to W. H. Arnott Young & Co and was broken up in the yard in which she had been built twenty-one years before. In all she had made ninety-nine voyages on the Atlantic, five trans-Pacific voyages and eight cruises for the company, in addition to her war service.

Empress of Scotland I (1922–30)

The *Kaiserin Auguste Victoria* had been laid down as the *Europa* by the Vulkan-Werke, Stettin, and built from plans supplied by Harland & Wolff of Belfast, who had just built the *Amerika* for the Hamburg Amerika Line. Reputed to be the largest ship built at that time, her launch was made a national occasion attended by the Kaiser and the Empress, who sponsored the liner. This was a great honour for the Hamburg Amerika Line and out of respect the name was changed to *Kaiserin Auguste Victoria*. The liner was 678ft in length, with a gross tonnage of 24,580, and was equipped with quadruple-expansion engines to give her a speed of seventeen knots. As flagship of the line she made her maiden voyage from Hamburg to New York in May 1906. Her passenger accommodation was luxurious and she became one of the most popular ships on the North Atlantic. In 1912, after the *Titanic* disaster, she was fitted with a powerful searchlight said to be capable of lighting up objects five miles away.

She arrived in Hamburg from New York at the beginning of August 1914, and remained in the harbour until she sailed for England in March 1919. At that time the homeward movement of troops was in full swing and the vessel was allocated to the United States by the Allies, sailing mostly between Brest and New York. She was finally transferred to Britain after the peace treaty was signed, and sailed on the North Atlantic under Cunard management until bought by Canadian Pacific in May 1921.

The Empress of Scotland *I, the 25,000 ton German liner* Kaiserin Auguste Victoria, *bought after World War I*

Renamed *Empress of Scotland*, she returned to Hamburg for a refit and conversion to oil fuel. Her tonnage was increased to 25,128grt, with accommodation for 460 first-class, 470 second-class and 530 third-class passengers, and a crew of 500. She ran trials in January 1922, and made her first Canadian Pacific voyage from Southampton to Halifax and New York, where she had been chartered by the Clark Travel Agency for a seventy-four-day Mediterranean cruise. After the cruise she inaugurated the company's service from Hamburg to Quebec via Southampton and Cherbourg; and in February 1923 was again chartered by the Clark Agency for a second Mediterranean cruise.

The year 1923 proved eventful for the *Scotland*. In January, while on her positioning voyage for her cruise from New York, she sighted the schooner *Clintonia* helpless in a severe storm. A lifeboat was launched and Captain A. Kearly and his crew of five were rescued. Owing to the severity of the storm several oars were lost and, as it was impossible to get the lifeboat back on board the *Empress*, it had to be abandoned. Passengers on the *Scotland* collected a purse of $400 for the crew of the schooner. Four months later, Captain Gillies was presented with a gold-headed silk umbrella, awarded annually by the Quebec Harbour Commission to the first foreign liner to reach Quebec after the winter freeze.

A two-berth cabin

When Miss Gertrude Ederle, a nineteen-year-old American, swam the English Channel in the record time of fourteen hours, thirty-one minutes on 7 August 1925, an all-out effort was made to help the press. When Miss Ederle arrived at Dover, after her record-breaking swim, photographs were taken and rushed to Southampton where the package was placed aboard the *Empress of Scotland*. Meanwhile, cable and radio messages regarding the photographs were sent to North America and the *Empress*. As the *Scotland* neared Anticosti Island at the mouth of the St Lawrence, a flying boat approached the ship and picked up the package which had been lowered into the water from the liner. The flying boat took the photographs to Rimouski where duplicate negatives were made. At 4pm two land-planes, each carrying a set of negatives, left for New York where they arrived at 2.30am on Saturday 14 August, in time for the photographs to be reproduced in the morning newspapers.

In December 1925 she sailed from New York on the first of her two round-the-world cruises. She was the largest vessel to have passed through the Panama Canal and paid $17,211.25 in tolls. Old records show that more than 123,000lb of meat, 48,000lb of fish and 35,000lb of sugar were consumed on the voyage, and a glance through old menus shows that in those days the first-class passengers were offered seventeen kinds of cereal, seventeen kinds of cheese, and could have their eggs cooked in a dozen different ways. The passengers on this first world cruise were so impressed by the warm welcome they received at Beppu, on the Japanese island of Kyushu, that they presented the mayor with a bronze tablet and silk flags of Japan, England and the United States. In September 1927, the Prince of Wales and Prince George, having completed their Canadian tour, returned from Quebec in the *Empress of Scotland*.

When the *Empress* arrived at Southampton in October 1930, after completing her seventy-first Atlantic voyage, she was laid-up at Southend until December when she was sold to the Hughes Bolckow Company for scrap. After her arrival at the Blyth yard for break-up, it was decided that the public should be given the chance to see her magnificent Chinese, Persian and Indian carpets; the maple, satinwood and other panelling; the damask, silk and velvet upholstery; and the oil paintings, some of which had been presented by the Kaiserin at the time of the launch.

The liner's elegant ballroom was prepared for a charity ball to aid the local hospital, but before this could take place fire broke out early one morning and rapidly spread throughout the ship. There were eight watchmen on board at the time, but, although the engineer turned off the oil supply to the boilers and fire hydrants were turned on, the men were driven off the ship by dense smoke. Fortunately the alarm had already been raised and several fire brigades and fire floats rushed to the scene. Under great difficulties ten holes were cut in the side of the ship, but the water pumped in merely caused the vessel to list, and the fire continued to burn for several days. Amidships, the steel plates became white hot and molten lead ran into the river. All the beautiful wood panelling and valuable fittings, which the breakers hoped to sell, were lost. The vessel settled in an upright position about fifty feet from the jetty, but when an attempt was made to move her she broke in two. Demolition was finally completed in October 1931.

The Monts

As memories of the value of merchant ships in wartime were still dominant, the three 'Monts' had gun rings and platform stiffenings built in; thus, in the event of another war, they could be quickly converted. Before World War I, when mail contracts were discussed before new ships were built and part of their earnings thus guaranteed, the provision of gun mountings was frequently part of the deal as were agreements relating to the turnover to the Admiralty and the carriage of troops. After the construction of the Monts the practice, so far as Canadian Pacific was concerned, fell into disuse and none of the later vessels was so equipped.

Their original double-reduction geared turbines caused some problems and were replaced by single-reduction gearing in the Harland & Wolff yard at Belfast during 1928–9. Accommodation originally provided for 554 cabin passengers in two- and four-berth state rooms, plus 1250 third-class passengers in two-, four- and six-berth rooms. This was later reduced to 520 cabin, 278 tourist and 850 third.

The Monts entered the Liverpool run in 1922 and this service was extended the following year to include calls at Greenock on the Clyde. Occasional calls were also made at Belfast. When the Duchesses began running out of Liverpool in 1929, the Monts made many of their summer sailings from the Continental ports of Antwerp or Hamburg, with calls at Southampton and Cherbourg. Because of falling traffic on the North Atlantic they were also used for short summer cruises from UK ports, mostly to the Canary Islands and the North African coast, from 1932 onwards.

The three Monts achieved a remarkably consistent service, chiefly out of Liverpool, between 1922 and 1939, making 484 North Atlantic voyages plus 142 cruises from the United Kingdom.

Montcalm (1922–42)

The *Montcalm* was launched from the John Brown yard by Lady Fisher, wife of the general manager, Canadian Pacific Ocean Services, on 3 July 1920. Leaving Liverpool for her maiden voyage on 17 January 1922, she made the headlines with the rescue of the crew of the Norwegian steamer *Mod* in the North Atlantic.

On Sunday 3 July 1927, whilst steaming slowly in dense fog through the Straits of Belle Isle, a huge iceberg suddenly loomed up, towering high above funnels and masts. With a loud crunching noise the vessel ran on to a submerged part of the berg. Fortunately in a few minutes the vessel slid off without any serious damage and was able to proceed on her way to the Clyde. During the summer of 1929, the *Montcalm* made five consecutive eastbound calls at Plymouth. Passengers travelled in special cars attached to the Cornish Riviera express,

One of three cabin-class liners built for the Liverpool service in 1921, the 16,000 ton Montcalm

reaching London in slightly over four hours. Under the command of Captain A. Rothwell, the crew of twenty-seven men and the captain's dog were rescued from the sinking salvage tug *Reindeer* off Halifax in heavy seas on 12 March 1932.

Returning to London from a cruise on 22 August 1939, she was requisitioned and sent to the Clyde from which she sailed with civilians and some troops on 2 September for Port Said. Adam Bremner, purser, who later became her paymaster with the rank of lieutenant-commander RNR, recalled an amusing incident on the first day of embarkation. An army officer informed the purser that he was embarkation staff officer, but didn't know what his duties were. The purser, whose staff were doing the job anyway, advised him to: 'stand at the foot of the gangway and look wise. If anybody complains about anything—stamp on him quickly.' The embarkation went ahead smoothly.

On her return from her first wartime voyage she was converted to armed merchant cruiser T98 and renamed HMS *Wolfe*. Disregarding Canadian Pacific's tactful choice of name for a ship plying the St Lawrence regularly, the Admiralty chose to honour the opponent of the marquis who lost his life on the Plains of Abraham, and named her for the victorious General James Wolfe. Based at Halifax, HMS *Wolfe* started her career escorting convoys on the North Atlantic. On one occasion a Focke-Wulf singled out *Wolfe* for attention and scored two hits; the first bounced off the boat deck into the sea, the second hit a ventilator and rebounded across the deck. Lieutenant Bremner recalled: 'The chief gunner's mate, on his way to repair a jammed gun, discovered it, rolled it into the scuppers and hove it overside.'

Arriving at Southampton in October 1941, she was paid off and her crew dispatched on some well-earned leave. On 8 January 1942 she left Milford Haven with

RAF personnel for Canada and then reported to the Admiralty repair mission at Baltimore for conversion to a submarine depot ship, which meant acting as parent vessel, maintaining and administering submarines, and housing their crews during off-duty periods. On her last day of requisition hire, 21 May 1942, she was bought by the Ministry of War Transport and in January 1943 became a destroyer depot ship. Withdrawn from service in February 1950, she was laid-up off Tighnabruaich in the Kyles of Bute. She was towed to Faslane on Gareloch on 7 November 1952, to be broken up.

Montrose II (1922–40)

Lady Raeburn, wife of the director-general of the Ministry of Shipping, named the *Montrose* when she was launched from the Fairfield yard on 14 December 1920. The vessel was originally to have been called *Montmorency*, after the great waterfall in Quebec, but this was changed before the launch. She sailed on her maiden voyage from Liverpool on 5 May 1922.

After leaving Saint John, the *Montrose* struck an iceberg on Easter Monday 1928 whilst steaming slowly in dense fog. With a deep crunching sound the bows of the vessel crumpled. The impact also caused a mass of ice to fall on the deck, killing two seamen. Fortunately she was able to continue her voyage to Liverpool under her own steam. In April and May 1929 two calls were made at Cardiff to pick up emigrant traffic from South Wales.

The Royal Empire Society chartered the *Montrose* on 18 May 1937 for a four-day cruise from Liverpool to Spithead for the coronation naval review. The occasion was made famous by Commander T. Woodroffe's expression, 'The fleet's lit up', broadcast to millions.

On 12 September 1939 the *Montrose* was requisitioned and renamed HMS *Forfar*. She moved to Portsmouth for the completion of her outfitting and then joined the northern patrol. When about 400 miles west of Ireland, on her way to meet a convoy from Halifax, she was attacked at 03.50 hours on 2 December 1940 by *U99* under the command of Otto Kretschmer. The first torpedo struck amidships, flooded the engine room and started several small fires. Half an hour later she was hit by a second and third torpedo, but it was not until two further torpedoes struck that she sank at 05.00 hours. HMCS *St Laurent* picked up seventeen men and three officers; two hundred other survivors were picked up by HMS *Viscount* and a tramp steamer. At the parish church

of Forfar in Scotland, on 30 March 1941, a brass tablet was unveiled:

> In proud memory
> Captain N. A. C. Hardy RN
> 41 officers and 143 men
> of
> HMS *Forfar*
> 2 December 1940
>
> Honour to all brave Captains
> and to all intrepid sailors
> and Mates and to all that
> went down doing their duty.

Montclare (1922–42)

The naming ceremony for the *Montclare* at the John Brown yard was carried out as arranged on Saturday 17 December 1921 by Lady Brown, wife of the European general manager of the CPR. Owing to a very high wind the launch was postponed until the next day. Originally to have been named *Matapedia* after a town on the Matapedia River at the head of Chaleur Bay, the name was changed before the launch. The *Montclare* sailed from Liverpool on her maiden voyage on 18 August 1922, under the command of Captain R. G. Latta, later to become general manager of Canadian Pacific Steamships.

In 1924 new radio equipment was fitted which was capable of relaying music to all parts of the ship, quite a novelty in those days.

The Firth of Clyde was enshrouded with dense fog on 21 March 1931 when the *Montclare*, making her way to Greenock, ran aground on Little Cumbrae. Passengers were disembarked without injury and later taken to Largs and thence to Glasgow by train. The *Montclare* was floated off the rocks the following day with the help of the tugs *Chieftain*, *Strongbow*, *Thunderer* and *Wrestler*, and was able to continue to Liverpool on her port engine, the starboard propeller having been damaged.

Like her sisters, the *Montclare* made short summer cruises from UK ports. It was on one such cruise, at Funchal on 28 August 1939, five days before war was declared, that Captain W. S. Brown received a secret radio message from the Admiralty to return home by the fastest possible means. As soon as the passengers had been landed at Liverpool, the ship set course for Barrow-in-

Furness where guns, fire-directors and magazines were fitted. Captain Brown was greatly honoured by the navy when, although he was not a member of the Royal Naval Reserve, he was commissioned as a commander RNR and asked to command HMS *Montclare* as an armed merchant cruiser.

Her first spell of duty was with the northern patrol, maintained by the Seventh and Twelfth Cruiser squadrons, reinforced by twenty-five converted liners. In March 1942 HMS *Montclare* was converted into a submarine depot ship and on 1 June was bought by the Ministry of War Transport and became flag ship to the fleet train (supply) in the Pacific. For a time she carried the flag of Rear-Admiral Fisher and in 1944 she also acted as 'base wireless repeating station'. In August 1944, Lieutenant-Commander F. W. S. Roberts RNR joined her as navigating officer. He had served in her as a junior watchkeeper before the war. In Sydney, Australia, on another occasion she was given her mooring by Commander J. P. Dobson DSC, RD, RNR, another Canadian Pacific officer, who was Admiralty berthing officer for that port. After the war HMS *Montclare* became the parent ship for the submarine flotillas at Rothesay until 12 October 1954, when she was laid-up at Gareloch, having served for seventeen years under the red-and-white chequered house flag and a further fifteen years under the White Ensign.

In February 1955 she was towed to Portsmouth by the Admiralty tugs *Warden* and *Enforcer*. In a storm on 4 February, when twenty-five miles west of the Scillies, she broke adrift. The following day two Dragonfly and one Whirlwind helicopter went to her assistance, transferring a doctor and helping to pass lines to the tugs. The *Montclare* was sold to the British Iron & Steel Corporation in January 1958 and towed to Inverkeithing by the tugs *Englishman* and *Merchantman*, arriving on 3 February to be broken up by T. W. Ward Ltd.

The Duchesses

At the time of building the Duchesses were the largest cabin steamers afloat and the largest liners to sail the St Lawrence as far as Montreal. With a length of 600ft, they provided accommodation for 580 cabin, 486 tourist and 500 third-class passengers on seven decks, but these figures were reduced several times over the years. They were oil-burners with two sets of steam turbines driving twin screws through single-reduction gearing. Water-tube boilers designed by John Johnson, the company's superintendent engineer, provided high-temperature steam at high pressure. Auxiliary diesel generators supplied electricity for all the lighting, heating and cooking requirements of the liners.

The John Brown yard at Clydebank and the Beardmore yard at Dalmuir each received an order for a 20,000 ton liner. The John Brown Company received a further order for two sister ships the following year. At the time it was rumoured that there were to be five liners. This probably arose because the name 'Duchess of Cornwall' was mentioned at the launch of the *Duchess of Bedford* and *Duchess of Richmond*. However, it was later decided that the vessel should be named *Duchess of York* instead. On another occasion a press release stated that five vessels had been ordered in 1926; in fact this referred to the two Duchesses and three cargo vessels.

From 1928 until the outbreak of the war the four Duchesses had made 458 Atlantic voyages, thirty-seven New York–Bermuda trips plus eighty-eight cruises, a wonderful record. Only the *Bedford* and *Richmond* survived the war, and they returned to the Clyde in 1946–7, to be reconditioned and elevated to first-class status. Most of the state rooms were rebuilt and enlarged to carry two classes: 441 first and 259 tourist, only 700 passengers instead of their original 1570. The public rooms were redecorated, the tourist lounge being extended to the full width of the ship and a new Empress Room built to act as a cinema and ballroom for both classes. The promenade deck was glassed in and the crew accommodation was also enlarged and improved. The hulls were painted white, with a green riband and green boot-topping. The red-and-white house flag was painted on the funnels, a new innovation.

Duchess of Atholl (1928–42)

The *Duchess of Atholl* was launched by Her Grace the Duchess on 23 November 1927. It had originally been intended that the ship would inaugurate the new service, but while fitting out, one of her turbines fell from a crane. Because of the delay, work on the *Duchess of Bedford* was hurried forward to enable her to take the first advertised sailing. The *Atholl* finally ran her trials on 5–6 June 1928. After taking a party of passenger agents for a two-day cruise she sailed on her maiden voyage from Liverpool to Montreal on 13 July. All the Duchesses made regular calls at Belfast and Greenock, both east and westbound.

Captain J. P. Dobson recalled in a letter that in 1928 an antelope was carried on the *Atholl* to Quebec and duly unloaded:

Minutes before we were due to sail for Montreal we were told that the papers for the beast were not in order and that we would have to take it back to England. As all the derricks were by this time secured, the animal was brought up the main passenger gangway in its crate and left outside the purser's office. On arrival in Montreal we spent three days arguing with the Department of Agriculture and Customs before we were allowed to land the antelope via the gangway, and then hoist it on to the deck near one of the holds. The gangway and everything had to be fumigated.

On the passage down the St Lawrence we received word to say that we could land the animal on to the passenger tender at Quebec and that it would be in quarantine for three months. It was duly landed and put into a field surrounded by an eight foot high fence. During the night it jumped over the fence and was never seen again.

The *Atholl* left Liverpool on 4 January 1929 to make her first cruise, to South America and South Africa. After disembarking her United Kingdom cruise passengers at Kingston she proceeded to New York to pick up American passengers, returning to Kingston on her way south. On Sunday 24 February she called at Tristan da Cunha and landed more than thirty tons of stores in three hours and twenty minutes. The stores had been organised through the auspices of the Imperial Order of Daughters of the Empire. Among the 314 items were:

An harmonium from Queen Mary, a wireless receiving set with complete outfit including batteries, loud speakers, jars of salammoniac [two years' supply], a mast and flagpole made on board, jams, preserves, baking powder, matches, cornflour, glycerine, cocoa, chocolate, tea, sugar, drugs, candy, salt, candles, tinned fruit, sewing machine, communion wafers, brooms, clocks, books, paints, boots, shoes, balls and cricket equipment, toys, hats, musical instruments, enamelware, axes, wallpaper, kitchen utensils, trousseaux, cobblers' kit, camera and plates, rat traps, crockery, stationery.

On an eastbound voyage in October 1935 the *Duchess* lost her rudder. On her arrival in the Mersey, the river was cleared of shipping and with half a dozen tugs in attendance, she was manoeuvred into the Gladstone Dock.

By the outbreak of war in 1939 the *Duchess of Atholl* had completed 109 round trips to Canada, three trips to Bermuda, plus forty-four cruises—sixteen from the United Kingdom and the remainder from Montreal and New York. Requisitioned in December 1939, she made several trooping voyages including the ferrying of troops and supplies between Marseilles and Alexandria. The *Atholl* returned to company service in May 1940; and on the first of six North Atlantic trips she carried 800 children who were being evacuated from the United Kingdom to Canada. Re-requisitioned on 15 November, she made more trooping voyages, mostly between the Clyde and the Middle East by way of Cape Town. In March 1941 the *Atholl* joined one of the largest troop convoys. It consisted of twenty-three ships including the *Duchess of York* and the *Empress of Canada*, plus an escort of four battleships and eight destroyers. In March 1942 the *Atholl* took part in the expedition to Madagascar, carrying 1900 troops and 820 tons of cargo, arriving home on 26 June.

The next and last voyage made by the *Duchess of Atholl* was to Suez, and on her way home she called at Cape Town to embark 529 passengers, including fifty-eight women and thirty-four children. Her crew for this voyage numbered 296. Among the passengers were twelve crew members from the *Princess Marguerite*, one of the company's British Columbia coastal steamers, which had been torpedoed a couple of months earlier near Port Said. The *Duchess* sailed from Cape Town on 3 October and by Saturday the tenth she was some 200 miles east of Ascension Isle (7.03'S, 11.12'W) when at 06.35 a torpedo struck in the centre of the engine room on the port side. Four engineers who were on duty at the time were killed and the lighting was extinguished. An SOS was broadcast, but as the receiving set had been put out of action by the explosion, no confirmation could be obtained that the signal had been heard. Twenty minutes later a second torpedo struck in almost the same spot. Captain Moore ordered the women and children away in the boats. Half an hour later a third torpedo exploded on the starboard side, forward of the bridge. As she began to settle, the order to abandon ship was given; fortunately she remained upright and within twenty minutes everybody had left the ship. Four of the ship's lifeboats were unserviceable; the remainder were launched safely with the 821 survivors aboard. The *U178* surfaced a few minutes before the *Duchess of Atholl* turned on her port side and slid gently down by the stern at 9.25am.

At 8.30 next morning, 11 October, smoke was seen on the horizon. This turned out to be the rescue ship HMS *Corinthian*, and by 13.30 all the survivors had been embarked. They were landed at Freetown and later returned to the Clyde aboard *Carnarvon Castle*. HMS *Corinthian* was also to rescue the survivors from the *Empress of Canada* nine months later. In a letter to Commander E. J. R. Pollitt RN, captain of HMS *Corinthian*, Captain Moore said:

My officers, ship's company, passengers and myself thank you for all the kindness and consideration we have received at your hands whilst guests on board your good ship. All our lives we shall remember the joy we felt when we first saw your smoke on the horizon and then gradually realised that you were steaming towards us, and we shall never forget the relief and pleasure that was ours when smiling faces greeted and willing hands helped us over the rail and guided us to a cup of tea.

Harry Dutton, chief catering superintendent, wrote in 1964:

At about 08.00 hours on the day she was torpedoed I was standing alongside D. N. Firth, Chief Barkeeper, awaiting final instructions to embark into a lifeboat. I said to him 'What about a bottle of whisky', he replied 'You would'. We sauntered along the deck to the smokeroom, he unlocked the bar door, then the locker. I then said 'I want two bottles of Black Label'. 'You would' he replied. These were produced, the locker, bar door and smokeroom securely locked and we returned to the open deck. About twenty-four hours later I passed the bottles along to more deserving cases and actually never had a tot from either, but thoroughly enjoyed the mug of steaming tea that was thrust into my hand when I was pulled aboard the rescue ship.

Captain H. A. Moore, whose father had also been a master with Canadian Pacific, was made an officer of the Order of the British Empire for meritorious service when attacked by the enemy.

It seems incredible that in the chaos that must have followed the explosion the purser was able to report:

I managed to open the safe in my office and obtain all the paper money contained therein to the value of £5222. Coin, of which there was a considerable amount owing to the Military having brought aboard £700 of silver, had to be left behind. . . .
It was extremely difficult working in the dark with only one torch!

He also managed to rescue the register, articles, log book, passenger and cargo manifests, which enabled an accurate roll-call to be taken on board the *Corinthian* and resulted in the quick relief of public anxiety when news of the sinking reached the United Kingdom. The purser and his staff went even further than saving documents. They were able to retrieve most of the valuables deposited by passengers for safe keeping and these were handed to the owners on the rescue ship.

In her three years of war service the *Duchess of Atholl* had steamed 159,600 miles and carried 36,556 military personnel, 905 civilian passengers and twelve prisoners of war, plus 75,800 tons of cargo.

Duchess of York (1929–43)

Originally to have been called *Duchess of Cornwall*, the name *Duchess of York* was finally chosen for yard No 524, when being built by the John Brown Company at Clydebank. However, it was found that a steam-engined pleasure boat with this name was plying the River Severn. This posed a problem for Canadian Pacific and it is said that the owner of the pleasure steamer was persuaded to sell the name for £250. With the registration problem solved, the new liner was launched by HRH the Duchess of York on 28 September 1928. This was the first occasion that a merchant vessel had been launched by a member of the Royal Family. The last of the four *Duchesses* to join the company's North Atlantic service, she ran her trials on 3 and 4 March 1929, and sailed on her maiden voyage from Liverpool on 22 March, calling at Belfast and Greenock on her way to Saint John NB.

In the early part of 1930, the *Duchess of York* made a record crossing from Liverpool to Saint John in six days, twenty-two hours, fourteen minutes, the first time such a crossing had been made in less than seven days. Soon after leaving Saint John on 21 March 1930, the British schooner *Faustina* was sighted about 235 miles south of Cape Race. She was flying her ensign upside down and it was learned by megaphone that she had been at sea for thirty-one days and was short of food. The necessary supplies were quickly transferred. On this eastbound trip the usual calls at Greenock and Belfast were omitted in the hope of enabling the ship to reach Liverpool in time for her passengers to see the Grand National if they so wished; unfortunately ice conditions delayed the ship.

The *York* was the only Duchess not to be employed for cruising; her only departures from the northern service out of Liverpool happened when she transferred to the New York–Bermuda run, making fifteen round trips in 1931, to be followed by ten more in 1932. Also in 1931, she made three trips on the southern service, sailing from Antwerp on 22 June, from Southampton on 15 August, and from Hamburg on 10 September. By the outbreak of war she had made 132 Atlantic voyages.

The *Duchess of York* was not as well known in the world's exotic ports as were her sisters. This righted itself as the war went on, and before her sinking by the Luftwaffe in 1943 she had shown the chequered house flag in Ana Fjord, St Nazaire, Freetown, Suez, Singapore, Bombay, Algiers, Oran, Cape Town, Durban, Gibraltar and even Pernambuco in South America. Although requisitioned in March 1940, it was not until June that she left her normal peacetime route. On 1 June she sailed from Liverpool to Ana Fjord to rescue 4000 troops and civilians from Norway. On her return to the Clyde she sailed for Brest with a group of French Foreign Legionnaires and then made her way to St Nazaire, where she was bombed all day but fortunately without being hit. After embarking 5000 British troops and nurses she returned to Liverpool in a convoy of twenty ships.

Leaving Liverpool for Canada on 21 June 1940, her entire passenger-list was made up of German prisoners of war and their guards. As there were only 250 armed guards to look after the 3000 prisoners, a request was made that the ship's officers should be allowed to carry side-arms, but this was turned down by the authorities. The prisoners virtually had the run of the ship and were allowed to visit the canteen to buy cigarettes and soft drinks and could take the bottles away. However, this privilege had to be stopped when one of the prisoners threatened a guard with his bottle and had to be shot. As a precaution, after this incident, it was decided to floodlight the decks after dark. An amusing result of this defensive measure was the noisy protests from the prisoners of war who thought this would make the ship too good a target for their U-boats. However, the *Duchess* reached Quebec without being attacked and then had to lie offshore for twenty-four hours because no prior arrangements had been made to receive the prisoners.

The official mind works in curious ways. On her next voyage from the United Kingdom the *York* carried 1100 children being evacuated to Canada to escape the bombing; and for this voyage each officer was issued with a .38 calibre revolver!

For her last voyage in 1940, the *Duchess* sailed to Suez via Cape Town, and in March 1941 carried reinforcements and supplies for the far eastern naval base at Singapore, which was soon to be lost to the Japanese. Returning to Liverpool towards the end of July, she next made two voyages to India. Late in 1942 and early 1943 the *York* made six trips with troops and supplies for the North African landings and was on several occasions the target of enemy air raids, but suffered no serious damage. Shortly after leaving Algiers she was hit on 14 March by a 500lb bomb which failed to explode. It fell through No 5 Oerlikon gun pit and through three decks. Two French naval ratings were in the gun pit and the fifth engineer was in his bed as the bomb passed through his room; but apart from shock none of these men was hurt. During its passage the top part of the bomb and its nose fuse were torn off and later found in 'A' deck alleyway. The remaining three feet of solid death lodged in an awkward and dangerous position on 'B' deck. The chief officer called for volunteers to manhandle it to the side door of 'B' deck, where it was pushed overboard. For this hazardous action R. V. Burns, who later became general manager of Canadian Pacific Steamships, was awarded the George Medal and Lloyd's medal. First Officer R. McKillop was made a member of the Order of the British Empire. Two other members of the crew were given the British Empire Medal and others were mentioned in dispatches.

The *Duchess of York* left King George V Dock, Glasgow, for the last time on 7 July 1943. She proceeded to the Clyde anchorage to join another convoy and escort which consisted of the Royal Canadian Navy destroyer *Iroquois*, Royal Naval destroyer *Douglas* plus HM frigates *Myola* and *Swale*. All went well until 8 pm on the evening of 11 July, when an unidentified aircraft was sighted. Later two Focke-Wulf aircraft, flying at approximately 15,000ft, were identified. At ten minutes past nine the *York* was hit by a stick of bombs. The centre of the ship quickly became a raging inferno and communication between the bridge and other parts of the ship became impossible. While the ship's guns continued to fire at the five aircraft, which were now attacking other ships in the convoy, efforts were also made to control the fire, but without success; the ship had to be abandoned.

Captain Busk-Wood and his chief engineer, Mr E. E. Vick, were the last to leave the ship, at approximately 22.40 hours. As the vessel continued to float, the escort destroyer *Douglas* fired a torpedo at the burning hulk in order to reduce the risk of the convoy being found by submarines. Eleven members of the crew, five members of the ship's permanent military staff and eleven RAF personnel were lost. The survivors were picked up by the escort vessels and taken to Casablanca where they were lodged in an American military camp until they embarked in the *Arundel Castle* for the Clyde. Eleven decorations and mentions in dispatches were awarded to the officers and men of the *Duchess* for outstanding service in the face of enemy attack.

The *Duchess of York* was the twelfth and last Canadian Pacific ship to be destroyed by enemy action in World War II. During her three and a half years of war service she had steamed 222,600 miles, carried 73,350 troops, 5800 prisoners of war, 4190 civilians plus 63,300 tons of cargo. In the March 1958 issue of the 'Crowsnest', the Royal Canadian Navy's magazine, the following appeared:

> In the after canopy of the Tribal class destroyer escort *Iroquois* there is a plaque which is displayed as proudly as any battle honour. It commemorates the rescue 15 years ago of survivors from SS *Duchess of York* sunk while on troop transport duty on 11 July 1943.

Duchess of Bedford (1928–48)
Empress of France (1948–60)

Mrs Stanley Baldwin, wife of the prime minister, launched the *Duchess of Bedford* on 24 January 1928 from the John Brown yard at Clydebank. The *Duchess* sailed on her maiden voyage from Liverpool to Montreal on 1 June 1928, with Captain H. Sibbons RNR in command. Thirty-two years later in December 1960 she made her last North Atlantic crossing, the last of the four Duchesses. On her second westbound voyage the *Bedford* set a new record of six days, nine and a half hours for the Liverpool–Montreal run.

In July 1933 the *Duchess* was in collision with an iceberg in the Straits of Belle Isle; fortunately there was no

serious damage. On 18 April 1938 she was the first foreign oceangoing vessel to pass the Montreal harbour clock after the winter freeze-up. To mark this achievement, Captain A. Meikle was awarded the traditional gold-headed cane presented annually by the Port of Montreal Authority. This tradition started around 1830 when the Montreal Harbour Trust Commission used to present the captain of the first ocean vessel to arrive in Montreal each spring with a top-hat. Since 1880 a more lasting souvenir has been presented, usually a straight malacca cane with a gold head bearing the coat of arms of Canada and an engraved inscription. The opening of the river to winter navigation since the 1960s has altered the significance of the award.

Five days before war was declared in 1939, the *Duchess of Bedford* was chartered for a voyage to Bombay with military personnel. Arriving back in Liverpool on 5 November, she returned to her normal Atlantic run but ran into a hurricane which blew for three days. For the eastbound leg of this voyage she joined the first troop convoy TC1 in company with the *Empress of Britain* and *Empress of Australia*, carrying the First Canadian Division, led by General A. G. L. McNaughton. The Atlantic escort consisted of the battleships *Repulse*, *Resolution* and the aircraft carrier *Furious*. Twelve destroyers from the Home Fleet were sent to meet the convoy. When in the north western approaches, a few hours from the end of the voyage, the liner *Samaria*, outward bound for Canada, steamed into the centre of the convoy, colliding with her fleet mate *Aquitania*, luckily without serious damage. Later, an inquiry revealed that the *Samaria* had been given a route close to the track of TC1, and that due to heavy security precautions the officer detailing outward routes had not been advised of incoming movements! This voyage is believed also to have set a naval precedent by virtue of having the senior naval officer of the escort act also as commodore of the convoy.

Eight more voyages to Canada followed in the first half of 1940. In August she began her trooping duties proper and made three voyages to Suez via Freetown and Cape Town. The *Duchess of Bedford* left Liverpool on 12 November 1941, on a five-month voyage which took her to Singapore with 4000 Indian troops and 40 nurses. Arriving at the end of January 1942, she embarked 875 women and children for evacuation to Batavia, Java. During her stay, Singapore suffered daily from aerial bombardment; although hit by bomb fragments and bullets, no vital damage was done, and she left on 31 January.

The 20,000 ton Empress of France II, *built in 1927 as the*
Duchess of Bedford

Although attacked on the way to Java she landed her passengers successfully and sailed for home on 4 February, arriving in Liverpool on 2 April 1942.

After two trips to Cape Town, the *Bedford* left Liverpool for Boston on 7 August 1942. Two days out of Liverpool, in a heavy sea, a U-boat was sighted about 400yd astern. Captain Busk-Wood altered course and opened fire at a range of only 100yd. The first shell hit the water, ricocheting the length of the U-boat. The second struck abaft the conning tower with a terrific explosion. Two more direct hits were scored, one entering the hull, the other hitting the conning tower. Immediately after these explosions the U-boat's bow rose 30ft out of the water

and the sub sank. A second U-boat was sighted shortly afterwards, three rounds were fired, but the enemy submerged quickly. For this action Captain Busk-Wood was made an officer of the Order of the British Empire.

The next appointment was at Oran on 7 November 1942, when three thousand troops were disembarked for the North African landing. On 26 November 1943, when approaching Philippeville, Algeria, she was attacked by German torpedo-bombers. The ship's gunners put up a terrific barrage and one enemy aircraft was brought down. After two trips to Algiers the *Bedford* also took part in the landings at Sicily and Salerno, where she came under very heavy attack from the enemy. The first half

from anxious to be repatriated and Purser Graham Crawford recalled that one officer was so certain of his reception that he slashed vital arteries and died on board. At Basra, the fabulous port at the junction of the rivers Tigris and Euphrates, special trains were waiting to carry the ex-prisoners north to Russia.

The *Bedford* was the largest ship to navigate the approaches to Basra and was escorted by the naval frigate HMS *Lochy*, also at that time commanded by a Canadian Pacific officer, Lieutenant W. J. P. Roberts RNR. When the pilot boarded for the return journey he told the master that he had prayed for him and would continue to do so. 'I pray that you never come here again with this big ship!' For this trip 400 Bokhara Jews together with their priceless Bokhara rugs were embarked and taken to Suez, where they entrained for Palestine.

In February 1945 the *Bedford* left Liverpool with more Russian ex-prisoners of war, this time bound for Odessa. On arrival the Russians searched the ship looking for 'White Russians'. After an eleven-day stay a large number of French, Canadian and American ex-prisoners of war were embarked. Just as they left the wharf about twenty men in Allied uniforms appeared and begged to be taken aboard. Captain Knight ordered a boat lowered and the men were rescued from the wharf despite threatening gestures by the guards.

The war in Europe had ended before she sailed on her next voyage. During 1946 she made four voyages to Bombay and Middle East ports, helping with the repatriation of Canadian and British troops. She returned to Liverpool from her last trip to Bombay on 21 February 1947, when she was released from government service and was sent to the Clyde to be reconditioned and refurbished as an Empress. *Empress of India* was chosen as her new name, but before she was ready for sea India had become a republic; so on 15 July 1948 she was renamed *Empress of France*. She sailed from Liverpool on 1 September 1948, on her first post-war voyage to Quebec and Montreal. The company was now back in the passenger business with two Empresses on the North Atlantic, *Empress of Canada* and the *Empress of France*.

The *Empress* continued to make regular crossings to Montreal in the summer season and to Saint John NB in the winter, averaging between fourteen and fifteen trips a year. When the *Empress of France* sailed from Liverpool on 19 February 1949 Captain B. Grant and six members of his crew were serving members of the Royal Naval Reserve and the *Empress* was thereby entitled to

of 1944 was taken up with two trips to New York and one to Bombay.

To Captain H. S. Knight fell the distinction of taking his *Duchess* to two ports unknown to most sea captains at that time—Basra and Odessa. Captain Knight had already collected many pilotage certificates, a worthwhile hobby while on naval service in World War I, as in those days the navigating officer was rewarded by a portion of the fees saved. Another of his spare-time occupations was composing organ music, which he performed for his own pleasure in many churches around the world. At the end of September 1944 the *Bedford* left Liverpool with more than 3000 Russian ex-prisoners of war. Some were far wear the Blue Ensign.

On 6 May 1950, when outward bound for Montreal, three Gaspe fishermen were found adrift in their boat off Matane, 400 miles downstream from Montreal. They were rescued and later transferred to an inbound steamer. When the *Empress* left Liverpool on 25 September 1951, cabins A32, 34 and 36 were occupied by Princess Elizabeth and the Duke of Edinburgh sailing for a tour of Canada.

Whilst undergoing her annual overhaul in February 1958 she was fitted with two new funnels, tapered from base to top, raking slightly aft and topped by black cowls. Peacetime trooping featured in her schedule for 1957, 1959 and 1960, when she made several voyages carrying Canadian troops between Canada and Rotterdam.

In May 1960 the third of the new Empresses to be built after the war had been launched. It was consequently decided to offer the thirty-two-year-old *Empress of France* for sale when she arrived at Liverpool on 7 December 1960 from Montreal, on her last passenger voyage for Canadian Pacific. She was bought by the British Iron & Steel Corporation for scrap and arrived at the Cashmore yard at Newport on 20 December. The Empress Bar was dismantled and incorporated as the Empress Room in the Barry Hotel, Barry, Glamorgan, where it can still be seen. In May 1961 the ship's bell was presented to Colonel John Wallis, Director of Movements, Army Headquarters, Ottawa.

From 1928 until the outbreak of war the *Duchess of Bedford* completed 131 round trips on the North Atlantic, nine round trips to Bermuda, plus thirteen cruises to the West Indies and four short cruises from Montreal to New York. On war service she steamed 413,000 miles carrying 146,678 troops, 11,390 prisoners of war, 21,739 civilians as well as 86,249 tons of cargo. As the *Empress of France* she made a further 186 voyages across the North Atlantic—a strenuous thirty-two years.

Duchess of Richmond (1929–47)
Empress of Canada II (1947–52)

The *Duchess of Richmond* was the third Duchess to be launched and this ceremony was performed at the John Brown yard on 18 June 1928 by Lady Augustus Nanton, whose husband was a director of Canadian Pacific Railway and the Hudson's Bay Company. The *Richmond* had a maiden voyage with a difference; she began her

Canadian Pacific career with a forty-one day cruise to Madeira, Las Palmas and the west coast of Africa, leaving Liverpool on 26 January 1929. Having had her first touch of the sun she returned to more prosaic duties and left on 8 March for her first North Atlantic crossing, from Liverpool to Saint John. On her second Atlantic voyage she was stranded off Partridge Isle and was out of commission until August, when she sailed from Southampton.

In January 1930 she made another cruise down the west coast of Africa and in the following year cruised to the West Indies with a second cruise into the Mediterranean. An experiment with a two-class cruise was tried in July 1932, when a five-day cruise was made from Liverpool to Santander, on the north coast of Spain. The minimum charges were cabin class £8.00 and tourist class £5.00. The passengers' preference for having the 'run of the ship' soon became apparent. In April 1934 she made a cruise to Istanbul which had been organised as a Royal Naval Division pilgrimage to Galipoli, for veterans and relatives of those who had lost their lives in the World War I campaign. Originally advertised for the *Montrose*, it proved so popular that it had to be switched to the larger *Duchess*. Also in 1934 she made four 'thrill cruises' from Montreal to New York. The West Indies cruise in January 1935 was exceptional in that the passenger list included the Duke and Duchess of Kent, who were on their honeymoon. Another rather unusual cruise started from Montreal in July 1939. After calling at New York the *Richmond* sailed through the Panama and up the West Coast of North America, calling at Los Angeles, Sitka and as far north as Juneau. The *Richmond* received her instructions to 'black-out' at Vera Cruz, on her way home to New York. So well were these instructions carried out that a long wait ensued at the approach to New York harbour. When the pilot finally climbed aboard he forestalled the captain's outburst with: 'You're so thoroughly blacked-out, sir, we didn't see you for some time.' She returned to Montreal on 8 September, just a few days after Britain declared war on Germany.

The *Richmond*'s first wartime voyage from Montreal to Liverpool lasted nineteen days. This must have been the longest transatlantic crossing by a crack liner for many years. The reason was the necessity of making a rendezvous at Halifax to join the first 'fast convoy' (ships able to steam at fifteen knots or better), plus the necessary zig-zagging and the more northerly course steered, which was half as long again as the normal 'great circle' course.

After this first crossing the *Duchess* remained on her normal North Atlantic run until the end of 1940, making fourteen more round trips.

On 30 August 1940 the *Duchess of Richmond* left Liverpool with one of the most important missions undertaken in the early days of the war. Professors Tizard and Cockroft took with them to the USA the latest British power-driven gun turrets, anti-submarine and anti-aircraft devices, a new predictor for the Bofors gun and, most important of all, the Randall & Boot cavity magnetron valve, which proved so important to our radar equipment. The aim of the mission was to prove Britain's intention of sharing her knowledge with her ally and additionally, swing the great manufacturing potential of the States behind the British war effort.

On the last of these Canadian trips, whilst proceeding westbound after the coastal escort had left, the *Richmond* picked up the SOS from the *Beaverford*, which was battling with the German 'pocket battleship' *Admiral Scheer* twenty miles to the north. Star shells and flashes of gunfire could be seen (see page 181). Carryings during this early period of the war were very light, averaging about 700 westbound and 500 eastbound. Many of these passengers were of course military personnel. Conversely, cargo loadings were, for a passenger liner, very high, averaging more than 4000 tons per voyage eastbound and 3000 tons westbound.

The *Duchess* finally started her trooping duties in January 1941, making two trips to Suez via the Cape, followed by two trips to India. In 1942 she made several trips into the Mediterranean with troops for the North African landings. In 1943 she had a couple of changes from her usual war-zone runs. In July she made a trip to the new air and naval base at Hvalfjord, Iceland, where the Canadian escort vessels used to refuel. December found her in New York, just in time for Christmas, which must have been a welcome break for her crew. The year 1944 was mostly taken up with trips to Mediterranean and African ports.

In March 1945 the *Richmond* sailed through the Mediterranean to Odessa, a port that no Canadian Pacific ship had visited in peacetime. She sailed from the Clyde with 3700 Russian prisoners of war who had been held in camps in France and released as the Allies had advanced. After some difficulties with the Russian authorities in Odessa, 900 British personnel were embarked for the return journey. Two of the British soldiers had married Russian girls, but the girls could not get permission to embark. However, on the following day, two women stowaways were found and arrangements were made to keep them hidden from the Russian naval officer who was attached to the ship. Shortly after the *Duchess* sailed, a signal was received requesting her to return as three women were missing from a Russian camp. In true Nelson fashion the signal was ignored and strangely enough a further search of the ship revealed the third stowaway, a Polish girl who had been smuggled on board in British battledress by a Polish member of the RAF.

In August the same year, the *Richmond* made a round trip to Quebec, arriving back in Liverpool on the twenty-seventh. This turned out to be her last wartime voyage. Her role was now reversed and she began to bring the troops home for demobilisation. The remainder of 1945 was spent with a voyage to Singapore and another to Gibraltar. In the early part of 1946 Bombay received two visits from the *Richmond* after which she was de-requisitioned. In May 1946 she left Liverpool for the Fairfield yard to be reconditioned.

Owing to the great shortages of materials and skilled labour the work took longer than expected and it was not until 16 July 1947 that she sailed from Liverpool on her first post-war voyage, under the command of Captain E. A. Shergold. To meet her new first-class status the *Duchess of Richmond* had been renamed *Empress of Canada* II on 12 July. A 'welcome back' message was sent to J. C. Patteson CMG, European general manager, Canadian Pacific Railway, London, by the Right Honourable W. L. MacKenzie King PC:

Canadians will be delighted to know that the Canadian Pacific post-war passenger service was inaugurated on 16th July by the sailing from Liverpool to Montreal of the *Empress of Canada*, formerly the *Duchess of Richmond*. We join in welcoming back to the North Atlantic routes a proud vessel bearing a storied name. To the captain, officers, members of the crew and all who sail on the *Empress of Canada* I send best wishes for the voyage and voyages to come.

After six years of active wartime service she returned to the relatively humdrum North Atlantic crossings to Quebec and Montreal in summer and to Saint John in winter, averaging fifteen trips per year until December 1952.

In January 1953 she was withdrawn for overhaul and after coming out of dry dock was berthed at the Gladstone Dock on 24 January. On the afternoon of Sunday the twenty-fifth a devastating fire broke out. At the time there was only a small security-crew aboard and they were able to get ashore. The fire had taken hold before it was discovered and by the time the fire-brigades reached the dock they were unable to control the blaze. Eventually the weight of water caused the vessel to turn on her side and she became a total loss. A reporter from the 'Liverpool Evening Express' wrote: 'Everywhere there is that almost impenetrable blackness and oil, where once were stately first-class bedroom suites, expansive dining saloons and airy lounges. Utter blackness, stark ruin was all that remained of this once glamorous scene.' The raising of the burned-out liner was the largest salvage operation ever undertaken in Europe. Preparatory work went on for fourteen months. Eleven air-filled buoyancy pontoons were attached under water to her port side. Sixteen steel tripods were erected on her starboard side. These were connected by steel hawsers to steam winches which had been set in concrete on the quay. On 6 March 1954 the vessel was righted and in August the hulk was sold to Cantiere di Portovenere, Genoa. She left Liverpool on 1 September, towed by the 836 ton Dutch tug *Zwarte Zee*, and arrived at Spezia on 10 October to be broken up.

From 1929 to 1940 the *Duchess of Richmond* had made 114 North Atlantic voyages plus twenty-seven cruises, five from Canada and twenty-two from the United Kingdom. During her war service she steamed 435,877 miles and carried 31,000 civilians, 26,110 prisoners of war, 12,387 military personnel plus 139,253 tons of cargo. As the *Empress of Canada* she made another eighty-two North Atlantic voyages for the company.

The Beaver cargo liners

The 1928 Beavers were 520ft in length, with a beam of 62ft. Their tonnage varied from 9874 to 10,042 and they were very easily distinguished by their five sets of twin kingposts (goal posts) which had topmasts on numbers one and four. They were coal-fired and were the first ships on the North Atlantic fitted with automatic stokers. About 2500 tons of bunker coal could be carried. Four water-tube boilers supplied super-heated steam at 250°C and at a pressure of 250lb. High, intermediate and low pressure turbines of the Parsons type were used to drive twin screws through single-reduction gearing, giving a speed of fourteen knots with a considerable reserve of

power. This was considered very fast for a cargo ship in those days. Eighty thousand cubic feet of insulated space was provided for the carriage of meat and other perishable cargoes. Four of the lower holds had special electric fan ventilation fitted for the carriage of apples. The general cargo holds could be converted for the carriage of grain, and cattle could be carried in the 'tween decks in specially built portable stalls. For the rapid handling of the cargo the deck equipment included twenty-seven derricks. The Beavers had black hulls, white deck-housing, buff funnels and green boot-topping.

CP's connection with the old Beaver Line was commemorated by using the prefix 'Beaver-' for the naming of the new cargo liners, which were built in three yards: W. Denny Brothers of Dumbarton built the *Beaverburn*, Barclay Curle of Scotstoun built the *Beaverford* and *Beaverhill*, and Armstrong Whitworth of Newcastle the *Beaverdale* and *Beaverbrae*.

In the twelve years from 1928, when they made their maiden voyage, until the outbreak of war in 1939, these five cargo liners had an uneventful but remarkably consistent career. Based on the Surrey Commercial Docks in London, regular calls were made at Hamburg and Antwerp; calls were also made at Le Havre between 1928 and 1934. They each made between 115 and 120 voyages between Europe and Canada, making an average of six sailings to Montreal each summer season and four to Saint John each winter.

Beaverburn (1927–40)

Mrs Peacock, wife of E. R. Peacock, a director of the CPR, launched the *Beaverburn* from the Wm Denny yard on 27 September 1927. She sailed on her maiden voyage from Glasgow on 24 December. In the following September she made a record crossing from Le Havre to Father Point in seven days, eight hours, twenty minutes.

Requisitioned at the beginning of the war, the Beavers continued on their normal route between the United Kingdom and Canada. Leaving London on 1 February 1940 on her fourth wartime crossing, the *Beaverburn* proceeded on her way to join convoy OB84 and its sole escort, HM Destroyer *Antelope*. She was commanded by Captain Thomas Jones, one of several Joneses in the Canadian Pacific fleet. He was known as 'Farmer Jones' although no one seemed to know why. At 13.12 hours on 5 February a torpedo struck. Recalling the incident later, Captain Jones said:

We were zig-zagging at nine knots, the speed of the slowest ship in the convoy, when there was a terrific explosion. It threw me up in the air. I ordered all hands to boat stations, rang the engine room telegraph to 'Stop' and then 'Finished with engines' (a warning to the engine room staff that all hands should make their way to the boats). The torpedo had struck right under the bridge and the jumper stay was slacking, which showed that the ship was breaking up; I ordered the boats to be lowered. She was still on an even keel as I walked aft to the engine room skylight where I could see water halfway up the engine room. I walked to the after rail, called to a boat to come closer, and leapt into the sea. She went down by the head and lifted her propellers out of the water and sank, about nine minutes after the torpedo had struck.

The US tanker *Narraganset* picked up the seventy-six survivors, only two of whom had to swim for it, Captain Jones and Third Engineer Henry Teare, who stayed to close the valves to minimise explosion risks. One other survivor was not quite dry, he had been taking a bath at the time and had to get into a lifeboat clad only in his lifebelt. Only one crew member was lost, the chief cook, who had returned to his room after being seen at his boatstation.

A report by Chief Officer David Ewing said:

I was on my way to the bridge and had my hand on the rail of the ladder when I felt the ship give a tremor, and lurch, that was all I felt.... After cutting the lashings of two of the lifeboats I went up to the bridge where I found the Captain standing in the wheelhouse. I thought it better to be out of the wheelhouse by that time and suggested to the Captain that we step outside. We did and a second later the wheelhouse collapsed as the ship was breaking in two amidships.

On the way to Falmouth, HMS *Antelope* came alongside the rescue ship and reported that it had pursued and sunk the U-boat.

An optimistic Irishman sent a postcard to the company: 'I picked up on this coast a name board from the *Beaverburn*. I have been told there is a reward of one pound for its recovery. Will you please let me know if this is correct.' A red-pencilled minute by Captain R. N. Stuart (the general manager) reads: 'If a stamped envel-ope has not been received with this query no reply is to be sent. RNS.' The telegraphic address of the Shipping Federation at Falmouth was Nemesis. On a telegram announcing the departure of the survivors for London was more red pencilling, 'Nemesis—what a code name. RNS.' That was his only recorded comment on the first war loss to be suffered by Canadian Pacific Steamships.

Beaverford (1928–40)

On 27 October 1927, Mrs H. P. Holt, daughter-in-law of a director of Canadian Pacific Railway, launched the *Beaverford* from the Whiteinch yard of Barclay Curle & Co. She made her maiden voyage from Glasgow on 21 January 1928. In June 1935 the *Beaverford* was involved in an act of salvage when she towed the *Kafiristan* to Sydney NS after this vessel had been in collision with the *Empress of Britain*.

The *Beaverford* had completed eight wartime voyages when she left Halifax NS in October 1940 to join convoy HX84 and its escort HMS *Jervis Bay*, the armed merchant cruiser that was to achieve world fame. Prior to sailing, Captain H. Pettigrew entertained two friends at an uptown restaurant. The friends were intrigued because he usually entertained them aboard ship. When asked why the change Captain Pettigrew replied: 'I have a feeling this will be our last lunch together, so I thought a change would be good.' George Pollock recounts in his story of the *Jervis Bay* that Lieutenant-Commander Morrison RNR had the same presentiment.

The convoy was formed in nine columns 600yd apart, the ships being 400yd apart from stern to bow in each column, and these were the stations that the masters had to endeavour to keep with signals by flag and whistle only. The *Beaverford* was the middle ship in the seventh column. For seven days there were no U-boat alarms and the convoy sailed eastwards uneventfully. Meantime, on 28 October, the German pocket battleship *Admiral Scheer* had sneaked out of Stavanger unobserved. Captain Krancke already knew that convoy HX84 had left Halifax, and on the morning of 5 November a reconnaissance plane from his ship had reported back after sighting the convoy.

The first warning to the convoy came at 3.45pm when smoke was seen on the horizon, by five o'clock the enemy raider had been recognised. The *Jervis Bay*, unarmoured and lightly armed, signalled 'Prepare to scatter' and 'Make smoke'; she then turned and made towards the raider. Her aim was to delay the battleship and so give the convoy a chance to get away. For nearly half an hour she engaged the *Admiral Scheer* before being sunk. Her captain, E. S. Fogarty Fegan RN, was awarded a posthumous VC. The *Beaverford* took over the fight and with her speed and the superb seamanship of Captain Pettigrew, but with only one 4in and one 3in gun and no gunnery-control equipment, succeeded in delaying the raider; it was not until 10.45pm that in a tremendous explosion the *Beaverford* sank with all hands. The *Admiral Scheer* had fired twelve rounds main armament plus seventy-one rounds of secondary armament at the *Beaverford* without sinking her. Three hits by main and sixteen by secondary armament were recorded, but to sink her the raider had to launch a torpedo.

The British official history, *The War at Sea*, volume 1, by Captain S. W. Roskill DSC, RN, credits the *Admiral Scheer* with having sunk the AMC *Jervis Bay* and five ships in the convoy HX84 action in November 1940. When it is remembered that the pocket battleship was armed with six 11in, eight 5.9in and six 4.1in high-angle guns, eight torpedo tubes, radar, range-finding equipment and gun-control systems, and that *Jervis Bay* and *Beaverford* had seven and two guns respectively, it becomes obvious that sheer determination coupled with superb seamanship can be credited with the salvation of the thirty-one ships that survived. According to the master of a ship which survived, *Beaverford* maintained an uneven fight for four or five hours while slower ships in the convoy made their escape.

Before the war the Downhills Central School, Tottenham, had 'adopted' the *Beaverford*. Under this scheme a strong personal interest developed from correspondence between the children and members of the crew, visits by the children while the ship was in port, and visits by the ship's officers to the school. When the loss of the ship became known, a fund was started for a memorial. A painting of the ship by S. Stott was purchased and hung in the school hall, with a bronze plaque:

> SS *Beaverford*
> Our ship
> Lost with all hands
> in action
> 5th November 1940.

The memorial was unveiled by Mrs M. Pettigrew, widow of the captain of the *Beaverford*. In addition a cheque for £125 was presented to the Seamen's Hospital Society.

Beaverdale (1928–41)

The *Beaverdale* was launched the day after the *Beaverburn*, 28 September 1927, from the Armstrong Whitworth yard at Newcastle. Two families much concerned in the history of Canadian Pacific were involved with the launch of this ship. In March 1891, when the company's first ocean liners were being built, the wife of the governor of the Hudson's Bay Company, Lady Stafford Northcote, was invited to launch the *Empress of China*. Lady Stafford's son later married the adopted daughter of Lord Mount Stephen, who as Lady Alice Northcote launched the *Beaverdale*.

In May 1933 rail track was laid on the deck of the *Beaverdale* to carry the Royal Scot, a crack London Midland & Scottish 4-6-0 locomotive, and eight coaches including an all-electric kitchen car, from London to Montreal. Together with her English crew the train made an eight-month trip around Canada and the United States, covering more than 11,000 miles before returning to the United Kingdom.

On the outbreak of war the *Beaverdale* made two voyages on government charter. With Captain Hugh Pettigrew on the bridge she sailed from Liverpool on 18 September 1939 to St Nazaire at the mouth of the Loire River, where she unloaded 571 tons of cargo on the twenty-sixth. Three days later she sailed, light, for Avonmouth, leaving the Bristol Channel port on 3 October for Nantes farther up the Loire with another small but highly significant cargo. Her next voyage, from Liverpool to Montreal where she arrived on 12 November, was the last to carry any sizeable tonnage westbound; she had 3750 tons. After that her Atlantic crossings followed the wartime pattern of heavy cargoes eastward, negligible tonnages to the west—Britain was too busy building up for war to be able to manufacture for export. Seven more trips to Canada followed without mishap.

The *Beaverdale* arrived at the London docks on 28 May 1940, at the time of the Dunkirk evacuation. Dave Ewing, the chief officer, took two of the ship's lifeboats downriver and across to Dunkirk. For five days they assisted with the evacuation from the beaches and eventually arrived back with the lifeboats intact.

On 26 March 1941 she left Saint John for the United Kingdom, but in the early hours of 1 April she was struck by a torpedo from the *U-48*. Half an hour later the crew of seventy-nine were in three of the ship's boats; no one had been injured. Two submarines then surfaced and started shelling the *Beaverdale*, which sank with a violent explosion. During the night, contact was lost with one of the lifeboats and next morning the remaining two boats set sail for Iceland, which Captain Draper reckoned was about 300 miles away. Later Captain Draper recalled, 'One day we had a great stroke of luck—a hail storm. We caught hail stones in the boat cover and ate them like candy.' The two boats kept in touch for three days, but then lost contact. Captain Draper's boat sighted land on the sixth day and the survivors were helped over the beach and taken to a farmhouse. The farmer made a twenty-mile journey to get a doctor and report their arrival.

Second Officer G. Mansell was in charge of the number 3 lifeboat, and after losing touch with Captain Draper continued to sail eastwards. The following day, fishing vessels were sighted and eventually the Icelandic trawler *Gulltoppur* took the men aboard and landed them at Reykjavik late that night. No trace was ever found of the number 2 lifeboat, with the first officer aboard. It was later assumed that the boat must have been destroyed by shells from the submarine when it was trying to sink the *Beaverdale*.

Beaverdale was the fifth Canadian Pacific vessel to be sunk in the first nineteen months of the war and the second casualty in 1941. Twenty-five years earlier, on 16 November 1916, Captain Draper had been serving on the *Monmouth* on a voyage from New York to Dunkirk when that vessel had been mined, off Cherbourg.

Beaverhill (1928–43)

Miss Mavis Gillies, daughter of Captain J. Gillies, general manager of Canadian Pacific Steamship Services, sponsored the *Beaverhill* when she was launched from the Scotstoun yard of Barclay Curle & Co on 8 November 1927. She made her maiden voyage from Glasgow on 18 February 1928.

When war broke out, *Beaverhill* was undergoing extensive repairs after her bow had been crushed in an encounter with an iceberg. She had arrived in London on 16 August 1939, but her repairs were not completed until the end of the following April. She ran trials on 1 May 1940, and was promptly requisitioned; for four and a half years she led a charmed life going about her 'lawful occasions', making no fewer than fifty-five crossings of

the North Atlantic, almost as regularly as in peacetime. She was never under attack by submarine or aircraft, and except for one or two occasions when the whole convoy was ordered to put up a barrage, never fired her guns 'in anger'. So good was her reputation as a lucky mascot that there was always a feeling of relief when it was learned that *Beaverhill* was to be part of a convoy.

En route to Liverpool on 26 May 1941, the lookout in the crowsnest reported a 'small flat object. Bearing red fifteen sir'. Eventually an inflated raft, almost awash, with two overall-clad figures waving frantically, came into sight. The ship was placed to windward of the raft and a scramblenet made fast on the port side. Two men made their way over the side of the ship to grab for the raft. Despite the lee made by the *Beaverhill*, the Atlantic surged up and down against the ship's side, alternately drenching the volunteers and then leaving them high—if not dry. With the aid of the watch on deck all four were helped aboard. The Fleet Air Arm pilot and observer had been adrift for fifty-seven hours and had almost given up hope. Lieutenant Furlong RNVR and Lieutenant Hoare RNVR had taken off from the aircraft carrier *Victorious* to search for the *Bismark*. Unfortunately when they returned to where they thought their carrier might be they failed to find her before running out of fuel. They had to ditch their aircraft and were extremely lucky to be found by the *Beaverhill*.

In September 1941 it was decided to add accommodation for 138 passengers. Immediately below the main deck, the upper 'tween deck extended from well forward to the after end of the ship, and was well above the waterline. In what had been number 1 hold a spacious lounge and bar were built. In 2 and 3 holds six berth rooms and a hospital were fitted. A dining saloon and galley were placed amidships. A refrigeration chamber for the extra food supplies needed was installed in number 4 hold. More accommodation was fitted in number 5 hold. Most of the passengers carried were RAF aircrew cadets travelling to and from Canada for initial flying training. Civilian passengers could be carried if space was not fully occupied by service personnel.

The nearest approach to real trouble experienced by the *Beaverhill* occurred in dense fog on 2 October 1943. When leaving Saint John she struck HMS *Anticosti*, a Canadian-built anti-submarine trawler. However, the damage was slight.

From 7 May 1940 until 24 November 1943, good fortune smiled on *Beaverhill*. She set up a cargo record for Canadian Pacific's war effort, 268,652 long tons plus 3680 passengers in 26½ voyages. Then a marine accident occurred in Saint John Harbour; a towing hawser snapped and wrapped itself around a propeller, and with a wrong set of wind and tide the *Beaverhill* was stranded on Hillyards reef, to break in half as the tide ebbed. On 11 December 1946 the stern section was refloated and eventually towed out to sea and scuttled off Grand Manan Island.

Beaverbrae (1928–41)

The fifth *Beaver* was launched from Armstrong Whitworth's yard on 24 November 1927 by Lady McLaren Brown, wife of the European general manager for the CPR in London. Four months later, on 15 March, she sailed on her maiden voyage from Newcastle to join the company's London and Continental cargo service. When she left Hamburg on 7 October 1931, a Junkers JV52 had been loaded, the largest ever single-engined aircraft to enter Canada. Canadian Airways had bought the aircraft to carry supplies to the Hudson's Bay Company's northern outposts.

The *Beaverbrae* arrived in London on the day war was declared, 3 September 1939, having completed 113 transatlantic voyages. Six days later she again sailed for Canada and made eleven round voyages totalling 75,408 miles, carrying 103,567 tons of cargo in the remaining eighteen months of her wartime life.

Apart from one voyage, Captain B. L. Leslie was on the bridge from the outbreak of war until 25 March 1941, when he jumped overboard to a waiting lifeboat after making sure that all hands were clear of the ship. On 23 March, *Beaverbrae* had sailed from Liverpool. At 08.05 hours on the morning of the twenty-fifth a Focke-Wulf attacked out of the sun and loosed a stick of bombs that opened the after deck. The same explosions tore up the upper and shelter decks, blew out the ship's side and sent several wooden hatchcovers clear over the funnel. All steam and water pipes were fractured and the engine-room bulkhead flattened. The hail of bullets from the ship's guns may have upset the aim of the pilot when he returned and loosed two more bombs which turned out to be near-misses, but his cannon and machine-gun fire caused two casualties. After a third attack the raider flew off. Thirty-five minutes after the first attack the chief officer reported that the efforts of the fire-damage-control parties had been unavailing and there was no possi-

bility of coping with the fire. The order to abandon ship was given at 08.45 hours. Captain Leslie stayed on board until 10.00 hours. During the next few hours a number of RAF planes appeared and proceeded to drop bags of provisions.

By 17.15 hours two destroyers had arrived and the whole ship's company were taken aboard. Captain Leslie discussed with the destroyer captain the possibility of boarding the *Beaverbrae* to extinguish the fire and take her in tow; but after circling the ship it was decided that this was not possible. The survivors were taken to Scapa Flow and later to Thurso, the northernmost railway station in the British Isles.

Empress of Britain II (1931–40)

The fastest, largest and most luxurious passenger liner to sail under the chequered house flag, the *Empress of Britain* II was the largest to sail between Commonwealth ports. By 1927 a new and fast liner had become necessary for the North Atlantic summer service, which would also provide the utmost luxury for the company's annual world cruise. It was intended that the shorter journey by the sheltered St Lawrence route, which was advertised as '39 per cent less ocean' would tap the vast tourist traffic from the United States' Midwest. Canadian Pacific built a new pier with the necessary rail connection at Wolfe's Cove, Quebec, but the maximum size of the ship was fixed by the need to pass through the Suez and Panama canals on her world cruise.

In 1928 an order was placed with the John Brown yard for the new liner, which was to be 760ft in length, 97½ft in breadth and have a gross tonnage of 42,348. The keel was laid on 28 November 1928.

The vessel was in an unusually advanced state by the time of her launch. A large part of her wood panelling and other internal fittings were already aboard. The launching ceremony, on 11 June 1930, was performed by HRH the Prince of Wales. At the luncheon which followed he said:

This vessel can be considered in construction as the last word in shipbuilding and as regards her appointments she will have no rivals. . . . She will represent the most ambitious undertaking of the CPR. . . . The liners built by this Company during the last three years constitute a record, I believe, unparalleled in the annals of the mercantile marine

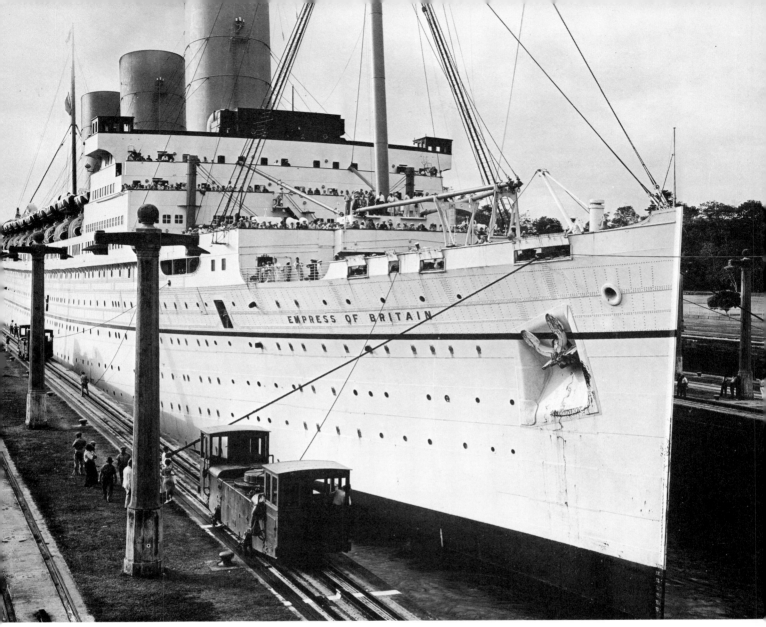

The pride of the fleet, the 42,000 ton Empress of Britain *II. The largest and fastest liner on the St Lawrence run*

throughout the world; sixteen vessels have been launched for the CPR in British yards, many of them on the Clyde.

The speeches were broadcast throughout the Commonwealth, the first time such an event had been broadcast round the world.

On 7 April when she left the Clyde, the 'Greenock Telegraph' reported:

Never before or since, in the history of up-river shipbuilding, has a vessel had such a welcome to the sea as was given the *Empress of Britain* when she manoeuvred slowly down from John Brown's yard. It was estimated that more than half a million people watched the passage to the Tail of the Bank in brilliant Spring sunshine and under the motherly and fussing guidance of five tugs and their 12-inch hawsers.

The *Empress* had a straight stem and cruiser stern, and was schooner-rigged fore and aft. Her ten decks included a sun deck, sports deck and a promenade deck.

Technically the ship was a masterpiece of British marine engineering and naval architecture. Her propelling machinery received high praise at the time of her sea-trials, which proved her to be the world's most economical steamship for fuel consumption per shaft-horsepower-hour.

John Johnson, chief engineer for Canadian Pacific Steamships, designed the propelling machinery which consisted of four sets of single-reduction geared turbines developing 62,500shp and giving a normal speed of twenty-four knots. The most outstanding feature was the 'Johnson boiler'. Its design reflected the very latest in metallurgy and the steam rate was greater than that of any other marine boiler of its day. The two inboard screws took two-thirds of the power and the two outboard screws the remaining third. When cruising, only the two inner screws were used; these were 19¼ft in diameter and were cast from forty-ton blocks of bronze, the heaviest ever cast. Four diesel generators and two turbine generators produced more than 3000kw of electricity and more than 320 miles of cable were used to feed the essential services, including twelve lifts, 407 electric motors and 200 clocks.

The *Empress of Britain* II was the first vessel to be equipped with a worldwide radio telephone service from passengers' rooms. On 31 May 1931, Lord Bessborough, Governor-General, telephoned from Ottawa to President Beatty on board the *Empress*. This was the first ever telephone message from shore to ship in Canada.

Many eminent artists were employed to design the furnishings and decorations for the *Empress*. The first-class dining saloon, Salle Jacques Cartier, occupied the full width of the ship on 'D' deck and, together with the two small private dining saloons, was designed by Frank Brangwyn, who also designed the cold buffet which rose in tiers from floor to ceiling in the centre of the room.

The other first-class public rooms were on the lounge deck. At the forward end was the Empress Ballroom, decorated to the design of Sir John Lavery. An outstanding feature of this room was the large dome on which was a representation of the heavens on the night of the launch. This room was also used as a cinema. In the Knickerbocker Bar, Heath Robinson designed an ingenious panoramic mural, 'The Legend of the Cocktail'. The humour of this artist was also allowed to run wild in the children's play room, where he illustrated nursery rhymes. The Mayfair Lounge was designed by Sir Charles Allom, who used many different woods for wall panelling, and at the forward end there was a large tapestry panel illustrating the hunting exploits of the Emperor Maximilian. In the smoking room, the Cathay Lounge, Edmund Dulac used Chinese lacquer vases and Chinese motifs on the walls and furnishings. At the head of the main staircase was a large painting, 13ft by 11ft, 'Champlain brings his wife to Quebec' by Maurice Griffenhagen RA.

The largest swimming bath in any liner, the Olympian Pool, was situated at the after end of 'F' deck. Water flowed into the pool from a large turtle carved in Portland stone and inlaid with blue mosaic. The pool was illuminated from below. Alongside the pool were Turkish baths and massage rooms. For the more energetic there were two gymnasia, one for adults and the other for children, a squash court on 'B' deck and a full-size tennis court on the sports deck. For morale boosting there was a hairdressing saloon and beauty parlour for the ladies but a mere barber's shop sufficed for the men. If any passenger was unlucky enough to be taken ill there was an operating theatre with extensive hospital accommodation; also a complete dental surgery, probably the first ever fitted in a liner.

The first-class passenger accommodation was also on a lavish scale. There were six deluxe suites, which included an entrance vestibule, sitting room, double bedroom, bathroom and box room. Two of these suites also had a sun verandah. There were also fourteen special two-berth state rooms in addition to the normal first-class bedrooms. Although naturally not so luxurious as the first-class, the tourist accommodation was said to be the finest afloat. The really large amount of space devoted to the passengers' comfort may be judged by comparing the *Empress* with the 20,000 ton Duchess liners which had accommodation for 1559 whilst the *Britain*, nearly 160ft longer, catered for only 1129.

After hull cleaning and painting, official trials began on 11 April, and a speed of 25.5 knots was recorded over the measured mile at Arran. After completing 1700 miles of sea-trials she arrived at Southampton on the sixteenth.

HRH the Prince of Wales flew to Southampton to wish her bon voyage before she sailed on her maiden voyage on 27 May 1931 under the command of Captain R. G. Latta. Just before the Prince arrived, a Rolls-Royce entered the dock and stopped at the foot of the gangway, where everyone stood smartly to attention and someone stepped forward and opened the door. Then to everyone's horror out staggered four 'merry' members of the crew.

The *Empress* was scheduled to make the Southampton to Quebec crossing in 5 days, including 1½ days in the sheltered St Lawrence. In conjunction with the *Empress of Japan* on the Pacific, the journey from London to Yokohama could be reduced by two days. On her first trip she arrived at Quebec in five days and thirty minutes after leaving Cherbourg, a record. Mail put on board at Southampton was taken off at Rimouski and flown to Montreal for delivery, creating another record. It had been hoped to transfer 800lb of mail to the CGS *Aranmore* in the Cabot Strait and to fly this westward from Sydney NS but bad weather put an end to this scheme.

From the 'Montreal Gazette', 2 June 1931:

A new page was written this evening in the history of St Lawrence shipping when the *Empress of Britain*, newest, largest and fastest liner in the Canadian Pacific fleet, glided easily into the new wharf at Wolfe's Cove at 10pm; 5 days, 13 hours and 25 minutes after she had left Southampton....

The mail plane destined to start the trans-Canada flight was the first to greet the *Empress* as it swung into Father Point 4 days, 19 hours and 20 minutes after she had left Cherbourg.... When the *Empress*, drew near Quebec the river was crowded with craft of all descriptions.... As the *Empress* passed along in front of Quebec City the Citadel and hills above were crowded with people.

Speaking later to the press Edward Beatty, president, said:

Naturally I am very glad that the Canadian Pacific has been the instrument through which such a vessel has been placed in this service, and my hope is that the results of her operation will justify a sister ship after she has been sufficiently tested.

Speaking to the press, film star Douglas Fairbanks said he found two faults: 'The voyage was too short because of the many attractions the ship offered; and the second was that these same attractions robbed one of the sense of being on an ocean voyage.'

On the evening of 2 June, after the *Empress* had arrived at Quebec, Edward Beatty, later Sir Edward, presided over a banquet in the Salle Jacques Cartier. Amongst those present were HE the Governor-General, the Lieutenant-governors of Quebec, New Brunswick and Prince Edward Island, the Prime Minister of Canada, and the Premier of Quebec. At the banquet, Mr Beatty announced that Captain Latta would henceforth be known as Commodore of the Canadian Pacific fleet.

Over the years the *Empress* continued to knock minutes off her time, her westbound record from Bishop Rock to Belle Isle being three days, two hours and forty minutes in October 1933. Eastbound her best time from Belle Isle to Bishop Rock was three days, one hour and thirty-six minutes in August 1934. In 1931 she made nine round trips to Quebec, returning to Southampton on 3 November, when she went into dry dock for the first overhaul. On 21 November she left for New York and her first world cruise, 146 days with seventy-one days in port for a minimum fare of £440. Some 400 lucky passengers made the cruise. During the cruise she became the largest ship to sail through the Suez and Panama canals, with only 7½ inches to spare on either side of the Panama locks.

The following figures will give some idea of the splendid performance of this ship. Returning from her second world cruise in April 1933, she made thirteen round trips from Southampton to Quebec between 3 May and 14 November:

Nautical miles steamed	73,727	
Fuel oil consumed	47,643	tons
Days at sea	133	
Days in port	62	
Passengers carried	3208	first
	3776	tourist
	4467	third
Automobiles	78	
Mail	59,955	bags
Cargo	3192	tons
Gold	524	boxes
Average crossing times westbound	4 days, 11 hours, 22 minutes	24.03k
Average crossing times eastbound	4 days, 8 hours, 13 minutes	24.74k

Speaking of the *Empress of Britain* at the Annual General Meeting in 1935, Beatty said: 'The service afforded by this ship has enabled the company, in the face of the most severe competition, to maintain a position in the shipping world which otherwise would not have been possible.'

A first-class suite on the Empress of Britain *II*

The Cathay Lounge, designed by Sir Edmund Dulac

The summer season on the North Atlantic, with the quick turn-rounds at Southampton and Quebec and almost continuous watchkeeping, left the crew of the *Empress of Britain* with little spare time for social activities, but the world cruises provided the opportunity for a thriving sports and social club to be built-up over the years. Activities included an orchestra which used to practise in the top of the dummy funnel, and a library of more than 1500 books, which would be changed by the Missions to Seamen Society at various ports of call. Cricket was a popular diversion and many games were played against various touring sides under such well-known leaders of the 1931–8 era as Jardine, Leverson-Gower and Lord Tennyson. Another highlight would be the match against the English colony at Los Angeles, where the host celebrities included film stars Aubrey Smith, Clarke Gable, Edward Everett Horton, Laurel and Hardy, with Joan Blondell and other stars adding glamour to the occasions.

The year 1935 was unlucky for the *Empress*. On 16 May, whilst passing through the Gatun Lock in the Panama Canal, she scraped the side and received minor damage. On 16 June, on her first eastbound passage, she rammed the 5000 ton collier *Kafiristan* in thick fog off the Madeleine Islands. The *Kafiristan* was badly damaged and set on fire, and was later towed to Sydney NS by the *Beaverford*. The *Britain* remained alongside until help arrived and then proceeded on her way. The hole in her starboard bow was repaired when she arrived at Southampton, causing her next westbound sailing to be delayed for fifteen hours.

Before the world cruise of 1937, two feet were lopped from her 208ft mast-tops to allow clearance under the new Golden Gate Bridge at San Francisco. It so happened that on the day the very moist atmosphere contracted the life-nets under the bridge, allowing ample clearance.

On 16 June 1939, under the command of Captain C. H. Sapsworth, the *Empress of Britain* sailed eastbound with her smallest but most illustrious passenger list, when she was chartered to carry HM King George VI and Queen Elizabeth, with their party of sixteen plus their staffs, from Conception Bay, St Johns, Newfoundland, to Southampton. The naval escort under Vice-Admiral Sir Dudley North KCVO consisted of HMS *Berwick*, *Glasgow* and *Southampton* with *Saguenay* and *Skeena*. As a compliment to the Merchant Navy, His Majesty ordered the *Britain* to fly the Red Ensign instead of the more usual White Ensign. Recalling the voyage many years later, Fred Evans, who had been relieved of watchkeeping duties and assigned to the Royal party for the voyage, recaptured something of the atmosphere:

> His Majesty asked if I could repair his movie camera. I said I would take it to a workshop and look see. But the King said 'No don't go to the workshop do it here.' So I sat on the deck and opened the camera. Meantime the King left and the Queen entered, expressed surprise and then asked if I smoked cigars and upon being told 'yes' took one from a humidor and gave it to me. I placed it in my uniform pocket and explained that I would smoke it after dinner, whereupon the Queen gave me a second cigar and asked me to smoke it then and there. So I lit up. The Queen left the room and soon the King returned. He sniffed the air and said 'Ah, I smell that someone smokes the same cigars as I do.' A bit embarrassing!

On the day before war was declared, 2 September 1939, on her last voyage for the company, she sailed with her largest-ever passenger list. Special permission was granted by the Board of Trade for temporary berths to be fitted, the squash court and other spaces being converted into dormitories, allowing 1143 passengers to be carried. By this time the *Britain* had already completed 100 round trips on the North Atlantic plus eight round-

the-world cruises, six to the West Indies and two to Bermuda.

When the *Britain* arrived at Quebec on 8 September 1939, after her last peacetime voyage, she was painted grey and laid-up awaiting orders. It was not until 25 November that she was requisitioned as a troopship and sailed for the Clyde on 10 December, as part of the first big convoy to cross the Atlantic from Canada. Early in 1940 she made three more trips across the Atlantic before leaving for Wellington, New Zealand, where she arrived on 14 April. Leaving on 2 May 1940, she joined the 'million-dollar convoy' (see page 140) which had originally been routed via Suez. The entry of Italy into the war, however, resulted in a change of direction to Cape Town, thence to the Clyde, where she arrived at the end of June.

On 6 August the *Empress* left Liverpool for Suez via Cape Town. On her return with 224 military personnel and their families, plus a crew of 419, she was given a course well clear of the Azores and far to the west of Ireland en route to the northwest approaches and Liverpool. Because of her high speed she travelled independently; a fighter patrol from RAF Coastal Command had been promised to meet the vessel off the northwest coast of Ireland. On the day concerned, however, no fighter planes appeared.

At 09.20 on 26 October an unidentified aircraft approached the ship on the port side. At the time of the attack the *Empress* was approximately sixty miles off the northwest coast of Ireland. The only armament she carried was one high-angle 3in gun and four Lewis guns. On the first attack a bomb hit the top deck, near the tennis court, where in happier days millionaires and film stars had enjoyed themselves. The bomb penetrated the Mayfair Lounge, setting it on fire, and wrought further damage on 'A', 'B', 'C' and 'D' decks below. The ship filled with black smoke; the lighting, water and communication systems were all put out of action. Consequently, all efforts to get the fire under control were unsuccessful. The whole of the midship section was quickly ablaze. The abandon ship signal was given. SOS signals were sent out and acknowledged; this was probably about thirty minutes after the first attack, and at about this time the aircraft was making its third and last attack, machine-gunning the bridge and scoring a direct bomb hit on the sun deck.

Those lifeboats which were not already on fire were lowered and eventually took off survivors. At four o'clock HMS *Echo* and some trawlers arrived and took on board all the survivors. It was then decided that the stricken vessel could be towed to port and HM tugs *Marauder* and *Thames* took the *Empress* in tow. In the forenoon of 27 October the *Britain* was sighted by *U32*. Under the command of Lieutenant-Commander Jenisch, the German U-boat succeeded in evading detection by the British destroyers, eventually got inside their protecting screen and after dark launched three torpedoes, two of which found their mark. The *Empress* heeled over to port and disappeared quickly under the sea.

The *U32* was attacked and sunk two days later by HMS *Harvester*. Among the survivors who were landed at Greenock as prisoners of war were the commander, Lieutenant-Commander Jenisch, and Lieutenant-Commander Fritz Wentzel, who was also aboard the *U32*. A few days later the crew, except for Commander Jenisch, were taken aboard the *Duchess of York* and travelled to Canada as prisoners of war. The master of the *Duchess* at this time was Captain C. H. Sapsworth, who had been the commander of the *Empress of Britain* when she was sunk. It is unlikely that the captain or the prisoners knew about this strange coincidence at that time.

By another coincidence, toward the end of 1964, Captain Hans Jenisch of the German navy was in England on a course with the Royal Navy at Portsmouth. Before he rejoined NATO staff at Kiel he was persuaded to pay a quick visit to the Trafalgar Square office. He confirmed that the *U32* had left Lorient on her last mission on 24 October 1940. On the following day he received a signal indicating that the Canadian Pacific liner, *Empress of Britain*, had been set on fire. By noon on 27 October, the *U32* had sighted the masts of the liner. By midnight the burning liner was again sighted and later attacked on the target's port beam. Two torpedoes were fired, but the first one was lost because of a malfunction of the fuse. So a third torpedo was then launched at the target. Immediately after the explosion, the escort destroyers and the *Sunderland* flying boat searched for the submarine, but she was able to avoid detection. Two days later on 30 October the *U32* was searching for an eastbound convoy which she did not find, but an independent ship was sighted during the forenoon. Attacking at noon, the submarine experienced another torpedo which malfunctioned. She was then attacked by a British destroyer dropping depth-charges. The second pattern of charges made a hit on the submarine, which was eventually able to surface to find two destroyers waiting. Shortly afterwards the submarine crew abandoned ship, having

opened the valves, and left the submarine with the hatch open to sink. Half an hour later both the destroyers, HMS *Highlander* and HMS *Harvester*, returned to the scene and picked up survivors. Nine of the submarine's crew were missing. The surviving officers and crew spent the rest of the war in Canadian and British prisoner-of-war camps and returned to Germany in 1947.

During her short life the *Empress* had been commanded by five masters, two of them, Captains R. G. Latta and R. N. Stuart VC, DSO, USNC, RD, RNR, later held office as general manager of Canadian Pacific Steamships. Completing the succession were Captains G. R. Parry, W. G. Busk-Wood OBE, and C. H. Sapsworth CVO. During her war service the *Empress* travelled 61,000 miles, carried 2850 tons of cargo, 9231 military personnel and 925 civilian passengers.

Three days after the bomb attack, Sir Edward Beatty, chairman and president of Canadian Pacific, received the following communication from the Governor-General of Canada: 'I have been asked by the King and Queen to convey to you and the Directors of the Canadian Pacific Railway their sincere sympathy in the loss of that fine ship the *Empress of Britain* in which their majesties had such a pleasant voyage from Canada last year.'

Among the many epitaphs printed by the world's great newspapers, that of the 'New York Times' of 29 October 1940 is perhaps the most fitting end to this story:

No ship ever fitted her name more than the *Empress of Britain*. She was, indeed, an empress, with pride and grace and dignity in every inch of her. She had millions of devoted subjects, in many countries, for she was primarily a cruise ship, and she had been seen and admired in more out-of-the-way harbours than any other liner. Her white paint was a coat of ermine that set her apart from the throng. It was always a thrill to see her come in the blue Mediterranean or in more distant ports of call; it was always an event in our own harbor when the great white *Empress* came in.

She had many proud moments in her reign of only a decade, notably when she brought the King and Queen home from Canada. But we suspect that the proudest of all were the months when the *Empress* wore her uniform of grey in wartime service. She carried thousands of troops from the free Dominions to the Old Country; she played her part in keeping England free. She now lies blackened and twisted on the ocean bottom, the largest of all ships that have gone down in this war; but she lived up to the traditions of her flag and to the very end, for the Admiralty has praised 'the resolution and efficient handling' of her anti-aircraft guns in her death struggle. The memory of this fine ship will survive until a new *Empress of Britain* inherits her name.

The name of this great ship was 'inherited' on 22 June 1955, when Her Majesty Queen Elizabeth II launched into the waters of the Clyde her 25,500 ton successor.

As recently as 1977 the *Britain*, in the form of a model, appeared on television in England. In 1934 to celebrate her record crossings, Harry Astley, the ship's chief confectioner, had made the model in sugar, corn starch and gelatine. Prior to the television appearance it had turned up in an antique dealer's shop and was bought by the company. Eventually, it was sent to Canada for display in the Château Frontenac, the Canadian Pacific hotel in Quebec.

Beaverbrae II (1947–54)

The company's second *Beaverbrae* was unusual in several ways. She was the only Beaver to carry passengers westbound and cargo eastbound. The only North Atlantic vessel operated by the company under Canadian registration and manned by a Canadian crew, she had a siren in her bows, audible for several miles over a wide forward arc but which could hardly be heard on board.

The *Beaverbrae* was a single-screw diesel-electric vessel of 9000 tons, 469ft in length and with a beam of 60ft. Built by Blohm & Voss at Hamburg as a cargo liner with accommodation for thirty-two passengers, she was named *Huascaran* after the highest mountain in Peru. Launched on 15 December 1938 for the Hamburg Amerika Line, she sailed on her maiden voyage from Hamburg to the Pacific coast of South America, and on her return was taken over by the German navy and became a submarine depot ship. She spent most of her time in Norway, where she was captured undamaged by the Allies in 1945. Having been taken over by the War Assets Corporation she arrived in Liverpool in April 1947 for a refit. In June she left for Montreal, as part of Canada's war reparations. The Canadian government allocated her to North American Transports Inc for use as a cargo liner and at that time she was the largest ship in the Canadian merchant navy.

In the aftermath of World War II thousands of refugees and displaced persons were stranded in camps across Europe. The Canadian government agreed to accept some of these people. To implement the rehabilitation scheme, Canadian Pacific bought the vessel in September 1947 and had her refitted at Sorel, Quebec, to carry the refugees from Europe. With a crew of 116 she was able to carry seventy-four passengers in cabins on the promenade deck and a further 699 in dormitory space. Canadian Pacific worked with the International Refugee Organisation and the Canadian Christian Council for the Relief of Refugees, which represented the Lutheran and Catholic Church voluntary organisations in Canada. The refugees were forwarded from collection depots on the German frontiers to the dispatching centre in Bremen. Here they were examined by Canadian government officials for health and security. Documentation and embarkation arrangements were handled at the Canadian Pacific office in Bremen. Because of numerous epidemics, ticketing and berthing were often a last-minute rush to ensure the maximum use of available berths.

The *Beaverbrae* made an average of one sailing each month and usually carried between 500 and 700 emigrants, of whom approximately one in five were children. They were destined for friends or relatives in Canada, but few could speak any English. Before the ship arrived at the Canadian port of entry, the purser would issue each passenger with an identification tag, indicating their destination.

When advice was received in Montreal that the *Beaverbrae* had left Bremerhaven, arrangements were made for two special trains with colonist and baggage cars to be assembled at the port of entry. The first train would usually be routed to Montreal and Toronto, and the second to Winnipeg and points west, almost every car destined to a different part of the country. A special three-car unit was attached to each train to feed the refugees. One car was fitted as a kitchen, the second as a dining car by day and a sleeper for the crew at night, the third being used as a dining and recreation car for the passengers. Church services were sometimes held in this car.

Renamed *Beaverbrae* II on 7 February 1948, she sailed from Saint John NB the following day with cargo for London. She left Bremerhaven on her first mission of mercy on 28 February.

When the *Beaverbrae* arrived at Montreal on 29 October 1948, a flaw was discovered in her crankshaft.

The ship of hope—the 9000 ton Beaverbrae *II ex* Huascaran,
*bought to carry displaced persons from Europe to a new life in
Canada between 1948 and 1954*

During November a special 5000lb steel bock, or clamp,
was made in the CPR Angus shops to strengthen the
shaft, until a new shaft could be fitted. The repair was
completed just in time for the ship to leave before the
winter freeze-up. She was in fact the last vessel to leave
Montreal that year.

She was unlucky in 1949 when, owing to a strike of
Canadian seamen, she was detained at the London docks
from 3 April until 26 July, and completed only four round

trips that year. For the next two years she sailed eastbound with cargo for Antwerp instead of London.

The *Beaverbrae* continued to average eight Atlantic
trips a year until 28 July 1954, when she left Bremen with
her last party of migrants. In all she had completed fifty-
two voyages and carried just over 38,000 refugees to
Canada. Burgomaster Kaiser of Bremen, soon after he
was appointed to take over from the Allied military
governor, wrote to Canadian Pacific's Bremen office,

thanking the company for happily rehabilitating many thousands of refugees to Canada.

The *Beaverbrae* was sold on 1 November 1954 to Compagnia Genovese d'Armamento, Genoa, and renamed *Aurelia*. She sailed from Genoa on the Cogedar Line service to South America with a call at Lisbon. On 13 September 1961 she arrived at Southampton to inaugurate a regular service to Australia. In 1970 she was sold to International Cruises SA of Greece and, under the name *Romanza*, is still cruising in the Mediterranean.

Post-war Empresses

After a number of trial specifications had been prepared amid much speculation as to the effect air transport would have on the future of the North Atlantic passenger trade, an order was placed with the Fairfield yard in 1952, for the company's first post-war passenger liner, the *Empress of Britain* III. A sister ship, the *Empress of England* was ordered from the Vickers Armstrong Walker-on-Tyne Tard, in the following year.

The new 25,500 ton *Empresses* were 640ft long with accommodation for 150 first and 900 tourist passengers, and 5000 tons of cargo. The main public rooms were on the promenade deck. The first-class drawing room, children's room, library and Empress room, were followed by the tourist smoking room and lounge, and a cinema used by both classes. A painting of Queen Elizabeth by W. E. Webster was hung in the Empress room on the *Britain*. By dividing the boiler room and engine room casing into two, port and starboard respectively, a vista of some 150ft was created from the forward end of the Empress room to the bulkhead of the cinema, where a mural of Windsor Castle hung. The idea was taken a step further to provide extra width to the central alleyway on the upper deck, through the first-class accommodation. This was later nicknamed 'The Broadway'. There was a sun lounge forward on the boat deck, the restaurants were on 'C' deck and there was a swimming pool on 'D' deck. Other post-war innovations included Denny Brown stabilisers and washing machines with drying and ironing rooms for the passengers. The *Empress of Britain* was the first British passenger liner to be fully air conditioned, including the crew quarters.

The double-reduction geared turbines, developing 30,000shp, were fitted with a reheat system between the high-pressure and intermediate turbines. Electrical power was provided by two 1200kw turbo-generators

and two 500kw diesel generators. The twin screws were four-bladed, 18ft in diameter, and weighed eighteen tons each.

Empress of Britain III (1956–64)

The Fairfield Company had built the first *Empress of Britain* fifty years earlier and it asked for the names of any of its staff who had worked on the earlier Empress. Fearing to give away their age, very few responded, but when it became known that they were to receive gold watches the list soon swelled to eighty.

The company's third *Empress of Britain* was launched by HM the Queen on 22 June 1955. When moving down the Clyde for her trials on 8 March 1956, she was caught by a squall and swung broadside against the quay wall of the King George V Dock and the stern of the tanker *British Sportsman*. Fortunately the damage was only very slight. The *Britain* sailed on her maiden voyage from Liverpool on 20 April 1956 under the command of Captain S. Keay.

The name *Empress of Britain* was commemorated by British Rail on 12 May 1960, when N. R. Crump, president of Canadian Pacific, named a new 2000hp diesel electric locomotive 'Empress of Britain' at Euston Station, London. The engine name-plate included a replica of a ship's wheel and the red-and-white house flag. This was the second occasion that Canadian Pacific had been commemorated by a British Rail locomotive. On 27 March 1942 a Southern Railway merchant navy class 4-6-2 steam locomotive had been named 'Canadian Pacific'. This recognised the importance of the special boat trains which were operated by the London, Midland and Southern Regions of British Railways between London, Liverpool and Southampton to carry passengers to and from the ports during the passenger liner era.

The *Britain* made her first cruise on 18 January 1960, from New York to the West Indies, and her first cruise from Liverpool on 13 February 1962.

During the early May 1963 westbound voyage an elderly lady passenger became ill and required treatment necessitating frequent transfusions of a particular kind of blood. It became clear that further supplies of blood plasma were urgently required and so a signal was sent to the coast guard stationed in Argentia, Newfoundland. It was established that supplies were available and the ship was asked to give her position, course, speed and weather and if an air drop after daylight, 5 May, would

Sir Anthony and Lady Eden returning from Canada

be acceptable. A message from the ship accepted the offer and so an RCAF rescue plane made the rendezvous and a successful drop at 06.07 hours on 5 May close to the vessel. The ship's number 9 motorboat was lowered at 06.08 and the vital blood plasma was recovered at 06.14 hours. The *Empress of Britain* proceeded full ahead at 06.18 hours.

By the early 1960s air travel was seriously affecting the summer season traffic on the North Atlantic and on 10 October 1963 the *Britain* arrived at Liverpool on completion of her 123rd and last Atlantic crossing for the company, only seven years after her maiden voyage. On 23 October she was chartered to the Travel Savings Association for cruising. She returned to Liverpool in 1964 and was sold to the Greek Line in November.

After an extensive overhaul she had the distinction of being named for a second time by a reigning monarch. At a ceremony in Piraeus attended by King Constantine, the prime minister of Greece, and more than 200 guests, Mr John Goulandris of the Greek Line formally requested the Queen of Greece to name the ship by unveiling a memorial plaque in the vessel's new Orpheus Room. As the *Queen Anna Maria*, she made her first voyage on 19 March under the Greek flag from Piraeus to Haifa, to start her fortnightly service to New York via Piraeus, Naples and Lisbon. She was also used for cruising by the Greek Line and continued in its service until 22 January 1975 when she was laid-up in Piraeus. In November she was bought by the Carnival Cruise Line and after an overhaul renamed *Carnivale* to join the

Mardi Gras (ex-*Empress of Canada*) cruising from Miami to the West Indies.

Empress of England (1957–70)

The promised sister ship was ordered from the Vickers Armstrong Company on 9 March 1954. The first three Empresses had been built at the Barrow yard of this company in 1890, and in 1927 it had built the *Beaverbrae* and *Beaverdale* at its Naval Yard, Walker-on-Tyne.

She was launched on 9 May 1956, and named *Empress of England* by Lady Eden (wife of the prime minister), but because of a strike in the builder's yard she was taken over and her trials, carried out by CP Steamships officers under the direction of Vickers personnel. Her maiden voyage began from Liverpool on 18 April 1957; in August she made record crossings, eastbound in four days, fifteen hours and westbound four days, fifteen hours and thirty minutes.

The *England* made her first cruise on 15 January 1958, from New York to the West Indies; in March 1962 she was chartered by the College of General Practice of Canada for an eight-day cruise to Bermuda and Nassau, possibly the first medical convention held on the high seas. After cruising for the Travel Savings Association in 1963, she returned to the North Atlantic in April 1964 and continued in the company's service until 28 November 1969, when she arrived in Liverpool after her 149th North-Atlantic run. During this period she also made four or five Canadian Pacific cruises out of Liverpool each winter, mostly to the Canary Isles, but also one longer cruise each winter to the West Indies. Her 60th and last cruise left Liverpool on 26 March 1970, and on 3 April she was sold to Shaw Savill, who renamed her *Ocean Monarch*. She joined the *Northern Star* on their round-the-world service and was also used for cruising.

In September 1970 she entered the Cammell Laird yard for a lengthy overhaul and conversion to a one class ship, with new cabins being built into part of her original cargo holds, bringing her accommodation to about 1400. Withdrawn from service in June 1975, she was sold for scrap and broken up at Kachsiung, Taiwan.

Empress of Canada III (1961–71): The Last Passenger Liner

Negotiations had begun in July 1957, and in January 1958 an order was placed with Vickers Armstrong for a third liner to join the *Empress of Britain* and *Empress of England*. The keel was laid at the Naval Yard on 27 January 1959, on the berth on which the *Empress of England* had been built four years previously. The new *Empress* was 650ft in length and 86ft in breadth, with a clipper bow and cruiser stern. She was fitted with a bulbous bow to reduce pitching, and stabilisers to reduce roll. The *Empress* was the largest passenger liner to be built on the Tyne since the 32,000 ton *Mauretania* in 1907.

On Tuesday 10 May 1960, Mrs J. G. Diefenbaker, wife of the Canadian prime minister, launched the 25,600 ton *Empress of Canada* III. A bottle of Canadian white wine was used for the ceremony and after the launch Mrs Diefenbaker was presented with a diamond brooch in the form of a spray of seven leaves.

Accommodation was provided for 192 first-class passengers on the Empress Deck and upper deck, including four blocks of suite rooms plus six verandah suites. Tourist rooms for 856 passengers were situated on the upper, main and restaurant decks, more than half being two-berth rooms. The machinery consisted of two sets of double-reduction geared turbines fed with steam at 850°F at a pressure of 590lb per square inch, with reheat between the high- and intermediate-pressure turbines, driving twin screws. Electrical power was supplied by two 1500kw turbo-generators and three 500kw diesel generators (sufficient to supply a town of 14,000 people). There were over 100 electric motors on board, totalling more than 4000hp. The main laundry could handle 10,000 pieces of linen each day and in addition there was a fully equipped launderette for the passengers. On her trials the *Empress* achieved twenty-three knots over the 'Arran mile', two more than her designed speed.

As late as the 1890s it was common for ships to carry live cows and hens to supply milk and eggs. The *Canada* had 26,000 cubic feet of insulated storage space and carried about 25,000lb of meat, 3000 gallons of fresh milk, six tons of flour, twelve tons of potatoes, nine tons of vegetables, 5000 oysters and many other items needed for the preparation of the 5000 meals that were served each day. She was also equipped to produce 70,000 gallons of fresh water each day.

Marconi radio telephone equipment enabled passengers to talk to any part of the world, privacy being ensured by speech invertors. Radar-track indicator equipment enabled the navigating officer to see the course and speed of each vessel on display. Two of the motor lifeboats also carried radio equipment.

The last passenger liner built for Canadian Pacific, the 27,000 ton Empress of Canada *III, passing the CP hotel Chateau Frontenac*

Patrick McBride and Paul Gell were responsible for the interior design, and an endeavour was made by the use of colour and decoration to capture the inanimate spirit of Canada in five of the public rooms, whilst the remainder provided an English atmosphere. The St Lawrence Club on the upper deck featured two murals by H. Cronyn, one with the brig *Jean* sailing up river in the early days and the other showing the commercial development that had taken place along the riverbanks. There were also three paintings of old sailing ships by Gordon Ellis. A carpet in deep blue-grey added to the river atmosphere, and coats of arms of French families associated with the river were used to decorate the wall behind the bar. The Canada Room, on the Empress Deck, had a dome 20ft above the dance floor, decorated with the moon and stars. A balcony ran round three sides of the room. Pale willow-wood panels were contrasted with dark-green curtains. The carpet, which was specially woven, had a golden background and incorporated the ten flower-emblems of Canada: the rose for Alberta, dogwood for

British Columbia, crocus for Manitoba, violet for New Brunswick, pitcher plant for Ontario, lady's-slipper for Prince Edward Island, iris for Quebec and the lily for Saskatchewan. To add to the floral effect, Canadian leaf motifs were etched on glass screens designed by Nan Elsan. The dance floor was made from maple, birch and mahogany.

The Banff Club had timbered walls and ceiling; behind the bar a carved mural, designed by Gertrude Hermes, depicted totem-pole motifs and animals of the West. A specially treated rawhide, burned with famous cattle brands, covered the entire front of the bar. When cruising, folding glass screens opened on to the deck area where a glass-fibre swimming pool was let into a cargo hatch. The first-class restaurant, Salle Frontenac, was named after the first Governor of Quebec. Figured sycamore and rosewood panels, with carpets and curtains in blue and gold with fleur-de-lis motifs, reflected the Comte de Frontenac period.

The Carleton Restaurant (tourist class) was named

197

after Sir Guy Carleton, the first Governor-General
of Upper Canada. Two large panoramic murals, by
Edward Bawden, portrayed the transition period from
French to English in Upper Canada. The Mayfair
Lounge was decorated with madrone wood panelling and
ice-blue curtains. One wall featured a large bough of
may-blossom designed by Sir Kenneth Clarke and was
executed in metal. The Windsor Lounge was given an
English atmosphere by paintings of English scenes
associated with the name of Windsor. The Coral Pool
was illuminated, under water, from both sides, and the
surrounding walls covered with mosaics depicting coral
and exotic fish.

The *Empress*, under the command of Captain J. P.
Dobson CBE, sailed from Liverpool on her maiden
voyage on 24 April 1961. She made regular crossings to
Montreal in summer and cruised each winter. She sailed
on her first cruise on 21 December 1961 from New York,
and made three cruises to the West Indies and one to the
Mediterranean. New York continued as her base for
cruises until 1969, except for two cruises to the West
Indies from Liverpool and Southampton in December
and January 1962–3. In 1969, twelve winter cruises out
of New York extended the season into May and she also
made four cruises from the United Kingdom during the
summer of that year, Atlantic crossings being reduced to
seven. On 5 April 1970 the *Canada* left New York for
a short cruise to Montreal, which included a trip up the
Saguenay River to Ha Ha Bay. She was the second largest
ship to sail the Saguenay and passed the steep rock cliffs
of Cape Trinity and Cape Eternity on the way to Port
Alfred and Chicoutimi. At Port Alfred, she was presented
with the flag of the 'Kingdom of Saguenay'.

When the *Canada* entered dry dock for her annual
overhaul at the beginning of November 1968, her funnel
was painted green and the new corporate symbol added;
a green band was also painted round her hull. Arriving
at Montreal on 26 August 1970, 1026 passengers disembarked, her longest ever passenger list.

On 23 November 1971 the *Empress of Canada* arrived
at Liverpool on her last voyage under the Canadian
Pacific flag. She had completed 121 North Atlantic
voyages and eighty-two cruises for the company, thus
ending seventy-eight years of Empress tradition and
sixty-nine years of passenger service on the North Atlantic. On 18 February 1972 she was handed over to her new

The Carleton restaurant on the Empress of Canada

A first-class suite on the Empress of Canada *III*

owners, Carnival Cruise Line, and renamed *Mardi Gras*. In 1975 she was joined by the *Empress of Britain*, which had been renamed *Carnivale*. Both liners still cruise out of Miami.

Adrian Waller of the 'Gazette', wrote under a banner headline on 18 November 1971:

LAST OF THE EMPRESSES SAILS INTO HISTORY

With her head high and a last defiant blast of her horn, the 26,000 ton *Empress of Canada* sailed into history yesterday.

She left Montreal at 7.30am, Liverpool bound with her crew's band playing and singing 'Now is the hour'. And hardly anyone waved goodbye.

Only 20 people stood at Pier Eight to see the flag-decked *Empress of Canada* eased into the St Lawrence River by two tugs. Three were CP officials, the remainder were friends of the mere 300 passengers on board the vessel, which has accommodation for more than 1000.

3 BC Coastal Steamships

The John Brown yard at Clydebank received an order in 1923 for two new passenger ferries for the British Columbia coastal service. For a cross-channel service these two sisters were very luxurious; with a length of 352ft and a gross tonnage of 5875, they were licensed for 1500 day passengers. Sixteen of their 147 first-class state rooms had their own bathrooms. The smoking rooms were decorated with Indian carvings. Their spacious dining rooms could seat 170 passengers.

Both vessels exceeded twenty-two knots on their trials and were able to maintain their tight schedule on the 'triangle' service, Vancouver–Victoria–Seattle, with ease. Although designed to carry thirty automobiles, this proved quite inadequate to meet the rapidly growing demand for this type of service.

The intensity with which this ferry service was operated in the days before the war, before the mass use of the motorcar and before the airliner had been accepted by the general traveller, may best be illustrated by an example. In an eleven-month period the *Princess Marguerite* maintained a continuous day and night service, apart from three days in dry dock, from 14 May 1938 until 13 April 1939, steaming 81,144 miles. Her longest period in port each day was two and a half hours! The *Princess Kathleen* sailed in the opposite direction from 16 March 1938 until 10 February 1939, apart from three days' break in dry dock.

The British Ministry of Shipping began negotiating for these two ships towards the end of 1941, and on 7 November of that year the two Princesses had been supplied with armament, strengthened for deep-sea service and sailed for Honolulu. It was intended that they should maintain an average speed of fifteen knots, but fog and southwesterly gales with squalls of hurricane force made the two little ships roll and pitch heavily; their

speed was considerably reduced. Better weather prevailed for their journey from Honolulu to Darwin via Fiji. The two ships left Darwin on 8 December; owing to the international date line it was still 7 December in Honolulu, the day the Japanese air force made its surprise attack on the USA. The Princesses heard about the attack in a wireless message and made for Java where they took on stores and fuel. For twelve days they played hide-and-seek with the Japanese fleet around the Netherlands East Indies. They then received orders to proceed to Colombo, Ceylon, and arrived on New Year's morning 1942.

Except for key ratings in deck, engine room and catering services, and the officers, the crews had come from a seamen's pool. By a stroke of good luck the *Empress of Russia* was also in Colombo and was paying off a Chinese crew. As there had been some trouble with some sections of the scratch crews, which had come to a head at Colombo, the two captains were able to recruit trusted Chinese ratings who had been with the company for many years—in the case of Saloon Number One Boy Chan For Sui, fifty-one years, later attested by the award of the OBE. Years later Captain L. C. Barry of the *Princess Kathleen* confided that for the first time in weeks the deck and engine-room officers had slept without clubs under their pillows.

Princess Marguerite (1925–42)

The Honourable Marguerite Shaughnessy, daughter of the former chairman of Canadian Pacific Railway, named the *Marguerite* on 29 November 1924, and on 25 March in the following year she sailed from the Clyde to Victoria by way of the Panama Canal, arriving on 20 April 1925. Then followed years of ferrying backwards and forwards

The 6000 ton Princess Marguerite *ii, taken over by the B C government in 1974*

across the Straits from the beginning of May to the end of September. During the winter when the frequency of the triangle service was reduced, some journeys would be made along the coast.

When King George VI and Queen Elizabeth toured Canada in 1939, they crossed from Vancouver to Victoria in the *Princess*.

When the *Princess Marguerite* arrived at Port Said on 18 January 1942, she was 'on station' for the start of her war service. However, there was great consternation when naval staff officers found out that these two speedy ships, in which they had planned to ship aviation fuel to Tobruk, were quite unsuited for that task, although ideal for trooping. The troop capacity of the *Marguerite* was approximately 800 but as Captain Leicester remarked in one of his reports: 'As appears usual with the Embarkation authorities, when they find that 800 men have been carried effectively, they are inclined to put 900 aboard on the following occasion, and then 1000 and so on. There is no saying what the "ceiling" is going to be.' There is no record of the number of individual voyages made, but Captain Leicester recalled later that they were continuously on the move, eight hours' steaming being followed by a quick turn-round with four hours in port, day after day.

The morning of 17 August 1942, just seven months after her arrival from Canada, was fine and clear when she embarked troops. Escorted by three destroyers and the armed merchant cruiser *Antwerp*, some of the troops were lulled into a false sense of security, with the result that many kept their heavy army boots on with, in some cases, disastrous results when they had eventually to take to the water. After leaving Port Said they made for Cyprus. All went well until 15.07 when a heavy explosion took place, shaking the ship violently from stem to stern, followed by the roar of escaping steam. The *Princess Marguerite* had been hit on the port side by a torpedo from *U83*. Fire spread rapidly from fore and aft and the order to abandon ship was given. Confidential books and papers were placed in weighted bags and thrown overside. To make matters more difficult, fuel oil spread on the water along the port side of the ship. This caught fire and it made a considerable blaze stretching the length of the ship. The ship was completely abandoned by 15.45 and sank by 15.56.

Although ten of the sixteen lifeboats and a number of floats had been lowered to the water, most of the men had to jump for it. Because of this it was impossible for HMS *Hero* to come alongside, because of the risk of crushing men between the two ships. In fact ninety-five per cent of the military and ninety-six per cent of the crew were saved.

Captain Leicester, after his ship had gone and he had assured himself that boats and rafts were taking care of survivors, asked a man holding on to the same raft as himself if he could swim, and they agreed to swim together towards the *Hero*. When the British soldier learned that the captain was a Canadian he inquired about Canada as a place to live. Captain Leicester gave him the fullest possible information during their swim.

A tragi-comedy took place when one of the Chinese crew, covered in oil and looking very bedraggled generally, had laboriously climbed nearly to the top of the net hung on the side of the *Hero*. A naval rating reached over to help him, grabbed at his belt to yank him over the side; the belt broke and he let the pieces fall as he grabbed the man under the arm. Without a single word but with what might have been a rueful look, he simply stood at the rail and watched the pieces of his belt slowly sink. They contained every dollar he had saved since he had left Hong Kong.

The British survivors were taken from Suez to Durban on the liner *Oronsay*. At Durban they transferred to the *Duchess of Atholl* for the journey home, only to be torpedoed and shipwrecked all over again on 10 October 1942. The Canadian survivors were taken to New York and went on to their homes in British Columbia from Montreal.

Princess Kathleen (1925–52)

Lady Mount Stephen, wife of the first president of Canadian Pacific Railway, launched the *Princess Kathleen* on 27 September 1924, and on 15 January 1925 she sailed from the Clyde to Panama and Vancouver, where she joined the famous triangle service.

The *Princess Kathleen* arrived on station in the Eastern Mediterranean on 24 January 1942. Her many journeys along the North African coast varied in length with the advance and retreat of the armies in the desert. In May 1942 the *Princess Kathleen* carried a thousand Italian prisoners of war from Masawa in Ethiopia to Port Sudan.

In June 1942 the evacuation of Egypt appeared to be a possibility because of the big advance by Rommel. The *Kathleen* was the last ship to leave Alexandria on 30 June. She carried 232 officers and ratings of the Women's Royal Naval Auxiliary, the Wrens. At Suez on 2 July, a number of civilian women and children were embarked

for transit to the South. By the end of 1942 the British were again advancing in the desert and on New Year's Day 1943 the *Princess Kathleen* arrived at Tobruk. On 18 February 1943 she was carrying troops to Tripoli. From Tripoli she made her first trip to the heroic island of Malta. Captain Barry recalled one of the brighter moments of the war: 'We had a grandstand view of the battleships *Italia*, *Vittorio Veneto*, four cruisers and four destroyers coming in like a flock of sheep herded by sheep dogs into the fold' (Alexandria harbour, 16 September 1943).

Later that year the Emir Mansour, son of Ibn Saud, and his entourage were to be entertained for two weeks in Suez. Special carpets were taken on board the *Princess Kathleen* for the Emir's quarters, and they also had to carry livestock to be killed in accordance with custom. After their stay, they returned to Djeddah. The Emir had thought to send the ship a gift of fifty live sheep. Fortunately they were able to get this changed to bags of rice, which were much more acceptable.

On 10 October 1943, Captain Barry and his Canadian crew left the *Princess Kathleen* for Canada. During the time the vessel had been at war she had made 131 voyages and travelled 67,000 miles and carried more than 59,800 personnel.

Captain Johnston, from the *Empress of Asia*, was the next master of the *Princess Kathleen*. He was in command for a year and ten months. During this time at least thirty-seven different voyages were made to many parts of the Mediterranean. The *Princess Kathleen* had the distinction of being the first troopship to reach Greece, and two days after VE-Day she was the first vessel to reach Rhodes where they took aboard as prisoners of war the German commander General Wagner and his staff. By the time her duties in the Mediterranean ended she had steamed more than a quarter of a million miles and her masters had been decorated: Captain L. C. Barry MBE, Captain L. H. Johnston OBE and Captain R. A. Leicester OBE. Battered and war-weary, with her interior fittings torn out and her deck warped, the *Princess Kathleen* returned to Vancouver for a major reconversion.

The smoking room was moved from the after end of the promenade deck and relocated above the forward observation room, which itself was refurnished to provide 200 seats with an uninterrupted view of the passing scenery. A mosaic in natural wood colours, of Lake Bennett in Alaska, was hung on the after bulkhead. A new structure on the boat deck doubled as a coffee bar on

The 42,000 ton Empress of Britain *passing the CP hotel Chateau Frontenac*

the tri-city run and a ballroom on the Alaska run. The dining saloon, seating 176, was decorated with a large mural of the Yukon River. A plaque commemorating the *Kathleen*'s round-the-world war service and inscribed with her major ports-of-call hung in the forward saloon. Eight deluxe rooms had twin beds which folded away to provide spacious day rooms. Fourteen semi-deluxe rooms were fitted with upper and lower berths which could be replaced by a settee for day use.

Trials after her conversion proved her engines to be as good as ever and she re-entered the Vancouver–Victoria–Seattle service on 22 June 1947, transferring to the Alaska run in June 1949.

On 30 August 1951 she was rammed by the *Prince Rupert*, and after all the passengers had been transferred, both ships made port where extensive repairs were carried out. On 7 September 1952, still dogged by bad luck, the *Princess Kathleen* ran aground on Lena Point. All the passengers were saved but as the tide fell the *Princess* slipped from the rocks and sank stern-first, rolling on to her port side as she went down. Divers have since reported that she now rests on a steep slope just west of Lena Point.

Part Three  Appendices

1 Allan Line

Alexander Allan was born in 1780, and went to sea at an early age. During the Peninsular War he commanded a store ship and later became part-owner of the brig *Jean*, a two-masted sailing ship 76ft in length. Probably because of his wartime trading, he adopted the French tricolour, but later reversed the colours.

The 'Glasgow Herald' for 11 June 1819 announced that the *Jean* had sailed for Quebec. In his first season he made two trips and in later years averaged three round trips during the summer season. Most ships at this time would sail as and when inducement offered, but Allan soon realised that the trade would be developed by regular sailings. By 1825 he had added a second ship, the *Favorite*, built in Montreal. On her first voyage to Montreal, Alexander's second son Hugh was aboard as a passenger, whilst his third son Bryce was also aboard learning to become a master mariner. Hugh settled in Canada and was later to set up the family business in Montreal.

In 1853 the Allan Line ordered its first iron-screw ship, the *Canadian*. She made her maiden voyage to Quebec in the following year. Her service was interrupted by the

A model of Andrew Allan's 76ft Jean. *The* Jean *made her first crossing from the Clyde to Montreal in 1819*

demands of the Crimean War, although such service could often prove profitable to shipowners.

By 1851 Nova Scotia, New Brunswick and the United Provinces had been granted control of their own postal services by the British government, and Canada had her first postmaster-general. Several abortive attempts were made by inexperienced companies with scratch fleets to secure the mail contract. The Allan Line, with a fleet of four specially built ships, the *Anglo Saxon*, *Canadian*, *Indian* and *North American*, secured a contract in 1856 for a fortnightly service from Liverpool to Quebec between April and October, and a monthly sailing to Portland, Maine, during the winter. At this time Portland was linked to Montreal by the Atlantic & St Lawrence Railway, whilst Halifax and Saint John were without a rail service. Over the next few years the Allan Line lost a number of ships on this treacherous route and it was only the perseverance of Hugh Allan that ensured the company's survival and eventually persuaded the government to improve the navigational facilities in the Gulf.

A regular steamship service from Glasgow to Montreal was added in 1861. Because of the large Irish emigration to North America, Moville, Co Donegal, became an important call. Queenstown, later Cobh, also appeared on sailing schedules by 1871.

Despite being unable to provide the twenty-knot service to Canada, the Allan Line had always been willing to pioneer. In 1880 it placed the first steel ship on the North Atlantic, the *Buenos Ayrean*, and in 1905 it was first with turbine engines in the *Victorian* and *Virginian*. When the CPR started its Empress service on the Pacific in 1891, the Allan Line was operating the following services to Canada:

Liverpool to Quebec and Montreal	weekly
Liverpool to St Johns NF and Halifax	fortnightly
Glasgow to Quebec and Montreal	weekly
London to Quebec and Montreal	fortnightly

The line also started a service from Glasgow to New York in that year.

The Allan Family

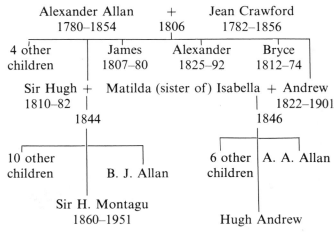

Notes

1 Alexander Allan founder of the Allan Line of sailing ships 1819.
2 James and Alexander founded J. & A. Allan, Glasgow, 1846.
3 Bryce founded the Liverpool office 1853.
4 The five brothers and others founded the Montreal Ocean Steamship Company in 1854.
5 Hugh and Andrew founded H. & A. Allan of Montreal 1860.
6 Sir Hugh Allan promoted the first Company to build the transcontinental railway in 1873, but before work began he became involved in a political scandal and the scheme was abandoned.
7 Allan Line Steamship Company, incorporated 1897, Andrew Allan, chairman.
8 Andrew Allan died 1901, the business was inherited by: Sir H. Montagu, B. J., Hugh Andrew and A. A. Allan.
9 Sir Hugh Allan, knighted 1871.
10 Sir H. Montagu Allan, knighted 1904.

For the story of the Allan family see *Ravenscrag: The Allan Royal Mail Line* by Thomas E. Appleton, published by McClelland & Stewart Ltd.

2 Beaver Line

In 1867 a number of Montreal merchants formed the Canada Shipping Company to trade from the St Lawrence to Liverpool, and in the following year they ordered four iron sailing ships from the Clyde, purchased a fifth, and named them after the Great Lakes. They chose a beaver on a white background with a blue surround as their house flag. Steamships, still with the prefix *Lake*, replaced sail in 1875. The first was the *Lake Champlain*, whilst the *Lake Ontario*, built by Laing of Sunderland in 1887, was the first British passenger ship on the North

Atlantic to be fitted with triple-expansion engines, and the last ship to be built for the original Beaver Line.

The Canada Shipping Company ran into serious financial difficulties in 1894 and Messrs D. & C. MacIver were appointed to act as managers. MacIvers' also acquired additional vessels which they operated under the name of Beaver Line Associated Steamers until they,

too, went into voluntary liquidation in 1900.

The Elder Dempster Company had entered the North Atlantic trade during the early 1890s. They took over the Dominion Lines's Avonmouth service in 1894, and in 1898 bought the original Beaver Line ships and ran them from Liverpool under the name Elder Dempster (Beaver Line). The line prospered and new tonnage was added.

3   Canadian Australasian Line

The Union Steamship Company of New Zealand had operated a joint service with the Oceanic Steamship Co, linking Australia and New Zealand to San Francisco in 1885. They were forced out of the business in 1900, when the Hawaiian Islands were annexed by the USA, who reserved the rights of the steamship trade to American-owned vessels. Canadian Pacific had always been interested in such a service. Writing to Harry Moody, CPR London, on 8 September 1885, Van Horne said:

If the same subsidy that has been paid to the Pacific Mail Co [to San Francisco] can be secured for a Line to Vancouver, the Canadian Government participating equitably, this Company will take immediate steps toward securing the necessary steamships.

It may be that the Line would have to be formed under the auspices of an independent company but I am strongly in favour, if it can be done, of having its control in the hands of Canadian Pacific.

And writing to George Stephen in London, 28 September 1885:

I have cabled you to see Mr Pearce of John Elder & Co about the South Sea business. He has been negotiating with the New Zealand Government. We will have Mr Pearce's opposition in any scheme that does not take care of his two boats.

Unfortunately Canadian Pacific was too late to clinch a deal, New Zealand continuing with the service to San Francisco, whilst Australia continued via Suez. The Canadian route was ridiculed in the Australian press and of course the P&O and the Pacific Mail companies were also in opposition. Van Horne wrote to Macdonald on 28 September 1885 that: 'It is certain there is not at present room for two steamship Lines from the West

coast of America to Australasia with all the subsidies that can be obtained. Only one line can live and we should have that one.'

James Huddart bought two new steamships from the Swan Hunter Company, the *Miowera* and *Warrimoo*, in 1891 and operated them between New Zealand and Australia in competition with the Union Steamship Company; this resulted in a disastrous rate-war and Huddart was forced to withdraw. He then turned his attention to the Canadian–Australian route and succeeded in obtaining a mail contract from New South Wales and Canada. He formed a new company, the Canadian Australian Line, in 1893. The term the 'all red route' now became significant.

James Huddart needed a partner to handle through-traffic from Vancouver to the United Kingdom. Canadian Pacific was in just that position to provide all the necessary facilities, since it was already operating its own service on the North Pacific, Vancouver to Hong Kong. Although the CPR did not yet have its own service on the Atlantic, it did have close arrangements with several Atlantic lines. When Huddart approached the CPR an agreement was quickly reached. A preliminary agreement dated 3 May 1893 enabled the *Miowera* to sail from Sydney on 18 May, whilst the final ten-year agreement dated 14 August 1893 affirmed that the CPR would represent the steamship line in all parts of the world except Australia and the Hawaiian Islands, where Huddart would act for the CPR. It also provided for a third vessel to be brought into the service at a later date. The *Miowera* arrived at Victoria on 8 June 1893 and was given a tremendous welcome. Canada was indeed on a 'highway'.

By 1897 a third vessel had become a necessity and a new company, the Canadian Australian Royal Mail Steamship Company, was incorporated in London by

Huddart and the New Zealand Shipping Company to buy the first *Aorangi*, built in 1883 by the John Elder Company. At this time Huddart undoubtedly believed that there would be a new fast service on the Atlantic (see page 20). Traffic did not reach expectations, however. Coupled with the cost of refitting the *Aorangi*, Huddart found himself in financial difficulties in 1898, and the New Zealand Shipping Company took over and maintained the service. The Union Steamship Company, which had been forced out of the San Francisco service in 1900, later purchased the three ships and became the owner of the line. Huddart died in 1901. An article in 'Sea Breezes', 'A Link of Commonwealth', described Huddart as 'a stout Imperialist who ruined himself and drove himself to a premature grave through following a loyal ideal'.

At this time the CPR was more concerned with its efforts to organise a satisfactory Atlantic service and made no attempt to enter the South Pacific service. The *Aorangi* made the first sailing for the Union Steamship Company's service on 3 April 1901. The *Miowera* was also retained but the *Warrimoo* was replaced by a faster ship, the *Moana*. By 1902 Suva was placed on the regular schedule, where a connection could be made to New Zealand. By 1911 Auckland was a regular port of call; the service was now Sydney, Auckland, Suva and Honolulu to Victoria and Vancouver, and the name was changed to Canadian Australasian Royal Mail Line.

In 1913 the Union Company placed a new triple-screw ship on the service. As a gesture to Canada they had asked Mrs Borden, wife of the Canadian prime minister, to name the vessel *Niagara* when she was launched from the John Brown yard (see page 153). In 1925 the second *Aorangi* was placed in service, the largest and fastest motor liner at that time (see page 156).

The world slump which followed World War I caused difficulties for all shipping companies and the Canada-to-Australia service also found itself in competition with the Matson Line, which was able to secure a much larger mail contract from the American government in addition to loans to build new vessels. On 2 July 1931 it was announced that the CPR with the Union Company had jointly formed a new company incorporated in Ottawa, the Canadian Australasian Line, to purchase and operate the two ships *Aorangi* and *Niagara* on a fifty-fifty basis.

The 'Journal of Commerce' of 6 August 1931 said:

... the agreement now reached should consolidate and strengthen the position of the line....

According to a New Zealand message the agreement has been reached as a reply to the extension of the activities of the United States Matson Line, which is building new tonnage for its service from San Francisco. Recently dockers at Auckland protested against unfair operating conditions, whereby the Matson Line were able to carry passengers between Sydney and Auckland although the Union Steamship Company were prohibited from so doing between Honolulu and San Francisco.

The sea voyage took twenty-three days, and a ship would leave Auckland and Vancouver every twenty-eight days.

The problems of ageing ships, competition and poor mail contracts remained. Another of the problems with the Australian and New Zealand subsidies had always been the fact that a service to both countries meant that one or other had an indirect service which was therefore slower than it need have been. Although it had been known for some years that the only hope for survival would be new and faster ships, it was not until 1938 that a glimmer of hope appeared. Sir Edward Beatty arrived in England on 14 July with the hope of placing orders for five new liners, a sister ship for the *Empress of Britain* and replacements for the *Empress of Asia*, *Empress of Russia*, *Aorangi* and *Niagara*; but on 22 July a statement was issued: 'Shipbuilding prices have reached an uneconomical peak and construction of ships is impracticable for the present.' The outbreak of war in the following year ended the matter.

The *Niagara* was lost by enemy action, but the *Aorangi* survived and resumed the service from Sydney on 19 August 1948. It soon became apparent that the service was losing money. There were many discussions between the governments concerned and subsidies were continued on an annual basis until 1953 when the service was finally withdrawn. The company was dissolved on 28 November 1955.

Canadian Pacific Airlines started a service from Vancouver to Sydney via Honolulu and Fiji in 1949, which was extended to Auckland, New Zealand, in 1951.

4 CP lifeboats

Making an appeal on behalf of the Royal National Lifeboat Institute at a meeting in Edinburgh on 21 November 1928, the Prince of Wales mentioned that he had recently heard from his friend Mr Beatty, president of Canadian Pacific, that his company would be pleased to give a modern lifeboat to the institute. The boat was built by S. E. Saunders Ltd of Cowes, and in June 1929 it was shown to Members of Parliament at the Speaker's steps and later proceeded to Richmond, Twickenham and Kingston. The lifeboat arrived at Selsey, Sussex, in the last week in June.

The Selsey station had been established in 1861, for the protection of the crews of vessels which stranded on the Ower's Banks and other shoals in the neighbourhood of Selsey Bill.

During her eight years on station *Canadian Pacific* was launched thirty-five times on service and rescued thirty lives. Unfortunately, in 1937, whilst undergoing an overhaul at Cowes, the vessel was destroyed by fire.

A second lifeboat, built by A. Robertson & Sons of Glasgow, went on station from 1938 until 1969. She was 46ft long and divided into nine watertight compartments. Two 40hp engines gave her a speed of eight knots and the capability of carrying ninety-five people in rough weather. On 31 May 1939, 'The Times' reported:

The Duchess of Norfolk, accompanied by the Duke of Norfolk, yesterday named the new Selsey lifeboat, which was afterwards launched fully manned. The boat, which is of the latest cabin type, has been provided from a gift of the Canadian Pacific Steamship Company, and was named *Canadian Pacific*.

It was dedicated by the Bishop of Chichester (Dr Bell) and Sir Godfrey Baring, Chairman of the RNLI, formally presented it to the Selsey branch.

During her thirty years she made 286 service launches and rescued 157 lives. This included fifty launches to rescue five lives during World War II.

Between 1969 and 1976 the vessel was in the Relief Fleet and served for short periods at various stations. During 1977 she was used for fund-raising activities on the River Thames, visiting many towns including Windsor, Maidenhead, Henley, Pangbourne and Reading. On 9 June 1977 she was one of three lifeboats in the Jubilee Pageant on the river. She made her last public appearance at Poole Lifeboat Day on 23 July 1977. In March 1978 she was sold to the Scrabster Harbour Trust, Thurso, Caithness—the northernmost port on the UK mainland. The harbourmaster, Captain I. McMillan, required a boat of exceptional sea-keeping qualities for use in the Pentland Firth to service the trawling fleet, for the boarding and landing of North Sea pilots from large ships, supplying stores and maintenance, attending to injured and sick crew-men and offering a pilotage service at Scrabster. Captain McMillan hopes for many years of service from the lifeboat.

The RNLB Canadian Pacific *on the Selsey station*

5 Early airmail

Early attempts were made in 1927 to collect mails off steamers at Rimouski or Father Point and fly them to Montreal. The *Empress of France* left Southampton on 3 September 1927 and mails were duly transferred at Rimouski; unfortunately the aircraft had an accident whilst trying to take off. The *Empress of Scotland*, which sailed from Southampton on 17 September, did not arrive at Rimouski until 19.30 hours on the twenty-third, when it was judged to be too late to permit a flight to Montreal. The mails were sent by rail.

On 21 September 1927, a Curtis seaplane left Montreal at 14.15 hours and arrived at Rimouski at 16.25. The mails were transferred to the *Empress of Australia* which arrived at Southampton on the twenty-eighth, enabling the mails to be delivered to the addressees in London the next day. The *Montnairn*, which left Southampton on 3 November 1927, arrived off Father Point at 16.30 on the eleventh. A Fairchild monoplane left at 18.15 and arrived at St Hubert airport at 21.18, the mail being delivered by 23.30, a saving of twenty-four hours. Mails on such flights were overstamped: 'This mail was carried by Postal airplane to Montreal'.

'The Times' of 26 September 1930, reported:

Mails delivered to the Empress of Australia by seaplane in the Strait of Belle Isle, opened a new mail service of less than 5 days between Canada and Great Britain. This means the saving of 48 hours in the time of delivery in Great Britain of mails posted in Montreal. Hitherto the mails were delivered at Father Point.

The 'Montreal Gazette' of 4 May 1928 reported:

Packages picked up from CP Liners to be carried to Three Cities. Canada's first regular package express air service was established yesterday when Canadian Pacific Express Company, a subsidiary of the CPR, entered into contract with the Canadian Trans Continental Airways Ltd and Canadian Airways Ltd respecting the carrying of packages between Rimouski and Montreal, Ottawa and Toronto. The two air transport companies had already entered into an agreement with the Canadian Government to carry first class mail between these points by Fairchild cabin monoplanes.

The new express service will be inaugurated tomorrow upon the arrival off Rimouski of the *Empress of Scotland*.

The 'Chatham Daily News' of 25 June 1928 said:

The first express parcel to be received in the city from overseas via steamship air and train service was delivered to A. Sheldrick & Son, merchant tailors, at 12.53 Saturday, eight days after the order was placed with a firm in London, England. ... A cable was sent from Chatham on Friday afternoon the 15th June, the parcel of silk was put aboard the *Empress of Scotland* on Saturday 16th June. The steamer arrived at Rimouski Friday afternoon 22nd June, when the parcel was flown to Montreal, where it was rushed across the city to Windsor Station and put on a train leaving at 11 o'clock. The parcel arrived in Chatham Saturday noon and was delivered at the Sheldrick store at 12.53 o'clock. 'The improved service just cuts a week off our previous record of quick deliveries by express from London, England,' said Mr Sheldrick in commenting upon the incident this morning.

The parcel was placed in the window of the Sheldrick store and attracted a great deal of attention Saturday afternoon and evening.

For the Imperial Conference at Ottawa in 1932, special arrangements were made to fly mail from London to Cherbourg to connect with the Empresses. On reaching Red Bay in the Strait of Belle Isle, mail was picked up by a Bellanca seaplane and flown 300 miles to Havre St Pierre, where a Vancouver flying boat was used for the 290 miles to Rimouski, the final 480 miles to Ottawa being accomplished by the regular Fairchild service to Ottawa. The first mails left London on 13 July, arriving in Ottawa on the eighteenth.

6 Silk traffic

Shortly after the opening of the CPR in 1887, Vancouver became one of the world's most important silk terminals. The silk traffic certainly made a valuable contribution to the development of the Empress service across the Pacific. The high value of the silk made insurance costly and speed was therefore essential. Special holds, fitted with side ports for speedy unloading, were built into the first white Empresses.

Silk was not a seasonal traffic and it would be loaded into an Empress at Shanghai, Kobe or Yokohama, destined mostly for New York. While tugs manoeuvred to warp the Empress to her berth at Vancouver, radio and telex facilities being still unheard of, the skipper on the bridge bawled 'silk talk' through his megaphone to agents and boss stevedores on the dock. Conveyors would be run through the open ports into the silk holds of the ship. Long before the passengers came down the gangway a steady stream of bales, uniformly wrapped in brown paper, would have reached the specially prepared platform where checkers determined their destination and pulled the bales on to the hand trucks of the waiting stevedores who trundled them to temporary resting places. Separated according to consignment, they were checked again by customs and railway officials and identified by serial number. They were then wheeled away to be loaded into the waiting 'silk train'. Speed, timing and organisation ensured that the silk would be out of the hold, checked and rechecked, and loaded into the silk train in the shortest possible time.

The silk train had specially designed cars, lined with varnished wood, sheathed in paper, airtight and sealed so that thieves and moisture could not reach the costly cargo. The cars were also shorter than the normal box-car, enabling them to take the curves at greater speed.

Each car could stow 470 bales and each bale was worth approximately $800. A typical silk train of fifteen cars could be worth between $5 million and $6 million. At least one train of more than forty cars (valued at more than $12 million) has been recorded.

The train of cars, with a powerful locomotive and a caboose, had only the train and engine crew plus guards as passengers. Stopping only at divisional points about 125 miles apart for fresh relays of locomotives and crews, the train had priority over everything on the rails. Silk trains did not run to a schedule, but went all out to beat the previous best time. Generally they lopped about twenty hours off the passenger-train times. Thus it was possible for a silk train to reach Toronto sixty hours after leaving Vancouver and save further time between there and New York.

Soon after the Empresses started running, the Japanese and the Americans built new ships and arranged special trains to run from San Francisco to New York, but they were unable to match the speed of the Empresses and the CPR. It was not until around 1908, when the Empresses were getting old, that some traffic was lost and this was soon regained when the new *Empress of Asia* and *Russia* appeared on the scene in 1913. In 1930 the second *Empress of Japan* had been built with special provision for silk stowage, but the trade was in fact disappearing. Man-made fibres had caused the price of silk to fall drastically. In 1924 the average price was $6.50 per lb, by 1934 it had fallen to $1.27; this meant that insurance was much cheaper and the speed of the Empresses less important, so much so that the Japanese began shipping in their own vessels via Panama. The silk trains stopped operating in 1933, and only odd shipments were handled until 1937, when they ceased altogether.

7 Senior officers, CPR

	joined CPR	president	president and chief executive officer	chairman and president	chairman and chief executive officer	chairman
George Stephen	1881	1881–8		—		—
W. C. Van Horne	1882	1888–99		—		1899–1910
T. G. Shaughnessy	1882	1899–1910		1910–18		1918–23
E. W. Beatty	1901	1918–24		1924–42		1942–3
D. C. Coleman	1904	1942		1943–7		—
W. M. Neal	1902	—		1947–8		
G. A. Walker	1891	—		—		1948–55
W. A. Mather	1904	1948–55				1955–61
N. R. Crump	1920	1955–61	—	1961–4	1964–9	1969–72
R. A. Emerson	1920	1964–6	—	—	—	—
I. D. Sinclair	1942	1966–9	1969–72	—	1972–	—
F. S. Burbidge	1947	1972–	—	—	—	—

George Stephen, born on 5 June 1829, Dufftown, Scotland; he emigrated to Canada in 1850 and became president of the Bank of Montreal in 1876. He formed the syndicate to build the CPR and became the first president (1881–8) before retiring to England. He was created Baronet in 1886, Baron Mount Stephen in 1891 and GCVO in 1905. He died on 29 November 1921

William Cornelius Van Horne, born on 3 February 1843, in Will County, Illinois. He began work in a railway station in 1857, and was general superintendent, Chicago Milwaukee & St Paul Railway by 1879. He joined the CPR as general manager, Winnipeg, in 1882, supervised the construction of the railway, was vice-president in 1884, president in 1888 and chairman in 1899. He resigned in 1911, was created KCMG in 1894 and died on 11 September 1915

Thomas George Shaughnessy, born on 6 October 1853, in Milwaukee, Wisconsin. He joined Chicago Milwaukee & St Paul Railway in 1869, joining the CPR as purchasing agent in 1882. He was president in 1899, chairman and president in 1911 and chairman in 1918. Knighted in 1901, he was created KCVO in 1907 and Baron Shaughnessy in 1916. He died on 10 December 1923

Edward Wentworth Beatty, born on 16 October 1877 in Thorold, Ontario. The son of Henry Beatty, who had developed CPR's Great Lakes steamships, he joined the law department of the CPR in 1901, becoming general solicitor in 1910, vice-president in 1914, president in 1918, chairman and president in 1924 and chairman in 1942. Appointed GBE in 1935, he died on 23 March 1943

R. Y. Pritchard (left) joined Canadian Pacific Steamships in Liverpool in 1953, becoming naval architect in 1956. Appointed manager operations in 1964, he became general manager in 1968 and managing director in 1972. He was elected chairman and managing director, CP Ships London, in 1976. I. D. Sinclair (centre) joined the CPR as an assistant solicitor in 1942, becoming vice-president and general counsel in 1960. He was elected president CPR in 1966, and chairman and chief executive in 1972. W. J. Stenason (right) joined the CPR as a research economist in 1952. He was appointed chairman of CP Ships in 1968, becoming vice-president Transport & Ships in 1969. In 1974 he became executive vice-president Canadian Pacific Investments (now CP Enterprises) and was appointed president of that company in 1979

8 Senior officers, CPSS

Canadian Pacific Railway Steamship Services

1883	H. Beatty	*manager SS lines and lake traffic, Montreal*
1891	A. Piers	*superintendent steamships*
1903	A. Piers	*manager SS lines, Montreal*
1908	A. Piers	*manager SS lines, Liverpool*
1914	H. M. Kersey	*manager CP Steamship Services, Montreal*

1915

Canadian Pacific Ocean Services

	chairman	managing director	general manager
1915	G. M. Bosworth, Montreal	H. M. Kersey, Montreal	
1919		*title in abeyance*	Sir Thomas Fisher RN

1921

Canadian Pacific Steamships

	chairman	managing director	general manager
1925	E. W. Beatty, Montreal		Captain J. Gillies
1935			Captain R. G. Latta
1938			Captain R. N. Stuart VC
1942	D. C. Coleman, Montreal		
1945		R. W. McMurray, Montreal	
1947	W. M. Neal, Montreal		
1948	W. A. Mather, Montreal		
1952		A. C. MacDonald, Montreal	Captain E. A. Shergold
1955		J. R. Johnston, Montreal	
1959			Captain R. Burns GC
1961	H. Arkle, London	D. K. Buik, London	
1963	G. H. Baillie, London		
1964			R. Y. Pritchard
1966		*title in abeyance*	
1968	W. J. Stenason, Montreal		

1969

CP Ships

	chairman	managing director	general manager
1972		R. Y. Pritchard, London	*title in abeyance*
1974	J. K. Dakin, Montreal		
1976	R. Y. Pritchard, London		

1964

CP (Bermuda) Ltd

	president		
1969	R. F. Lynch, Bermuda		
1976	A. F. Joplin, Bermuda		R. K. Gamey
1979			D. G. Toole

9 Chronology

	Canadian population in 000s	year	
		1819	Alexander Allan's *Jean*, Greenock–Quebec
SS *Genova*, Liverpool–Quebec 20 days		1853	
	3229	1861	
Confederation		1867	
	4324	1881	CPR incorporated
first Parsons steam turbine		1884	Great Lakes service started
		1885	The 'last spike'
		1886	*W. B. Flint* arrives Port Moody
		1887	chartered steamships on Pacific
	4833	1891	Pacific Empresses
		1893	BC Lake and River Service
first diesel engine		1897	Allan Line Steamship Co formed
first radio signal across Atlantic	5371	1901	BC Coastal Steamships
		1903	purchase of Beaver Line
		1906	first Atlantic Empresses
first aeroplane flight in Canada		1909	control of Allan Line
	7206	1911	
		1915	Canadian Pacific Ocean Services formed
first Atlantic flight by Alcock and Brown		1919	
	8787	1921	name changed to Canadian Pacific Steamships Ltd
		1922	first Canadian Pacific cruise
		1923	*Motor Princess* first CP motor ship
R100 England to Montreal		1930	launch of *Empress of Britain* II
	10,376	1931	Canadian Australasian Line formed
	11,506	1941	last CP Pacific sailing, Hong Kong to Vancouver
BOAC and Trans-Canada Airline service, Montreal–London		1947	
		1949	CP Air, Vancouver–Sydney
		1950	first post-war CP cruise
	14,009	1951	
		1953	Canadian Australasian Line service ended
		1955	CP Air, Vancouver–Amsterdam
		1956	*Empress of Britain* III first post-war CP passenger liner
St Lawrence Seaway opened		1959	
	18,238	1961	
		1964	CP (Bermuda) Ltd formed
	21,568	1971	CP Atlantic passenger service ended *CP Discoverer*, *CP Trader* and *CP Voyageur* enter service

10 Staff for a passenger liner

main duties

Master—in sole command of the ship.

Staff captain or staff commander—to relieve Master of much routine on a large ship; policy may vary from company to company.

Chief officer—the 'mate'; working boss of the deck department; arranges day's work for the crew; chief cargo officer.

First officer—senior watchkeeper; navigation.

Second officer—watchkeeper, life-saving equipment, mail, etc; a number of junior officers depending upon the size of the ship.

Chief engineer—overall responsibility for all mechanical/electrical equipment on board.

Staff chief—working chief, supervising all routine maintenance for machinery and hotel services on board.

Second engineers—watchkeepers with specialised responsibilities; a number of junior engineers according to the size of the ship.

Surgeon—ship's doctor.

Purser—accountant and chief clerk, foreign exchange, wages, passenger and freight manifests.

Chief steward—provisioning, preparation and service of food and drink, passenger accommodation.

Chefs—many specialists, butchers and kitchen staff.

Stewards, stewardesses, storekeepers, barkeepers, waiters, etc, according to the number of passengers being carried. There may also be hairdressers, musicians, printers, shop attendants, stenographers, etc.

Manning Levels	1901	1903	1931	1956	1946	1965	1971	1973
	E/Japan I	Lake Champlain	E/Britain II	E/Britain III	Beaver cargo	Beaveroak	container ship	VLCC
deck	48	46	120	92	22	17	14	18
engine	20	37	130	68	26	11	11	11
catering & stewards	50	80	380	300	12	7	7	16
total	118	163	630	460	60	35	32	45

Notes
1 These figures are approximate only and could vary from voyage to voyage.
2 Deck figures for passenger vessels could include shop attendants, baggage staff, printers, musicians.
3 The engine-room crew for the *Lake Champlain* included seventeen firemen and six trimmers; thirty-two cattlemen were also carried on this voyage.

11 Changes of name during CP service

1	*Alsatian*	1909–15
	Empress of France I	1915–31
	Balfour see no. 21	
	Bawtry see no. 22	
2	*Beavercove*	1946–52
	Maplecove	1952–6
	Beavercove	1956–63
3	*Beaverdell*	1945–52
	Mapledell	1952–6
	Beaverdell	1956–63
4	*Beaveroak*	1965–70
	CP Ambassador	1970–3
5	*Beaverpine*	1962–71
	CP Explorer	1971–3
	Bedwyn see no. 21	
	Berwyn see no. 18	
	Bolingbroke see no. 20	
	Borden see no. 19	
	Bosworth see no. 33	
	Bothwell see no. 32	
	Brandon see no. 13	
	Brecon see no. 9	
	Bredon see no. 13	
	Bruton see no. 28	
	CP Ambassador see no. 4	
	CP Explorer see no. 5	
6	*Corsican*	1909–22
	Marvale	1922–3
7	*Duchess of Bedford*	1928–48
	Empress of France II	1948–60
8	*Duchess of Richmond*	1929–47
	Empress of Canada II	1947–53
9	*Dunbridge*	1918–23
	Brecon	1923–8
10	*Elk* (tug)	1915–19
	Wapiti	1919–45
	Empress of Australia I see no. 29	
11	*Empress of Britain* I	1906–24
	Montroyal	1924–30
	Empress of Canada II see no. 8	
	Empress of China II see no. 26	
	Empress of China III see no. 29	
	Empress of France I see no. 1	
	Empress of France II see no. 7	
	Empress of India II see no. 26	
12	*Empress of Japan* II	1930–42
	Empress of Scotland II	1942–57
	Empress of Scotland I see no. 14	
	Empress of Scotland II see no. 12	
	Fort St John see no. 23	
	Henry Osborne see no. 25	
13	*Holbrook*	1918–23
	Bredon	1923
	Brandon	1923–8
14	*Kaiserin Auguste Victoria*	1921
	Empress of Scotland I	1921–30
15	*König Friedrich August*	1920–1
	Montreal II	1921–7
16	*Lake Champlain*	1903–13
	Ruthenia	1913–14
17	*Lake Erie*	1903–13
	Tyrolia	1913–14
	Maplecove see no. 2	
	Mapledell see no. 3	
	Marburn see no. 30	
	Marglen see no. 27	
	Marloch see no. 31	
	Marvale see no. 6	
18	*Mattawa*	1915–23
	Berwyn	1923–8
19	*Methven*	1917–23
	Borden	1923–4
20	*Montcalm* II	1917–20
	Bolingbroke	1920–9
21	*Montezuma* II	1918–23
	Bedwyn	1923
	Balfour	1923–8
	Montlaurier see no. 26	
	Montnairn see no. 26	
	Montreal II see no. 15	
	Montroyal see no. 11	
22	*Mottisfont*	1918–23
	Bawtry	1923–7
23	*Pacific Logger*	1969–77
	Fort St John	1977–
24	*Princess Norah*	1928–55
	Queen of the North	1955–8
	Princess of Acadia I see no. 25	
25	*Princess of Nanaimo*	1950–63
	Princess of Acadia I	1963–71
	Princess of Nanaimo	1971–2
	Henry Osborne	1972–4
26	*Prinz Friedrich Wilhelm*	1921
	Empress of China II	1921
	Empress of India II	1922
	Montlaurier	1922–5
	Montnairn	1925–8
	Queen of the North see no. 24	
	Ruthenia see no. 16	
27	*Scotian*	1909–22
	Marglen	1922–6
28	*Sicilian*	1909–23
	Bruton	1923
29	*Tirpitz*	1921
	Empress of China III	1921–2
	Empress of Australia I	1922–52
30	*Tunisian*	1909–22
	Marburn	1922–8

Tyrolia see no. 17		32 *War Beryl*	1919–20
31 *Victorian*	1909–22	*Bothwell*	1920–9
Marloch	1922–8	33 *War Peridot*	1919–20
Wapiti see no. 10		*Bosworth*	1920–8

12 Sponsors

Abbreviations: ch—chairman; dir—director; Etm—European traffic manager; gm—general manager; m—manager; md—managing director; mdE—managing director for Europe; sec—secretary; vp—vice-president.

Canadian Pacific Fleet

Date of launch		
3.07.1883	*Athabasca*	Miss Govan
12.07.1883	*Alberta*	Miss M'Lellan (daughter of Canadian minister of marine)
31.07.1883	*Algoma*	Miss Schaw[1]
30.08.1890	*Empress of India*	Lady Louise Egerton (sister of Lord Hartington)[2]
13.12.1890	*Empress of Japan*	Lady Alice Stanley (daughter-in-law of gov-gen of Canada)
25.03.1891	*Empress of China*	Lady Stafford Northcote (wife of gov Hudson's Bay Co)
22.05.1894	*Prince Rupert*	
22.10.1898	*Moyie*	Mrs Troup (wife of Capt J. Troup)
18.11.1902	*Princess Victoria*	Mrs Archer Baker (wife of Etm CPR London)
10.09.1903	*Princess Beatrice*	Mrs F. Bullen (wife of md Bullen's Yard)
11.11.1905	*Empress of Britain*	Mrs Arthur Piers (wife of manager SS Lines CPR)
27.01.1906	*Empress of Ireland*	Mrs Alex Gracie (wife of md Fairfields)
1.09.1906	*Princess Royal*	Mrs R. Marpole (wife of gen-supt CPR)
4.09.1906	*Bison* (tender)	Mrs Mowat (wife of Capt Mowat CPR)
25.06.1907	*Assiniboia*	Mrs G. M. Bosworth (wife of vp CPR)
6.07.1907	*Keewatin*	Miss Piers (daughter of m SS Lines CPR)
22.09.1907	*Princess Ena*	
27.06.1908	*Princess Charlotte*	Mrs Marpole (wife of gen-supt Pacific Division CPR)
10.07.1910	*Princess Adelaide*	Mrs A. Piers (wife of m SS Lines CPR)
21.09.1910	*Princess Mary*	Mrs Pritchard (daughter of m SS Lines CPR)
20.09.1910	*Musquash* (tug)	
11.1910	*Gopher* (tug)	
29.05.1911	*Princess Alice*	Mrs A. Piers (wife of m SS Lines CPR)
8.11.1911	*Princess Sophia*	Miss Piers (daughter of m SS Lines CPR)
28.08.1912	*Empress of Russia*	Mrs W. Beauclerk (daughter of Sir T. Shaughnessy, ch CPR)
23.11.1912	*Empress of Asia*	Mrs G. Bosworth (wife of vp CPR)
24.12.1912	*Princess Maquinna*	Mrs H. Bullen (wife of md BC Marine Railway Co)
20.10.1914	*Princess Irene*	Mrs J. A. Heritage (wife of chief eng *Princess Margaret*)
22.06.1914	*Missanabie*	Mrs G. McLaren Brown (wife of Egm CPR London)
24.06.1914	*Princess Margaret*	Mrs R. Redmond (daughter of Sir T. Shaughnessy, ch CPR)
19.11.1914	*Metagama*	Lady Biles (wife of Sir J. H. Biles)[3]
09.1915	*Moose* (tug)	
1915	*Elk* (tug)	
21.04.1917	*Melita*	Mrs Martin (wife of m CPOS Ltd, London)
7.06.1917	*Montcalm* II	Lady Fisher (wife of gm CPOS Ltd, London)
17.10.1917	*Minnedosa*	Mrs Rodan (wife of sec Allan Line)
3.07.1920	*Montcalm* III	Lady Fisher (wife of gm CPOS Ltd, London)
17.08.1920	*Empress of Canada*	Mrs G. M. Bosworth (wife of ch CPOS Ltd)

Date of launch

Date of launch	Ship	Sponsor
14.12.1920	*Montrose*	Lady Raeburn (wife of dir-gen ministry of shipping)
29.08.1921	*Princess Louise* II	Mrs J. W. Troup (wife of m BCCSS)
18.12.1921	*Montclare*	Lady McLaren Brown (wife of Egm CPR, London)
27.09.1924	*Princess Kathleen*	Lady Mount Stephen (wife of former pres CPR)
29.11.1924	*Princess Marguerite*	Hon Marguerite Shaughnessy (daughter of former ch CPR)
27.09.1927	*Beaverburn*	Mrs E. R. Peacock (wife of dir CPR)
28.09.1927	*Beaverdale*	Lady Alice Northcote[4] (wife of former dir CPR)
26.10.1927	*Princess Elaine*	Mrs Stockwell Day (daughter of Mr Grant Hall, vp CPR)
27.10.1927	*Beaverford*	Mrs H. Holt (wife of dir CPR)
8.11.1927	*Beaverhill*	Miss M. Gillies (daughter of gm CPSS Ltd)
23.11.1927	*Duchess of Atholl*	Her Grace the Duchess of Atholl
24.11.1927	*Beaverbrae*	Lady McLaren Brown (wife of Egm CPR, London)
24.01.1928	*Duchess of Bedford*	Mrs Stanley Baldwin (wife of prime minister)
18.06.1928	*Duchess of Richmond*	Lady Augustus Nanton (wife of dir CPR)
27.09.1928	*Princess Norah*	Miss M. Gillies (daughter of gm CPSS Ltd)
28.09.1928	*Duchess of York*	HRH Duchess of York
17.12.1929	*Empress of Japan* II	Mrs E. R. Peacock (wife of dir CPR)
16.01.1930	*Princess Elizabeth*	Mrs Redford (daughter of W. R. MacInnes, vp CPR)
4.02.1930	*Princess Joan*	Mrs Bircher (daughter of Sir A. Nanton, dir CPR)
12.05.1930	*Princess Helene*	Miss Nesta Gillies (daughter of gm CPSS Ltd)
12.05.1930	*Traverse* (tug)	Mrs M. L. Duffy (wife of m CPR, Liverpool)
11.06.1930	*Empress of Britain* II	HRH Prince of Wales
11.09.1930	*Prescotont*	Mrs Duff (wife of m Great Lakes Service)
27.08.1945	*Beaverdell*	Mrs D. C. Coleman (wife of pres CPR)
10.12.1945	*Beaverglen*	Mrs J. Johnson (wife of supt eng CPSS Ltd)
20.05.1946	*Beaverlake*	Mrs W. Baird (wife of SS pass traffic manager)
16.07.1946	*Beavercove*	Mrs J. C. Patteson (wife of Egm CPR, London)
5.10.1948	*Princess Patricia* II	Lady Patricia Ramsey (daughter of Duke of Connaught)
26.05.1948	*Princess Marguerite*	Mrs R. W. McMurray (wife of md CPSS Ltd)
14.09.1950	*Princess of Nanaimo*	Lady Anderson (wife of dir CPR)
7.03.1954	*Princess of Vancouver*	Mrs H. Arkle (wife mdE CPR, London)
22.06.1955	*Empress of Britain* III	HM The Queen
9.05.1956	*Empress of England*	Lady Eden (wife of prime minister)
10.05.1960	*Empress of Canada* III	Mrs Diefenbaker (wife of Canadian prime minister)
22.03.1961	*Beaverfir*	Mrs D. K. Buik (wife of deputy md CPSS, London)
18.06.1962	*Beaverpine*	Miss Janice Crump (daughter of ch CPR)
31.03.1965	*Beaveroak*	Mrs G. H. Baillie (wife of mdE CPR, London)
19.08.1969	*CP Voyageur*	Mrs D. C. Jamieson (wife of Canadian minister of transport); naming ceremony 24.01.1970
	Princess of Acadia II	Mrs G. E. Benoit (wife of vp CP Ltd); naming ceremony 15.05.1971
28.01.1971	*CP Trader*	Mrs A. Jiskoot (wife of dir CP Ltd)
26.03.1971	*CP Discoverer*	Mrs F. S. Burbidge (wife of pres CP Ltd)
20.02.1973	*Carrier Princess*	Mrs R. Strachan (wife of minister of highways)
28.02.1974	*Incan Superior*	Mrs M. Carter (wife of pres Gt Lakes Paper Co)

Notes

1 Daughter of partner in the firm M'Crindell Schaw & Co, who, with Henry Beatty, supervised the building of the three ships.
2 Chairman, Naval Construction & Armament Co.
3 Professor of Naval Architecture at Glasgow University, who had helped design the first Pacific Empresses in 1890.
4 Lady Alice Northcote was an adopted daughter of Lord Mount Stephen and married the son of Lady Stafford Northcote, who had sponsored the *Empress of China* in 1891.

CP (Bermuda) fleet

Date of launch		
3.08.1966	*Lord Mount Stephen*	Mrs J. R. Herrington (daughter of ch CPR)
15.11.1966	*Lord Strathcona*	Mrs I. D. Sinclair (wife of pres CPR)
31.10.1967	*H R MacMillan*	Mrs J. Lecky (wife of vp MacMillan Bloedel)
3.02.1968	*J V Clyne*	Mrs A. W. Gamage (daughter of ch MacMillan Bloedel)
8.03.1969	*N R Crump*	Mrs D. G. Cook (daughter of ch CPR)
8.07.1969	*Fort St John*	Mrs M. Echigo (wife of pres C Itoh Co) as *Pacific Logger*
15.08.1969	*T Akasaka*	Mrs T. Akasaka (wife of pres NKK)
11.03.1970	*W C Van Horne*	Mrs I. D. Sinclair (wife of pres CPR)
4.04.1970	*Port Hawkesbury*	Mrs. G. I. Smith (wife of premier NS)
26.10.1970	*T G Shaughnessy*	Mrs W. A. Stenason (wife of vp CPR)
2.09.1972	*G A Walker*	Mrs R. Haupt (wife of dir tpt Ford Co)
27.01.1973	*W A Mather*	Mrs A. F. Dickson (wife of Capt Dickson, Shell Co)
22.06.1973	*E W Beatty*	Mrs H. Hyama (wife of pres Marubeni Corp)
7.07.1973	*R A Emerson*	Mrs W. A. Stenason (wife of vp CPR)
8.10.1973	*D C Coleman*	Mrs Sugayoshi (daughter of dir NKK)
20.10.1973	*Fort MacLeod*	Mrs J. Lunderville (wife of vp Domtar)
29.03.1974	*I D Sinclair*	Mrs Veillon (daughter of ch CPR)
10.05.1974	*W M Neal*	Mrs. G. L. Morton (daughter of ch CPR)
27.07.1974	*Fort Steele*	Mrs J. Johnston (wife of gm CP Ships)
12.10.1974	*Fort Edmonton*	Lady Richards (wife of premier, Bermuda)
8.03.1975	*Fort Kipp*	Mrs R. Burrough (wife of ch J. Burrough Ltd)
28.05.1975	*Fort Nelson*	Mrs E. Pritchard (wife of md CP Ships)
18.10.1975	*Fort Coulonge*	Mrs Clerihue (wife of ch Celanese Canada)
18.12.1975	*Fort Calgary*	Mrs Sinclair (daughter-in-law of ch CP Ltd)
22.07.1976	*Fort Kamloops*	Mrs Moriasu (wife of pres Kobe Steel Corp)
11.11.1976	*Port Vancouver*	Baroness Bekaert (wife of ch Bekaert Ind Ltd)
15.11.1976	*Fort Victoria*	Mrs M. Prus (wife of pres Carey Canadian Mines)
17.02.1977	*Port Quebec*	Mrs I. Messel (wife of pres Lake Asbestos Co)
17.03.1977	*Fort Yale*	Mrs Billingsley (wife of ch Reed Paper Corp)
27.07.1977	*Fort Walsh*	Mrs R. Gillett (wife of Lord Mayor of London)
14.10.1977	*Fort Carleton*	Mrs K. Tohji (wife of dir Kobe Steel Ltd)
23.12.1977	*Fort Hamilton*	Mrs A. F. Joplin (wife of pres CP (Bermuda))
7.12.1979	*Fort Assiniboine*	Mrs Vines (wife of R. Vines, Alcoa, Australia)
14.03.1980	*Fort Garry*	Mrs J. Bolger (wife of pres Shell Chemical Company, Canada)

13 CP passenger liners 1887-1971

CP voyages

		Atlantic	Pacific
Abyssinia	1887–91	—	17
Batavia	1887–91	—	15
Parthia	1887–91	—	20
Empress of India I	1891–1914	—	119
Empress of Japan I	1891–1922	—	157
Empress of China I	1891–1911	—	n/a
Athenia	1898–1907	—	n/a
Tartar	1898–1907	—	n/a

Beaver Line fleet from 1903

		Atlantic	Pacific
Lake Champlain ⎫	1903–13	84	—
Ruthenia ⎭	1913–14	10	—
Lake Erie ⎫	1903–13	62	—
Tyrolia ⎭	1913–14	9	—
Lake Manitoba	1903–18	99	—
Lake Michigan	1903–18	76	—
Monmouth	1903–19	19	—
Montcalm	1903–14	23	—
Monteagle	1903–24	6	n/a
Montezuma	1903–14	63	—
Montfort	1903–14	42	—
Montreal I	1903–14	69	—
Montrose I	1903–14	66	—
Mount Royal	1903–14	25	—
Mount Temple	1903–16	72	—
Empress of Britain I ⎫	1906–24	137	—
Montroyal ⎭	1924–30	50	—
Empress of Ireland	1906–14	96	—
Empress of Asia	1913–41	1	153
Empress of Russia	1913–40	2	154
Missanabie	1914–18	38	—
Metagama	1915–31	152	—
Melita	1918–35	145	—
Minnedosa	1918–35	128	—

Allan Line fleet from 1919

		Atlantic	Pacific
Empress of France I	1919–31	99	5
Corsican ⎫	1919–22	32	—
Marvale ⎭	1922–3	1	—

		Atlantic	Pacific
Grampian	1919–21	21	—
Pretorian	1919–22	22	—
Scandinavian	1919–23	31	—
Scotian ⎫	1919–22	20	—
Marglen ⎭	1922–6	1	—
Sicilian ⎫	1919–23	15	—
Bruton ⎭	1923	1	—
Tunisian ⎫	1919–22	32	—
Marburn ⎭	1922–8	40	—
Victorian ⎫	1919–22	25	—
Marloch ⎭	1922–8	39	—
Montreal II	1921–7	21	—
Prinz Fredk Wilhelm ⎫	1921	3	—
Empress of India II ⎪	1922	3	—
Montlaurier ⎬	1922–5	21	—
Montnairn ⎭	1925–8	36	—
Montcalm III	1922–42	162	—
Empress of Scotland I	1922–30	71	—
Empress of Canada I	1922–43	1	98
Montrose II	1922–40	152	—
Empress of Australia I	1922–52	83	21
Montclare	1922–42	170	—
Duchess of Bedford ⎫	1928–48	131	—
Empress of France II ⎭	1948–60	186	—
Duchess of Atholl	1928–42	109	—
Duchess of Richmond ⎫	1929–47	114	—
Empress of Canada II ⎭	1947–53	82	—
Duchess of York	1929–40	132	—
Empress of Japan II ⎫	1930–42	1	58
Empress of Scotland II ⎭	1942–57	90	—
Empress of Britain II	1931–40	100	—
Beaverbrae II	1948–54	51	—
Empress of Australia II	1953–5	38	—
Empress of Britain III	1956–63	109	—
Empress of England	1957–70	149	—
Empress of Canada III	1961–71	121	—

14 CP passenger sailings to Canada — major European services

	Liverpool	Glasgow direct	Southampton Cherbourg	Antwerp direct	Antwerp Southampton	Hamburg Southampton Cherbourg	London Le Havre
1903–14	489			393			
1909–14*	412	212					175
World War I							
1919–31		218					26
1919–39	1125				263		
1922–33						111	
1922–39			306				
World War II							
1947–71	1033						
Total	3059	430	306	393	263	111	201

Notes
*1 Allan Line sailing under CP control.
2 From 1922 some Glasgow sailings made via Belfast.
3 From 1923 some Liverpool sailings via Greenock and Belfast
4 Between 1950 and 1955 and 1957 and 1968 some Liverpool sailings via Greenock.

15 CP passenger carryings

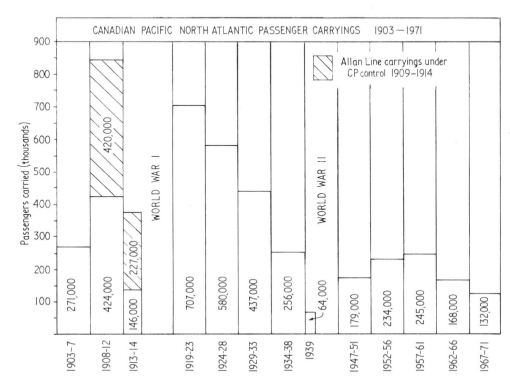

CANADIAN PACIFIC NORTH ATLANTIC PASSENGER CARRYINGS 1903–1971

Allan Line carryings under CP control 1909–1914

Passengers carried (thousands)

1903–7	1908–12	1913–14	1919–23	1924–28	1929–33	1934–38	1939	1947–51	1952–56	1957–61	1962–66	1967–71
271,000	424,000 / 420,000	146,000 / 227,000	707,000	580,000	437,000	256,000	64,000	179,000	234,000	245,000	168,000	132,000

Europe–Canada 1903–1971

	1903–14	1909–14	1919–39	1947–71	Total
westbound	626,000	469,000	1,260,000	552,000	2,907,000
eastbound	215,000	178,000	783,000	406,000	1,582,000
	841,000	647,000	2,043,000	958,000	4,489,000

Notes
1 Allan Line carryings under CP control 1909–14.
2 Between 1915 and 1918 CP operated a limited service from Liverpool carrying military and government personnel; 82 trips with 88,000 passengers. Allan Line figures are not available.
3 Included in the above figures are a limited number of passengers carried on Beaver cargo liners between 1947 and 1960.

16 CP cruising fleet

		World	West Indies	Mediterranean	Canaries	Scandinavia	Others	*Total*	New York	United Kingdom	South Africa
									From		
Empress of France	1922–31	2		5			1	8	8		
Empress of Scotland	1922–30	2		7				9	9		
Empress of Britain ⎫	1922–4		6					6	6		
Montroyal ⎭	1925–8		8			1		9	8	1	
Marloch	1923					1		1		1	
Empress of Canada	1924	1					1*	2	2		
Montreal	1925			1				1		1	
Empress of Australia	1927–39	4	23	13	2	13	4	59	30	29	
Duchess of Bedford	1928–34		13				4	17	17		
Duchess of Atholl	1929–39		4	9			31	44	28	16	
Duchess of Richmond	1929–39		8	7	1		11	27	5	22	
Empress of Britain II	1931–9	8	6				2	16	16		
Melita	1932–4			7	3	2	9	21		21	
Montcalm	1932–9			24	17	4	3	48		48	
Montclare	1932–9			23	17	6	2	48		48	
Montrose	1932–9			17	20	3	7	47		47	
		17	68	113	60	30	75	363	129	234	
World War II											
Empress of Scotland II	1950–7		28				1	29	26	3	
Empress of England	1958–70		29	2	19		10	60	24	30	6
Empress of Britain III	1960–4		4	5	6		8	23	4	17	2
Empress of Canada III	1961–71		72	4	1	2	3	82	75	7	
			133	11	26	2	22	194	129	57	8
grand totals		17	201	124	86	32	97	557	258	291	8

*Vancouver to New York via Panama

17 CP cruises 1922-71

year	World	West Indies	Mediterranean	Canaries	Scandinavia	Others	*Total*	North America	United Kingdom	South Africa
								From		
1922		2	2				4	4		
1923	1	2	1	1			5	4	1	
1924	1	2	1			1	5	5		
1925	2[1]	2	2				6	5	1	
1926	1	2	1	1			5	4	1	
1927	1	2	1				4	4		
1928	1	3	1			1	6	6		
1929	1	3	1			2	7	6	1	
1930	1	3	2			1	7	5	2	
1931	1	5	2		2	4	14	9	5	
1932	1	4	13	3	3	13	37	9	28	
1933	[1]	3	22	12	4	10	51	7	44	
1934	1	4	22	6	3	8	44	10	34	
1935	1	2	13	7	1	10	34	7	27	
1936	1	7	8	8	4	7	35	11	24	
1937	1	9	14	5	5	8	42	13	29	
1938	1	10	3	12	5	6	37	14	23	
1939	1	3	4	7	1	4	20	6	14	
	17	68	113	60	30	75	363	129	234	
World War II										
1950–61[2]		49				1	50	47	3	
1962		6	1	3			10	7	3	
1963		6	3	4		2	15	6	7	2[3]
1964		7	3	2		12	24	7	11	6
1965		9	2	4			15	8	7	
1966		9		2		1	12	8	4	
1967		9		2		1	12	8	4	
1968		9		2		1	12	8	4	
1969		12	2	5	1	2	22	13	9	
1970		9		2	1	1	13	9	4	
1971		8				1	9	8	1	
		133	11	26	2	22	194	129	57	8
grand totals	17	201	124	86	32	97	557	258	291	8

Notes

1 During 1923–5 world cruises had sailed in January. In 1925 it was decided to sail in December, hence two world cruises left in 1925. In 1933 it was decided to make a short cruise with the *Empress of Britain* over the Christmas–New Year holiday and to sail the world cruise in January.

2 1950–61 collected to save space. The *Empress of Scotland* II made one cruise to South America in 1953. In 1951–3 one cruise per year to the West Indies sailed from the United Kingdom.

3 Travel Savings Association charters.

18 CP cargo liners

	years	Pacific	West Indies	St Lawrence	Saint John	total
Mattawa	1915–23	17	5	26	—	48
Berwyn	1923–8	—	29	2	3	34
Medora	1915–18	—	—	—	—	—
Miniota	1916–17	—	—	—	—	—
Methven	1917–23	11	1	3	—	15
Borden	1923–4	—	8	1	1	10
Montcalm II	1917–20	—	—	9	8	17
Bolingbroke	1920–9	—	—	37	25	62
Montezuma II	1918–23	—	7	10	6	23
Bedwyn	1923	—	1	—	—	1
Balfour	1923–8	—	13	12	6	31
Holbrook	1918–23	—	2	13	8	23
Bredon	1923	—	—	—	1	1
Brandon	1923–8	—	—	21	13	34
Dunbridge	1918–23	—	—	18	10	28
Brecon	1923–8	—	—	20	13	33
Mottisfont[1]	1918–23	—	—	9	10	19
Bawtry	1923–7	—	—	11	8	19
Batsford[2]	1918–26	—	—	24	18	42

voyages (1915–29)

War Peridot ⎱	1919–20	—	—	4	4	8
Bosworth ⎰	1920–8	—	—	33	19	52
War Beryl ⎱	1919–20	—	—	5	2	7
Bothwell ⎰	1920–9	—	—	39	16	55

		voyages (1927–79)			
		Saint John	St Lawrence	Great Lakes	*total*
Beaverburn	1927–40	47	74	—	121
Beaverford	1928–40	49	78	—	127
Beaverdale	1928–41	49	77	—	126
Beaverhill	1928–44	58	85	—	143
Beaverbrae	1928–41	45	81	—	126
Beaverdell	1946–62	38	95	—	133[3]
Beaverburn II	1946–60	37	87	—	124
Beaverglen	1946–63	41	108	—	149
Beaverford II	1946–62	39	104	—	143
Beaverlake	1946–62	38	99	—	137
Beavercove	1947–63	37	87	—	124[4]
Beaverlodge	1952–60	16	48	—	64
Beaverfir	1961–72	17	18	30	65
Beaverpine ⎱	1962–71	9	11	33	53
CP Explorer ⎰	1971–3	—	28	—	28
Beaverelm	1962–71	18	5	31	54
Beaverash	1963–9	17	5	25	47
Beaveroak ⎱	1965–70	3	24	15	42
CP Ambassador ⎰	1970–3	—	45	—	45
CP Voyageur	1970–	—	138	—	—
CP Trader	1971–	—	131	—	—
CP Discoverer	1971–	—	127	—	—
CP Hunter	1980–	—	—	—	—

Notes
1 Made three trooping voyages, one to South America plus two to North America.
2 Plus two charter voyages to New York, 1918.
3 Plus nine trans-Pacific voyages as *Mapledell* 1952–4.
4 Plus seven trans-Pacific voyages as *Maplecove* 1952–4.

19 Charters into the Lakes 1957-69

		voyages				
A. M. Kruger	1966–7/69	15	Finnpulp	1968	2
Alex	1968–9	5	Heinrich Schulte	1961–2	9
Angelica Schulte	1960–2	9	Herman Schulte	1959–63	23
Arion	1964	2	Kirsten Skov	1968–9	3
Arctic Tern	1962–3	2	Lillevan	1963–4	3
Auguste Schulte	1957–9	15	Lord Viking	1963–8	39
Beate Bolton	1965	4	Ludolf Oldendorf	1960–7	27
Bonita	1963	2	Maria Anna Schulte	1960–3	18
Christiane Schulte	1960/62	2	Medicine Hat	1964–8	29
Damtor	1958	6	Moose Jaw	1963–8	36
Dora Oldendorf	1960–4	33	Nordvest	1968–9	2
Elise Schulte	1959–64	30	Otto Nubel	1957–9	15
Elizabeth Schulte	1962–3	6	Polydora	1964–9	31
Erika Schulte	1960–4	24	Rhein	1968–9	5
Erich Schroder	1964–5	6	Rosita	1961/63	4
Ernst Schroder	1964	5	Rosto	1963–8	5
Erwin Schroder	1964–5	16	Tariq	1968	2
Eudora	1965–6	10	Uranus	1965/67	8

Many other vessels were chartered for single voyages.
Some voyages terminated at Montreal and Saint John NB

20 Charters for container service 1969-72

		voyages
Beavermondo	1969–71	26
Beaverrando	1970–1	22
Bernd Wesch	1969	2
Christine Isle	1971	1
Eemstroom	1969–71	33
Hope Isle	1969–71	25
Hother Isle	1970–2	33
Iris	1969	4
Rapallo	1969–70	15
Weser Isle	1970	9
Yarkino Adventurer	1969	2

The 1500 ton German motor ship Beaverrando, chartered to start the container service in 1970–1

21 BC coastal services

The following are some of the more important routes and the vessels that became associated with them.

Triangle Route
Operated continuously during the summer with a reduced winter schedule. On the night run Seattle–Vancouver (145 miles), the vessels would sail from Vancouver at 23.00hrs and from Seattle 23.30hrs, arriving at 08.00hrs next morning. No call was made at Victoria on the night run, which was discontinued in 1948.

Princess Victoria	1909–25	Princess Alice	1912–30
Princess Charlotte	1909–25	Princess Adelaide	1911–30
,, ,,	1941–2	Princess Marguerite	1925–41
,, ,,	1947–8	Princess Kathleen	1925–41
			1947–8

Vancouver–Victoria–Seattle
Princess Beatrice	1904–07	Princess Alice	1941–7
Princess Victoria	1908–25	Princess Charlotte	1941–9
		Princess Kathleen	1947–9

Vancouver–Victoria–Seattle: Tri City
(No overnight)
Princess Patricia	1949–60	Princess Elizabeth	1949–59
Princess Marguerite	1949–60	Princess Joan	1949–59

Vancouver–Victoria
(83 miles; night service)
Princess Adelaide	1911–30	Princess Elizabeth	1930–59
Princess Alice	1911–30	Princess Joan	1930–59

Vancouver–Nanaimo
Nanaimo is the main distribution centre for traffic from Vancouver. Usually two round trips daily (40 miles) during the summer.

Joan	1905–12	*Princess Joan*	1930–59
Princess Mary	1910	*Princess Victoria*	1931–50
Princess Patricia I	1912–28	*Princess of Nanaimo*	1951–62
Charmer	1919–30	*Princess Marguerite*	1949–62
Motor Princess	1926–8	*Princess Patricia*	1949–62
Princess Elaine	1928–62	*Princess of Vancouver*	1955–
Princess Elizabeth	1930–59	*Carrier Princess*	1973–

Vancouver–Prince Rupert
(478 miles) CNR terminus at the mouth of the Skeena River.

Princess Beatrice	1909–28	*Princess Adelaide*	1932–48
Princess Royal	1928–30	*Princess Norah*	1951–8
Princess Mary	1930–2		

Vancouver–Skagway, Alaska
(895 miles) Terminus White Pass & Yukon Railway. Freight and passengers to and from Yukon, plus summer cruises.

Amur	1901–08	*Princess Mary*	1918–28
Danube	1901–08	*Princess Louise* II	1922–62
Princess Beatrice	1905–11	*Princess Kathleen*	1928–52
Princess Sophia	1912–18	*Princess Norah*	1929–52
Princess Alice	1914–41	*Yukon Princess*	1951–6
Princess Charlotte	1916–41	*Princess Patricia* II	1963–

Victoria–Vancouver
(83 miles; night service one way)

Charmer	1901–10	*Princess Charlotte*	1909
Princess Victoria	1907		

Victoria–Port Angeles
Three round voyages (20 miles) a day, by the steamer arriving at Victoria from Vancouver each morning. Summer only.

Princess Elizabeth	1953–8	*Princess Marguerite* II	1966–74
Princess Joan	1953–8		

West Coast of Vancouver Island
Usually one round voyage a week with approximately twenty ports of call.

Queen City	1901–07	*Princess Norah*	1929–41
Tees	1907–13	*Veta C*	1952–3
Princess Maquinna	1913–52	*Princess Alberni*	1953–8

Gulf Islands
Mid-way between Vancouver and Victoria: Gabriola, Galiano, James, Kuper, Mayne, Moresby, North and South Pender, Salt Spring, Saturna, Sidney, Thetis, etc. Most of these islands would receive a call from once to three times a week.

Joan	1911–14	*Princess Royal*	1926–32
Charmer	1911–28	*Princess Mary*	1932–51
Queen City	1914–16	*Princess Elaine*	1952–4
Otter	1916–31	*Princess Norah*	1953–4
Island Princess	1918–30	*Princess Alberni*	1954

General Freight Service

Otter	1901–15	*Will W. Case* (barge)	1910–21
Princess Ena	1907–31	*Nootka*	1927–49

The Princess Maquinna *sailed the west coast of Vancouver Island for thirty-nine years, 1913–53*

The 400 ton Otter, *a wooden general-purpose cargo ship, taken over from the Canadian Pacific Navigation Co, 1901–31*

22 Derivation of ship names

Akasaka T.	1900–71, president Nippon Kokan Kaisha, Tokyo.
Alberta	Province named by Marquis of Lorne.
Algoma	District of Ontario.
Angus R.B.	1831–1922, joined CPR syndicate 1880, remained a director until his death.
Aorangi	Maori name for Mount Cook, 'Sky Piercer'.
Assiniboia	District of NW Territories
Athabasca	River in Alberta.
Beatty E.W.	1877–1943, joined CPR 1902, president 1918–42.
Borden Sir R.L.	1854–1937, prime minister of Canada.
Brandon	City in Manitoba.
Clyne J.V.	b. 1902, chairman, MacMillan Bloedel Co.
Coleman D.C.	1879–1956, joined CPR 1899, president 1942, retired 1947.
Constantine	Captain C., inspector NW Mounted Police.
Crump N.R.	b. 1904, joined CPR 1920, president 1955, retired 1972.
Columbia	Named by Captain R. Gray 1892, after his ship.
Dalton	Jack, explorer and trader.
Dawson	George M. 1849–1901, head of geological survey.
Duchesnay	E. J., divisional engineer CPR.
Emerson R.A.	1911–66, joined CPR 1928, president 1964.
Fort Assiniboine	Built 1793, by the NW Company.
Fort Calgary	Built 1875 by NWMP, junction Bow and Elbow rivers.
Fort Carleton	Built 1795 by NW Company between Red River and Edmonton.
Fort Coulonge	After fort built by Louis d'Ailleboust Sieur de Coulonge governor of New France 1648–51
Fort Edmonton	Built 1796, by Hudson's Bay Co, named after deputy governor, who came from Edmonton, Middlesex
Fort Garry	Built 1822, by Hudson's Bay Co.
Fort Hamilton	Built 1869, by two traders Healy and Hamilton.
Fort Kamloops	Built 1812, at confluence North and South Thompson rivers.
Fort Kipp	Built 1874, by J. Kipp, whiskey trader, between Lethbridge and Fort MacLeod, Alberta.
Fort MacLeod	Built 1874, by NWMP under command of Col J. F. MacLeod, 106 miles south of Calgary.
Fort Nelson	Built 1800, by NW Co, 300 miles NW Dawson Creek.
Fort Rouge	Built 1738, by Hudson's Bay Co, on Assiniboine River.
Fort St John	Built 1805, by NW Co, on Peace River.
Fort Steele	Built 1887, by NWMP under Supt S. B. Steele.
Fort Victoria	Built 1843, by Hudson's Bay Co.
Fort Walsh	Built 1875, by NWMP, SW Saskatchewan.
Fort Yale	Built 1848, by Hudson's Bay Co, after J. M. Yale, 102 miles NE Vancouver.
Grant Hall	1863–1934, joined CPR 1880, v-p 1915–34.
Hamlin	L. B., engineer CPR.
Henry Osborne	First governor of Newfoundland.
Hosmer	Chas. R. H., manager CPR Telegraphs.
Illecillewaet	Indian word meaning 'Swift Water'.
Jean	Wife of Alexander Allan.
Joan	Wife of Robert Dunsmuir.
Kaleden	Town on Skaha Lake BC.
Keewatin	District of NW Territories.
Kelowna	Indian word meaning 'Grizzly Bear'.
Kokanee	Indian word meaning 'Red Fish', salmon.
Kootenay	Indian word meaning 'Water People'.
Kyuquot	Indian tribe.
Lord Strathcona	1820–1914, as Donald A. Smith, cousin of George Stephen, joined CPR syndicate 1880. Drove the 'last spike' 1885. Canadian high commissioner in London 1896–1914.
Lytton	Sir Edward Bulwer-Lytton, 1803–73. Secretary-of-State for Colonies.
McConnell	R. G., geologist and surveyor.
MacMillan H.R.	1885–1976, chairman MacMillan Bloedel Co.
Mather W.A.	1885–1961, joined CPR 1918, president 1948, retired 1961.
Mattawa	Town on CPR in Ontario.
Melita	Town on CPR in Manitoba.
Metagama	Station on CPR in Ontario.
Miniota	Town on CPR in Manitoba.
Minnedosa	Station on CPR in Ontario.
Minto	Earl of, governor-general of Canada 1898–1904.
Missanabie	Station on CPR.
Montcalm	Marquis de, French general 1712–59.
Monteagle	Lord, 1790–1866, secretary for the Colonies.
Montmorency	River and Falls in Quebec.
Nakusp	Indian word meaning 'closed in'.
Naramata	Aborigine word meaning 'Place of Water'.
Nasookin	Indian word meaning 'Queen of the Lakes'.
Neal W.M.	1886–1961, joined CPR 1902, president 1947, retired 1948.
Nelson	Hon Hugh, Lt-governor British Columbia.
Nitinat	Indian tribe.
Nootka	Named by Captain J. Cook 1778.
Niagara	Indian word meaning 'Thunder of Waters'.
Ogilvie	W., commissioner Yukon Territory.
Okanagan	River and Lake in British Columbia.
Port Hawkesbury	Gulf Oil refinery on Strait of Canso NS.
Port Quebec	Founded 1608, by Samuel de Champlain, incorporated as city 1832.
Port Vancouver	Captain George, 1792, incorporated as city 1886.
Prince Rupert	First governor of the Hudson's Bay Co.

Princess Alberni	Port W coast Vancouver Island, after Don Pedro de Alberni, military commander from Mexico 1793.
Princess Helene	Wife of Samuel de Champlain.
Princess Irene	Granddaughter of Queen Victoria.
Princess Kathleen	Hon Marguerite Kathleen Shaughnessy.
Princess May	Duchess of Cornwall, after a visit to Canada.
Princess Patricia	Princess Pat of Connaught.
Princess of Nanaimo	After city of Nanaimo.
Procter	T. G., manager Kootenay Valley Company.
Rithet R.P.	Chairman, Canadian Pacific Navigation Co.
Rosebery	5th Earl of, 1847–1929.
Rossland	Ross Thompson, established the town site.
Ruthenia	Area of Central Europe inhabited by Ukrainians.
Sandon	Jack, prospector.
Schwatka	F., 1849–92, explorer.
Shaughnessy T.G.	1853–1923, joined CPR 1882, president 1899, ch 1918–23.
Sicamous	Indian 'Shimmering Water'.
Sinclair I.D.	b. 1913, joined CPR 1942, president 1966, ch 1972.
Tyrell	J. B., 1858–1957, surveyor.
Tyrolia	Former crown land of Austria–Hungary.
Valhalla	Range of mountains in West Kootenay.
Van Horne W.C.	1843–1915, joined CPR 1882, president 1888–99.
Walsh	J. M., 1843–1905, first commissioner Yukon District.
Walker G.A.	1879–1959, joined CPR 1891, chairman 1948, retired 1955.

23 Sample crossing times

Pacific

				days	hrs	mins
1891	April	*Empress of India*	Yokohama–Race Rocks	11	7	27
1891	Aug	*Empress of Japan*	Yokohama–Race Rocks	10	13	10
1897	June	*Empress of Japan*	Yokohama–Race Rocks	10	10	—
1914	May	*Empress of Russia*	Yokohama–Race Rocks	8	18	31
1923	June	*Empress of Canada* I	Yokohama–Race Rocks	8	10	53
1924	July	*Empress of Asia*	Yokohama–Race Rocks	8	14	48
1931	Feb	*Empress of Japan* II	Yokohama–Race Rocks	8	3	18
1931	April	*Empress of Japan* II	Yokohama–Race Rocks	7	20	16

North Atlantic: UK to Canada

				days	hrs	mins
1819		*Jean*	Greenock–Montreal	30–40	—	—
1854	Sept	*Canadian*	Liverpool–Quebec	12	—	—
1898	June	*Parisian*	Liverpool–Montreal	8	21	30
1906	June	*Empress of Britain* I	Moville–Rimouski	5	21	17
1907	Jan	*Empress of Britain* I	Liverpool–Halifax	5	8	18
1908	July	*Empress of Britain* I	Liverpool–Quebec	6	2	—
1920	Aug	*Empress of France*	Liverpool–Quebec	5	20	6
1924	Aug	*Montcalm*	Liverpool–Montreal	6	12	—
1928	July	*Duchess of Bedford*	Liverpool–Montreal	6	9	30
1929	Sept	*Beaverburn*	Le Havre–Father Point	7	8	20
1930	April	*Duchess of York*	Liverpool–St John	6	22	14
1930	Sept	*Duchess of York*	Greenock–Quebec	5	17	40
1932	June	*Empress of Britain* II	Cherbourg–Father Point	4	8	27
1933	Oct	*Empress of Britain* II	Bishop Rock–Belle Isle	3	2	40
1950	May	*Empress of Scotland* II	Liverpool–Quebec	5	0	36
1957	Sept	*Empress of Britain* III	Greenock–Father Point	4	18	48

24 Working boats

Between 1882 and 1895 the CPR made use of a number of small steamboats and/or tugs to ferry men and materials during the building of the railway, in the area of the Great Lakes and in British Columbia. So far it has been possible to identify only eight of these as being owned by the company.

Devil's Gap Lodge, Lake of the Woods, Ontario, was opened by the CPR on 1 July 1923. From then until 1961, when the Lodge and the surviving boats were sold, some seven motor launches had sailed the Lake under the chequered house flag. Some were used to tow small 'otter' boats with guests to fish the distant parts of the Lake; others to ferry guests and their luggage between Kenora station and the Lodge.

From 1924 until the present time the company has operated two small motor launches, *Green Jade* numbers 1 and 2, in Vancouver harbour, to reposition camels and fenders.

For fleet list see page 264.

The Nipigonian, *a motor launch used for fishing excursions for guests at Devil's Gap Lodge on Lake of the Woods, Ontario*

25 War service

CP Fleet in World War I

Alsatian	survived	
Batsford	survived	
Calgarian	1.3.1918	t *U19* 11 miles off Rathlin Island, **49** died
Carthaginian	14.6.1917	mined off Innistrahull
Corinthian	survived	
Corsican	survived	
Dunbridge	survived	
Empress of Asia	survived	
Empress of Britain I	survived	
Empress of India	7.12.1914	sold to Maharajah of Gwalior to be hospital ship *Loyalty*
Empress of Japan I	survived	
Empress of Russia	survived	
Grampian	survived	
Hesparian	4.9.1915	t off Fastnet, **32** died
Holbrook	survived	
Ionian	20.10.1917	mined off St Gowans Head, *UC51*, **7** died
Lake Manitoba	26.8.1918	gutted by fire at Montreal
Lake Michigan	16.4.1918	t *U100* off Eagle Island, **1** died
Mattawa	survived	
Medora	2.5.1918	t *U86* off Mull of Galloway
Melita	survived	
Metagama	survived	
Methven	survived	
Milwaukee	31.8.1918	t *U105* 260 miles SW Fastnet, **1** died
Miniota	31.8.1917	t *U62* 30 miles SE Start Point, **3** died
Missanabie	9.9.1918	t *UB87* S Daunts Rock, **45** died
Mongolian	1914	sold to Admiralty 21.7.1918, t **36** died
Monmouth	survived	
Montcalm I	29.1.1916	sold to Admiralty
Montcalm II	survived	
Monteagle	survived	
Montezuma I	7.7.1915	sold to Admiralty 25.7.1917, t *UC41*
Montezuma II	survived	
Montfort	1.10.1918	t *U55* 170 miles W Bishops Rock, **5** died
Montreal I	30.1.1918	rammed and sunk in Mersey
Montrose I	28.10.1914	sold to Admiralty, wrecked 28.12.1914
Mount Royal	10.7.1916	sold to Admiralty
Mount Temple	6.12.1916	captured and sunk by *Moewe*, **3** died
Numidian	3.12.1914	sold to Admiralty
Pomeranian	15.4.1918	t *UC77* off Portland Bill, **55** died
Pretorian	survived	
Princess Irene	3.1915	sold to Admiralty, sunk 27.5.1915
Princess Margaret	3.1915	sold to Admiralty, survived
Ruthenia	29.1.1916	sold to Admiralty
Sardinian	survived	
Scandinavian	survived	
Scotian	survived	
Sicilian	survived	
Tunisian	survived	
Tyrolia	27.6.1916	sold to Admiralty
Victorian	survived	
Virginian	survived	

Vessels chartered during World War I

Ardgarroch	Nov	1914
Avristan	Aug	1915
Cape Finisterre	Nov	1915
Franklyn	Nov	1915
Ikala	Sept	1915
Ikbal	Oct	1915
Indore	Sept	1915
Kelvinbrae	Oct	1915
Knight of the Thistle	June	1915
Mascara	Nov	1914
Rio Tiete	Nov	1914
Saxon Monarch	May	1916
Yarrowdale	June	1915

It has not been possible to trace the number of voyages made.

CP Fleet in World War II

Aorangi	survived	
Beaverbrae I	25.3.1941	bombed and sunk 60.12N 09.00W, all saved
Beaverburn I	5.2.1940	t *U41* 49.20N 10.07W, 1 died
Beaverdale	1.4.1941	t *U48* 60.50N 29.19W, 21 died
Beaverford I	5.11.1940	sunk by *Admiral Scheer* 52.66N 32.34W, 77 died
Beaverhill	24.11.1944	stranded Hillyards Reef, Saint John NB
Duchess of Atholl	10.10.1942	t *U178* 07.03S 11.12W, 4 died
Duchess of Bedford	survived	
Duchess of Richmond	survived	
Duchess of York	11.7.1943	bombed and sunk 41.18N 15.24W, 27 died
Empress of Asia	5.6.1942	bombed off Singapore, 7 died
Empress of Australia I	survived	
Empress of Britain II	28.10.1940	t *U32* 55.16N 09.50W, 49 died
Empress of Canada I	14.3.1943	t *Leonardo da Vinci* 01.13S 09.57W, 392 died
Empress of Japan II	survived	
Empress of Russia	8.9.1945	gutted by fire at Barrow
Montcalm III	22.5.1942	sold to Admiralty, survived
Montclare	2.6.1942	sold to Admiralty, survived
Montrose II	2.12.1940	t *U99*, 185 died
Niagara	18.6.1940	mined, Hauraki Gulf NZ, all saved
Princess Kathleen	survived	
Princess Marguerite	17.8.1942	t *U83* N Port Said, 49 died

	miles steamed	cargo carried tons	troops and/or passengers carried
Empress of Asia	46,993	3,495	7,923
Empress of Australia	315,161	20,000	139,794
Empress of Britain	61,000	2,850	10,156
Empress of Canada	202,249	13,584	39,535
Empress of Russia	160,056	6,230	60,241
Empress of Scotland	719,783	30,867	258,292
Duchess of Atholl	759,600	75,800	39,173
Duchess of Bedford	413,044	86,249	179,807
Duchess of Richmond	435,877	139,253	187,327
Duchess of York	222,617	65,300	83,343
Beaverbrae	75,408	103,567	—
Beaverburn	19,320	18,090	—
Beaverdale	65,075	65,881	—
Beaverford	55,263	77,315	—
Beaverhill	178,397	268,652	3,680
	3,729,843	977,133	1,009,271

Park Ships managed/loaded on CP berths in World War II

Park		built by	CP interest years	voyages
Alder	1944	United Shipyards, Montreal	1944–6	7
Bellwoods	1943	Marine Industries, Sorel	1945	1
Crystal	1944	N Vancouver SB Co	1944–6	6
Dentonia	1944	United Shipyards, Montreal	1944–6	12
Eastwood	1944	United Shipyards, Montreal	1944	1
Gatineau	1942	Davie SB Co, Lauzon	1942–6	19
Glacier	1942	Marine Industries, Sorel	1946	2
Grafton	1944	United Shipyards, Montreal	1944–6	6
Hampstead	1944	United Shipyards, Montreal	1944–6	5
Kawartha	1944	Marine Industries, Sorel	1944–5	2
Lakeside	1944	Victoria Mchy Depot, BC	1944–6	3
Lakeview	1944	Marine Industries, Sorel	1946	1
Montebello	1945	Victoria Mchy Depot, BC	1946	2
Portland	1944	United Shipyards, Montreal	1944	1
Riverdale	1943	Davie SB Co, Lauzon	1945–6	2
Riverview	1943	Davie SB Co, Lauzon	1943–6	15
Rosedale	1944	United Shipyards, Montreal	1944–6	11
Strathcona	1943	Burrard Dry Dock, Vancouver	1946	1
Wellington	1944	United Shipyards, Montreal	1945–6	2
Westmount	1943	United Shipyards, Montreal	1945	1
Whiteshell	1944	United Shipyards, Montreal	1944–6	9
Yamaska	1944	Marine Industries, Sorel	1946	1

Empire Ships

Many ships came under the control of the Ministry of War Transport during World War II and were given the prefix *Empire-*. These vessels mostly came from the following groups:

1 Vessels built too late for World War I and which had been laid-up in America.

2 Enemy ships seized in Allied ports or captured on the high seas.

3 Cargo vessels and military transports built in the USA.

4 Standard designs built in British yards.

A number of these ships were managed by Canadian Pacific on behalf of the Ministry of War Transport, many for only a single voyage, but others for longer periods.

Empire Ships managed/loaded on CP berths in World War II

Empire		built by	grt	CP interest years	voyages
Allenby	1945	J. L. Thompson, Sunderland	9904	1945	1
Balfour	1944	Lithgows, Glasgow	7201	1944	1
Bittern	1902	Harland & Wolff, Belfast	8546	1943–4	2
Buffalo	1919	Skinner & Eddy, Seattle	6404	1942	1
Camp	1943	Short Bros, Sunderland	7046	1944	1
Cromer	1944	Short Bros, Sunderland	7058	1944	1
Cutlass	1943	Consol Steel Corp, Wilmington, Mass	7177	1943–5	3
Dabchick	1919	Atlantic Corp, Portsmouth, NH	6089	1942	1
Dorado	1920	Atlantic Corp, Portsmouth, NH	5595	1941	1
Flame	1941	Cammell Laird, Birkenhead	7069	1943	1
Gannet	1941	J. Duthie, Seattle	5673	1941	1
Gazelle	1920	Todd Constn Corp, Tacoma	4828	1945	1
Glen	1941	C. Connell & Co, Glasgow	6327	1944–5	3
Grange	1943	Harland & Wolff, Belfast	6981	1943	1
Kitchener[1]	1944	Caledon SB Co, Dundee	9881	1944–5	3
Lady	1944	Shipbldg Corp, Newcastle	7046	1944	1
Lance[2]	1943	Consol Steel Corp, Wilmington, Mass	7177	1943–8	14
Magpie	1919	Federal SB Corp, Kearny, NJ	6211	1940–5	16
Mariner	1922	Deutsche Werke, Hamburg	4957	1943–4	3
Mist	1941	W. Doxford & Co, Sunderland	7241	1945	1
Mouflon	1921	Hanlon SB Co, Oakland, Cal	3234	1944–5	7
Moulmein	1944	Readhead & Sons, South Shields	7047	1944–5	3
Ploughman	1943	W. Gray & Co, West Hartlepool	7045	1944	1
Prowess	1943	W. Gray & Co, West Hartlepool	7058	1944	1
Reindeer	1919	Federal SB Corp, Kearny, NJ	7058	1940–2	4
Rosalind	1943	Burntisland SB Co, Burntisland	7290	1945	1
Sailor	1926	Stablimento Tech, Trieste	6086	1940–2	6
Tamar	1907	Workman Clark, Belfast	6604	1943	1
Thrush	1919	Federal SB Corp, Kearny, NJ	6213	1940–2	2
Union	1924	Stablimento Tech, Trieste	5952	1941–2	9
Woodlark	1913	New York SB, Camden, NJ	7793	1941–5	5
Yukon	1921	Stablimento Tech, Trieste	7651	1942	16

Notes
1 Delivered to Canadian Pacific 8.12.1944; bought 12.6.1947, renamed *Beaverford* II.
2 December 1944 made 40 voyages Southampton–Le Havre–Southampton with some trips to the Channel Islands. During 1946 also made 33 voyages Hull–Cuxhaven–Hull.
In addition to the Empire and Park ships many other vessels were operated by Canadian Pacific for the British government during World War II.

Part Four   Fleet Lists

1 Liners

(The dates in brackets following the name of the vessel indicate the years in Canadian Pacific service.)

1
Abyssinia (1887–91), 63765, 3651g, 364 × 42 × 34ft, iron.
Engine: 1882 by J. Jones & Son, 1S 11k.
3.3.1870 launched by J. & G. Thomson, Clydebank, for Cunard.
1880 to J. & G. Thomson. 1881 to S. B. Guion. 1885 to Sir Wm Pearce. 11.2.1887 loaned to Canadian Pacific. 17.5.1887 ex Hong Kong. 14.6.1887 arr Vancouver. 28.1.1891 ex Vancouver. 10.1891 returned to Guion SS Co. 18.12.1891 destroyed by fire at sea.

2
Batavia (1887–91), 63756, 2549g, 327 × 39 × 27ft, iron.
Engine: builder, C, 2cy. 1884 J. Elder, C 4cy 1S 11k.
1.2.1870 launched by Wm Denny & Bros, Dumbarton, for Cunard.
1884 to Sir Wm Pearce. 11.2.1887 loaned to Canadian Pacific. 27.12.1887 arr Vancouver from Hong Kong. 3.1891 ex Vancouver, returned to Guion SS Co. 5.1892 to Northern Pacific SS Co. 12.1892 renamed *Tacoma*. 10.1898 to Guion SS Co. 1901 to Northern Pacific SS Co. 2.1904 to Northwestern SS Co. 15.3.1905 seized by Japanese. To R. Yamashima, renamed *Shikotan Maru*. 3.10.1924 aground on Japanese coast. Broken up in China.

3
Parthia (1887–91), 63797, 3167g, 361 × 40 × 34ft, iron.
Engine: 1885 by Elder, T 3cy 1S 11k.
1870 launched by Wm Denny & Bros, Dumbarton, for Cunard.
11.2.1887 loaned to Canadian Pacific. 4.7.1887 arr Vancouver ex Hong Kong. 20.8.1891 ex Vancouver, returned to Guion SS Co, renamed *Victoria*. 5.1892 to Northern Pacific SS Co. 10.1898 to North American Mail SS Co. 1901 to Northern Pacific SS Co. 2.1904 to Northwestern SS Co. 1908 to Alaska SS Co. 1924 oil fuel. 1936 laid-up. 1941-7 to War Shipping Admin. 11.1950 bell presented to new *Parthia*. 8.1952 laid-up. 1954 to Dulien Steel Products for scrapping. Hull became barge for Straits Towing Co, Vancouver. 1955 renamed *Straits No 27*. 1956 towed across Pacific by tug *Sudbury* as *Straits Maru*. 16.10.1956 arr Osaka, scrapped.

Note: above three steamers were placed on the Vancouver–Shanghai run by arrangement between the CPR, Sir W. Pearce and Adamson Bell & Co, from February 1887 until replaced by the Pacific Empresses in 1891 (see page 13).

4
Empress of India I (1891–1914), 98887, 5905g, 456 × 51 × 33ft.
Engine: builder, T 6cy 2S 16k.
30.8.1890 launched by Naval Construction & Armament Co, Barrow, y. no 179.
8.2.1891 m/v ex Liverpool to Hong Kong via Suez. 16.3.1891 arr Hong Kong. 7.4.1891 ex Hong Kong. 28.4.1891 arr Vancouver. 8.1914 ex Vancouver for Bombay. 7.12.1914 to Maharajah of Gwalior. 19.1.1915 renamed *Loyalty* (hospital ship). 3.1919 to Scindia Steam Navigation Co. 3.1921 laid-up Bombay. 2.1923 to Maneckchand Jiyray & Co, Bombay. Scrapped.

5
Empress of Japan I (1891–1922), 98911, 5905g, 456 × 51 × 33ft.
Engine: builder, T 6cy 2S 16k.
13.12.1890 launched by Naval Construction & Armament Co, Barrow, y. no 180.
11.4.1891 m/v ex Liverpool to Hong Kong via Suez. 22.6.1891 arr Victoria. 13.8.1914 requisitioned. 27.10.1915 returned to Pacific service. 18.7.1922 laid-up. 1925 to V. Lamken. 31.3.1926 to R. E. Mahaffay, Burrard Inlet. Broken up by R. J. Christian, North Vancouver. Bell to Merchants Exchange, Vancouver.

6
Empress of China I (1891–1911), 98953, 5905g, 456 × 51 × 33ft.
Engine: builder, T 6cy 2S 16k.
25.3.1891 launched by Naval Construction & Armament Co, Barrow, y. no 181.
6.7.1891 trials. 15.7.1891 m/v ex Liverpool to Hong Kong via Suez. 23.9.1891 arr Vancouver. 27.7.1911 wrecked on Mera Reef, Tokyo Bay. 12.1911 refloated. 9.1912 to Sasso Shojiro for scrapping at Yokohama.

7
Athenian (1897–1907), 82425, 3877g, 365 × 46 × 29ft, iron.
Engine: J. & J. Thomson, Glasgow, C 1S 15k.
7.12.1881 launched by Aitken & Mansell, Glasgow, for Union Line.
29.12.1897 to Canadian Pacific. 12.2.1898 ex Southampton for Vancouver via Cape Horn. 7.1899–2.1901 to US government on charter. 22.8.1907 ex Vancouver. 14.9.1907 to K. Kishimoto, Osaka, for scrap.

8
Tartar (1897–1907), 86336, 4339g, 377 × 47 × 30ft, iron.
Engine: J. & J. Thomson, Glasgow, C 1S 14k.
25.1.1883 launched by Aitken & Mansell, Glasgow, for Union Line.
29.12.1897 to Canadian Pacific. 5.2.1898 ex Southampton for Vancouver via Cape Horn. 12.1898 first CP call at Honolulu. 7.1899 to 4.1900 to US government on charter. 17.10.1907 collision with *Charmer* (No *303*). 3.1908 broken up at Osaka.

Beaver Line vessels taken over 6.4.1903

* Adapted for carriage of oil in cylindrical tanks, World War I.

9
Lake Champlain* (1903–16), 110650, 7392g, 446 × 52 × 28ft.
Engine: builders, T 6cy 2S 13k.
31.3.1900 launched by Barclay Curle & Co, Glasgow, y. no 422.
21.5.1901 first radio apparatus on a merchant ship. 6.4.1903 to Canadian Pacific. 14.4.1903 first CP sailing. 7.3.1913 renamed *Ruthenia*. 8.1914 requisitioned. 29.1.1916 to Admiralty. 1942 captured by Japanese, renamed *Choran Maru*. 1945 recaptured. 18.6.1949 broken up at Dalmuir.

10

Lake Erie* (1903–16), 110631, 7550g, 446 × 52 × 31ft.
Engine: builders, T 6cy 2S 13k.
21.11.1899 launched by Barclay Curle & Co, Glasgow, y. no 420.
6.4.1903 to Canadian Pacific. 8.5.1903 arr Montreal on her first CP crossing. 29.3.1913 renamed *Tyrolia* for Trieste service (see page 32). 28.10.1914 requisitioned as troop transport, later became a store ship. 27.6.1916 to Admiralty, fitted with tanks to become an oiler. Renamed *Saxol*. 7.10.1916 to Lane & MacAndrew Ltd. Renamed *Aspenleaf.* 7.11.1917 to Shipping Controller. 12.9.1919 to Anglo-Saxon Petroleum Co. 11.1.1921 renamed *Prygona*. 6.2.1925 to Petersen & Albeck, Copenhagen, for scrap.

11

Lake Manitoba (1903–18), 113497, 8850g, 469 × 56 × 32ft.
Engine: Richardson & Westgarth, T 6cy 2S 12k.
6.6.1901 launched by C. S. Swan & Hunter Ltd, Newcastle, y. no 263.
24.9.1901 m/v Liverpool to Montreal. 6.4.1903 to Canadian Pacific. Tonnage 9674g. 16.5.1903 arr Montreal on her first CP crossing. 26.8.1918 gutted by fire at Montreal, scuttled. 9.1918 refloated. 8.10.1918 to Bishop Navigation Co. Refitted Halifax. Renamed *Iver Heath*. 28.9.1921 to Canada Steamship Lines Ltd. 25.7.1923 to Stelp & Leighton Ltd (Crete Shipping Co). 1924 scrapped.

12

Lake Michigan (1903–18), 115252, 8200g, 469 × 56 × 32ft.
Engine: Richardson & Westgarth, Hartlepool, T 6cy 2S 12k.
28.9.1901 launched by C. S. Swan & Hunter Ltd, Newcastle, y. no 264.
6.4.1903 to Canadian Pacific. 21.2.1904 collision with *Matterhorn*. Beached at Dungeness. 25.2.1904 refloated, towed to Gravesend. 15.11.1916 mined off Brest, towed into port. 16.4.1918 torpedoed 93 miles NW of Eagle Island by *U100*.

13

Milwaukee (1903–18), 106834, 7317g, 470 × 56 × 32ft.
Engine: NE Marine Engineering Co Ltd, Newcastle, T 3cy 1S 12k.
7.11.1896 launched by C. S. Swan &

Hunter Ltd, Newcastle, y. no 214.
16.9.1898 ashore near Cruden Bay, Aberdeen. Split by dynamite. 180ft of fore-end left on rocks, remainder towed to Tyne. 12.4.1899 new fore-part built and launched. 6.4.1903 to Canadian Pacific. 31.8.1918 torpedoed 260 miles SW of Fastnet by *U105*.

14

Monmouth* (1903–19), 113379, 4078g, 375 × 48 × 26ft.
Engine: Furness, Westgarth Ltd, Middlesbrough, T 3cy 1S 12k.
1.5.1900 launched by Sir R. Dixon Ltd, Middlesbrough, y. no 467.
6.4.1903 to Canadian Pacific. 16.11.1916 mined off Cherbourg. 27.9.1917 Liverpool to Murmansk and Archangel. 31.12.1919 to Imperial Oil Co, Toronto. 1922 to Stillmar, Sarnia, Ontario. 1923 to Kishimoto KK Japan. 1925 renamed *Shinzan Maru*. 1929 to Dalgosrybtrest, Vladivostok. Renamed *Treti Krabolov*. 1960 no information.

15

Montcalm I* (1903–16), 106869, 5478g, 445 × 53 × 28ft.
Engine: builders, T 3cy 1S 13k.
17.5.1897 launched by Palmers Shipbuilding Co, Jarrow, y. no 724.
6.4.1903 to Canadian Pacific. 1914 requisitioned as BEF transport. 1915 store ship. 29.1.1916 to Admiralty. 18.2.1916 to Leyland Line. 26.10.1916 to Anglo-Saxon Petroleum Co. 18.11.1916 renamed *Crenella*. 11.10.1917 to Shipping Controller. 26.11.1917 torpedoed off SW Ireland. 26.11.1919 to Anglo-Saxon Petroleum Co. 19.10.1920 to Velefa SS Co. 20.6.1923 to C. Nielsen & Co, Norway. Whaling depot ship. 10.1923 renamed *Rey Alfonso*. 1925 to H.M. Wrangell & Co, Norway. 1927 to Anglo-Norse Co. Renamed *Anglo-Norse*. 8.1929 to Falkland Whaling Co. Renamed *Polar Chief*. 2.7.1941 to Ministry of War Transport. 17.11.1941 renamed *Empire Chief*. 3.8.1946 to South Georgia Co Ltd. Renamed *Polar Chief*. 29.4.1952 arr Dalmuir, broken up by W. H. Arnott Young & Co Ltd.

16

Monteagle (1903–26), 110554, 5498g, 445 × 52 × 28ft.
Engine: builders, T 6cy 2S 13k.

13.12.1898 launched by Palmers SB Co, Jarrow, y. no 738.
1899 requisitioned as troop transport No 87. Boer War. 6.4.1903 to Canadian Pacific. 30.5.1903 arr Montreal, first Canadian Pacific sailing from Bristol. 1904 refit at Liverpool, 97 cabin-class berths. Tonnage 6163g. 3.1906 to Hong Kong via Cape of Good Hope. 2.5.1906 ex Hong Kong, laid-up until 3.1907. 9.1914 requi arr Vancouver. 18.9.1906 ashore Hong Kong, laid up until 3.1907. 9.1914 requisitioned as troop ship. 24.2.1915 returned to trans-Pacific service. 11.1918–5.1919 three trips to Vladivostok repatriate POWs. 4.1921 rescued crew of *Hsin Tien* off China coast. Capt A. J. Hosken awarded Medaille d'Honneur de Sauvetage by French government. 22.9.1922 ex Vancouver for Montreal. 17.11.1922 ex Montreal for Avonmouth. 29.1.1923 arr London. Laid-up. Renamed *Belton*. 15.4.1926 to Hughes Bolckow Shipbreaking Co. 27.4.1926 arr. Blyth.

17

Monterey (1903), 109427, 5455g, 445 × 52 × 28ft.
Engine: builders, T 3cy 1S 13k.
25.11.1897 launched by Palmers SB Co, Jarrow, y. no 728.
6.4.1903 to Canadian Pacific. 4.7.1903 arr Montreal from Bristol. 14.7.1903 wrecked at Plata Point, Little Miquelon.

18

Montezuma I* (1903–15), 110604, 7345g, 485 × 59 × 31ft.
Engine: builders, T 6cy 2S 13k.
11.7.1899 launched by A. Stephen & Sons, Linthouse, Glasgow, y. no 383.
6.4.1903 to Canadian Pacific. 10.1914 requisitioned. 7.7.1915 to Admiralty, converted to be an oiler. Renamed *Abadol*. 7.2.1917 to Lane & MacAndrew Ltd. Renamed *Oakleaf*. 25.7.1917 torpedoed by *UC41* 64 miles NW from Butt of Lewis.

19

Montfort (1903–18), 110568, 5481g, 445 × 52 × 28ft.
Engine: builders, T 6cy 2S 12k.
13.2.1899 launched by Palmers SB Co, Jarrow, y. no 739.
6.4.1903 to Canadian Pacific. 1.10.1918 torpedoed by *U55* 170 miles W of Bishop Rock.

20

Montreal I (1903–18), 113373, 6960g, 469 × 56 × 32ft.
Engine: Wallsend Slipway, T 6cy 2S 12k.
28.4.1899 launched by C. S. Swan & Hunter Ltd, Newcastle, y. no 252.
6.4.1903 to Canadian Pacific. 8.1914 left Antwerp towed by *Montrose*. 1.4.1915 requisitioned. 29.1.1918 rammed by *Cedric*. 30.1.1918 sank 14 miles from the Bar, Liverpool.

21

Montrose I (1903–14), 108251, 5431g,, 444 × 52 × 28ft.
Engine: T. Richardson & Son, Hartlepool, T 3cy 1S 13k.
17.6.1897 launched by Sir R. Dixon & Co, Middlesbrough, y. no 441.
6.4.1903 to Canadian Pacific. 22.7.1910 radio message which led to arrest of Crippen. 28.10.1914 to Admiralty. 28.12.1914 wrecked on Goodwins.

22

Mount Royal (1903–16), 109498, 7044g, 470 × 56 × 32ft.
Engine: Central Marine Eng Works. W Hartlepool, T 3cy 1S 12k.
17.8.1898 launched by C. S. Swan & Hunter Ltd, Newcastle, y. no 230.
6.4.1903 to Canadian Pacific. 10.1914 requisitioned. Converted to oiler. Renamed *Rangol*. 10.7.1916 to Admiralty. 17.11.1916 to Lane & MacAndrew Ltd. Renamed *Mapleleaf*. 7.11.1917 to Shipping Controller. 4.10.1919 to British Tanker Co Ltd. 19.10.1920 renamed *British Maple*. 6.6. 1922 bunker depot ship Southampton. 10.12.1932 to Metal Industries Ltd for scrap. 25.1.1933 Rosyth.

23

Mount Temple (1903–16), 113496, 8790g, 485 × 59 × 30ft.
Engine: Wallsend Slipway, Newcastle, T 6cy 2S 12k.
18.6.1901 launched by Sir W. G. Armstrong Whitworth Ltd, Newcastle, y. no 709.
6.4.1903 to Canadian Pacific. 1.12.1907 stranded W Ironbound Island, Lahave NS. 600 rescued by breeches buoy. 16.4.1908 refloated. 6.1908 towed to Newport News by tug *Covington*. 6.12.1916 captured and sunk by German raider *Moewe* 620 miles W of Fastnet.

24

Empress of Britain I (1906–30), 120940, 14,188g, 550 × 65 × 37ft.
Engine: builders, Q 8cy 2S 18k.
11.11.1905 launched by Fairfield S&E Co, Govan, y. no 442.
5.5.1906 m/v Liverpool–Quebec. 27.7.1912 collided with and sank *Helvetia* in fog off Cape Madeleine. 16.8.1914 requisitioned as AMC. 12.12.1915 passing eastwards through Straits of Gibraltar, collided with and sank Greek steamer. 8.1919 converted to oil fuel at Fairfield. 16.4.1924 converted to cabin class. Renamed *Montroyal*. 17.6.1930 to Stavanger Shipbreaking Co.

25

Empress of Ireland (1906–14), 123972, 14,191g, 550 × 65 × 37ft.
Engine: builders, Q 8cy 2S 18k.
27.1.1906 launched by Fairfield S&E Co, Govan, y. no 443.
29.6.1906 m/v Liverpool–Quebec. 29.5.1914 sank near Father Point after collision with *Storstad*. 7.1964 wreckage located by skin divers.

26

Empress of Russia (1913–45), 135197, 16,810g, 570 × 68 × 42ft.
Engine: builders, 4ST 4S 19k.
28.8.1912 launched by Fairfield S&E Co. Govan, y. no 484.
1.4.1913 m/v Liverpool–Hong Kong via Suez. 23.8.1914 requisitioned as AMC. 12.2.1916 returned to Pacific service. 6.5.1918 requisitioned, trooping on Atlantic. 8.3.1919 returned to Pacific service. 28.11.1940 requisitioned as troopship. 8.9.1945 gutted by fire at Barrow whilst refitting. Broken up by T. W. Ward Ltd, Barrow.

27

Empress of Asia (1913–42), 135226, 16,908g, 570 × 68 × 42ft.
Engine: builders, 4ST 4S 19k.
23.11.1912 launched by Fairfield S&E Co, Govan, y. no 485.
14.6.1913 m/v Liverpool–Hong Kong via Cape Town. 2.8.1914 requisitioned at Hong Kong as AMC. 20.3.1916 returned to the company's service. 3.5.1918 left Vancouver for New York via Panama and made six trooping voyages across Atlantic. 2.1.1919 left Liverpool for Vancouver

via Panama. 10.2.1919 returned to Pacific service. 11.11.1926 in collision with and sank the small freighter *Tung Shing* below Shanghai. 11.1.1941 arrived Vancouver. 2.1941 requisitioned as troopship, leaving Vancouver 13.2.1941 for UK via Panama. 5.2.1942 sunk by Japanese aircraft off Singapore.

28

Missanabie (1914–18), 136705, 12,469g, 501 × 64 × 38ft.
Engine: builders, Q 8cy 2S 15k.
22.6.1914 launched by Barclay Curle & Co, Scotstoun, y. no 510.
7.10.1914 m/v Liverpool–Montreal. 9.9.1918 torpedoed by *U87* 52 miles S by E from Daunts Rock.

29

Metagama (1915–34), 136791, 12,420g, 501 × 64 × 38ft.
Engine: builders, Q 8cy 2S 15k.
19.11.1914 launched by Barclay Curle & Co, Scotstoun, y. no 511.
26.3.1915 m/v Liverpool–Saint John. 26.5.1923 collision with *Baron Vernon* in the Clyde. 19.6.1924 collision with *Clara Camus* off Cape Race. 1931–3 laid-up Southend. 3.4.1934 to P. & W. McLellan Ltd. Broken up Bo'ness, Firth of Forth.

30

Mattawa (1915–28), 131444, 4874g, 398 × 52 × 27ft.
Engine: D. Rowan, Glasgow, T 3cy 1S 10k.
15.6.1912 launched by A. McMillan & Son Ltd, Dumbarton, y. no 443, as *St Hugo* for British & Foreign SS Co Ltd. 6.2.1915 to Palace Shipping Co Ltd. Renamed *Franktor*. 10.9.1915 to Canadian Pacific. 13.9.1915 first CP voyage. 21.10.1915 renamed *Mattawa*. 23.4.1920 ex Liverpool for the Pacific via Suez and Karachi. 15.7.1922 Montreal–W Indies service. 19.2.1923 renamed *Berwyn*. 2.3.1926 arr Glasgow laid-up. 15.10.1926 N Atlantic service. 12.1.1928 arr Glasgow. 30.1.1928 to Kintyre SS Co. 2.2.1928 renamed *Kingarth*. 7.1932 to G. & F. Bozzo, Italy. Renamed *Beppe*. 19.10.1942 torpedoed 28 miles off Lampedusa Island by 4M s/m *Unbending*.

31
Medora (1915–18), 131438, 5135g, 410 × 52 × 29ft.
Engine: D. Rowan, Glasgow, T 3cy 1S 11k.
26.4.1912 launched by Russell & Co, Port Glasgow, y. no 632, as *Frankmount* for Palace Shipping Co. 18.5.1915 to Canadian Pacific. 29.6.1915 renamed *Medora*. 2.5.1918 torpedoed *U86* 11 miles WSW of Mull of Galloway.

Allan Line
16 vessels (Nos 32–47), officially taken over 1.10.1915; financial control from 1909 (see page 27).

32
Alsatian (1915–34), 136266, 18,481g, 571 × 72 × 42ft.
Engine: builders, 4ST 4S 18k.
22.3.1913 launched by W. Beardmore & Co, Glasgow, y. no 509.
17.1.1914 m/v Liverpool–Halifax. 7.8.1914 requisitioned as AMC. 1.10.1915 to Canadian Pacific. 18.1.1919 refit at Beardmore's. 4.4.1919 renamed *Empress of France* I. 26.9.1919 first post war CP voyage, Liverpool–Quebec. 30.5.1922 Hamburg–Southampton–Cherbourg–Quebec service. 24.11.1923 arr Beardmore's for conversion to oil fuel. 31.10.1928 ex Southampton for the Pacific via Suez. 17.10.1929 ex Hong Kong for Liverpool. 28.9.1931 laid-up on Clyde. 20.10.1934 to Arnott Young & Co for scrap. 24.11.1934 arr Dalmuir.

33
Calgarian (1915–18), 136277, 17,515g, 569 × 70 × 42ft.
Engine: builders, 4ST 4S 18k.
19.4.1913 launched by Fairfield SB&E Co, Govan, y. no 487.
15.9.1914 requisitioned as AMC. 1.10.1915 to Canadian Pacific. 1.3.1918 torpedoed by *U19* off Rathlin Island.

34
Carthaginian (1915–17), 89990, 4214g, 386 × 45 × 22ft.
Engine: J. & J. Thompson, Glasgow, C 2cy.
9.10.1884 launched by Govan SB Co, Glasgow, y. no 140.
1.10.1915 to Canadian Pacific. 14.6.1917 sunk by mine off Innistrahull.

35
Corinthian (1915–18), 111257, 6227g, 430 × 54 × 28ft.
Engine: builders, T 3cy 1S 12k.
19.3.1900 launched by Workman Clark & Co, Belfast, y. no 160.
1910 converted to cabin class. 1.10.1915 to Canadian Pacific. 14.12.1918 stranded NW Ledges, Brier Island, Bay of Fundy.

36
Corsican (1915–23), 124191, 11,436g, 500 × 61 × 38ft.
Engine: builders, T 6cy 2S 16k.
29.4.1907 launched by Barclay Curle & Co, Scotstoun, y. no 467.
8.8.1914 requisitioned as troop ship. 1.10.1915 to Canadian Pacific. 16.11.1922 renamed *Marvale*, converted cabin class at Liverpool. 21.5.1923 wrecked on Freels Rock off Cape Pine NF.

37
Grampian (1915–21), 124220, 9598g, 480 × 60 × 38ft.
Engine: builders, T 6cy 2S 15k.
25.7.1907 launched by A. Stephen & Sons Ltd, Linthouse, y. no 422.
1.10.1915 to Canadian Pacific. 26.1.1921 arr Antwerp. 13.3.1921 gutted by fire at Antwerp. 10.7.1925 to F. Rysdyk Industries Ltd, Rotterdam, for scrap.

38
Ionian (1915–17), 113989, 8265g, 470 × 57 × 37ft.
Engine: builders, T 6cy 2S 14k.
12.9.1901 launched by Workman Clark & Co, Belfast, y. no 127.
1.10.1915 to Canadian Pacific. 20.10.1917 wrecked by mine two miles W of St Gowans Head. Laid by *UC51* 14.10.1917.

39
Pomeranian (1915–18), 85193, 4364g, 381 × 44 × 33ft.
Engine: builders, C 2cy 1S 12k.
6.5.1882 launched by Earle's SB&E Co, Hull, y. no 241, as *Grecian Monarch* for Monarch Line.
6.9.1887 to Allan Line. Renamed *Pomeranian*. 1.10.1915 to Canadian Pacific. 15.4.1918 torpedoed by *UC77* nine miles from Portland Bill.

40
Pretorian (1915–22), 113969, 6436g, 437 × 53 × 30ft.

Engine: Richardson & Westgarth, Hartlepool, T 3cy 1S 13k.
22.12.1900 launched by Furness Withy & Co, Hartlepool, y. no 253.
1910 converted to cabin class. 1.10.1915 to Canadian Pacific. 31.5.1919 to Murmansk and Archangel. 9.3.1922 laid-up Gareloch. 20.2.1926 to J. King & Co, Garston for scrap.

41
Sardinian (1915–20), 71695, 4376g, 400 × 42 × 35ft.
Engine: builders, C 2cy 1S, 1897 Denny, T 3cy 13k.
3.6.1874 launched by R. Steele & Co, Greenock, y. no 81.
29.7.1875 m/v. 10.5.1878 caught fire at Moville, scuttled and refloated. 26.11.1901 ex Liverpool with Marconi and equipment for first radio station St Johns NF. 1.10.1915 to Canadian Pacific. 8.12.1920 to Astoreca Azqueta & Co, to be hulk at Vigo. 1934 to Compania Carbonera. 22.6.1938 for Bilbao in tow for scrap.

42
Scandinavian (1915–23), 109441, 11,394g, 555 × 59 × 39ft.
Engine: builders, T 8cy 2S 14k.
17.4.1898 launched by Harland & Wolff Ltd, Belfast, y. no 315, as *New England* for Dominion Line.
1903 to White Star renamed *Romanic*. 1.1912 to Allan Line renamed *Scandinavian*. 1.10.1915 to Canadian Pacific. 9.7.1923 to Rysdyk Industries Rotterdam. 16.7.1923 to Klasmann & Lentze, Emden, for scrap.

43
Scotian (1915–26), 129547, 10,319g, 515 × 60 × 24ft.
Engine: builders, T 6cy 2S 14k.
7.5.1898 launched by Harland & Wolff Ltd, Belfast, y. no 320, as *Statendam* for Holland America Line.
23.3.1911 to Allan Line renamed *Scotian*. 1914 trooping for Canadian army. 1.10.1915 to Canadian Pacific. 16.11.1922 renamed *Marglen*. 1921–6 15 government trooping charters. 30.12.1926 to D.L. Pittaluga, Genoa, for scrap.

44
Sicilian (1915–23), 111225, 6224g, 430 × 54 × 28ft.

Engine: builders, T 3cy 1S 12k.
28.8.1899 launched by Workman Clark Ltd, Belfast, y. no 158.
28.10.1899 chartered as *Transport 57*. 1910 converted to cabin class. 1.10.1915 to Canadian Pacific. 12.1921 Montreal–West Indies, cargo service. 12.4.1923 renamed *Bruton*. 19.9.1923 laid-up Falmouth. 8.5.1925 to Franchi Gregorini, Italy, for scrap.

45
Tunisian (1915–28), 111248, 10,576g, 500 × 59 × 40ft.
Engine: builders, T 6cy 2S 14k.
17.1.1900 launched by A. Stephen & Sons, Linthouse, y. no 384.
1.10.1915 to Canadian Pacific. 1920 re-engined, oil fuel, converted to cabin class by D. W. Henderson & Co. 16.11.1922 renamed *Marburn*. 5.7.1927 laid-up Southend. 3.3.1928 two voyages to Saint John. 9.5.1928 laid-up Southampton. 17.9.1928 to Soc A. Co-operative Ligure Demolitori Navi, Genoa.

46
Victorian (1915–28), 121216, 10,629g, 520 × 60 × 38ft.
Engine: Parsons, ST 3S 18k.
25.8.1904 launched by Workman Clark & Co, Belfast, y. no 206.
17.8.1914 requisitioned as AMC. 1.10.1915 to Canadian Pacific. 11.12.1922 renamed *Marloch*, cabin class. 19.9.1928 laid-up Southend. 5.4.1929 to T. W. Ward Ltd, broken up Pembroke Dock.

47
Virginian (1915–20), 121219, 10,757g, 520 × 60 × 38ft.
Engine: Parsons, ST 3S 18k.
22.12.1904 launched by A. Stephen & Sons, Linthouse, y. no 405.
13.11.1914 requisitioned as AMC. 1.10.1915 to Canadian Pacific but did not sail for CP. 31.1.1920 released. 14.2.1920 to Swedish Amerika Line. Renamed *Drottningholm*. 1945 to Home Lines. 8.4.1948 first voyage as *Brasil* for South Atlantic Lines. 1.6.1951 renamed *Homeland*. 2.1955 ti SIDARMA. 29.3.1955 arr Trieste.

48
Miniota (1916–17), 135311, 4928g, 420 × 55 × 24ft.
Engine: Cent Marine Eng Works, Hartle-pool, T 3cy 1S 10k.
27.11.1913 launched by W. Gray & Co, West Hartlepool, y. no 834, as *Hackness* for London & Northern SS Co.
28.9.1916 to Canadian Pacific. 17.10.1916 renamed *Miniota*. 31.8.1917 torpedoed by *U62*, 30 miles SE of Start Point.

49
Methven (1917–24), 120650, 4700g, 390 × 53 × 27ft.
Engine: builders, T 3cy 1S 12k.
1.2.1905 launched by D. & W. Henderson & Co, Glasgow, y. no 448, as *Helipolis* for Alliance SS Co.
4.3.1908 to Century Shipping Co. 17.2.1913 to Admiralty to be hospital ship *Mediator*. 1914 renamed *Maine* II, conversion not completed. 7.3.1916 to Harris & Dixon Ltd as *Heliopolis*. 15.5.1917 to Canadian Pacific. 24.6.1916 ex Barry first CP voyage. 20.8.1917 renamed *Methven*. 18.12.1918 ex London for Vancouver via Panama. 22.3.1922 ex Hong Kong via Suez. 13.6.1922 New York–West Indies. 16.8.1922 Montreal–London service. 22.3.1923 renamed *Borden*. 26.6.1923 Montreal–West Indies service, 8 voyages. 25.7.1924 laid-up Falmouth. 26.10.1926 to G. E. Kulukundis, Greece, renamed *Perseus*. 1932 to F. Bertorello, broken up Genoa.

50
Montcalm II (1917–29), 140349, 6608g, 420 × 53 × 36ft.
Engine: NE Marine Eng Co, Newcastle, T 3cy 1S 11k.
7.6.1917 launched by Northumberland Shipbuilding Co, Newcastle, y. no 235.
12.9.1917 m/v London–Montreal. 25.8.1920 renamed *Bolingbroke*. 13.7.1929 arr Falmouth. Laid-up. 27.12.1933 to W. H. Arnott Young & Co. 2.1934 arr Troon to be broken up.

51
Melita (1918–35), 136367, 13,967g, 520 × 67 × 42ft.
Engine: Harland & Wolff Ltd, Belfast, T 8cy + LP turbine 3S 17k.
21.4.1917 launched by Barclay Curle & Co, Scotstoun, y. no 517.
2.6.1917 to Belfast to be completed. 12.1.1918 delivered to be troop ship. 25.1.1918 ex Liverpool first CP voyage. 1925 refit Palmers SB Co, Jarrow. 5.4.1935 to Ricuperi Metallici, Turin. Towed to Genoa by *Zwarte Zee*. To Italia Line as troop ship. Renamed *Liguria*. 22.1.1941 scuttled at Tobruk. 1950 raised. 19.8.1950 towed to Savona by *Ursus* for scrap.

52
Montezuma II (1918–28), 142423, 5038g, 405 × 53 × 27ft.
Engine: J. Kincaide & Co, Greenock, T 3cy 1S 11k.
28.3.1917 launched by R. Duncan & Co, Glasgow, y. no 330, as *Camperdown* for Glen & Co.
16.5.1918 to Canadian Pacific prior completion. Renamed *Montezuma* II. 23.5.1918 m/v ex Glasgow. 14.5.1923 renamed *Bedwyn*. 19.6.1923 renamed *Balfour*. 6.1924 Montreal–West Indies. 1.1926 returned to North Atlantic. 22.1.1928 arr Antwerp. 4.2.1928 to Lyle SS Co. 9.2.1928 renamed *Cape Verde*. 6.1935 to Fan Shien Ho, China. Renamed *Shang Ho*. 7.1938 to Mayachi Kisen KK, Japan, renamed *Kizan Maru*. 27.9.1943 destroyed at Singapore by British underground forces.

53
Holbrook (1918–28), 140409, 6655g, 412 × 55 × 27ft.
Engine: Blair & Co, Stockton, T 3cy 1S 11k.
17.7.1917 launched by J. L. Thompson & Sons, Sunderland, y. no 524, for Century Shipping Co.
24.6.1918 to Canadian Pacific. 28.6.1918 ex Liverpool, first CP voyage. 2.3.1923 renamed *Bredon*. 19.5.1923 renamed *Brandon*. 27.2.1928 arr Rotterdam. 3.3.1928 to South Georgia Co, whaling depot ship. 8.12.1939 torpedoed by *U48* south of Cork.

54
Dunbridge (1918–28), 142305, 6650g, 412 × 55 × 27ft.
Engine: Blair & Co, Stockton, T 3cy 1S 10k.
1.10.1917 launched by J. L. Thompson & Sons, Sunderland, y. no 525, for Century Shipping Co.
10.6.1918 to Canadian Pacific. 5.9.1918 ex Liverpool first CP voyage. 24.2.1923 renamed *Brecon*. 2.3.1928 arr Glasgow. 15.3.1928 to Goulandris Bros, Greece, renamed *Frangoula B. Goulandris*. 7.6.1940 torpedoed by *U26* SW of Cape Clear.

55

Mottisfont (1918–27), 140262, 5692g, 400 × 52 × 33ft.
Engine: NE Marine Eng Co, T 3cy 1S 10k.
11.11.1917 launched by W. Dobson & Co, Newcastle, y. no 197, for Harris & Dixon Ltd.
5.6.1918 to Canadian Pacific. 9.8.1918 m/v ex Barry. 22.3.1923 renamed *Bawtry*. 22.2.1927 to Livanos Bros, Greece, renamed *Archangelos*. 5.1935 to Theofano Maritime Co, Greece. 6.1950 to Kemal Sadikoglu, Turkey, renamed *K. Sadikoglu*. 9.1961 broken up at Kalafatyeri, Turkey.

56

Batsford (1918–27), 136641, 4782g, 388 × 54 × 27ft.
Engine: J. Dickinson, Sunderland, T 3cy 1S 11k.
11.12.1913 launched by J. L. Thompson & Sons, Sunderland, y. no 503, for Century Shipping Co.
11.6.1918 to Canadian Pacific. 26.9.1918 ex Weymouth, first CP voyage. 18.1.1927 to Turnbull Coal & Shipping Co. 28.1.1927 renamed *Hamdale*. 12.4.1937 to Barry Shipping Co. 29.4.1937 renamed *St Mellons*. 8.1937 to Okada Gumi KK, Japan, renamed *Tozan Maru*. 6.3.1938 wrecked on Goto Island on passage from Yawata to Keelung.

57

Minnedosa (1918–35), 142717, 13,972g, 520 × 67 × 42ft.
Engine: Harland & Wolff, Belfast, T 8cy + 1p turbine 3S 17k.
17.10.1917 launched by Barclay Curle & Co, Scotstoun, y. no 518.
2.5.1918 arr Belfast for completion by Harland & Wolff Ltd. 21.11.1918 delivered as troop ship. 5.12.1918 ex Liverpool first CP voyage. 1925 refit by R. & W. Hawthorne Leslie & Co. 5.4.1935 to Ricuperi Metallici, Turin. Towed to Savona for break-up, but transferred to Italia Line as troop ship, renamed *Piemonte*. 15.8.1943 scuttled at Messina. 27.7.1949 towed to Spezia for scrap.

58

Bosworth (1919–28), 143043, 6660g, 412 × 55 × 27ft.
Engine: J. Dickinson, Sunderland, T 3cy 1S 10k.

31.12.1918 launched by J. L. Thompson & Sons, Sunderland, y. no 527, as *War Peridot* for Shipping Controller.
7.3.1919 to Canadian Pacific. 15.3.1919 m/v ex Sunderland. 14.6.1920 renamed *Bosworth*. 11.1.1928 arr Antwerp. 5.3.1928 to H. M. Thomson. 10.7.1944 requisitioned. 4.9.1944 sunk off Normandy as part of Mulberry Harbour. Later refloated. 4.5.1949 arr Dalmuir for scrap by W. H. Arnott Young & Co.

59

Bothwell (1919–29), 143057, 6723g, 412 × 55 × 27ft.
Engine: builders, T 3cy 1S 11k.
7.12.1918 launched by W. Doxford & Sons, Sunderland, y. no 533, as *War Beryl* for Shipping Controller.
15.4.1919 to Canadian Pacific. 25.4.1919 m/v ex Sunderland. 23.6.1920 renamed *Bothwell*. 10.7.1929 laid-up at Falmouth. 27.11.1933 to Tramp Shipping Development Co. 23.3.1934 to Tower Shipping Co. 6.4.1934 renamed *Tower Crown*. 10.1937 to Kulukundis Shipping Co, Greece, renamed *Mount Ossa*. 4.1939 to R. Bornhofen, renamed *Robert Bornhofen*, requisitioned as auxiliary mine sweeper, renamed *Sperrbrecher*. 17.5.1940 became target vessel. 12.9.1942 sunk by mine off Honnigsvag, Porsanger Fjord, Finland.

60

Montreal II (1920–7), 143162, 9720g, 476 × 55 × 30ft.
Engine: builders, Q 8cy 2S 16k.
4.7.1906 launched by Blohm & Voss, Hamburg, y. no 184, as *Konig Friedrich August* for Hamburg Amerika Line.
1918 to Reparations Commission. 6.11.1920 to Canadian Pacific. 3.2.1921 renamed *Montreal* II. 5.2.1921 to Antwerp for refit. 1.6.1921 ex Antwerp first CP voyage. 1923 converted to cabin class. 22.5.1927 laid-up Southend. 4.5.1928 to Fabre Line, renamed *Alesia*. 10.1931 laid-up Marseilles. 3.11.1933 arr Genoa for break-up.

61

Montlaurier (1921–9), 144402, 17,500g, 590 × 68 × 39ft.
Engine: builders, Q 8cy 2S 16k.
21.10.1907 launched by J. C. Tecklenborg AG Geestemunde, y. no 211, as *Prinz Friedrich Wilhelm* for Norddeutscher Lloyd.

1918 to Reparations Commission. 13.5.1921 to Canadian Pacific but made several voyages on charter. 2.8.1921 renamed *Empress of China* II. 12.10.1921 renamed *Empress of India* II. 23.6.1922 ex Liverpool first CP voyage. 13.12.1922 renamed *Montlaurier*. 2.7.1925 renamed *Montnairn*. 7.10.1928 arr Southampton. 23.12.1929 to Soc A. Co-operative Ligure Demolitori Naiva, Genoa.

62

Montcalm III (1922–42), 145903, 16,418g, 546 × 70 × 40ft.
Engine: builders, 6 ST(dr) 2S 16k.
3.7.1920 launched by John Brown & Co, Glasgow, y. no 464.
17.1.1922 m/v ex Liverpool rescued crew Norwegian SS *Mod*. 6.12.1928 arr Harland & Wolff re-engined ST(sr). 25.8.1939 requisitioned as AMC. 17.10.1939 renamed HMS *Wolfe*. 22.5.1942 to Admiralty. 1952 to British Iron & Steel Corp. 7.11.1952 towed to Metal Industries (Salvage) Ltd, Faslane.

63

Empress of Scotland I (1921–30), 144371, 24,581g, 678 × 77 × 50ft.
Engine: builders, Q 8cy 2S 17k.
29.8.1905 launched by Vulcan Werke AG, Stettin, y. no 264, as *Kaiserin Auguste Victoria* for Hamburg Amerika Line.
3.1919 to Reparations Commission. 13.5.1921 to Canadian Pacific. 5.8.1921 renamed *Empress of Scotland*. 22.1.1922 ex Southampton first CP voyage. 2.12.1930 to Hughes-Bolckow Co, Blyth. 10.12.1930 caught fire. 17.10.1931 demolition completed.

64

Empress of Canada I (1922–43), 146215, 21,516g, 625 × 78 × 42ft.
Engine: builders, 8 ST(sr) 2S 22k.
17.8.1920 launched by Fairfield SB Co, Govan, y. no 528.
5.5.1922 m/v ex Falmouth to Hong Kong via Suez. 1.11.1928 ex Vancouver for Fairfield yard to be re-engined. 27.8.1929 ex Southampton–Quebec. 18.9.1929 ex Southampton for Vancouver via Panama. 29.11.1939 requisitioned. 14.3.1943 torpedoed by *Leonardo da Vinci* in South Atlantic.

65
Montrose II (1922–40), 145919, 16,401g, 546 × 70 × 40ft.
Engine: builders, 6 ST(dr) 2S 16k.
14.12.1920 launched by Fairfield SB Co, Govan, y. no 529.
5.5.1922 m/v ex Liverpool. 1931 re-engined by Harland & Wolff. 3.9.1939 requisitioned as AMC, renamed HMS *Forfar*. 2.12.1940 torpedoed by *U99* off West coast of Ireland.

66
Empress of Australia I (1922–52), 145300, 21,860g, 590 × 75 × 41ft.
Engine: builders, 2 ST 2S 17k.
20.12.1913 launched by Vulcan Werke AG, Stettin, y. no 333, as *Tirpitz* for Hamburg Amerika Line.
1919 to Reparations Commission—trooping. 25.7.1921 to Canadian Pacific.
28.7.1921 renamed *Empress of China* III.
2.6.1922 renamed *Empress of Australia*.
16.6.1922 ex Clyde for Pacific via Panama.
1.9.1923 at Yokohama earthquake.
4.8.1926 ex Hong Kong via Suez for Fairfield yard. 25.6.1927 ex Southampton–Quebec. 17.9.1939 requisitioned. Continued trooping until 1952. 10.5.1952 arr Inverkeithing for scrap.

67
Montclare (1922–42), 145964, 16,314g, 546 × 70 × 40ft.
Engine: builders, 6 ST(dr) 2S 16k.
18.12.1921 launched by John Brown & Co, Clydebank, y. no 465.
18.8.1922 m/v ex Liverpool. 22.3.1931 ashore Little Cumbrae, 300 passengers disembarked. 28.8.1939 requisitioned AMC. 2.6.1942 to Admiralty. 3.2.1958 arr Inverkeithing for scrap.

68
Beaverburn I (1927–40), 160187, 9874g, 503 × 62 × 38ft.
Engine: builders, 6 ST(sr) 2S 14k.
27.9.1927 launched by W. Denny Bros, Dumbarton, y. no 1192.
24.12.1927 m/v ex Glasgow. 5.2.1940 torpedoed by *U41*, North Atlantic.

69
Beaverford I (1928–40), 149983, 10,042g, 503 × 62 × 38ft.
Engine: Parsons Marine ST Co, 6 ST 2S 14k.
27.10.1927 launched by Barclay Curle & Co, Scotstoun, y. no 617.
21.1.1928 m/v ex Glasgow. 22.2.1940 requisitioned. 5.11.1940 sunk by *Admiral Scheer*, North Atlantic.

70
Beaverdale (1928–41), 149987, 9957g, 503 × 62 × 38ft.
Engine: Parsons Marine ST Co, 6 ST 2S 14k.
28.9.1927 launched by Sir W. G. Armstrong Whitworth & Co, Newcastle, y. no 1019.
1.2.1928 m/v ex Newcastle. 13.9.1939 requisitioned. 1.4.1941 torpedoed *U48*, North Atlantic.

71
Beaverhill (1928–44), 160362, 10,041g, 503 × 62 × 38ft.
Engine: Parsons Marine ST Co, 6 ST 2S 14k.
8.11.1927 launched by Barclay Curle & Co, Scotstoun, y. no 618.
18.2.1928 m/v ex Glasgow. 3.5.1940 requisitioned. 10.1941 fitted to carry 138 passengers. 24.11.1944 stranded Hillyards Reef, Saint John NB.

72
Beaverbrae I (1928–41), 160836, 9956g, 503 × 62 × 38ft.
Engine: Parsons Marine ST Co, 6 ST 2S 14k.
24.11.1927 launched by Sir W. G. Armstrong Whitworth & Co, Newcastle, y. no 102.
15.3.1928 m/v ex Newcastle. 11.3.1940 requisitioned. 25.3.1941 sunk by enemy aircraft, North Atlantic.

73
Duchess of Bedford (1928–60), 160482, 20,123g, 582 × 75 × 42ft.
Engine: builders, 6 ST(sr) 2S 18k.
24.1.1928 launched by John Brown & Co, Clydebank, y. no 518.
1.6.1928 m/v ex Liverpool. 29.8.1939 requisitioned as troop ship. 3.3.1947 refitted at Fairfields. 15.7.1948 renamed *Empress of France* II. 1.9.1948 ex Liverpool first post-war voyage. 22.12.1960 to John Cashmore Ltd, Uskside, scrapped.

74
Duchess of Atholl (1928–42), 160505, 20,119g, 582 × 75 × 42ft.
Engine: builders, 6 ST(sr) 2S 18k.
23.11.1927 launched by W. Beardmore & Co, Dalmuir, y. no 648.
13.7.1928 m/v ex Liverpool. 30.12.1939 requisitioned as troop ship. 10.10.1942 torpedoed *U178* 200 miles east Ascension Isle.

75
Duchess of Richmond (1929–53), 160631, 20,022g, 582 × 75 × 42ft.
Engine: builders, 6 ST(sr) 2S 18k.
18.6.1928 launched by John Brown & Co, Clydebank, y. no 523.
15.3.1929 m/v ex Liverpool. 14.2.1940 requisitioned as troop ship. 19.5.1946 refitted at Fairfields. 12.7.1947 renamed *Empress of Canada* II. 16.7.1947 ex Liverpool first post-war voyage. 25.1.1953 gutted by fire at Gladstone Dock. 8.1954 to Cantiere di Portovenere, Genoa. 1.9.1954 ex Liverpool in tow by *Zwarte Zee*. 10.10.1954 arr Spezia.

76
Duchess of York (1929–43), 161202, 20,021g, 582 × 75 × 42ft.
Engine: builders, 6 ST(sr) 2S 18k.
28.9.1928 launched by John Brown & Co, Clydebank, y. no 524.
22.3.1929 m/v ex Liverpool. 7.3.1940 requisitioned as troop ship. 11.7.1943 sunk by enemy aircraft off Morocco.

77
Empress of Japan II (1930–57), 161430, 26,032g, 644 × 84 × 45ft.
Engine: builders, 6 ST(sr) 2S 21k.
17.12.1929 launched by Fairfield SB Co, Govan, y. no 634.
14.6.1930 m/v ex Liverpool–Quebec. 12.7.1930 ex Southampton for Hong Kong via Suez. 7.8.1930 ex Hong Kong first trans-Pacific voyage. 26.11.1939 requisitioned as troop ship. 16.10.1942 renamed *Empress of Scotland* II. 3.5.1948 arr Liverpool on completion of war service. 9.5.1950 ex Liverpool to Quebec, first post-war voyage. 13.5.1952 first voyage to Montreal. 25.11.1957 arr Liverpool. 13.1.1958 to Hamburg-Atlantic Line. 22.1.1958 renamed *Hanseatic*. 7.9.1966 caught fire at New York. 23.9.1966 ex New York in tow by tugs *Atlantic* and *Pacific*. 11.1966 to Eckhardt & Co, Hamburg, for scrap.

78
Empress of Britain II (1931–40), 162582, 42,348g, 733 × 98 × 56ft.
Engine: builders, 12 ST(sr) 4S 24k.
11.6.1930 launched by John Brown & Co, Clydebank, y. no 530.
27.5.1931 m/v ex Southampton–Quebec. 25.11.1939 requisitioned. 26.10.1940 set on fire by enemy aircraft. 28.10.1940 torpedoed by *U32*, North Atlantic.

The two following ships were owned jointly with the Union Steamship Co and operated as the Canadian Australasian Line (see page 209).

79
Aorangi (1931–53), 148515, 17,491g, 580 × 72 × 43ft.
Engine: builders, 4 × 2SA 4S 17k.
17.6.1924 launched by Fairfield SB Co, Govan, y. no 603, for Union SS Co of New Zealand.
3.1.1925 ex Southampton m/v to Victoria via Panama. 2.7.1931 to Canadian Australasian Line. 10.2.1940 requisitioned as troop ship. 5.1946 to Sydney for refit. 19.8.1948 ex Sydney first post-war voyage. 14.5.1953 ex Vancouver last voyage to Sydney. 9.6.1953 to British Iron & Steel Corp. 25.7.1953 arr Dalmuir, break-up by W. H. Arnott Young & Co.

80
Niagara (1931–40), 135193, 13,414g, 523 × 66 × 35ft.
Engine: builders, T 8cy + LP turbine 3S 18k.
17.8.1912 launched by John Brown & Co, Clydebank, y. no 415, for Union SS Co, New Zealand.
2.7.1931 to Canadian Australasian Line. 18.6.1940 sunk by mine off Hauraki Gulf, New Zealand.

———

81
Beaverdell (1946–62), 180818, 9901g, 476 × 64 × 40ft.
Engine: Parsons, TE 1S 16k.
27.8.1945 launched by Lithgows Ltd, Port Glasgow, y. no 1001.
28.2.1946 m/v ex Liverpool. 28.8.1952 renamed *Mapledell* for Pacific service. 30.8.52 ex Montreal for Vancouver via Panama. 27.6.1954 ex Vancouver for London via Panama. 21.12.1956 renamed *Beaverdell*. 12.11.1962 arr London. 11.1.1963 to Giacomo Costa Fu Andrea,

Genoa, renamed *Luisa Costa*. 29.3.1971 arr Spezia. 1.1972 demolition by Terrestre Marittima SpA.

82
Beaverburn II (1946–60), 166217, 9875g, 476 × 64 × 40ft.
Engine: Parsons, 2 ST(dr) 1S 15k.
25.2.1944 launched by Caledon S&E Co, Dundee, y. no 404, as *Empire Captain* for M of War Transport.
15.5.1946 to Canadian Pacific. 17.5.1946 renamed *Beaverburn* II. 19.5.1946 ex Liverpool first CP voyage. 3.1948 passenger accommodation reduced from 35 to 12. 21.3.1960 arr Antwerp. 25.3.1960 to Ben Line. 30.3.1960 renamed *Bennachie*. 2.7.1960 caught fire, towed into Singapore. 9.1964 to Atlantic Navigation Corp, renamed *Silvana*. 1969 to Outerocean Nav Co, Kaohsiung, Taiwan. 15.4.1971 arr Kaohsiung for scrap.

83
Beaverglen (1946–63), 180858, 9824g, 476 × 64 × 40ft.
Engine: Parsons, TE 1S 16k.
10.12.1945 launched by Lithgows Ltd, Port Glasgow, y. no 1002.
24.5.1946 m/v ex Liverpool. 11.8.1963 arr London. 24.9.1963 to Hibiscus Ltd, Hamilton, Bermuda, renamed *Bermuda Hibiscus*. 4.1965 to Teh-Hu SS Co, Hong Kong, renamed *Ping An*. 24.11.1965 aground near Hook of Holland, to H.P. Heuvelman NV as lies for scrap.

84
Beaverford II (1946–62), 166218, 9881g, 476 × 64 × 40ft.
Engine: Metropolitan Vickers Ltd, ST(dr) 1S 15k.
18.8.1944 launched by Caledon SB&E Co, Dundee, y. no 406, as *Empire Kitchener* for M of War Transport.
12.6.1946 to Canadian Pacific, renamed *Beaverford* II. 16.6.1946 ex Liverpool first CP voyage. 3.1948 passenger accommodation reduced from 35 to 12. 10.6.1960 passenger accommodation withdrawn. 29.8.1962 laid-up at Antwerp. 3.12.1962 to Alliance Marine Corp, Hong Kong, renamed *Hulda*. 1966 to Int Marine Development Corp. 18.8.1969 damaged by hurricane Camille—ashore Gulfport, Mississippi, constructive total loss—as lies to Coastal Metal Processors Inc. P&W Industries Inc.

85
Beaverlake (1946–62), 180954, 9824g, 476 × 64 × 40ft.
Engine: Parsons, TE 1S 16k.
20.5.1946 launched by Lithgows Ltd, Port Glasgow, y. no 1003.
25.10.1946 m/v ex Liverpool. 18.6.1962 to Lloyd Tirrenico SpA Genoa, renamed *Bice Costa*. 1964 to Giacomo Costa Fu Andrea. 1968 to Costa Armatori SpA. 23.4.1971 arr Spezia for scrap.

86
Beavercove (1947–63), 181659, 9824g, 476 × 64 × 40ft.
Engine: Parsons, TE 1S 16k.
16.7.1946 launched by Fairfield SB Co, Govan, y. no 728.
3.9.1947 m/v ex London. 22.7.1952 renamed *Maplecove*. 15.8.1952 arr Vancouver. 13.5.1954 ex Vancouver. 13.7.1954 arr London. 1.12.1956 renamed *Beavercove*. 19.8.1963 to Giacomo Costa Fu Andrea, renamed *Giovanna Costa*. 1968 to Costa Armatori SpA. 24.3.1971 for demolition by Cantieri Navali Santa Maria, at Spezia.

87
Beaverbrae II (1948–54), 177895, 9034g, 469 × 60 × 35ft.
Engine: builders, 2 SA DE 1S 16k.
15.12.1938 launched by Blohm & Voss, Hamburg, y. no 518, as *Huascaran* for Hamburg Amerika Line.
1945 captured by Allies. 2.9.1947 to Canadian Pacific. 8.2.1948 ex Saint John as *Beaverbrae* II, first CP voyage. 1.11.1954 to Compagnia Genovese d'Armamento, Genoa, renamed *Aurelia*. 1970 to International Cruises SA, Panama, renamed *Romanza*. 17.10.1979 aground Dhenousa Island. 19.10.1979 refloated, to Syros for repairs.

88
Beaverlodge (1952–60), 164865, 9904g, 476 × 64 × 40ft.
Engine: builders, 2 ST(dr) 1S 15k.
17.7.1943 launched by Furness SB Co, Haverton-Hill on Tees, y. no 335, as *Empire Regent* for M of War Transport.
13.8.1946 to Furness Withy & Co, renamed *Black Prince*. 19.5.1949 renamed *Zealandic*. 3.10.1952 to Canadian Pacific, renamed *Beaverlodge*. 1.11.1952 ex Liverpool first CP voyage. 16.3.1960 to Ben Line, renamed *Benhiant*. 1970 to Witty

CIA Nav SA, Cyprus, renamed *Venus*. 14.7.1971 arr Kaohsiung, Taiwan, for scrap.

89
Empress of Australia II (1953–6), 185887, 17,707g, 552 × 72 × 42ft.
Engine: builders, ST(sr) 2S 16k.
23.2.1924 launched by Cammell Laird & Co, Birkenhead, y. no 886, as *De Grasse* for French Line.
1940 seized by Germans. 30.8.1944 sunk by Germans. 1945 refloated. 7.1947 Le Havre–New York. 26.3.1953 to Canadian Pacific. 27.4.1953 renamed *Empress of Australia* II. 28.4.1953 ex Liverpool first CP voyage. 15.2.1956 to Fratelli Grimaldi, Genoa, renamed *Venezuela*. 28.8.1962 to Soc Armamente Santa Rosalia SpA, Spezia, for scrap. When ordered it was intended to name the vessel *Suffren*.

90
Empress of Britain III (1956–64), 187376, 25,516g, 640 × 85 × 48ft.
Engine: builders, 6 ST(dr) 2S 20k.
22.6.1955 launched by Fairfield SB Co, Govan, y. no 731.
20.4.1956 m/v ex Liverpool. 23.10.1963 chartered to Travel Savings Assoc. 16.11.1964 to Greek Line. 15.3.1965 renamed *Queen Anna Maria*. 22.1.1975 laid-up Piraeus. 11.1975 to Carnival Cruise Line, renamed *Carnivale*. 1976 to Fairweather Int Corp, Panama.

91
Empress of England (1957–70), 187544, 25,585g, 640 × 85 × 48ft.
Engine: builders, 6 ST(dr) 2S 20k.
9.5.1956 launched by Vickers Armstrong SB Ltd, Walker on Tyne, y. no 155.
18.4.1957 m/v ex Liverpool. 23.10.1963 chartered to TSA. 28.4.1964 returned to N Atlantic service. 14.4.1970 to Shaw Saville Ltd, renamed *Ocean Monarch*. 6.1975 to Chi Shun Hwa Steel Co. 17.7.1975 arr Kaohsiung, Taiwan, for scrap.

92
Empress of Canada III (1961–72), 302597, 27,300g, 650 × 76 × 48ft.

Engine: builders, 6 ST(dr) 2S 21k.
10.5.1960 launched by Vickers Armstrong SB Ltd, Walker on Tyne, y. no 171.
24.4.1961 m/v ex Liverpool. 18.2.1972 to Carnival Cruise Line, renamed *Mardi Gras*.

93
Beaverfir (1961–72), 302712, 4539g, 374 × 51 × 25ft.
Engine: Burmeister & Wain, 2SA 6cy 1S.
22.3.1961 launched by Sarpsborg Mek Verksted A/S, y. no 32.
5.7.1961 m/v ex Antwerp. 21.4.1972 to Arion Shipping Corp, Monrovia, renamed *Arion*. 11.1975 to Linea Manaure CA, Venezuela, renamed *Manaure* II.

94
Beaverpine (1962–73), 304365, 4514g, 371 × 53 × 24ft.
Engine: Fairfield-Sulzer, 2SA 6cy 1S.
18.6.1962 launched by Burntisland SB Co, Burntisland, y. no 403.
23.10.1962 m/v ex London. 2.9.1971 converted to cellular container ship. 13.12.1971 renamed *CP Explorer*. 28.12.1973 to Arion Shipping Corp, Monrovia, renamed *Moira*.

95
Beaverelm (1962–71), 304325, 3959g, 355 × 49 × 30ft.
Engine: Burmeister & Wain, 2SA 7cy 1S.
19.5.1960 launched by Moss Vaerft & Dokk A/S, Norway, y. no 144, as *Roga* for Aktieselskapet Asplund, Moss, Norway. 9.1960 m/v ex Riga. 9.8.1962 to Canadian Pacific, renamed *Beaverelm*. 1.9.1962 first CP voyage ex Antwerp. 28.9.1971 to Nan-Yang Shipping Co, Macao, renamed *Hengshan*. 1976 to Fortune Sea Transport Corp, Panama. 1977 to China Ocean Shipping Co, renamed *Yong Kang*.

96
Beaverash (1963–9), 304451, 4529g, 375 × 50 × 23ft.
Engine: Burmeister & Wain, 2SA 7cy 1S.
19.5.1958 launched by A/B Ekensbergs

Varv, Stockholm, y. no 214, as *Mimer* for M. Thorviks Rederi A/S, Oslo.
10.1.1963 to Canadian Pacific, renamed *Beaverash*. 12.2.1963 first CP voyage ex Antwerp. 26.11.1969 to Friendship Shipping Co, SA, renamed *Zanet*. 1977 to Zanet Navigation Corp.

97
Beaveroak (1965–73), 307911, 6165g, 408 × 58 × 33ft.
Engine: Sulzer, 2SA 6cy 1S.
31.3.1965 launched by Vickers Armstrong SB Co, Walker on Tyne, y. no 182.
7.9.1965 m/v ex Antwerp. 10.7.1970 converted to cellular container ship, 2.10.1970 renamed *CP Ambassador*. 24.12.1973 to Arion Shipping Corp, renamed *Atalanta*.

98
CP Voyageur (1970–), 341152, 15,680g, 548 × 84 × 30ft.
Engine: Burmeister & Wain, 2SA 8cy 1S 19k.
19.8.1970 launched by Cammell Laird & Co, Birkenhead, y. no 1343.
29.11.1970 m/v ex Liverpool.

99
CP Trader (1971–), 341333, 15,680g, 548 × 84 × 30ft.
Engine: Burmeister & Wain, 2SA 8cy 1S 19k.
28.1.1971 launched by Cammell Laird & Co, Birkenhead, y. no 1344.
2.6.1971 towed to Cork for completion by Verolme Dockyard. 2.7.1971 m/v ex Cork.

100
CP Discoverer (1971–), 342762, 15,680g, 548 × 84 × 30ft.
Engine: Burmeister & Wain, 2SA 8cy 1S 19k.
26.3.1971 launched by Cammell Laird & Co, Birkenhead, y. no 1345.
28.7.1971 m/v ex Liverpool.

101
CP Hunter (1980–), 19,663dwt.
Chartered from Ernst Russ, Hamburg.
16.1.1980 ex Hamburg, first CP voyage.
22.6.1980 arr Rotterdam off hire.

2 Tankers and bulk carriers

Abbreviations: Types of vessel CC—crude carrier; VLCC—very large crude carrier; GBC—geared bulk carrier; BC—gearless bulk carrier; PC—product carrier. *Builders* MHI—Mitsubishi Heavy Industries; San—Sanoyasu Dockyard; NKK—Nippon Kokan Kaisha; VDG—Van der Giessen; B&W—Burmeister & Wain.

151
R. B. Angus (1965–67), GBC.
317140, 13,100d, 503 × 62 × 30ft.
2.11.1958 launched by Brodogradiliste Split, as *Sunrise*.
29.8.1963 renamed *Modena*. 19.11.1965 to CP(B), renamed *R. B. Angus*. 3.12.1965 ex Grimstad, Norway for Vancouver. 25.11.1967 ex Chemainus BC for Tokyo. 17.12.1967 abandoned during storm 620 miles ENE Tokyo.

152
Lord Mount Stephen (1966–), CC.
317155, 65,000d, 758 × 118 × 57ft.
Engine: Sulzer, 2SA, 9cy, 16k.
3.8.1966 launched by MHI, y. no 1623.
10.11.1966 m/v Nagasaki to Ras Tanura.

153
Lord Strathcona (1967–), CC.
317156, 71,747d, 758 × 118 × 57ft.
Engine: Sulzer, 2SA, 9cy, 16k.
15.11.1966 launched by MHI, y. no 1624.
14.2.1967 m/v Nagasaki to Mina al Ahmadi.

154
H. R. MacMillan (1968–78), GBC.
317163, 28,947d, 594 × 96 × 52ft.
Engine: Sulzer, 2SA, 7cy, 15k.
31.10.1967 launched by MHI, y. no 191.
26.1.1968 m/v Hiroshima to Nanaimo, BC. 14.6.1978 to Pender Shipping Corp Panama, renamed *Grand Reliance*.

155
J. V. Clyne (1968–79), GBC.
317169, 28,899d, 594 × 96 × 52ft.
Engine: Sulzer, 2SA, 7cy, 15k.
3.2.1968 launched by MHI, y. no 192.
26.4.1968 m/v Hiroshima to Port Alberni, BC. 31.3.1979 to Korean Shipping Corp Panama, renamed *West Sunori*.

156
N. R. Crump (1969–79), GBC.
317180, 28,939d, 594 × 96 × 52ft.
Engine: Sulzer, 2SA, 7cy, 15k.
8.3.1969 launched by MHI, y. no 204.
31.5.1969 m/v Hiroshima to Nanaimo, BC. 27.2.1979 to Korean Shipping Corp Panama, renamed *West Jinuri*.
1980 to Azufrera Panamericana SA Mexico, renamed *Texistepec*

157
Fort St John (1969–), GBC.
332490, 15,925d, 487 × 70 × 40ft.
Engine: Sulzer, 2SA, 7cy, 15k.
8.7.1969 launched by Sanoyasu, y. no 275, as *Pacific Logger*. 6.9.1969 m/v Osaka to Seattle. 18.12.1974 shaft damaged in storm. 28.3.1977 renamed *Fort St John*.

158
T. Akasaka (1969–), BC.
332498, 57,138d, 744 × 102 × 58ft.
Engine: B&W, 2SA, 7cy, 15k.
15.8.1969 launched by NKK, y. no 860.
22.11.1969 m/v Yokohama to Dampier.

159
W. C. Van Horne (1970–), BC.
332503, 57,114d, 744 × 102 × 58ft.
Engine: B&W, 2SA, 7cy, 15k.
11.3.1970 launched by NKK, y. no 861.
10.6.1970 m/v Yokohama to Vancouver, BC.

160
Port Hawkesbury (1970–), VLCC.
332661, 252,970d, 1109 × 170 × 88ft.
Engine: B&W, 2SA, 9cy, 15.5k.
26.10.1970 launched by NKK, y. no 2.
16.7.1970 m/v Tsu to Mina al Ahmadi.

161
T. G. Shaughnessy (1971–), VLCC.
332669, 252,820d, 1109 × 170 × 88ft.
Engine: B&W, 2SA, 9cy, 15.5k.
4.4.1970 launched by NKK, y. no 4.
29.1.1971 m/v Tsu to Mina al Ahmadi.

162
G. A. Walker (1973–), PC.
332687, 30,606d, 650 × 85 × 47ft.
Engine: B&W, 2SA, 6cy, 15.5k.
2.9.1972 launched by VDG, y. no 888.
20.3.1973 m/v Rotterdam to Salem, Mass.

163
W. A. Mather (1973–), PC.
332695, 30,606d, 650 × 85 × 47ft.
Engine: B&W, 2SA, 6cy, 15.5k.
27.1.1973 launched by VDG, y. no 889.
1.8.1973 m/v Rotterdam to Boston.

164
E. W. Beatty (1973–), BC.
356275, 123,132d, 853 × 137 × 78ft.
Engine: B&W, 2SA, 9cy, 15.5k.
22.6.1973 launched by NKK, y. no 893.
28.9.1973 m/v Yokohama to Port Hedland.

165
R. A. Emerson (1973–), PC.
356277, 30,606d, 560 × 85 × 47ft.
Engine: B&W, 2SA, 6cy, 15.5k.
7.7.1973 launched by VDG, y. no 890.
2.11.1973 m/v Rotterdam to Portland.

166
D. C. Coleman (1974–), BC.
356285, 123,132d, 853 × 137 × 78ft.
Engine: B&W, 2SA, 9cy, 15.5k.
8.10.1973 launched by NKK, y. no 894.
19.1.1974 m/v Yokohama to Proudhoe.

167
Fort MacLeod (1974–), PC.
356290, 30,782d, 560 × 85 × 47ft.
Engine: B&W, 2SA, 6cy, 15.5k.
20.10.1973 launched by VDG, y. no 893.
4.3.1974 m/v Rotterdam to Port Jefferson.

168
I. D. Sinclair (1974–), VLCC.
356299, 250,713d, 1109 × 170 × 88ft.
Engine: B&W, 2SA, 10cy, 15.3k.
29.3.1974 launched by NKK, y. no 27.
20.7.1974 m/v Tsu to Dubai.

169
W. M. Neal (1974–), BC.
356300, 123,132d, 853 × 137 × 78ft.
Engine: B&W, 2SA, 9cy, 15.5k.
10.5.1974 launched by NKK, y. no 899.
8.8.1974 m/v Yokohama to Port Hedland.

170
Fort Steele (1974–), PC.
356305, 30,782d, 560 × 85 × 47ft.
Engine: B&W, 2SA, 6cy, 15.5k.
27.7.1974 launched by VDG, y. no 894.
30.11.1974 m/v Rotterdam to Ventspils.

171
Fort Edmonton (1975–   ), PC.
356312, 30,782d, 560 × 85 × 47ft.
Engine: B&W, 2SA, 7cy, 15.5k.
12.10.1974 launched by VDG, y. no 900.
1.3.1975 m/v Rotterdam to Callao, Peru.

172
Fort Kipp (1975–   ), PC.
356320, 30,782d, 560 × 85 × 47ft.
Engine: B&W, 2SA, 7cy, 15.5k.
8.3.1975 launched by VDG, y. no 901.
3.7.1975 m/v Rotterdam to Gibraltar.

173
Fort Nelson (1975–   ), GBC.
356728, 35,414d, 604 × 92 × 51ft.
Engine: B&W, 2SA, 7cy, 15k.
28.5.1975 launched by San, y. no 343.
12.8.1975 m/v Osaka to Suez.

174
Fort Coulonge (1976–   ), PC.
356734, 30,782d, 560 × 85 × 47ft.
Engine: B&W, 2SA, 7cy, 15.5k.
18.10.1975 launched by VDG, y. no 902.
20.2.1976 m/v Rotterdam to Amuay Bay.

175
Fort Calgary (1976–   ), GBC.
356741, 35,414d, 604 × 92 × 51ft.
Engine: B&W, 2SA, 7cy, 15k.
18.12.1975 launched by San, y. no 345.
26.3.1976 m/v Osaka to Tripoli.

176
Fort Kamloops (1976–   ), GBC.
356764, 27,960d, 568 × 84 × 47ft.
Engine: B&W, 2SA, 7cy, 15k.
22.7.1976 launched by San, y. no 357.
28.10.1976 m/v Osaka to Vancouver.

177
Port Vancouver (1977–   ), BC.
356773, 59,898d, 738 × 106 × 59ft.
Engine: B&W, 2SA, 7cy, 15k.
11.11.1976 launched by B&W, y. no 871.
14.1.1977 m/v Copenhagen to Tubarao.

178
Fort Victoria (1977–   ), GBC.
356775, 27,960d, 568 × 84 × 47ft.
Engine: B&W, 2SA, 7cy, 15k.
15.11.1976 launched by San, y. no 358.
28.2.1977 m/v Osaka to Marseilles.

179
Port Quebec (1977–   ), BC.
373247, 59,898d, 738 × 106 × 59ft.
Engine: B&W, 2SA, 7cy, 15k.
17.2.1977 launched by B&W, y. no 873.
18.4.1977 m/v Copenhagen to Contre-coeur.

180
Fort Yale (1977–   ), GBC.
373249, 27,960d, 568 × 84 × 47ft.
Engine: B&W, 2SA, 7cy, 15k.
17.3.1977 launched by San, y. no 359.
2.8.1977 m/v Osaka to Newcastle, NSW.

181
Fort Walsh (1978–   ), GBC.
373271, 21,824d, 528 × 75 × 44ft.
Engine: B&W, 2SA, 6cy, 15k.
27.7.1977 launched by San, y. no 364.
17.1.1978 m/v Osaka to Karachi.

182
Fort Carleton (1978–   ), GBC.
373273, 21,824d, 528 × 75 × 44ft.
Engine: B&W, 2SA, 6cy, 15k.
14.10.1977 launched by San, y. no 365.
15.3.1978 m/v Osaka to Suez.

183
Fort Hamilton (1978–   ), GBC.
373276, 21,824d, 528 × 75 × 44ft.
Engine: B&W, 2SA, 6cy, 15k.
23.12.1977 launched by San, y. no 366.
27.3.1978 m/v Osaka to New York.

184
Fort Norman (1979–   ), BC.
680551, 55, 120d, 714 × 97 × 42ft.
Engine: B&W, 2SA, 8cy, 15k.
1968 launched by Eriksbergs M/v Gothen-burg as *Rona* for A/S Kosmos 1972 to
A/S Agnes. 1978 to Owen Corp Liberia,
renamed *Pilot Trader*. 1979 to Pacheia Ship-ping Corp Liberia, renamed *Norman
Trader*. To CP(B) renamed *Fort Norman*.
14.12.1979 first CP voyage.

185
Fort Fraser (1980–   ), BC.
670785, 74,422d, 825 × 106 × 45ft.
Engine: B&W, 2SA, 9cy, 16k.
1967 launched by Mitsuizosen, Tm, as
Fernie for P & O SN Co. 1979 to Alcyone
Shipping Corp Liberia, renamed *Alcyone*.
1980 to CP(B), renamed *Fort Fraser*.
8.2.1980 first CP voyage Tamano to Port
Hedland.

186
Fort Douglas (1980–   ), BC.
681,574, 105,439d/820 × 134 × 49ft.
Engine: Sulzer, 2SA/10cy.
1968 launched by Ishikawajlma–Harima
Kur. as *Sidney Spiro* for General Ore Int
Corp. 1979 to Docynia Shipping Corp
Liberia, renamed *Docynia*. 1980 to CP(B),
renamed *Fort Douglas*. 18.2.1980 first CP
voyage, Mizushima to Dampier WA.

187
Fort Erie (1980–   ), BC.
671,282, 57,567d/ 743 × 102 × 39ft.
Engine: Sulzer, 2SA/8cy/16.5k.
1967 launched by NKK Tsu as *Jasaka* for
Anders Jahre, Norway. 1978 to Arion Ship-ping Corp Liberia, renamed *Nemesis*. 1979
to Nemesis Shipping Corp. 1980 to CP(B),
renamed *Fort Erie*. 7.3.1980 first CP voyage,
Yokohama to Roberts Bank BC.

188
Fort Nanaimo (1980–   ), GBC.
—   35,414d, 604 × 92 × 51ft.
Engine: B&W, 2SA/7cy/15k.
12.9.1975 launched by San, y. no 344 as
Leda for Leda Shipping Co. 3.1980 to
CP(B), renamed *Fort Nanaimo*. 24.3.1980
first CP voyage Tampa to Vancouver.

189
Fort Assiniboine (1980–   ), PC.
388396, 31,766d/525 × 89 × 48ft.
Engine: B&W, 2SA.
7.12.1979 launched by San, y. no 1033.
15.6.1980 m/v Osaka to Kwinana.

190
Fort Garry (1980–   ), PC.
—   31,000d, 525 × 89 × 48ft.
Engine: B&W, 2SA.
14.3.1980 launched by San y. no 1034.

191
Fort Rouge (1980–   ), PC.
— 31,000d, 525 × 89 × 48ft.
Engine: B&W, 2SA.
29.5.1980 launched by San y. no 1035

192
Fort Toronto (1980–   ), PC.
—   31,000d, 525 × 89 × 48ft.
Engine: B&W, 2SA.
— launched by San, y. no 1036.
191–192 inder construction.

3 BC coastal ships

The following fourteen vessels were taken over from Canadian Pacific Navigation Co 1901, see page 75.

301
Amur (1901–11), 98073, 907g, 216 × 28 × 11ft.
Engine: NE Marine Co, T3cy 1S 12k.
1890 launched by Strand Slipway Co, Sunderland.
1895 to Lombard SS Co. 1898 to Klondyke Mining Co. 1899 to CPN Co. 11.1.1901 to Canadian Pacific. 1911 to Coastwise SS & Barge Co. 2.1924 stranded. 1924 to A. Berquist, renamed *Famous*. 1926 wrecked Skeena River—salvaged. 1929 dismantled and sunk North Arm, Burrard Inlet.

302
Beaver (1901–19), 107096, 545g, 140 × 28 × 5ft, stern wheeler.
1898 launched by Albion Iron Works, Victoria BC, for CPN Co.
11.1.1901 to Canadian Pacific. 1913 New Westminster–Chilliwack. 1919 to BC government. 1930 scrapped.

303
Charmer (1901–35), 150413, 1081g, 200 × 42 × 13ft.
Engine: builders, T3cy 1S 13k.
1887 launched by Union Iron Works, San Francisco, for CPN Co as *Premier*.
18.10.1892 struck *Willamette* and beached at Bush Point. Towed to Victoria, renamed *Charmer*. 11.1.1901 to Canadian Pacific. 17.10.1907 collision with *Tartar*. 26.2.1916 rammed and sunk *Quadra* in fog off Nanaimo. 1933 dressing room for bathers Newcastle Island. 1935 dismantled, hull burned off Albert Head.

304
Danube (1901–5), 62279, 887g, 215 × 28 × 11ft, iron.
Engine: builders, C2cy 1S.
1869 launched by J. Elder & Co, Clyde, for D. R. MacGregor.
6.6.1884 to Scottish Oriental SS Co. 1888 chartered by CPR for Vancouver–Portland service and to San Francisco in connection with trans-Pacific service. 2.8.1890 to CPN Co. 11.1.1901 to Canadian Pacific. 20.10.1905 to BC Salvage Co. 4.11.1905 Renamed *Salvor*. 3.8.1918 to J. P. Davies, Montreal. 1920 to A. Menchaca, Bilbao, renamed *Nervion*. 1936 scrapped.

305
Islander (1901–), 95093, 1495g, 240 × 42 × 14ft.
Engine: Dunsmuir & Jackson, Govan, T3cy 15k.
1888 launched by Napier Shanks & Bell, Glasgow, y. no 41, for CPN Co.
22.9.1888 left Clyde, 9.12.1888 arr Victoria. 11.1.1901 to Canadian Pacific. 15.8.1901 struck iceberg in Lynn Canal with loss of 42 lives. 8.1934 raised and beached on Admiralty Island. 1952 scrapped.

306
Maude (1901–3), 64136, 175g, 113 × 21 × 9ft, wooden side-wheeler.
Engine: Albion Iron Works, Victoria, C2cy 1S (1898).
4.1.1872 launched by Burr & Smith, San Juan, for East Coast Mail Line.
1883 to CPN Co. 1885 fitted with compound engine and screw. 11.1.1901 to Canadian Pacific. 1903 to BC Salvage Co. 1914 dismantled, hull used as barge.

307
Otter (1901–31), 107832, 366g, 128 × 24 × 11ft, wooden.
Engine: from *Rainbow*.
1900 launched at Victoria for Canadian Pacific Navigation Co.
11.1.1901 to Canadian Pacific. 7.10.1915 ashore south of Sidney Island, salvaged and reconditioned. 1928 withdrawn. 1931 to Gibson Bros, Vancouver Island. 12.5.1937 lost by fire whilst at anchor Malksope Inlet, west coast Vancouver Island.

308
Princess Louise I (1901–6), 72682, 932g, 180 × 30 × 13ft, wooden side-wheeler.
Engine: J. Roach & Son, New York, C2cy.
1869 launched by J. Inglis, New York as *Olympia*.
7.12.1869 m/v via Cape Horn. 10.1878 to Hudson's Bay Co. 1879 renamed *Princess Louise*. 1883 to CPN Co. 24.7.1886 carried Sir John and Lady MacDonald from Port Moody to Victoria. 11.1.1901 to Canadian Pacific. 1906 to Marpole MacDonald, Victoria. 1908 to Vancouver Dredging & Salvage Co. 1916 to Britannia Mining & Smelter Co. 1917 to Whalen Pulp & Paper Mills. 1919 sank at Port Alice.

309
Queen City (1901–16), 103482, 207g, 116 × 27 × 10ft, wooden schooner.
Engine: 1898, fitted with compound engine, Albion Iron Works.
1895 launched by R. Brown, Vancouver.
1898 to CPN Co. 11.1.1901 to Canadian Pacific. 9.9.1916 damaged by fire, Victoria; to Vancouver Dredge & Salvage Co. 1917 to Pacific Lime Co Ltd, Vancouver; rebuilt and re-engined. 1918 to Kingsley Nav Co, Vancouver. 1920 converted to barge. 11.11.1920 whilst in tow by *Prospective*, *No 2* gasoline tank exploded, total loss, off Beaver Cove, Vancouver Island.

310
R. P. Rithet (1901–9), 85316, 686g, 117 × 33 × 8ft, wooden stern-wheeler.
Engine: C2cy.
20.4.1882 launched by A. Watson, Victoria, for Capt J. Irving.
11.1.1901 to Canadian Pacific. 4.1909 to Terminal Steam Nav Co, renamed *Baramba*. 1917 to Pacific Lime Co, Vancouver, as barge. 1918 to Kingsley Nav Co, Vancouver. 1922 to J. Wray, Blubber Bay BC. 1923 to Capt G. Smith. 1928 (?) beached at Sturt Bay, Texada Island.

311
Tees (1901–18), 95929, 679g, 165 × 26 × 11ft.
Engine: Blair & Co, Stockton, T3cy 1S.
1893 launched by Richardson Duck Co, Thornaby on Tees, for Union SS Co.

1896 to Hudson's Bay Co (pass accom added). 1897 to CPN Co. 11.1.1901 to Canadian Pacific. 1918 chartered to Pacific Salvage Co. 1925 to Pacific Salvage Co, renamed *Salvage Queen*. 1930 to Island Tug & Barge Co, renamed *Island Queen*. 1937 smashed by her barge in storm; towed to Capital Iron Works, Victoria, burned for scrap off Albert Head.

312
Transfer (1901–9), 100794, 264g, 122 × 24 × 5ft, wooden stern-wheeler.
1893 launched by A. Watson, New Westminster BC, for CPN Co Fraser River Service.
11.1.1901 to Canadian Pacific. 1909 to R. Jardine, New Westminster, became power plant for cannery, Redonda Bay.

313
Willapa (1901–2), 81313, 331g, 136 × 22 × 17ft, wood.
Engine: Pusey & Jones, Wilmington Cal, C2cy 1s.
1882 launched at Astoria, Oregon, as *General Miles*.
1891 renamed *Willapa*. 19.3.1896 stranded Regarth Reef, salvaged. 1898 to CPN Co. 11.1.1901 to Canadian Pacific. 1902 to Bellingham Bay Transportation Co, renamed *Bellingham*. 1912 to Inland Nav Co. 1919 laid-up. 1950 burned at Seattle Seafair.

314
Yosemite (1901–6), 27550, 1525g, 282 × 35 × 12ft, wooden side-wheeler.
Engine: Allaire Works, New York, 1cy.
1862 launched by J. W. North, San Francisco, for Central Pacific Railroad.
1883 to J. Irving. 1890 to CPN Co. 11.1.1901 to Canadian Pacific. 11.1906 to T Grant. 9.7.1909 wrecked near Bremerton Wash; total loss.

315
Princess May (1901–19), 109860, 1394g, 250 × 34 × 18ft.
Engine: builders, T6cy 1S.
29.2.1888 launched by Hawthorn Leslie, Newcastle, y. no 278, as *Cass* for Formosa Trading Corp.

1894 renamed *Arthur*. 1896 to govt China, renamed *Ningchow*. 1899 to Marty & D'Abbadie, renamed *Hating*. 12.5.1901 arr *Vancouver* for Canadian Pacific, renamed *Princess May*. 1905 rebuilt by BC Maritime Co; 1717g, 150 berths. 1906 Alaska service. 5.8.1910 aground on Sentinel Island. 2.9.1910 salvaged by *Santa Cruz* and *W. Jolliffe*. 13.9.10 arr Esquimalt. 5.1911 converted oil fuel. 8.1919 to Princess May SS Co, for West Indies banana trade. 1930 scuttled off Kingston.

316
Princess Beatrice (1904–29), 116405, 1290g, 193 × 37 × 15ft, wood.
Engine: Bow McLachlan, Paisley, T3cy 1S 13k. 10.9.1903 launched by BC Marine Rly Co, Esquimalt. 20.1.1904 started Victoria–Seattle service. 1.1929 to B.L. Johnson, hull to be cannery on West Coast.

317
Princess Victoria (1903–50), 115953, 1943g, 300 × 40 × 15ft.
Engine: Hawthorn Leslie, T8cy 2S 19½k.
18.11.1902 launched by Swan Hunter & Co, Newcastle.
26.1.1903 trials. 28.1.1903 ex Tyne without superstructure. 28.3.1903 arr Victoria; superstructure built by Robertson & Hackett, Vancouver. 17.8.1903 entered service, Victoria–Vancouver. 21.7.1906 rammed and sank tug *Chehais* off Burnaby. 26.8.1914 collided with *Admiral Sampson*, Puget Sound. 1930 converted to carry 50 cars, beam incr 17ft, 3167g. 1934 floating hotel at Newcastle Island. 21.8.1950 last trip Vancouver–Nanaimo; laid-up; bell to BC Archives. 2.1952 to Tahsis & Co, to be fuel carrier *Tahsis No 3*; whistle to *Princess of Nanaimo*. 10.3.1953 sank Welcome Pass.
In 1905 the CPR took over the Esquimalt & Nanaimo Railway from the Dunsmuir interests, together with the three following ships.

318
City of Nanaimo (1905–12), 96995, 761g, 159 × 32 × 9ft, wood.
Engine: J. Doty Eng Co, Toronto, C2cy 1S 13k.
1891 launched by McAlpine & Allan, Vancouver, for Mainland & Nanaimo Steam Nav Co.

1897 to E&N Rly. 1905 to Canadian Pacific. 28.6.1911 started Gulf Islands service. 1912 to Terminal Steam Nav Co, Vancouver, renamed *Bowena*. 1922 to Union SS Co, renamed *Cheam*. 1926 to American company as bunk house.

319
Joan (1905–14), 100635, 821g, 177 × 30 × 11ft, wood.
Engine: builders, C4cy 1S 13k.
1892 launched by Albion Iron Works, Victoria, for E&N Rly.
1905 to Canadian Pacific. 5.1914 to Terminal Steam Nav Co, renamed *Ballena*. 13.11.1920 burnt out at Vancouver; to Vancouver Dredging & Salvage Co for scrap.

320
Czar (1905–14), 103907, 152g, 101 × 21 × 11ft, wooden tug.
Engine: Hinckly Spears & Hayes, S. Francisco, Q4cy.
1897 launched by T. H. Trackey, Victoria.
1902 to E&N Rly. 1905 to Canadian Pacific. 1914 to Greer Coyle & Co. 1918 to Imperial Munitions Board. 1919 to Pacific Construction Co. 1927 to Dominion Tug & Barge Co. 19? hull sank off Prince Rupert.

321
Princess Ena (1907–31), 122387, 1368g, 195 × 38 × 15ft.
Engine: Crabtree & Co, C2cy 1S 10k.
22.9.1907 launched by H. & C. Grayson, Garston, y. no 63.
31.10.1907 ex Mersey via Straits of Magellan. 22.1.1908 arr Victoria. 14.10.1933 stranded entrance to Jedway. 1935–6 laid-up Coal Harbour. To Dulien Steel Co for scrap.

322
Princess Royal (1907–31), 121988, 1997g, 228 × 40 × 16ft, wood.
Engine: Bow McLachlan, T3cy 1S 15k.
1.9.1906 launched by BC Marine Rly Co, Esquimalt.
1931 sold; hull converted to sawdust carrier. 3.1932 to H. B. Elworthy for

scrap. Bell to Japanese Mission, Ocean Falls.

323

Nanoose (1908–46), 122397, 305g, 116 × 24 × 14ft, tug.
Engine: builders, C2cy 1S 12k.
1908 launched by BC Marine Rly Co, Victoria.
1911 salvaged *Tees* after she had foundered.
1940 withdrawn. 1946 to Comox Logging & Rly Co; sunk as breakwater.

324

Princess Charlotte (1909–49), 12636, 3925g, 330 × 46 × 23ft.
Engine: builders, T8cy 2S 19k.
27.6.1908 launched by Fairfields, Govan, y. no 457.
2.11.1908 ex Clyde. 30.12.1908 arr Victoria. 12.1.1909. Vancouver–Victoria service. 1926 refit, ballroom added. 30.8.1927 struck Vichnefski Rock, Wrangell. 4.2.1935 collision with *Chelhosin*. 7.3.1941 collision with *Caverhill*. 6.1949 laid-up Thetis Cove. 12.1949 to Typaldos Bros. 17.6.1950 ex Vancouver; renamed *Mediterranean* (Venice–Piraeus–Istanbul). 3.1965 to Sidiremboriki SA Perema, for scrap.

325

Princess Adelaide (1911–49), 126948, 3061g, 290 × 46 × 17ft.
Engine: builders, T4cy 1S 18k.
10.7.1910 launched by Fairfields, Govan, y. no 474.
4.10.1910 ex Clyde via Straits of Magellan. 12.12.1910 arr Victoria. 24.1.1911 Vancouver–Victoria–Seattle route. 19.12.1928 holed by *Hampholm*, towed to Vancouver. 14.10.1948 withdrawn. 7.1949 to Typaldos Bros, renamed *Angelika*. 17.9.1949 ex Victoria. 1967 to Genoa for scrap.

326

Princess Mary (1910–52), 126950, 1697g, 210 × 40 × 14ft.
Engine: builders, T6cy 2S 15k.
21.9.1910 launched by Bow McLachlan, Paisley, y. no 261.
22.11.1910 m/v ex Clyde via Straits of Magellan. 15.2.1911 arr Victoria.

15.3.1911 Victoria–Nanaimo–Comox. 1913 lengthened at Yarrows, oil fuel, 2155g. 3.7.1926 cruise round Vancouver Island. 11.1951 withdrawn. 4.1952 to Union SS Co, renamed *Bulk Carrier No 2*. Superstructure removed to become restaurant. 15.4.1954 broke from tug *Chelan*. 19.4.1954 lost off Cape Decision, Alaska.

327

Will W. Case (1910–24), 80661, 538g, 143 × 31 × 17ft, wooden barque.
1878 launched by S. Starrat, Rockland Me. 1910 to Canadian Pacific. 1924 to Canadian govt, sunk as breakwater, Sidney BC.

328

Melanope (1911–46), 74550, 1686g, 258 × 40 × 24ft, iron sailing ship.
1876 launched by W. H. Potter, Liverpool, for Australasian Shipping Co.
12.1906 abandoned in storm, drifted into Columbia River. 1907 converted to barge. 1911 to Canadian Pacific as coal barge. 1946 to Comox Logging Co, sunk as breakwater, Royston BC.

329

Princess Alice (1911–49), 130609, 3099g, 290 × 46 × 14ft.
Engine: Wallsend Slipway, T 4cy 1S 18k.
29.5.1911 launched by Swan Hunter and W. Richardson, y. no 883.
22.9.1911 ex Tyne via Straits of Magellen. 17.1.1912 Victoria–Vancouver service. 6.1947 laid-up. 6.1949 to Typaldos, renamed *Aegaeon*. 19.11.1949 ex Victoria. 2.12.1966 ran aground Civitavecchia, Italy, whilst in tow by *Eyforia*, to be broken up at La Spezia.

330

Qualicum (1911–46), 130607, 200g, 96 × 22 × 12ft, tug.
Engine: builders, C2cy 1S.
1904 launched by Neafie & Levy, Philadelphia, as *Colima* (worked on construction of Panama Canal).
1911 to Canadian Pacific, renamed *Qualicum*. 1946, sold; sunk as breakwater.

331

Princess Patricia I (1912–37), 115685, 1157g, 270 × 32 × 11ft.
Engine: Parsons Marine, 3ST 3S 20k.
Second ST pass ship. 8.4.1902 launched by Denny Bros, Dumbarton, y. no 970, as *Queen Alexandra* for Turbine Steamers Ltd.
9.1911 to Canadian Pacific; reconditioned by Denny Bros, 1158g, renamed *Princess Patricia*. 1932 laid-up Esquimalt. 5.1937 to Capital Iron & Metals Co, Victoria, for scrap.

332

Princess Sophia (1912–18), 130620, 2320g, 245 × 44 × 24ft.
Engine: builders, T3cy 1S 14k.
8.11.1911 launched by Bow McLachlan, Paisley, y. no 272.
19.2.1912 ex Clyde. 20.5.1912 arr Victoria. 7.6.1912 entered service Alaska route. 1913 converted oil fuel. 23.10.1918 struck Vanderbilt Reef, Lynn Channel. 25.10.1918 broke up; all passengers and crew lost. 1919 salvage attempted.

333

Princess Maquinna (1913–53), 133769, 1777g, 232 × 38 × 14ft.
Engine: Bow McLachlan, Paisley, T3cy 1S 13k.
24.12.1912 launched by BC Marine Rly Co, Esquimalt.
20.7.1913 m/v ex Victoria, west coast Vancouver Island. 11.1952 laid-up. 23.2.1953 to Union SS Co, ore barge, renamed *Taku*. 7.1962 to General Shipbreaking Co, False Creek Vancouver.

334

Nitinat (1914–24), 91255, 322g, 149 × 26 × 14ft, iron tug.
Engine: builders, C2cy 1S.
1885 launched by J. Readhead, S. Shields, as *William Jolliffe*.
1907 to BC Salvage Co. 1914 to Canadian Pacific, renamed *Nitinat*. 1924 to Pacific Salvage Co, renamed *Salvage Chief*. 7.2.1925 wrecked Merry Island, Wellcome Pass.

335

Princess Irene (1914), 5900g, 395 × 54 × 28ft.
Engine: builders, 4ST 2S.
20.10.1914 launched by Wm Denny, Dumbarton, y. no 1006.
20.1.1915 taken over by Admiralty, to be minelayer. 27.5.1915 sunk by explosion Sheerness harbour. 11.9.1962 two boilers recovered.

336
Princess Margaret (1914),
5934g, 395 × 54 × 28ft.
Engine: builders, 4ST 2S.
24.6.1914 launched by Wm Denny, Dumbarton, y. no 1005.
23.10.1914 trials (23.15k). 26.12.1914 taken over by Admiralty, flagship minelaying squadron. 1919 bought by Admiralty for service in Baltic sea. 1921 refitted as Admiralty yacht. 2.7.1929 arr Blyth by tug *Seaman* for demolition by Hughes Bolckow & Co.

337
Dola (1917–33), 122517, 176g, 96 × 22 × 11ft, wooden tug.
Engine: McKie & Baxter, Glasgow, T3cy 1S.
1907 launched by Wallace Shipyard, Vancouver, for Vancouver Tug & Barge Co. 1917 to Canadian Pacific. 1933 to Dola Tug Co. 28.10.1953 lost in collision with *Lady Cynthia* in Howe Sound BC.

338
Island Princess (1918–30), 339g, 116 × 25 × 8ft, wood.
Engine: S. F. Hodge, Detroit, T3cy 1S.
1913 launched by M.McDowell, Tacoma, as *Daily*.
1.6.1918 to Canadian Pacific. 19.6.1918 renamed *Island Princess*, Gulf Islands service. 1930 to Gulf Islands Ferry Co, Victoria, renamed *Cy Peck*; diesel engine; 1956 rebuilt car capacity 40. 1961 to BC Toll Highways Authority. 1964 to BC Ferries (Swartz Bay–Fulford Harbour route). 1965 laid-up. 1966 to J. H. Todd & Co, Vancouver; supply store for fishermen. 1975 to J. W. Russell, Ganges BC. 30.12.1978 anchored off Fanny Bay wharf after being raised from a sinking.

339
Princess Louise II (1921–63),
150555, 4032g, 327 × 48 × 34ft.
Engine: builders, T4cy 1S 17k.
29.8.1921 launched by Wallace SB&DD Co, Vancouver, y. no 108.
26.2.1964 to Shoreline Holdings, Vancouver; engine and boiler removed. 1966 to Princess Louise Corp. 6.1966 ex Vancouver in tow of tug *La Pointe* for Los Angeles—restaurant.

340
Motor Princess (1923–55),
150894, 1243g, 165 × 43 × 9ft, wood.
Engine: McIntosh & Seymour, diesel 4SA 12cy 14k.
31.3.1923 launched by Yarrows Ltd, Esquimalt BC. 1.1955 to Gulf Island Ferry Co (1951). 1961 to BC Toll Highways; rebuilt, renamed *Pender Queen*. 1964 to BC Ferry Authority; 1980 laid-up.

341
Kyuquot (1925–62), 143307, 419g, 135 × 29 × 14ft, tug.
Engine: Fawcett Preston, T3cy 1S.
1919 launched by J. Crichton & Co, Chester, as *St Florence* for British Admiralty.
1925 to Canadian Pacific, renamed *Kyuquot*. 25.1.1925 ex Leith via Panama. 21.3.1925 arr Victoria. 10.11.1931 ran ashore Porlier Passage whilst towing carbarge Vancouver–Ladysmith. 26.2.1932 salvaged. 12.1957 laid-up; bell to Brockville Yacht Club. 11.7.1962 to General Shipbreaking Co, Vancouver. Last CPR tug on BC coast.

342
Princess Kathleen (1925–52),
150908, 5875g, 352 × 60 × 26ft.
Engine: builders, 4ST 2S 22k.
27.9.1924 launched by J. Brown, Clydebank, y. no 504.
15.1.1925 m/v ex Clyde. 13.2.1925 arr Vancouver. 6.1925 triangle service. 9.1939–7.1946 war service. 3.8.1946 overhaul Victoria Mchy Depot—5908g. 22.6.1947 re-entered service. 30.8.1951 holed by *Prince Rupert*. 7.9.1952 ran aground Lena Point, total loss, all saved.

343
Princess Marguerite I (1925–42), 150910, 5875g, 350 × 60 × 26ft.
Engine: builders, 4ST 2S 22k.
29.11.1924 launched by J. Brown, Clydebank, y. no 505.
25.3.1925 m/v ex Clyde. 20.4.1925 arr Victoria. 9.1941 requisitioned. 17.8.1942 torpedoed by *U83* on voyage Port Said to Cyprus.

344
Nootka (1926–55), 14186, 2069g, 251 × 44 × 20ft.
Engine: builders, T3cy 1S.

1919 launched by Port Arthur Shipbuilding Co, y. no 41, as *Canadian Adventurer* for Canadian Merchant Marine.
1925 renamed *Emperor of Port McNicoll*.
1926 to Canadian Pacific. 12.11.1926 ex Montreal with hay for Newfoundland; loaded steel at Sydney for Vancouver via Panama; renamed *Nootka*. 1928 converted to oil fuel, fitted with cargo tank capacity of 171,000gal to serve pilchard industry. 1955 to Commercio Amazonas, Lima, Peru. 1960 broken up in Peru.

345
Princess Elaine (1928–63),
154739, 2125g, 299 × 48 × 16ft.
Engine: builders, 3ST 3S 19k.
26.10.1927 launched by J. Brown, Clydebank, y. no 520.
17.3.1928 m/v ex Clyde. 25.4.1928 arr Victoria. 7.5.1928 took over from P/*Patricia*, Vancouver–Nanaimo. 13.10.1955 collision with barge *VT 25* entrance Vancouver harbour. 11.1.1960 collision with *Alaska Prince*. 1.10.1962 withdrawn. 30.12.1963 towed to Blaine, Washington to be restaurant. 12.1967 to Mrs T. Rogers, towed to Seattle as restaurant; both unsuccessful. 1977 scrapped.

346
Princess Norah (1929–58),
154848, 2731g, 262 × 48 × 26ft.
Engine: builders, T4cy 1S 16k.
27.9.1928 launched by Fairfields, Govan, y. no 632.
20.12.1928 m/v ex Clyde. 23.1.1929 arr Victoria. 9.1955 renamed *Queen of the North* for joint service with CNR to Kitimat. 31.12.1957 joint service withdrawn; reverted to *Princess Norah*. 7.1958 to Northland Nav Co, renamed *Canadian Prince*. 10.1964 engine and boilers removed; renamed *Beachcomber*, towed to Kodiak, Alaska, by *Hecate Prince* to be restaurant and dance hall.

347
Princess Elizabeth (1930–60),
156463, 5251g, 366 × 52 × 28ft.
Engine: builders, 8Qcy 2S 16k.
16.1.1930 launched by Fairfields, Govan, y. no 638.
27.3.1930 m/v ex Clyde via Panama. 3.5.1930 arr Victoria. 12.1960 to Epirotiki Line, renamed *Pegasus* (Venice–Piraeus–Haifa). 13.12.1960 ex Victoria. 2.1973 chartered by contractors to provide tem-

255

porary accommodation for North Sea oil workers. 1.3.1973 arr Nigg Bay, Inverness; renamed *Highland Queen*. 2.1976 to Brugge Scheepssloperij NV for scrap. 20.3.1976 arr Tees in tow. 23.3.1976 left for Zeebrugge.

348
Princess Joan (1930–60), 156465, 5251g, 366 × 52 × 28ft.
Engine: builders, Q8cy 2S 16k.
4.2.1930 launched by Fairfields, Govan, y. no 639.
15.4.1930 m/v ex Clyde via Panama. 16.5.1930 arr Victoria. 24.2.1959 last night run Vancouver to Victoria. 27.3.1959 withdrawn. 12.1960 to Epirotiki Line. 13.12.1960 ex Victoria. 1961 renamed *Hermes* (Venice–Piraeus–Haifa). 1970 to L. Dupes & Ass, Cyprus. 22.10.1973 arr Nigg Bay (see *347* above). 29.8.1974 arr Inverkeithing for break-up by T. W. Ward Ltd.

349
Princess Marguerite II (1949–75), 190660, 5911g, 359 × 56 × 25ft.
Engine: BTH, Rugby, 2ST–EL 2S 23k.
26.5.1948 launched by Fairfields, Govan, y. no 729.
6.3.1949 m/v ex Clyde via Panama. 6.4.1949 arr Victoria. 1972 refit at Yarrows, Victoria. 9.1974 withdrawn. 4.1975 to BC government. 12.1979 withdrawn.

350
Princess Patricia II (1949–), 190663, 5911g, 374 × 56 × 16ft.
Engine: BTH, Rugby, TE 2S 23k.
5.10.1948 launched by Fairfields, Govan, y. no 730.
10.5.1949 m/v ex Clyde. 3.6.1949 arr Esquimalt. 15.6.1949 entered tri-city service. 1963 converted for Alaska cruising, 6062g. Winter 1965–6 & 1966–7 chartered to Princess Cruises, Los Angeles–Acapulco. 1979 still cruising to Alaska for CP.

351
Yukon Princess (1950–8), 176046, 1334g, 224 × 38 × 20ft.
Engine: Allis Chalmers, T3cy 1S 10k cargo.
28.11.1945 launched by Pacific DD Co, Vancouver, y. no. 159, as *Ottawa Parapet* for war service Far East—too late.
1947 to Clarke SS Co, renamed *Island Connector*. 12.1950 to Canadian Pacific.

29.1.1951 arr Vancouver from Halifax; renamed *Yukon Princess*. 2.1951 fitted with 25 ton crane and reefer space. 1956 laid-up. 4.1958 to Cia Vapores David, Monrovia, renamed *West Princess*. 1959 to La Lutz Mines Ltd, Monrovia, renamed *Rosita*. 21.6.1963 ran aground Cape Gracias, Nicaragua; to Southern Scrap Material Co. 1.1964 broken up at New Orleans.

352
Veta C (1952–3), 193774, 520g, 141 × 33 × 15ft, wood.
Engine: F-Morse, Chicago, 5cy oil engine 1S.
1951 launched by North Western SB Co, Bellingham, Washington, for Union SS Co.
17.10.1952 chartered by Canadian Pacific to replace *Princess Maquinna*. 1953 reverted to Union SS Co, renamed *Chelan*. 15.4.1954 foundered off Cape Decision, Alaska.

353
Princess Alberni (1953–8), 195786, 538g, 142 × 33 × 17ft, wood.
Engine: F-Morse, Chicago, 5cy CSA 1S 13k.
1945 launched by Martinolich SS Co, San Francisco, as *Pomare* for US Army—supply duties.
1947 to Cia Pesquera Ambas Costa, Mexico. 4.1953 to Canadian Pacific, renamed *Princess Alberni*. 7.1958 to Northland Nav Co, renamed *Nootka Prince*. 1959 to Great West Towing & Salvage Co. 1959 to Canadian Tugboat Co (Crown Zellerbach); renamed *Ocean Crown*. 4.1978 to Techno Maritime Ltd, Sept Isles Quebec, renamed *Techno Crown*—hydrographic survey work in the St Lawrence River.

354
Princess of Vancouver (1955–), 197858, 5554g, 420 × 65 × 19ft.
Engine: 4 National diesels, 5600shp 2S 15½k.
7.3.1955 launched by A. Stephen, Linthouse, y. no 646.
29.4.1955 m/v ex Clyde. 7.6.1955 arr Vancouver. 21.6.1955 entered service Vancouver–Nanaimo. 4.1963 refit Yarrows, Victoria. Auto capacity incr 1973, new engines, 8600 bhp.

355
Trailer Princess (1966–), 327072, 2689g 308 × 57ft.
Engine: General Motors, 2 oil 12cy 11k.
1944 launched by US Navy Yard, Boston, as *LST 1003*.
29.6.1944 commissioned. 11.7.1944 converted to repair ship at Bethlehem Key Highway Shipyard, Baltimore. 28.11.1944 recommissioned as USS *Coronis*. 7.1966 to Canadian Pacific; renamed *Trailer Princess*. 29.8.1966 Vancouver–Swartz Bay service.

356
Greg Yorke (1964–8), 323224, 2443g, 325 × 57 × 13ft.
Engine: NV Werkspoor, Amsterdam, 2S twin rudders.
1964 launched by Allied Shipbuilders, Vancouver, for F. M. Yorke & Sons.
1.10.1964 chartered to Canadian Pacific. Vancouver-Nanaimo; 25 rail-cars on four sets of track. 10.4.1968 replaced by *Doris Yorke*. 2.1975 to Aqua Transportation, renamed *Seaspan Greg*.

357
Doris Yorke (1968–74), 328327, 2000g, 325 × 57 × 19ft.
Engine: Caterpillar Tractor, 4 oil 4SA 8cy.
1967 launched by Victoria Machy Co, y. no 145, for F. M. Yorke & Sons. 10.4.1968 chartered to Canadian Pacific. 2.1975 to Aqua Transportation Ltd, renamed *Seaspan Doris*.

358
Haida Transporter (1969–), 329516, 2553g, 326 × 56 × 13ft.
Engine: NV Werkspoor, Amsterdam, 2 oil 4SA 6cy 9k.
1969 launched by Allied Shipbuilders, Vancouver, y. no 162, for Kingcome Navigation Co, Vancouver. 7.1969 leased to Canadian Pacific.

359
Carrier Princess (1973–), 347756, 4353g, 380 × 66 × 24ft.
Engine: General Motors, 4Vee 2SA 16cy 2S 18k.
20.2.1973 launched by Burrard DD Co, Vancouver.
1.6.1973 m/v Vancouver–Nanaimo; 260 passengers, 150 autos or 30 rail-cars; three round trips per day.

Transfer barges, handling rail box-cars on BC coast

The first barge was acquired when CPR took over the Esquimalt & Nanaimo Railway in 1905, many others followed:

Transfer No 1 1905–19
No 2 1907–30
No 3 1911–57
No 4 1913–46
No 6 1917–27
No 7 1920–51
No 8 1921–51

371
Transfer No 4 II (1952–   ), 1593g, 308 × 53ft.
1946 built as US landing craft.
1952 to CPR, remodelled by Victoria Machinery Depot for Vancouver–Nanaimo service, to carry 33 trucks or 24 rail-cars.

372
Transfer No 9 (1929–64),155240, 1396g, 231 × 43ft.
1929 built by Canadian Vickers, Montreal, as barge No 16 for Kootenay Lake. 1941 cut in sections; by rail to Esquimalt to be rebuilt; lengthened to 271ft, freeboard increased by 4ft, wheelhouse and

steering gear added; to carry 17 rail-cars, renamed *Transfer No 9*; Vancouver–Ladysmith. 1.12.1964 to Island Tug & Barge Co.

373
Prospect Point (1942–51), 173632, 1038g, 232ft (14 rail-cars).
2.2.1942 launched by Star Shipyard, New Westminster, for Wartime Shipping Board; leased to CPR until 1951.

374
Island Logger (1951–64), built for Island Tug & Barge Co.
6.1951 leased to CPR until 3.1964, when contract to supply tug and barge service passed to F. M. Yorke & Sons.

Northland Navigation Ltd

The following three tugs and four barges were leased to Canadian Pacific from 1 January 1978 for six years.

381
Ocean Prince II (1978–9), 182g, 87ft, tug.
1962 built at Owen Sound as *Manicouagan*.

382
Northland Fury (1978–9), 330469, 118g, 63ft, tug.
1969 built at New Westminster as *Pacific Fury*.

383
Squamish Warrior (1978–9), 345659, 15g, 38ft, tug.
1970 built at Delta BC.

384
Kemano IV (1978–   ), 198987, 689g, 130ft, barge.
1955 built at Vancouver BC.

385
Lakelse (1978–9), 319343, 803g, 160ft, barge.
1962 built at North Vancouver.

386
Northland 101 (1978–9), 328960, 2468g, 203ft, barge.
1968 built at North Vancouver.

387
Northland Transporter (1978–9), 369085, 2002g, 255ft, barge.
1974 built at North Vancouver.

4 BC lake and river steamers

401
Aberdeen (1893–1919), 100675, 554g, 146 × 30 × 7ft, wood stern-wheeler.
Engine: BC Iron Works, 2cy horiz.
22.5.1893 launched by CPR at Okanagan Landing.
8.6.1893 m/v Okanagan Landing–Penticton. 1902 converted to coal. 1916 withdrawn. 1919 to B. Johnson, dismantled and beached as houseboat.

402
Denver (1897–1907), 103310, 9g, 36 × 9 × 4ft, wood screw tug.
1896 built at New Westminster; assembled at Slocan City for W. F. Wardroper, New Denver BC.
1897 to Canadian Pacific to tow freight barges Slocan to Rosebery. 1903 shipped to Shuswap Lake to be tender for CPR houseboat. 1907 sold.

The following seven steamers plus ten barges were bought from the Columbia & Kootenay Navigation Co, 1 February 1897.

403
Columbia I (1897–1920), 103892, 50g, 77 × 15 × 6ft, wood screw tug.
1896 launched at Nakusp, for CKSN Co.
1.2.1897 to Canadian Pacific, towing Nakusp–Arrowhead. 1920 withdrawn; rebuilt to become *Columbia* II (see No 444).

404
Illecillewaet (1897–1902), 100683, 98g, 78 × 15 × 4ft, wood stern-wheeler.
Engine: from *Despatch*.
30.10.1892 launched at Revelstoke for CKSN Co. 1.2.1897 to Canadian Pacific,

Arrowhead–Beaton. 8.1898 withdrawn. 1902 dismantled to become barge.

405
Kokanee (1897–1923), 103305, 348g, 143 × 25 × 6ft, wood stern-wheeler.
Engine: Harlan & Hollingsworth, Wilmington, 1cy.
7.4.1896 launched by T. J. Bulger, Nelson, for CKSN Co.
1.2.1897 to CP. 1923 dismantled to be fishing lodge, Mr Deane of Deanshaven. 1930 sank.

406
Lytton (1897–1903), 94904, 452g, 131 × 25 × 5ft, wood stern-wheeler.
5.1890 launched by A. Watson, Revelstoke, for CKSN Co. 2.7.1890 m/v Revelstoke–Little Dalles, Washington (Capt F.

Odin); Sir W. Van Horne and other CP officials sailed on this trip. 1.2.1897 to CP. 8.1897 Arrowhead to Laporte via Revelstoke with hydraulic machinery for the French Creek Co. 1903 beached at Robson.

407
Nakusp (1897), 1083g, 171 × 34, wood stern-wheeler.
Engine: Iowa Iron Works.
1.7.1895 launched by T. Bulger, Nakusp, for CKSN Co.
15.8.1895 m/v. 1.2.1897 to CP. 23.12.1897 burnt out at Arrowhead.

408
Nelson I (1897–1913), 96987, 496g, 134 × 27ft, wood stern-wheeler.
11.6.1891 launched by A. Watson, Revelstoke, for CKSN Co.
1.2.1897 to CP. 1913 withdrawn and machinery sold. 16.7.1914 hull burned at firework carnival, Nelson.

409
Trail (1897–1902), 103306, 633g, 165 × 31 × 5ft, wood stern-wheeler.
1896 launched by T. Bulger, Nakusp, for CKSN Co. 1.2.1897 to CP. 1900 withdrawn. 1902 burnt out at Robson West.

Stikine River Steamers

The following ten steamers were built for a proposed service from Glenora BC to Wrangell, Alaska (see page 102).

410
Constantine (1897–8), 150ft, stern-wheeler.
1897 launched at Port Blakely, Seattle.
22.6.1898 towed to Alaska. 11.1898 sold. 4.7.1899 lost.

411
Dalton (1897–1901), 552g, 145 × 30ft.
1897 launched at Port Blakely, Seattle.
1.1901 to White Pass & Yukon Rly, renamed *US Capital City*. 1919 abandoned.

412
Dawson (1897–9), 107836, 779g, 167 × 34 × 4ft, wood paddle-steamer.

1897 launched by CPR at False Creek, Vancouver.
Remained in builders yard until 6.1899, when sold. 1901 rebuilt at Dawson for British Yukon Nav Co. 1926 wrecked on Tache Reef, Rink Rapids, Yukon.

413
Duchesnay (1898–9), 107151, 277g, 120 × 21 × 4ft, wood paddle-steamer.
1898 launched by CPR at False Creek, Vancouver.
6.1899 to E. T. Rathbone, renamed *General Jefferson C. Davis*.

414
Hamlin (1898–1901), 107144, 515g, 146 × 31 × 5ft, wood paddle-steamer.
1898 launched by CPR at False Creek, Vancouver.
20.3.1901 to British Yukon Nav Co. 14.1.1903 to Wm McCallum. 15.2.1904 to T. J. Kickham. 9.6.1910 to E. J. Coyle. 2.3.1911 to Hamlin Tug Boat Co, Victoria. 2.12.1913 to J. H. Greer, Vancouver. 28.7.1917 to Defiance Packing Co, Vancouver. Lost in Fraser River BC.

415
McConnell (1898–1901), 107152, 727g, 142 × 30 × 5ft, wood paddle-steamer.
1898 launched by CPR, False Creek, Vancouver.
20.3.1901 to British Yukon Nav Co. 4.9.1901 broken up at Skagway.

416
Ogilvie (1898–1901), 107148, 741g, 147 × 30 × 5ft, wood paddle-steamer.
1898 launched by CPR, False Creek, Vancouver.
20.3.1901 to British Yukon Nav Co. 4.9.1901 broken up at Skagway.

417
Schwatka (1897–1904), 484g, wood.
1897 launched at Port Blakely, Seattle.
8.1904 sold.

418
Tyrell (1897–8), 678g, 142 × 30 × 5ft, wood paddle-steamer.
1897 launched by CPR at False Creek, Vancouver.

7.1898 to British American Corp. 1905 to D. W. Davis, Yukon. 1915 to British Yukon Nav Co.

419
Walsh (1897–1902), wood.
1897 launched at Port Blakely, Seattle. Laid-up Lulu Island. 9.1902 sold.

———————

420
Kootenay (1897–1920), 103164, 1117g, 184 × 33 × 6ft, wood stern-wheeler.
4.1897 launched by CPR, Nakusp (4 rudders with steam-powered steering).
19.5.1897 m/v Nakusp–Trail. 1919 withdrawn. 1920 to Capt Sanderson, houseboat at Nakusp. 1942 burnt out.

421
Rossland (1897–1917), 107142, 884g, 183 × 29 × 7ft, wood stern-wheeler.
Engine: BC Iron Works, Vancouver, 1cy.
18.11.1897 launched by CPR at Nakusp.
2.5.1898 m/v Nakusp–Trail. 1908 hull rebuilt, superstructure replaced with additional accommodation. 12.1916 sank at Nakusp by weight of snow. 3.1917 raised and sold to Capt Forslund to be wharf near Needles, Lower Arrow Lake.

422
Slocan I (1897–1905), 103168, 578g, 156 × 25 × 6ft, wood stern-wheeler.
Engine: BC Iron Works.
22.5.1897 launched by CPR, Rosebery.
1905 withdrawn and rebuilt (see No *432*).

423
Minto (1898–1954), 107453, 829g, 162 × 30 × 6ft, wood stern-wheeler.
19.11.1898 launched by CPR, Nakusp, after being shipped in parts by rail from Bertram Iron Works, Toronto.
1940s freighting farm produce. 23.4.1954 left Robson on last round trip to Arrowhead. 1956 hull towed to Galena Bay, Upper Arrow Lake. 1.8.1968 burned. 1978 name board on display Selkirk College, Castlegar.

424
Moyie (1898–1957), 107454, 835g, 162 × 30 × 6ft, wood stern-wheeler.
22.10.1898 launched by CPR, Nelson (see *Minto* 423).
7.12.1898 m/v Nelson–Lardo. 27.4.1957

last trip; towed by *Granthall* to Kaslo and beached.

425
Sandon (1898–1927), 107451, 97g, 76 × 17 × 6ft, wood screw tug.
10.1898 launched by CPR, Rosebery, Slocan Lake, towing rail-car barges.
1927 dismantled.

426
William Hunter (1897–1903), 100690, 51g, 59 × 13 × 3ft, wood screw tug.
7.11.1892 launched by W. Hunter & A. McKinnon, New Denver, for Slocan Trading & Navigation Co. 1897 to CP. 1903 withdrawn.

427
Ymir (1899–1928), 107452, 90g, 86 × 17 × 6ft, wood screw tug.
27.2.1899 launched by CPR, Nelson, towing rail-car barges Nelson–Kootenay Landing.
1929 scuttled in Kootenay Lake.

428
Procter (1900–17), 107452, 43g, 65 × 14 × 5ft, wood screw tug.
1900 launched by CPR, Nelson.
1904–17 Trout Lake. 1917 to W. A. Foote, Revelstoke; continued to operate on the lake until 1921.

429
Valhalla (1901–31), 11541, 153g, 103 × 21 × 9ft, wood tug.
Engine: Polson Iron Works, Owen Sound, C 2cy.
1901 launched by CPR, Nelson.
1930 withdrawn. 1931 to R. Dill, beached in cement foundation and converted to home.

430
York (1902–32), 111979, 134g, 88 × 16 × 5ft, steel twin-screw tug.
Engine: builders.
18.1.1902 launched Okanagan Landing, built in sections by Bartram Engine Works, Toronto. 1921 transferred to Skaha Lake. 1932 dismantled, hull to C.S. Leaky, Nakusp.

431
Victoria (1900–1904), 107530, 107g, 75 × 15 × 4ft, wood stern-wheeler.

1898 launched by Capt N. P. Roman, Trout Lake.
1900 to CP, Trout Lake City–Gerrard.
1904 beached and used as wharf and freight shed on Trout Lake.

432
Slocan II (1905–28), 121680, 605g, 158 × 28ft, wood stern-wheeler.
1905 launched by CPR, Rosebery.
5.1928 sold to become warehouse for logging camp, north end of Slocan Lake.

433
Kuskanook (1906–30), 121758, 1008g, 194 × 31 × 7ft, wood stern-wheeler.
Engine: Pelson Iron Works, Owen Sound.
1906 launched by CPR, Nelson; Nelson–Kootenay.
31.12.1930 last run. 1931 dismantled and used as hotel at Nelson.

434
Okanagan I (1907–38), 122378, 1078g, 193 × 32 × 8ft, wood stern-wheeler.
16.4.1907 launched by CPR, Okanagan Landing; Okanagan–Penticton.
1928 freight only. 1934 laid-up. 1938 sold as hulk; boiler installed in cannery at Kelowna.

435
Hosmer (1909–34), 126551, 154g, 110 × 21 × 8ft, wood screw tug.
1909 launched by CPR, Nelson.
1925 burnt to waterline and rebuilt. 1931 withdrawn. 1934 beached near Nelson, converted to houseboat.

436
Whatshan (1909–20), 126552, 106g, 90 × 19 × 8ft, wood screw tug.
1909 launched by CPR, Nakusp.
1919 withdrawn. 9.1920 dismantled, engine and boiler to *Kelowna*, No *445*.

437
Kaleden (1910–20), 130297, 180g, 94 × 18 × 4ft, wood stern-wheeler.
Engine: from *Victoria*, No *431*.
23.7.1910 launched by CPR, Okanagan Landing. 1917 laid-up. 1920 dismantled.

438
Bonnington (1911–42), 130555, 1700g, 202 × 39 × 7ft, stern-wheeler.
1911 launched by CPR, Nakusp.

1931 withdrawn. 1942 to BC government. 1946 dismantled, converted to barge.

439
Castlegar (1911–25), 130556, 104g, 94 × 19 × 8ft, wood screw tug.
Engine: Collingwood SB Co, C 2cy.
12.4.1911 launched by CPR, Okanagan Landing, to tow two 8-car barges. 1925 dismantled.

440
Nasookin (1913–32), 133855, 1869g, 200 × 40ft, steel stern-wheeler.
1913 launched by CPR, Nelson; built in sections by Western Dry Dock Co, Port Arthur. 1.6.1913 m/v. 1920s used as car ferry. 31.12.1930 last trip. 1932 to BC government. 1942 fitted with boiler from *Bonnington*. 1947 taken over by Navy League. 1948 ran aground, dismantled.

441
Naramata (1914–69), 134271, 150g, 90 × 19 × 8ft, steel screw tug.
20.4.1914 launched by CPR, Okanagan Landing; built in sections by Western Dry Dock Co, Port Arthur.
1967 withdrawn. 6.1969 sold to Calgary syndicate.

442
Nelson II (1913–20), 134085, 25g, 61 × 11 × 4ft, wood screw tug.
1913 launched by CPR, Nelson.
1919 laid-up. 1920 sold.

443
Sicamous (1914–49), 134276, 1787g, 201 × 40 × 8ft, steel stern-wheeler.
26.5.1914 launched by CPR, Okanagan Landing.
1.7.1914 m/v Okanagan–Penticton. 1930 converted for cargo. 3.1.1935 last voyage. 6.1949 to city of Penticton as museum.

444
Columbia II (1920–48), 150597, 90g, 72 × 15 × 7ft, wood screw tug.
Engine: from *Columbia* I, No *403*.
1920 launched by CPR, Nakusp. 1948 sold to be houseboat, Robson West.

445
Kelowna (1920–57), 150271, 96g, 89 × 19 × 8ft, wood screw tug.
Engine: from *Whatshan*, No *436*.

259

1920 launched by CPR, Okanagan Landing.
1956 laid-up. 5.1957 to P. Ellergodt, Penticton.

446
Rosebery I (1928–43), 154688, 133g, 92 × 20 × 7ft, wood screw tug.
Engine: from *Castlegar* No *439*.
19.4.1928 launched by CPR, Rosebery.
1943 laid-up; machinery to *Rosebery* II, No *448*.

447
Granthall (1928–64), 154663, 164g, 92 × 24 × 10ft, steel tug.
7.3.1928 launched by CPR, Nelson; built in sections by Canadian Vickers, Mon-

treal; Kootenay Landing–Procter.
1957 laid-up. 1965 sold to Mardell Ltd, Edmonton.

448
Rosebery II (1943–58), 166g, 98 × 20ft, tug.
Engine: from *Castlegar* No *439*.
1943 launched by CPR, Rosebery; built in sections at Montreal.
5.11.1943 m/v Rosebery–Slocan. 1957 laid-up. 21.7.1958 to Fowler & Martin for scrap; beached at New Denver, burned.

449
Okanagan II (1947–72), 178045, 204g, 110 × 24 × 12ft, tug.
18.2.1947 launched by CPR, Okanagan

Landing; built in sections by Westcoast Shipbuilders, Vancouver; handled fruit crop to railheads at Penticton and Kelowna.
31.5.1972 last trip, service withdrawn. End of BC Lake & River services of CPR. Sold to Fintry Estates with barge No 8.

450
Columbia III (1948–54), 22g, 50 × 11ft, wood tug.
Launched at Vancouver as *Surfco* for Alberni Canal Co.
1948 to CP, to replace *Columbia* II, renamed *Columbia* III. 24.4.1954 to Ivan Horie, who had sailed her for the CPR. 1968 sank. 1969 raised; shipped to Vancouver.
Last ship acquired for the BC Lake & River service.

5 Bay of Fundy ships

CPR took over 501–506 from the Dominion Atlantic Railway in 1911.

501
Boston (1911–12), 98595, 1694g, 245 × 36 × 21ft.
Engine: builders, T 3cy.
1890 launched by A. Stephen, Linthouse, y. no 328, for Yarmouth SS Co.
6.1901 DAR took over the Yarmouth SS Co. 1911 to CP. 20.8.1912 to Eastern Steamship Corp. 1920 scrapped.

502
Prince George (1911–12), 110003, 1990g, 290 × 38 × 16ft.
Engine: builders, T 8cy 2S.
1898 launched by Earle & Co, Hull, y. no 430, for DAR.
11.1898 arr Boston for the Boston–Yarmouth service. 1911 to CP. 20.8.1912 to Eastern Steamship Corp. 1931 to Boston Iron & Metal Co for scrap.

503
Prince Arthur (1911–12), 110131, 2041g, 290 × 38 × 16ft.
Engine: builders, T 8cy 2S.
1899 launched by Earle & Co, Hull, y. no 439, for DAR; 6.1899 arr Boston.
4.7.1899 first trip Boston–Yarmouth. 1911 to CP. 20.8.1912 to Eastern Steamship Corp. 1929 to Boston Iron & Metal Co for scrap.

504
Prince Albert (1911–27), 107349, 112g, 97 × 20 × 8ft, wood.
Engine:
1899 launched by J. McGill, Shelburne NS, as *Messenger* for Harbinger Steam Trawler Co, Yarmouth.
1904 to DAR; renamed *Prince Albert*; Kingsport–Parrsboro. 1911 to CP. 1927 to Albert SS Co. 5.3.1929 lost in ice, Mulgrave NS.

505
Prince Rupert (1911–19), 104789, 1159g, 260 × 32 × 11ft, steel paddlewheeler.
Engine: builders, T 3cy.
22.5.1894 launched by W. Denny, Dumbarton, y. no 496, for T. G. Shaughnessy (CPR).
21.5.1895 to DAR. 1911 to CP. 1919 to US interests. 1924 broken up.

506
Yarmouth (1911–18), 93373, 1452g, 220 × 35 × 13ft.
Engine: D. Rowan, Glasgow, T 3cy 1S.
1887 launched by A. McMillan & Sons, Dumbarton, y. no 276, for Yarmouth SS Co.
1901 to DAR. 1911 to CP. 1918 to North American SS Corp. 1924 to Pottstown Steel Co, USA, for scrap.

507
St George (1913–17), 123673, 2456g, 352 × 41 × 16ft.
Engine: builders, 3ST 3S 20k.
1906 launched by Cammell Laird, Birkenhead, y. no 665, for GW Rly. 5.1913 to CP. 1917 to UK to be hospital ship. 6.1919 to GE Rly; Harwich–Hook service. 10.1929 to Hughes Bolckow & Co, Blyth, for scrap.

508
Empress (1916–34), 116309, 1342g, 235 × 34 × 20ft.
Engine: builders, T 6cy 2S.
1906 launched by Swan Hunter, Newcastle, y. no 274, for Charlottetown SS Nav Co, PEI.
1916 to CP. 8.1930 replaced by *Princess Helene*. 22.6.1931 caught fire West Saint John NB. 2.11.1934 to Dominion Coal Co as hulk.

509
Kipawo (1925–41), 150498, 200g, 123 × 26 × 9ft.
Engine: Fairbanks Morse, oil 2SA.
1925 launched by Saint John DD&SB Co, to replace *Prince Albert*; Kingsport–Parrsboro service.
1940 service withdrawn. 1941 requisitioned as supply ship for military bases on coast of NF. 20.9.1946 to Crosbie & Co, St Johns NF. 20.11.1952 to Terra

Nova Transportation Ltd. 13.1.1953 re-engined with Ruston & Hornsby 4 stroke diesel; running between Conception Bay ports. 12.11.1974 to Fogo Transportation Ltd, Fogo NF. 6.6.1975 to Bonavista Bay Boats Ltd, Trinity Bay NF.

510
Princess Helene (1930–63),
156707, 4505g, 320 × 51 × 27ft.
Engine: builders, 6 ST 2S 19k.
12.5.1930 launched by Wm Denny, Dumbarton, y. no 1244.
5.8.1930 trials. 22.8.1930 arr Saint John NB. 1950 major o'haul. 2. 1963 withdrawn.
5.1963 to Marvic Nav Inc, Monrovia.
11.7.1963 ex Saint-John NB as *Helene*, to be car ferry in Mediterranean, renamed *Carina* II. 11.1967 to International Cruises

SA, renamed *Carina*. 7.3.1977 to Kyriazi Bros, Perama, for demolition.

511
Princess of Acadia (1951–73),
193326, 6787g, 358 × 62 × 14ft.
Engine: builders, 4ST.
14.9.1950 launched by Fairfields, Govan, y. no 750, as *Princess of Nanaimo*.
2.5.1951 m/v ex Clyde. 11.6.1951 arr Esquimalt. 27.6.1951 Vancouver–Nanaimo service. 30.9.1962 last trip Vancouver–Nanaimo. 28.2.1963 ex Victoria for Halifax. 20.3.1963 arr Halifax. 24.4.1963 Saint John–Digby service; renamed *Princess of Acadia*. 27.5.1971 laid-up, reverted to *P/Nanaimo*; passenger accommodation removed, vehicle capacity incr to 225. 14.11.1972 renamed

Henry Osborne; first voyage Saint John NB to St Johns NF. 16.5.1973 ran ashore, Saint John NB. 27.10.1973 sold to Union Pipe & Mchy Co, Montreal. 1.1974 ex Saint John under tow by *Hansa* for Bilbao for break-up.

512
Princess of Acadia II (1971–4),
10051g, 480 × 66 × 15ft.
Engine: 4 General Motors diesels to twin screws.
1971 launched by Saint John SB&DD Co.
27.5.1971 m/v Saint John–Digby.
24.12.1974 sold to Canadian government, but continued to be operated by CP.
1.9.1976 transferred to East Coast Marine & Ferry Service, CN.

6 Great Lakes ships

Note: Nos 601 and 605 are not used.

602
Athabasca (1883–1946), 85764, 2269g, 263 × 38 × 23ft.
Engine: D. Rowan, Glasgow, C2cy.
3.7.1883 launched by Aitken & Mansell, Kelvinhaugh, y. no 123.
2.11.1883 ex Montreal after being halved for transit to Buffalo where rejoined; 13.10.1909 aground Flower Pot Island, Owen Sound; 1910 rebuilt at Collingwood, length 299ft, 2784g; 1913 re-engined Western DD & SB Co, Port Arthur; 1916 freight service; 8.1946 to Florida as fruit carrier; 1948 scrapped.

603
Alberta (1883–1946), 85765, 2282g, 264 × 38 × 23ft.
Engine: D. Rowan, Glasgow, C2cy.
12.7.1883 launched by Connell & Co, Glasgow, y. no 136.
10.11.1883 ex Montreal after being halved for transit to Buffalo where rejoined; 1911 rebuilt at Collingwood, length 310ft, 2829g; 1916 freight service; 8.1946 to Florida as fruit carrier; 1948 scrapped.

604
Algoma (1883–85), 85766, 1773g.
Engine: D. Rowan, Glasgow, C2cy.

31.7.1883 launched by Aitken & Mansell, Kelvinhaugh.
4.11.1883 ex Montreal after being halved for transit to Buffalo where rejoined; 11.5.1884 first voyage ex Owen Sound to start the Great Lakes service; 7.11.1885 wrecked on Greenstone Island; engine salvaged and transferred to *Manitoba*.

606
Manitoba (1888–1950), 94879, 2616g, 303 × 38 × 15ft.
Engine: From *Algoma*.
4.5.1888 launched by Polson Iron Works, Owen Sound.
1950 withdrawn; 1951 scrapped.

Train Ferries—Windsor–Detroit

607
Ontario (1890–1924), 94885, 1615g, 297 × 41 × 15ft, steel paddle.
Engine: builder.
1890 launched by Polson Iron Works, Owen Sound.
25.4.1890 m/v Owen Sound to Windsor; 1924 to Newaygo Co as barge. 13.10.1927 sunk, Lake Superior.

608
Michigan (1890–1924), 98904, 1730g, 296 × 41 × 15ft, steel paddle.
Engine: S. F. Hodge, Detroit, C2cy.

30.10.1890 launched by F. W. Wheeler, Michigan.
1924 to Newaygo Co as barge; 14.11.1942 wrecked Hope Island, Georgian Bay.

609
Assiniboia (1908–68), 125984, 3880g, 337 × 44 × 15ft.
Engine: builder, Q4cy.
25.6.1907 launched by Fairfields, Govan, y. no 452.
9.1907 m/v ex Clyde to Levis, Que. Halved at Davie Shipyard rejoined at the Buffalo Dry Dock Co. 18.11.1907 to Owen Sound to be fitted out; 4.7.1908 entered service Owen Sound–Fort William; 9.6.1909 accident at Soo Lock; winter 1950–51 steel bulkheads fitted at Midland shipyard, 3 wooden masts replaced by 2 steel; winter 1953–4 4 scotch boilers replaced by 2 water tube boilers and oil fuel; 10.1965 withdrawn from passenger service; continued as freighter; 24.11.67 ex Fort William, last CP voyage; 19.5.1968 to Jal SS Co, 9.11.1969 destroyed by fire at Philadelphia.

610
Keewatin (1908–68), 125985, 3856g, 337 × 44 × 15ft.
Engine: builder, Q4cy.
6.7.1907 launched by Fairfields, Govan, y. no 456.

14.9.1907 ex Clyde with cargo drain pipes, 23.9.1907 arr Montreal; 5.10.1907 arr Davie Shipyard, Levis; 15.10.1907 towed to Buffalo Dry Dock, rejoined; 19.12.1907 ex Buffalo; 25.12.07 arr Owen Sound 7.10.1908 entered service; winter 1950–1 steel bulkheads and 2 steel masts fitted; 1956 echo-sounder and radar fitted; 10.1965 withdrawn from passenger service. 8.11.1966 to Marine Salvage, Port Colborne. 1967 to River Queen Boat Works, Gary, Indiana. 27.6.1967 arr Saugatuck to be Museum.

Incan Marine Ltd was formed in 1972, with the Inchcape Group of London (see page 113).

611
Incan Superior (1974–   ), 348515, 3838g, 382 × 66 × 24ft, rail-car ferry.
Engine: two SA General Motors, 12cy diesels.
28.2.1974 launched by Burrard Dry Dock Co. N. Vancouver, y. no 211.
6.1974 m/v Thunder Bay to Superior.

612
Incan St Laurent (1975–6), 369371, 3800g, 382 × 66 × 24ft, rail-car ferry.
Engine: two SA General Motors, 12cy diesels.
18.12.1974 launched by Burrard Dry Dock Co, N. Vancouver, y. no 212.
6.1975 chartered to Alaska Trainship Corporation for service between Whittier, Alaska and New Westminster. 4.1.77 to CN Marine. 5.11.77 renamed *Georges Alexandre Lebel*; service between Matane and Baie Comeau.

7 Rail Ferry ships

Pennysylvania–Ontario Transportation Co

Formed 16.2.1906 as a joint venture with the Pennsylvania Railroad Co. Dissolved 29.9.1961 (see page 110).

621
Ashtabula (1906–58), 203071, 2670g, 338 × 56 × 17ft.
Engine: builders, T 3cy 2S.
1906 launched by Gt Lakes Engineering Works, St Clair, Michigan; Ashtabula–Port Burwell, Ontario.
18.9.1958 in collision with *Ben Moreel* in Ashtabula Harbour; salvaged and sold for scrap.

Toronto Hamilton & Buffalo Navigation Co

622
Maitland No 1 (1916–35), 214213, 2757g, 338 × 56 × 18ft.
Engine: builders, T 6cy 2S.

1915 launched by Gt Lakes Engineering Works, Ecorse, Michigan; Ashtabula–Port Maitland.
21.8.1926 rescued crew of the *Howard S. Gerken*. 28.6.1932 service withdrawn, laid-up at Ashtabula. 1935 leased to Nicholson Steamship Co. 8.1942 requisitioned by War Shipping Administration; dismantled, hull to J. Roen as barge.

CP Car & Passenger Transfer Co

Bought by CPR 1.9.1929 and owned jointly with the New York Central Railroad 1930–72 (see page 110).

631
Charles Lyon (1929–36), 125975, 1658g, 280 × 40 × 20ft.
1908 launched by Polson Iron Works, Toronto, for Capt D. H. Lyon.
1929 to CP. 1935 withdrawn. 1937 to J. P. Porter & Sons as barge. 1941 scrapped at Hamilton.

632
Ogdensburg (1930–72), 162504, 1405g, 290 × 45 × 12ft, rail-car float.
1930 launched by American Shipbuilding Co, Lorain, Ohio, y. no 806.
2.11.1930 entered service with *Prescotont*.
1958 passenger car service withdrawn.
25.9.1970 freight service withdrawn.
10.1.1972 to Windsor Detroit Barge Line Ltd, Detroit, Mich.

633
Prescotont (1930–72), 155297, 302g, 117 × 28 × 12ft, D-Electric tug.
Engine: Winton Engineering Co, Cleveland, 4SA, 12cy, 11k.
11.9.1930 launched by Davie Shipbuilding Co, Lauzon, Que, y. no 508.
1958 passenger car service withdrawn.
25.9.1970 freight service withdrawn.
10.1.1972 to Windsor Detroit Barge Line Ltd, Detroit, Mich, where still in use moving containers with 632.

8 Tugs

Quebec Salvage & Wrecking Co

Formed 1914, sold to Foundation Company of Canada 1944 (see page 123).

641
G.T.D. (1914–30), 97096, 333g, 123 × 30 × 12ft, wood schooner.
1891 launched by T. A. Wilson, Bridgewater NS, as *Tyree*.

1907 to G. T. Davie & Sons, renamed *G.T.D.* 1914 to Quebec Salvage & Wrecking Co; 1930 scrapped.

642
Lord Strathcona (1914–19), 99478, 495g, 160 × 27 × 13ft, tug.
1902 launched by J. P. Rennoldson, South Shields for G. T. Davie & Sons, Quebec.

1914 to Quebec Salvage & Wrecking Co. 1919 to Foundation Maritime Co. 1947 scrapped.

643
Traverse (1930–44), 161435, 317g, 130 × 26 × 10ft, tug.
Engine: Worthington Simpson, Newark, 2SA, 4cy.

12.5.1930 launched by G. Brown & Co, Greenock, y. no 172.
23.6.1930 m/v ex Greenock. 14.7.1930 arr Quebec. 1944 to Foundation Co of Canada. 1952 to Levis Shipping Co, Quebec, renamed *Fort Levis*. 1958 to R. L. Leclerc. 1961 to B. Dufour. 20.3.1964 crushed in ice off Magdalen Island, later broken up, St Laurent, Îles d' Orleans.

Note: *Gopher* and *Musquash* arrived Quebec 20.6.1914 .to join Quebec Salvage & Wrecking Co, see Nos *656* and *657*.

Mersey Towing Co

Three following tugs bought from the Elder Dempster Co, 1903.

651
Beaver (1903–22), 105185, 154g, 106 × 20 × 11ft.
Engine: , C 1S.
1898 launched by Elliot & Jeffrey, Cardiff, y. no 4, as *Powerful*.
1899 renamed *Lady Lewis*. 1901 to Elder Dempster, renamed *Beaver*. 1903 to CP. 1922 to J. Davies, Cardiff. 1938 broken up by Reese & Co, Llanelly.

652
Otter (1903–22), 89213, 145g, 105 × 20 × 14ft, iron tender.
Engine: builders, C 2cy.
1887 launched by Elliot & Jeffrey, Cardiff, y. no 2, as *Sir W. T. Lewis*. 1901 to Elder Dempster; renamed *African*. 1903 to CP. 10.1906 refit with one funnel and renamed *Otter*. 1922 to Liverpool Screw Towing & Lighterage Co, renamed *Marshcock*. 27.5.1946 to Rootledge & Co. 1948 broken up at Bromborough, Port Rainbow.

653
Panther (1903–21), 89188, 150g, 105 × 20 × 11ft, iron tug.
Engine: builders, C2cy 1S.

1884 launched by Elliot & Jeffrey, Cardiff, y. no 1, as *Elliot & Jeffrey*, 1901 to Elder Dempster, renamed *Panther*. 1903 to CP. 1921 to Coulson Tug Co. 1925 to France Fenwick. 1926 broken up.

654
Bison (1906–46), 124020, 274g, 125 × 24 × 11ft, tender.
Engine: Crabtree & Co, Gt Yarmouth, T 3cy 1S.
1906 launched by H. & C. Grayson, Garston, y. no 57.
1915–19 war service. 1936 passenger licence increased to 537 plus crew of 11. 4.5.1941 sunk by air attack in Mersey; salvaged. 9.11.1946 to J. S. Lastis. 1.1947 renamed *Niki*. 1954 to N. Lambiris; re-engined and renamed *Hydra*. 1957 renamed *Nicholas* I. 1964 to A. Alexiadis & P. Iliadis, Piraeus, renamed *Aghios Georgios*. 5.11.1968 sank off Mitlene Island.

655
Cruizer (1907–13), 104606, 380g, 150 × 24 × 13ft, tug.
Engine: Rankin & Blackmore, Greenock, T 3cy 1S.
1895 launched by W. Hamilton & Co, Glasgow, y. no 119, as *Flying Buzzard*.
1900 to Liverpool Steam Tug Co; renamed *Cruizer*. 1907 to CP. 1913 to C. Bristler & Co, Halifax NS. 1925 to Cruizer Shipping Co. 1952 to Dominion Steel Co for scrap.

656
Gopher (1910–23), 131308, 198g, 100 × 23 × 12ft, tug.
Engine: Crabtree & Co, Gt Yarmouth, T 3cy.
11.1910 launched by H. & C. Grayson, Garston, y. no 67.
1914 requisitioned by Admiralty. 3.6.1914 ex Liverpool with *Musquash*. 20.6.1914 arr Quebec for Quebec Salvage & Wrecking

Co. Also worked out of Saint John NB. 1923 to Saint John DD Co, renamed *Ocean King*. 1926 to Davie SB & Repair Co, renamed *Chateau*. 30.10.1961 broken up.

657
Musquash (1910–20), 131307, 198g, 100 × 23 × 12ft, tug.
Engine: Crabtree & Co, Gt Yarmouth, T 3cy 1S.
20.9.1910 launched by H. & C. Grayson, Garston, y. no 66.
3.6.1914 ex Liverpool with *Gopher*. 20.6.1914 arr Quebec for Quebec Salvage & Wrecking Co. 1920 to Atlantic Salvage Co, Halifax NS. 4.8.1921 sunk in collision off Anticosti Island.

658
Moose (1915–46), 137482, 208g, 105 × 25 × 13ft, tug.
Engine: Crabtree & Co, Gt Yarmouth, T 3cy 1S.
9.1915 launched by H. & C. Grayson, Garston, y. no 94.
1915 requisitioned; war service in Dardenelles and N Russia. 20.10.1919 returned to CP. 28.7.1945 sunk in collision with *Kawartha Park*. 2.8.1945 refloated. 1.2.1946 to Liverpool Screw Towing Co, renamed *Prairie Cock*. 5.1959 broken up.

659
Wapiti (1915–45), 137488, 208g, 101 × 25 × 12ft, tug.
Engine: Crabtree & Co, Gt Yarmouth, T 3cy 1S.
1915 launched by H. & C. Grayson, Garston, y. no 95, as *Elk*; requisitioned; war service in Dardenelles and N Russia.
12.6.1919 returned to CP, renamed *Wapiti*. 1945 to Liverpool Screw Towing Co, renamed *Weather Cock*. 16.8.1958 arr Barrow in tow by *Rosegarth*, for scrap.

9 Working boats

(See page 234.)

Great Lakes

901
Champion II (1883–5)
Sidewheeler 74297 323g 131 × 23 × 11ft.
1877 launched by G. T. Davie, Levis Que.
1883 to CP: 1885 sold; 1887 rebuilt at
Owen Sound.

902
Dolphin
No information.

903
Emily
33ft keel.
16.7.1885 sold by CP to J. Whelan.
No other information.

904
Georgian (1884–8)
80596 377g 130 × 22 × 11ft.
1864 launched by J. Potter, Georgian Bay
for J. C. Graham; 1.4.1884 to CP;
9.5.1888 sank Owen Sound.

905
Juliette
1878 launched at Burlington, Ont.
21.11.1883 sank Pine Tree harbour, Ont.

906
Magdalena
71115 18g 48 × 12 × 5ft.
1875 launched Buffalo, New York.

907
Siskiwit (1883–94)
92287 61g 67 × 16 × 8ft.
1879 launched at Buffalo N.Y.
1883 to CP towing on Kaministikwia
River.
1894 sold to C. Drinkwater, Montreal.

British Columbia

911
Skuzzy II (1884–90)
297 g 133ft.
1884 launched at Savona BC for CP with
machinery from *Skuzzy I* for use on
Thompson & Shuswap Rivers. 1890 sold.
The first and famous *Skuzzy* was built for
Andrew Onderdonk, who had a contract
from the Canadian government in 1879, to
build 127 miles of railway in the Frazer
Canyon, from Yale to Kamloops Lake.
120ft long, powered by two horizontal
engines, she had a steam winch in her bows
for warping through rapids.

Lake of the Woods, Ontario

921
CPR No 1 (1923–52)
26ft wooden motor launch, 14k.

922
CPR No 2 (1923–52)
30ft wooden launch, 10k.

923
Nipigonian (1923–52)
34ft wooden launch 16k.

924
Misty Maid (1954)
26ft cabin cruiser 17k.
1954 launched by Turner Boat Works
Vancouver; 17.5.1954 exploded & caught
fire whilst being driven by H. S. Walker,
manager of the Lodge.

925
Misty Mist (1953–6)
25ft wooden motor launch to replace
CPR Nos 1 & 2.
1956 exploded at Kenora dock.

926
Canadiana (1954–61)
26ft cabin cruiser built by Richardson
Boat Works, Meaford, Ont.
1961 sold with the Lodge.

927
20ft wood and fibreglass outboard built
in Winnipeg.
1961 sold with the Lodge.
Now owned by a commercial fisherman.

Vancouver Harbour

931
Green Jade I (1924–52)
1924 26ft motor boat built in N. Vancouver.

932
Green Jade II
1952 17ft motor boat built by S. Madil,
Nanaimo BC, still in use.

Bibliography

Affleck, E. L., *Sternwheelers, Sandbars and Switchbacks*, Alexander Nicolls Press, Vancouver, 1973

Appleton, T. E., *Ravenscrag, The Allan Royal Mail Line*, McClelland, Stewart, Toronto, 1974

Armstrong, G. H., *Origin of Place Names in Canada*

Babcock, F. L., *Spanning the Atlantic*, A. Knopf, New York, 1931

Barry, J. P., *Ships of the Great Lakes*, Howell-North, Berkeley, 1973

Barstow, D. H. M., *Beatty of the CPR*, McClelland, Stewart, Toronto, 1951

Benson, R. M., *Steamboats and Motorships of the West Coast*, Superior Publications, Seattle, 1968

Berton, P., *The National Dream*, McClelland, Stewart, Toronto, 1970

Bonsor, N. R. P., *North Atlantic Seaway*, Brookside Publications, Jersey, 1979

Bowen, F. C., *A century of Atlantic travel*

— —, *History of the Canadian Pacific Line*, Sampson Low, Marston, London

Charlebois, Dr P., *Sternwheelers and Sidewheelers*, NC Press, Toronto, 1978

Creighton, D., *J. A. Macdonald*, Macmillan, Toronto, 1955

Croal, J., *Fourteen Minutes: Last voyage of the 'Empress of Ireland'*, Michael Joseph, London, 1978

Currie, A. W., *Economics of Canadian Transportation*, University of Toronto, 1959

Curwood, J. O., *The Great Lakes*, Putnam, New York, 1909

Daem, M., *History of Revelstoke*

Davies, Sir R. H., *Deep Diving*

Downs, A., *Paddlewheels on the Frontier*, Outdoors Magazine, Cloverdale, 1971

Gibbon, J. M., *Steel of Empire*, Rich & Cowan, London, 1935

Gilbert, H., *Awakening Continent: Life of Lord Mount Stephen*, Aberdeen University Press, 1965

Glazebrook, G. P., *History of Transportation in Canada*, Ryerson Press, Toronto, 1938

Greene, R., *Personality ships of BC*, Marine Tapestry Publication, W Vancouver, 1969

Hamilton, R. H., *The All Red Route*, BC Historical Quarterly, 1956

Hedges, J. B., *Building of the Canadian West*, Macmillan, New York, 1939

Hilton, G. W., *Great Lakes Car Ferries*, 1962

— —, *The Night Boat*, Howell-North Books, 1968

Hocking, C., *Disasters at Sea*, Lloyds Register, London, 1969

Innis, H. A., *History of the CPR*, P. S. King & Sons, London, 1923

Lamb, Dr. W. Kaye and Hacking, N. R., *The Princess Story*, Mitchell Press, Vancouver, 1974

— —, *History of the CPR*, Macmillan, New York, 1977

Lamb, Dr W. Kaye and Hacking, N. R., *The Princess Story*, Mitchell Press, Vancouver, 1974

Lavallée, Omer, *Van Horne's Road*, Railfare Enterprises, Montreal, 1974

McDougall, J. L., *Canadian Pacific*, McGill University Press, Montreal, 1968

Maginnis, A. J., *The Atlantic Ferry*, Whittaker & Co, London, 1892

Marshall, L., *Tragic story of the 'Empress of Ireland'*, Patrick Stephens, London, 1972

Martin, C., *Gold Rush—Narrow Gauge*, Trans-Anglo Books, Los Angeles, 1969

Mills, R., *Sternwheelers up Columbia*

Mitchell, W. H. and Sawyer, L. A., *Wartime Standard Ships*, Journal of Commerce, Liverpool, 1965

Nicholson, G., *Vancouver Island's West Coast*, published by the author, Victoria BC, 1962

Ormsby, M., *British Columbia—A History*, Macmillan, Vancouver, 1958

Plowden, D., *Farewell to Steam*

Pope, Sir J., *Correspondence of Sir J. A. Macdonald*, Oxford University Press

— —, *Memoirs of Sir J. A. Macdonald*

Roskill, Capt. S. W., *The War at Sea*

Rushton, G., *Whistle up the Inlet*, J. J. Douglas, N Vancouver, 1974

Taylor, J., *Gold from the Sea*

Turner, R. D., *Vancouver Island Railroads*, Golden West Books, San Marino, 1973

— —, *The Pacific Princesses*, Sono Nis Press, Victoria, 1977

Vaughan, W., *Life and Work of Sir W Van Horne*, Oxford University Press, 1926

Waters, S. D., *The Union Line*

Wilson, B., *Life of Lord Strathcona*

265

Index

Numbers in bold indicate illustrations. References to ships in the Fleet Lists on pages 239–64 are given as 244/40, indicating ship number 40 on page 244.

266